D0239963

THE FOUNDATIONS OF MODERN EUROPE 1789–1871

M. E. BARLEN, M.A.

LONDON
G. BELL AND SONS, LTD
1968

PREFACE

IT has become generally accepted that the particular interests and prejudices of every generation are reflected in its writing of history. The Middle Ages provided their militant chronicles and monastic commentators. The Victorians created heroes and burrowed into the constitutional and political undergrowth. Early twentieth-century historians probed the economic foundations of human behaviour. Today, the emphasis has swung towards a closer analysis of the social structure and administrative framework, and to a study of the ideological relationships of classes and creeds all tending to reflect the conflicts and tensions of our own generation.

At the same time these developments have been accompanied by attempts to formulate a more scientific and objective approach, one that sees historical events as the outcome of a series of innumerable, interlocking factors rather than as the product of any one movement or of any one towering personality. This trend has been fostered by a calculated examination of the social and economic foundations of human behaviour and thought; 'sociometric' analysis in France and the careful exploration of ideological backgrounds carried out by American historians have opened up new fields of historical investigation and clarified many areas that had remained obscure or had been the subject of broad and misleading generalisations.

Any attempt to analyse events as the mere outcome of a series of desiccated relationships can, however, create a somewhat deadening effect. Here, therefore, an attempt has been made to combine analysis with a narrative that retains some impression of the disordered complexity of events. Though history is not a logical process, yet, in the general mêlée some occasional patterns may be discerned. It is in the hope that readers and students will be able to piece together the many and varied strands making up the historical process that this book has been arranged in its present form.

The first two chapters try to set out the eighteenth-century environment, the framework of existing institutions and the elements of change, all providing the broad canvas upon which the personalities and the particular economic, social and ideological factors were to operate. Subsequent chapters explore the growth of revolutionary movements and the continuity of basic human attitudes and behaviour patterns. Chapter Eight examines the new wave of stimulating developments introduced by the scientific, technological, economic and philosophical advances of the late eighteenth and mid-nineteenth centuries. The concluding chapters examine the working of these influences upon the structure of European society and politics.

Out of these conflicts emerged states, societies, economies and ideals that still condition the development of present-day Europe. Though the superstructure has been altered on several occasions the essential foundations were clearly laid. Class distinctions, economic developments, scientific and technological discovery, ideological debates and political solutions began to assume a familiar shape and created problems and policies which still appear relevant today.

In writing this book I have been assisted and encouraged by many, all of whom deserve thanks. In particular I wish to acknowledge a debt to my former tutor, Mr. F. M. H. Markham, for reading lengthy sections of the manuscript and for offering valuable advice. Also I would extend thanks to the Warden and Fellows of New College, Oxford, for electing me to a Schoolmaster Studentship which afforded an essential opportunity for much needed revision and research, and to Mr. W. M. Brown, Headmaster of Bedford School, for the necessary term's leave. Lastly to my wife for the Index and a patient scrutiny of the text which removed innumerable inaccuracies and inconsistencies. For any remaining errors and for any general opinions expressed I am of course entirely responsible.

M.E.B.

CONTENTS

MAPS

I · EUROPE IN 1789: THE FRAMEWORK OF THE PAST

1. *Introduction*

IN 1789 Europe was divided into a wide variety of separate and often isolated regions. The mass of the population was still tied to the land and sparsely distributed. Estates and villages lay cut off by tracts of scrub and semi-cultivation. Many towns were merely focal points of particular or provincial interests. In France, Arthur Young estimated that an area the size of England lay waste. In Spain massive ranges stood out uncultivated and bare. The forests of Germany and the plains of eastern Europe captivated the imagination of travellers. Behind a carefully planted Mediterranean coastline, deep valleys, swamps and rocky outcrops isolated communities and made travel by sea generally preferable to a land journey.

Social, political and commercial activity was concentrated in towns. Of these, the capital cities of Europe had already acquired unique importance. London, with a population of nearly a million, had begun to dominate the nation. Paris, with half a million, was to determine the tempo of change. Lisbon, Madrid, Berlin, Vienna, Warsaw and St. Petersburg, with 100,000–200,000, all exercised a measure of control over state affairs and were centres of court and cultural activity. Some towns retained importance because of their traditional associations with the past: Moscow, the ancient capital of Russia; Milan, dominating trade and politics in Lombardy; Rome, the heart of the Roman Catholic Church. All exceeded 100,000 at the turn of the century. Others, expanding through industry or by trade, were becoming increasingly prominent, especially in the West; here Lyons, Marseilles, Barcelona, Amsterdam and Hamburg had already established a commanding lead.

Urbanization, however, remained a gradual process, and the population in cities rose more slowly than in healthier rural areas. Most provincial towns were barely distinguishable from larger villages. Though detached from the country by their clustered buildings and corporate rights they remained tied to the economy of their region. The market exchanged rural produce for artisan wares; many townsmen owned extensive gardens outside city walls and lived, in part, off the profits of the surrounding countryside.

The sense of separation was enhanced by the slow speed of communication. Travel was restricted to the few. Roads were often little more than tracks, impassable in bad weather. In western Europe paved or 'metalled' surfaces, *chaussées,* had become more widespread, especially between the larger cities. France had a road system radiating from Paris. It extended into the Netherlands, into southern Germany as far as Vienna, and into the north of Italy. But the by-ways remained poor; in north and eastern Europe even the main roads were often rutted to the axle. France and Germany were covered by a regular service of stage coaches and post stations for private and public use. These, however, could only cater for a small minority and travel between towns was both costly and irregular.

News was slow to spread and hearsay remained the source of most opinion. Lack of accurate information did much to spread rumour and panic. Papers were few and only available in the largest towns. Censorship encouraged ignorance and a resigned acceptance of existing horizons. Only in the great cities, ports and universities and in a scattering of courts and country houses had a more cosmopolitan society really taken root. Even here ideas spread slowly. The great rivers of France and central Europe encouraged exchange. Wealth and power accumulated at the cross roads of commerce and in state capitals. But national issues were often debated in alarming ignorance of any economic or political facts. Censuses and statistics only developed in the nineteenth century and were to remain imperfect for much of that period.

The frontiers of Europe had hardly begun to acquire their present outline. In the West, boundaries had become more defined. France had stabilized her eastern frontier from Dunkirk to the Rhine, but it still followed an irregular and mountainous course from Geneva to the Mediterranean. Central Europe remained confused and divided: Italy was

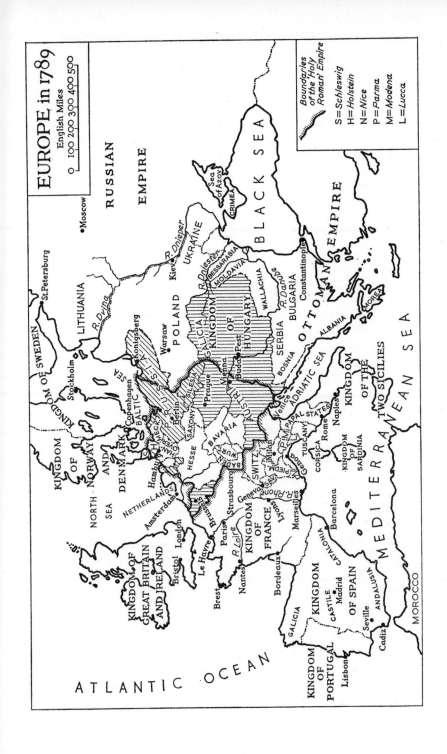

split into some dozen states of varying size; the 'Empire' was severed into an even greater assortment of fragments. The Austrian Habsburgs were the dominant power. From Vienna they controlled the southern Netherlands, the Tyrol, Austria, Milan, Bohemia, Hungary, Croatia and the intervening lands. Prussia, in the North, had assumed a position of growing importance. Frederick the Great had seized Silesia and by joining Brandenburg to East Prussia had consolidated his kingdom.

Fossilized between Prussian and Austrian territory lay a variety of petty princes, courts, prelates and free cities. They enjoyed the nebulous benefits of membership of the 'Holy Roman Empire', an entity that had little geographical, economic or political significance. Its frontiers cut through the middle of Austrian and Prussian territory, and divided Holstein from the Kingdom of Denmark. These arbitrary boundaries were to be the cause of frequent conflict during the next hundred years. Only the Swiss Confederation and the Dutch Republic bore any resemblance to their present outline.

Eastern Europe was even more fluid. Russian expansion had acquired new momentum under Peter the Great and this had been maintained by Catherine (1762–96). She pressed forward into Poland and the Ottoman Empire, using every favourable opportunity to extend Russian territory to the West and round the shores of the Black Sea. By 1789 Russia had occupied the Crimea and consolidated her frontier on the Dnieper and Dvina. The next decade was to see further extensive gains. Poland and the Ottoman Empire were quite unable to resist the predatory demands of their neighbours. Both lacked geographical unity and political cohesion; both appealed for aid to the other great powers, and the problem of their survival was to remain one of the major issues of European history for much of the nineteenth and twentieth centuries.

Alterations to the map, rates of growth and patterns of change were the outcome of factors embracing almost every aspect of human behaviour. The social order, the economy, governments, foreign and imperial designs still reflected the ideas and needs of the past. These had become sanctified by custom and by the accepted traditions of church and state.

But other factors were already acquiring a greater significance. The Industrial Revolution, science and technology,
the ideas of the rational and scientific mind had begun to
undermine the established framework; romantics and revolutionaries were attacking the very foundations of the old order
and planning to build new states and new societies upon the
ruins.

2. *The Social Order*

Eighteenth-century society was dominated by the ambitions of a landowning aristocracy. Their property and privileges gave them power; their actions and interests determined
the fate of millions. Though varied in composition they did
display a number of similar characteristics. Their authority
was generally founded upon their estates. In Spain, one third
of the cultivated acreage was in the hands of four powerful
families. In France the aristocracy possessed at least a fifth of
all property. In Lombardy one per cent of the population
owned half the land, while in Russia half a million nobles
controlled some nineteen and a half million serfs. Aristocratic
privileges included exemption from direct taxation and
labour dues, as well as special feudal rights. These powers of
'*justice seigneuriale*' prevailed in France and Spain and
throughout most of central and eastern Europe. Manorial
courts and customs assured control over a tenant's land, living
and private life; rents and services, fees and fines provided a
basic source of income for the lord.

From estates, power spread to the provinces. Courts and
country houses conditioned employment and demand. Control of municipal office or administrative machinery was
usually in the hands of local magnates. In Lombardy the
patricians controlled the magistracy, in Spain the gentry
monopolized local government. Prussian landowners were
officials with control over anything from peasant taxation to
cemetery inspection. In France, provincial assemblies and
regional offices were all dominated by the aristocracy. Provincial power, however, was not enough to satisfy the demands of noble ambition. The apex of an aristocratic society
was a royal court where official appointment could lead to
further powers, privileges, influence and estate. In Poland
some control over court offices had already been achieved.

Elsewhere, hopes of profit and promotion brought nobles flocking to St. Petersburg, Vienna or Versailles. Here amid a ritual of etiquette and intrigue positions of honour, posts and pensions, marriages and alliances were negotiated and sealed.

Younger sons could find alternative employment in the army or in the Church. In Prussia, France and Russia regimental officers were drawn exclusively from the aristocracy. In Poland, where nobles had won exemption from military service, the Church provided a profitable alternative. Throughout much of Europe high ecclesiastical livings had become almost exclusively an aristocratic preserve. In France every bishop with one exception was noble. In Habsburg territories prebends were awarded from the age of fourteen. Except in Spain and in a few protestant countries, the close links between the Church and the aristocracy offered further opportunities for the exercise of patronage and power.

Aristocratic privileges were emphasized by a general attitude of exclusiveness that elevated the élite above the rest of society and kept all property in noble hands. Strict entailing prevented the division or sale of estates. In Italy, Spain and Austria the eldest was guaranteed the inheritance. In Prussia any heir could inherit, but estates could not be divided or sold outside the nobility by laws designed to maintain an exclusive and aristocratic caste. In France the law varied and subdivision of land and competing interests did much to promote friction between the social orders.

But beyond these general similarities the aristocracy was sharply divided between the old and the new, between the Court and the provinces. The old nobility, the *noblesse d'épée* in France, the grandees of Spain, Hungarian magnates, all claimed descent from warrior invaders of the medieval past. In France they competed for pensions and precedence at court. Elsewhere they struggled for administrative authority and military rank. A few tried to improve their property and invested in their estates. Enlightened nobles in France and Germany were praised for their agricultural experiments and liberal reforms. In Italy the close connection between patricians and land ownership promoted investment and rising productivity. Elsewhere, however, the majority lived off the land but seldom on it. In Spain overgrazing reduced wide areas into desert; in Russia peasants and property were ruthlessly exploited.

Among the old nobility there were many who had neither the fortune nor the favour to reach high office and who kept to the provinces. Though reduced to poverty they still retained their pride and their privileges. Jealous of the powerful and the wealthy they retreated behind a barrier of caution and contempt. The Magyar gentry, Prussian Junkers and French *hobereaux* were to maintain a tradition of bitter opposition to any modification in their privileged position or established rights.

Whatever the divisions within the old aristocracy, all were united in opposition to the new. These had reached high status by royal favour, finance, the law and occasionally commerce. It had become accepted practice for the Crown to create a new aristocracy to undermine the ambition of the old. In time some of these elements had fused, though distinctions of precedence nearly always remained. In France the *noblesse de robe* had already held hereditary titles for some 200 years. Originally lawyers whose role had been to verify laws at sessions of *parlements* in Paris and the provinces, they had become in time a closed caste entrenched behind a barrier of vested interests. Their position, however, was rather unique. Many ennoblements were intimately associated with royal policy – in Spain to reinforce the Crown against the established grandees; in Austria to rally support for the dynasty. Such new creations inevitably caused resentment among the older orders.

In many parts of Europe high financiers had also been able to acquire noble status. In France tax collection was farmed out to wealthy *fermiers-généraux* who could advance loans to the government in anticipation of tax returns. These men were soon able to buy their office, a title and extensive estates. In the towns, merchants and magistrates also aspired to 'live nobly', creating petty provincial castes. Similar penetration occurred in Italy where bankers rose to become patricians; even the Habsburgs and Tsars promoted financiers and industrialists. But in Prussia traditional barriers stood firm, while Spain lacked the wealth to promote an independent financial class. In these countries, and throughout much of eastern Europe, the aristocracy remained united and well prepared to resist any change. The intrusion of new wealth split the nobility into rival fragments. Factions at court and in the capital created dangerous divisions at a moment when violent discontents were also beginning to agitate society at almost every level.

The bourgeoisie, or middle classes, were unevenly distributed. In eastern Europe their role was still barely significant. In Russia, where only some 3 per cent of the population was urban, town life remained backward. Mining, production and trade were largely run under the patronage of the nobility or by the State. International exchange was maintained by itinerant merchants, and contacts with the West encouraged by foreign immigrants, especially German and by the activities of Jews and Baltic traders. In Poland and south-east Europe the picture was very similar. Only in the West and in some central states had the middle classes become a recognizable political factor. Their range, however, was ill-defined and showed wide variation in social and economic status.

The upper bourgeoisie included leading lawyers, state officials, financiers and wealthy manufacturers. They often aspired to nobility, won titles at court or acquired provincial status allowing them to 'live nobly'. The lawyers claimed superiority though they often found such claims hard to justify in face of the wealth accumulated by their rivals. In France they filled the highest posts of the magistracy. Elsewhere they were closely associated with the royal administration. In Germany they supervised the law, taxation and tolls. In Spain they acted as general administrators for the Crown both at court and in the provinces. Isolated between the privileged and the wealthy, they often appeared critical and aloof. The financiers, on the other hand, soon cut across every social barrier. In France they were received at court, married their daughters into the nobility and quickly bought lands and titles. Their intrusion was resented but their claims were too powerful to ignore.

The merchants played a varied role. Accumulating wealth through trade and investment, they dominated the ports and cities of western Europe. In Germany their power was entrenched in the corporations governing Hamburg, Frankfurt and the larger cities. In Italy they were the core of the new patrician aristocracy. But in France their influence often competed with the nobility, the lawyers and the upper bourgeoisie. Lacking the wealth to 'live nobly' they helped to swell the middle reaches of society and press for economic and political reforms. Their capital promoted new enterprise and encouraged industrial reorganization, but met frequent obstruction from vested interests at every other level.

An intellectual and professional core of doctors, teachers, provincial lawyers and university men was also to become increasingly influential. Their role was varied and their status elusive. Some became administrators in Prussian and petty state bureaucracies and gradually made their way to the top. Others joined the freer salons and café houses of Paris and Lombardy to discuss the state of society and speculate upon the need for reform. Many became private tutors in aristocratic households. Educated in classics, law, languages, science and philosophy, their position generally depended upon their ability. Fostered by a network of universities, notably in Germany, their ideas were to become the articulate voice of the middle classes, often vague and divided, yet clear in its claims for increased influence and power.

The *petit bourgeois,* or lower middle class, were divided among artisans, shopkeepers, clerks and workmen grading from masters to apprentices. They were the basis of urban economic life and were often lumped together as 'the people' in popular literature. Their life centred on the regional market. A carefully regulated guild organization protected their trade from foreign competition and maintained a strict hierarchy within each craft. They resented the influence of new investment which undermined their security – especially in France and in the German states. They were opposed to both the privileges of the aristocracy and the financial interests of the upper bourgeoisie, although this was not always apparent at first sight. Their status had been maintained by centuries of traditional craftsmanship and a corporate town life that protected them from the servile conditions which persisted outside city walls. Fear of foreigners, vagrants and unemployment dominated their lives and made them equally opposed to middle-class or peasant competition.

The great mass of the population – the peasantry – remained poverty-stricken and inarticulate. They represented some 80 per cent of the population in France, at least 75 per cent in the German states, and sometimes as much as 95 per cent in eastern Europe. They carried the economic burdens of society and were generally regarded with pity or contempt by everyone else. Their status varied: only a few were genuine freeholders, but pockets of small freeholds did exist in Norway, Holland, Holstein and even in parts of France. The majority in western Europe were tenant pro-prietors holding lands from a lord of the manor in return for labour services or rent. Many had established their right to free sale and limited security of tenure and had commuted their services for 'quit rents' or *cens*.

But a wide variety of feudal obligations remained. These were both a financial burden and a permanent reminder that tenants were not after all fully free. They differed from region to region but included service in a lord's court, com-pulsory use of his wine press, oven and mill, work on the roads, *corvées*, and submission to game laws which sacrificed crops in the interest of the local hunt. When to these were added the tithes paid to the Church, royal taxation on property, *taille*, and in France the salt tax, *gabelle*, as well as possible military service, *milice*, the position of the peasant became barely tolerable. Many were described by travellers as wretchedly poor or living in 'misery and vermin'. Never-theless, a few did achieve a limited degree of prosperity particularly in northern Spain, north Italy, parts of France and the Rhineland – where this type of tenant smallholding was typical of up to 40 per cent of the population.

On the whole, however, most peasants lived at even lower levels of servility. In France some 50 per cent were *métayers* or share-croppers provided with stock, seeds and tools by a lord in return for half the produce. With dues and taxes they were barely able to subsist. They lacked the security and the incentive to improve their holdings. About one million were serfs tied entirely to their lord. East of the Elbe serfdom was almost universal. The peasant was bound to the law, customs and routine of a manorial estate. Lacking security of tenure he needed permission to move or to marry. In Russia a serf could be flogged, drafted into the army and even auctioned without appeal.

Monarchs often tried to soften the extremes of hardship

and terror inflicted by the aristocratic élite. In Russia, state peasants were subject to taxation, conscription and rents or services; but on the whole their condition was less intolerable. Living in communes they were able to work their land holdings according to customary law and practice. The gradual extension of serfdom by royal grants, especially in the South, forced half the peasantry into subjection, while the dependence of the Crown upon aristocratic support made any state intervention largely ineffective. Attempts to promote reform in Habsburg territories also met bitter opposition. Throughout eastern Europe the peasantry continued to live dependent, downtrodden and depressed.

3. The Economy

In 1789 agriculture was still the essential basis of economic life. Europe was overwhelmingly rural with agrarian village communities generally managing to subsist in self-sufficient isolation. The routine of daily living appeared very similar: across the great northern plain from the Loire valley to the Volga, land working followed a traditional two crop, open field system. A third of the land was left fallow; common pastures provided for sheep and cattle, and wastes and woodland for timber and fuel. Craftsmen and cottagers made the clothing and implements needed for everyday use. The village consumed over two-thirds of its produce and sold any surplus at a local market in exchange for luxuries and hardware goods. Some degree of specialization had already developed. Vineyards in France and the Rhineland, cereal crops in Poland and Russia, timber in the North all produced growing surpluses. Crop yields, however, remained low – five-fold in Silesia, four-fold in Hungary. Cultivation was extensive, handicapped by lack of fertilizers and tools. Wooden ploughs and brushwood harrows were widespread. In Italy the implements of the Roman Empire were still in general use, especially in the South.

Exploitation of the soil led to frequent exhaustion. Southern Europe was covered by wasted corn lands and arid pastures. In Hungary and the Balkans primitive one crop cultivation impoverished peasant holdings. Elsewhere more enlightened methods had slowly begun to create the basis of a sounder economy. Rice plantations were gradually extended along the Po valley, flax and hemp were cultivated in Russia, and cattle breeding improved in the Netherlands. In areas where the peasantry held securer tenures agriculture flourished and prosperity was increasingly noticeable. Catalonia, south-west France, and independent mountain villages balanced cereal, cattle and timber production with crops of olives and fruit. In Flanders, Holland and Holstein, dairy farming had already begun to make significant progress. Elsewhere, however, a mass of the semi-free, the servile and illiterate struggled to survive and to produce enough for the tithes, taxes and feudal dues needed to support the rest of the economy.

Industry was slowly emerging from its medieval shell. In Russia and eastern Europe basic necessities were still produced by family enterprise in villages or on estates. In the West, however, output had become concentrated in towns, where guilds provided protection and markets encouraged exchange. Self-sufficiency was again the ideal. The town produced enough for its own needs and for the surrounding area. Specialized goods were exchanged at neighbouring fairs or in exceptional circumstances were sent further afield. Guild organizations made up of masters, journeymen and apprentices regulated standards, controlled prices and wages, and excluded possible rivals. This led to a growing number of restrictive practices, and eventually encouraged alternative methods of production. Merchants began to co-ordinate cottage and village industries by 'putting-out' tools and raw materials which could be worked at home and the finished product then returned for sale. Flanders cloth, Lyons silk, and German paper developed rapidly in this way. The system spread from Catalonia to Russia where nobles put out materials for making knives, locks, boots and samovars to their peasants.

State action and the gradual concentration of capital led to a steady growth of large-scale enterprise. In Russia, Peter the Great and his successors exploited the mineral resources of the Urals by setting up mines and foundries. Later many were leased out to nobles who often set up factories for flax, linen and smaller crafts on their own account. In Spain, Prussia, Hungary and France the State encouraged similar development with varying success. Hungary lacked the capital and Spain the enterprise to make much progress. But in Prussia royal policies led to the increased exploitation of the Silesian mines and encouraged new silk, cloth and dyeing industries. In France the Crown promoted coal mines at Anzin, iron works at Le Creusot, Sèvres pottery, luxury silks and tapestry works, while royal concessions encouraged the construction of dockyards, sugar refineries and textile mills.

These developments had already met mounting opposition from guilds and trade corporations. Artisans and workmen, masters and apprentices soon felt themselves threatened by such new capitalist enterprise. Competition endangered their livelihood and opened up bleak prospects of vagrancy and unemployment. Governments quickly began to bring in a measure of control in order to pacify guild agitation. Prussia took the lead and most German states followed her example. In France guilds were generally retained as useful agents for the regulation of tolls, and for revenue collection and militia service. Indeed, they were quickly recognized as essential props of the old order. The growing competition between new capitalists and established corporations caused frequent disturbances and added new economic fears to existing social grievances.

The expansion of credit and the increase in state spending also led to a rapid rise in prices. In Russia the pressure of demand created by new buildings and government expenditure caused a runaway inflation. In France prices rose by about 65 per cent between 1730 and 1789. This provided increased profits for bankers, entrepreneurs and stockholders which in turn promoted further growth. Wages, however, trailed behind and rose by only 22 per cent during the same period bringing increased hardship to many workers and artisans. Any failure in the food supply had disastrous effects. The bad harvests of 1787 and 1788 sent the price of bread soaring and created violent, revolutionary unrest.

Trade, however, appeared to flourish. In spite of internal obstruction from provincial and state tolls, and from inadequate roads and communications, it more than doubled in much of Europe during the second half of the eighteenth century. Though customs barriers crippled many of the smaller inland states, commerce continued to expand from the Baltic to the Mediterranean. Prussia and Russia encouraged exports while protecting their own industries. In Russia the progressive abolition of tolls and the partial reduction of tariffs brought a three-fold rise in foreign trade. The Baltic with its Polish grains, Swedish iron ore, timber products and naval stores was indeed one of the major sources of raw materials for the West.

In Germany, Prussia and Saxony competed for control over the eastern trade routes. The Leipzig fairs attracted goods from all parts of Europe and Prussian rulers tried to direct commercial traffic into their own territories by building new canals and by the development of dockyards at Stettin and Königsberg. The maritime powers held the whip hand, and the older centres in the South gradually declined. Only Strasbourg and Frankfurt retained their position as commercial entrepôts. The Habsburgs also limited internal tolls and attempted to stimulate trade and industry but with little success. Lacking capital, middle-class enterprise and a natural coastline, their Empire remained landlocked and became increasingly isolated.

The most spectacular development occurred on the Atlantic and North Sea coasts. Hamburg, Amsterdam, Le Havre, Nantes and Bordeaux prospered. French colonial trade accounted for some 40 per cent of her total commerce. Sugar, rum, cotton, wine and fruits promoted wealth, financed harbours and brought booming returns. Manufactured goods, leather and textiles, which with wine formed the basis of French exports, were, however, unable to balance a rise in imports, and the trade balance seems to have been unfavourable for much of the second half of the eighteenth century.

Nevertheless, the general picture was one of increased prosperity in the ports, in capital cities and in the newer industrial centres. Wealth was diffused among financiers, merchants and bourgeois manufacturers while prices increased and profits rose. Governments became preoccupied with the needs of industry, finance and trade, and the interests of capitalist enterprise were carefully protected, encouraged or controlled. Even in Spain efforts were made to revive a once flourishing industry by the relaxation of prohibitive taxation. Excess control had a restricting impact on commercial enterprise, and trade flourished best where government was directly influenced by the mercantile community.

4. *Government*

In most European states effective rule depended upon royal initiative. For centuries monarchs had consolidated their estates, developed an administrative machine and extended their authority. Leadership in war, the preservation of law and order, and the protection of trade had become elevated by religious sanction into a divine absolutism. The Crown had become the personification of government, the fountain of law, commander-in-chief, and father of the people. Louis XIV claimed '*l'état c'est moi*'; Kings of Prussia asserted '*a sovereignty of bronze*'; and Russian Tsars proclaimed their laws to be '*of God*'. In practice sovereigns did not always live up to expectation. Louis' successors were inept; Tsars were occasionally mad; while some monarchs allowed their kingdoms to lapse into confusion.

The machinery of government followed much the same pattern. Royal instructions were dictated by the sovereign with the aid of ministers or secretaries. Some separation of function had already emerged and officials were becoming increasingly divided among several departments of state – legal, financial, military, foreign and domestic. A Chancellor often acquired responsibility for foreign affairs – a key role. The growing importance of finance and trade were reflected in the rise of a Controller-General in France and a Procurator-General in Russia. Responsibility for the police was sometimes held by ministers but was more often under immediate royal control. The Secret Chancellery of Catherine the Great eliminated rebels; the Habsburg police imposed a strict censorship and checked correspondence. Monarchs were able to choose ministers at will and were under no obligation to accept ministerial proposals. They were responsible only to themselves and would often prefer the suggestions of wives or mistresses to any official advice.

Ministers and court officials were generally assisted by bureaucrats who did most of the work. French *Conseils*, Prussian Colleges and Habsburg Councils collected information and drafted royal commands.[1] In Russia a Senate wrote out

[1] See p. 42.

imperial decrees and checked their enforcement. Numerous advisory councils also existed but played a varied role. In France the Councils of State were filled with lawyers and aristocrats and had become almost entirely decorative. In Russia the executive Colleges set up by Peter the Great had been absorbed into new ministerial Boards. In Prussia the central government was rather more effectively organized with departmental Colleges advising a General Directory of ministers. But on the whole organization at court remained ill defined. Real power lay with the King, an inner council of intimate advisors and a growing number of professional bureaucrats.

The efficiency of the central government thus depended on the drive of the monarch and the loyalty of his councillors and secretaries. The efforts of kings to replace an acquisitive nobility by new middle class assistants inevitably aroused growing resentment. Only the most powerful rulers were successful. Any signs of weakness were rapidly exploited by nobles who were determined to retain their traditional place in the King's councils. The interplay of autocracy, ambition and ignorance generally reduced government to a desperate series of improvisations. Only outstanding sovereigns were able to bring these conflicting interests into any semblance of order.

While monarchs were able to exercise some immediate control over the Court, their influence in the provinces was far more precarious. The administration was often slow to penetrate the far corners of the realm where the powers of the aristocracy remained entrenched. Effectiveness varied, control was nowhere complete. The Prussian system was to become among the most efficient. Landowners of regional Circles met in local diets to elect a *Landrat* who was responsible for a variety of administrative tasks such as roads and poor relief. He was guided, however, by local War and Domain Chambers set up by the Crown and responsible to the General Directory. These Chambers were run by officials who co-ordinated royal policies and provincial interests.[1]

Elsewhere the interests of the Crown and the aristocracy seldom tallied. Russia, divided into fifty provinces, was far too large for effective control. Regional governors reported to the Senate and tried to pass on imperial instructions through local boards. But in 1785 a Charter to the Nobility had encouraged landowners to elect their own local corporations with independent officials to administer justice and implement government decrees. The towns had gained similar privileges and contention between local men and government officials became a basic feature of Russian life. The authority of a remote, omnipotent Tsar might inspire terror, but his actual powers were often lost amid the wastes of Siberia and the obstructions of a serf-owning aristocracy.

In Habsburg territories the Crown made a more determined effort to consolidate its authority. Each province was to be controlled by a College responsible to the Chancellery. Provinces were divided into Circles with Captains to check taxes, enforce laws and deal with conscription. Their activities, however, provoked bitter opposition from the nobility and the towns, and both entered into a period of prolonged conflict with the central government.

In France the position was equally confused. In the seventeenth century the Crown had created *intendants* as executive agents to govern the provinces in the name of the King and to undermine the influence of the local aristocracy. This process, however, had never been completed and the nobility had retained most of their powers. In the *Pays d'Election* the interests of the *noblesse de robe* were jealously defended in the *parlements*. The *Parlement* of Paris was of special significance due to its influence in the capital and its jurisdiction over one third of the country. In the *Pays d'Etat* the regional Estates were still powerful. They represented the local landowners who were prepared to ally with the upper bourgeoisie to reject taxation and any instructions from the Court. Their powers, however, were seldom a real threat to the Crown as mutual rivalry prevented any united opposition. Nevertheless, if any monarch failed to maintain the initiative their influence inevitably revived.

Following the death of Louis XIV there were signs of a noticeable aristocratic revival in France. The Estates and *parlements* became increasingly active while the aristocracy infiltrated into the *intendances* and began to occupy many of the chief offices of state. By 1789 most of the *intendants* were noble and tied to a variety of provincial interests. Their subordinates lacked the authority to impose royal decrees and soon abandoned any pretence of loyalty to the Crown in a scramble for privileges and profit. This inevitably weakened royal authority and whetted noble appetite for even greater powers. Rivalry and intrigue permeated the Court where the whole administrative structure appeared in imminent danger of collapse.

5. Politics and Powers

The purpose of royal policy was to enhance the power of the Crown by consolidating its authority, harnessing its resources and increasing its prestige. Once a measure of control over the Court and the provinces had been assured, it became essential to raise adequate funds to pay for the administrative and military establishment upon which the security of the monarch so often depended. This created a close association between the Crown and other legal, financial and commercial interests. At the same time military needs could only be met by drawing upon nobles and landowners who provided the officers and supplied regular peasant levies from their estates. All these demands created an intimate network of interests that formed the basis of national and international affairs.

Finance was a glaring weakness in most European states. There was no concept of a balanced budget. Money was accumulated from royal estates, customs dues, loans and taxes, distributed as necessary among government departments and spent, often recklessly, at royal caprice. A considerable proportion of the tax revenue went to pay collectors and receivers, who frequently embezzled further large sums. The whole was fundamentally unbalanced, geared to extract a maximum from the peasantry and unprotected bourgeois while leaving most of the nobility and the wealthy exempt from any direct charges. Efforts at reform invariably foundered upon this fundamental weakness. Collection could be co-ordinated and audited, economies were frequently improvised, but every attempt to re-cast the tax structure inevitably met universal opposition from the privileged classes.

The Crown was thus forced to turn to other sources of revenue. In Prussia the royal house owned one third of the arable land and was able, through new short leases and low interest loans, to double the income from its estates. Else-where the revenue was augmented by clerical levies or the seizure of church property. Banking was exploited by a reck-less issue of notes. Recourse could be made to loans, generally at ruinous rates of interest. These financed the expansion of Russia and maintained the French Court until, on the eve of the Revolution, half the revenue had to be set aside to pay off the debt interest.

The most significant increase in revenue came from in-dustry and trade. 'A country without industry is a body with-out life,' wrote Frederick William I of Prussia. Kings were quick to realize the advantages of an expanding economy for tax purposes. Towns were given special privileges. Tariffs were raised to stop the import of manufactured goods from abroad in order to protect new industries at home. This 'mercantile policy' was designed to promote both the wealth and the self-sufficiency of the State. Economic development increased royal revenue. In Prussia the urban excise rose by 50 per cent. In Spain royal income trebled. Exports were en-couraged and imports reduced. This helped to create a favourable trade balance, enhanced national prosperity and augmented national gold reserves.

A subsequent need for wider markets and new sources of raw materials stimulated imperial expansion and the acquisi-tion of exclusive colonial rights. English Navigation Acts, the French *exclusif*, and Spanish commercial regulations were designed to create wider self-sufficient units and to exclude foreign competition. Though most countries in eastern Europe lacked an opportunity for similar colonial expansion their land-locked empires followed much the same policy. The Habsburgs created a Danubian customs union. Russia expanded into Siberia and opened up new spheres of in-fluence round the Caspian and on the shores of the Black Sea.

Policies of mercantilism and imperial expansion created growing rivalry and led to eventual war. Austria and Russia competed for control on the Danube. Prussian expansion was inevitably resented by her neighbours. In the West the Dutch had occupied the Cape of Good Hope and the East Indies; the Portuguese had settled in wide areas of Africa, India and Brazil. Both had to struggle against rivals in order to safe-guard their possessions. Spain had consolidated her territories in South and Central America and had tried to exclude British and French trade. Meanwhile Britain and France fought for supremacy in India and North America. Trade and empire brought prosperity to the State and power to its ruling dynasties. But it also embroiled the European powers in a series of conflicts that dominated the middle years of the eighteenth century.

The struggles for colonial domination and for power in Europe fused into two great wars. Conflicts between England and Spain, provoked by mercantile competition in South America, merged with the War of the Austrian Succession when Frederick the Great seized Silesia in 1740. France, anxious to weaken Habsburg influence, joined Prussia while Spain attacked the Austrians in Italy. In the Seven Years' War the increasing rivalry between France and England made conflict between them inevitable. War broke out in 1755 and rapidly merged into a general European conflagration. England's alliance with Prussia forced Austria to find allies elsewhere to help recover her lost Silesian province. This led to a reversal of alliances when France joined Austria and Russia in a determined effort to cripple Prussian expansion.[1]

The wars were disastrous for France who lost Canada, her Indian territories and her military prestige. Her armies, officered by exclusive and opinionated nobles, were no match for the well-drilled regiments of Frederick the Great. These survived unparalleled onslaught from French, Austrian and Russian troops. Eventually all sides resigned themselves to a period of peace and reconstruction. But Prussia retained Silesia and also established a firm hold upon the imagination of Germany and the politics of Europe.

In eastern Europe, Russian expansion led to conflict with the Poles and the Ottoman Empire which alarmed the Austrians but created an understanding between Russia and Prussia, fostered by a lively correspondence between Frederick and Catherine the Great. They combined to prevent Polish reconstruction and engineered the election of one of Catherine's lovers to the Polish throne. Continued Russian pressure provoked increasing resistance and led to the creation of a Polish Confederation of Bar. Allied to the Ottoman Empire, the Poles launched a war against the creep-

[1] For fuller details see L. W. Cowie, *Eighteenth Century Europe*.

ing advance of their eastern neighbour. But Catherine emerged victorious, occupied the Danubian principalities of Moldavia and Wallachia, invaded the Crimea and decisively defeated the Ottoman fleet in the Mediterranean.

Russia's rapid penetration alarmed Austria and Prussia. Both were anxious to avoid war and agreed with Catherine to the first partition of Poland in 1772. Russia acquired Polish territory in exchange for her Danubian gains, thus pacifying Austria; Prussia linked her estates in the East with her Brandenburg lands, while the Habsburgs acquired Galicia to counterbalance the acquisitions of her neighbours. In 1774 the Treaty of Kutchuk-Kainardji gave Russia access to Azov and the Black Sea, control over the mouth of the Danube, and allowed her dangerously vague rights of protection over Orthodox Christians in the Ottoman Empire.

War was generally accepted as a normal extension of policy. Its costs were great; expenditure under Catherine rose from 17 to over 70 million roubles a year largely as a result of foreign expansion; in France the State Treasury emerged bankrupt after every major contest. Nevertheless, its effects were often localized. The State lacked the machinery to embark on 'total' war. Resources were limited and exhaustion brought a rapid conclusion to any conflict. Recovery was often equally swift. Peace created prosperity; trade soon revived to refill the exchequer in readiness for further hostilities.

Military forces were limited to professional armies, or to navies whose fighting strength was seldom sufficient to be decisive. Officers were drawn from the nobility and fought their battles in a spirit of aristocratic bravado. In France the purchase of commissions by old and new led to rivalry and increasing incompetence. The Austrians remained tied to wars of slow manoeuvres, divided attacks and lengthy sieges. The Prussian army, however, had built up a disciplined officer class and developed a speed in tactical deployment that gave it a decisive advantage.

Manpower was a constant problem. The towns as sources of profit and trade were often exempt from military service. The major burden fell on the peasantry. Russian press gangs and Prussian recruiting officers raided the countryside for men; France extracted militia service; Austria raised a peasant levy. Discipline could only be maintained by rigid subordination and a brutal reliance on flogging and knouting. Soldiers felt little loyalty to their officers or to the Crown. Frederick the Great seized conscripts from every German state and absorbed whole detachments from his defeated rivals; after every battle they deserted in thousands. Russian officers maintained a brutal discipline and would even beat an offending man to death. The French treated their troops with greater consideration but retained class distinctions at every level and so weakened effectiveness.

Armies were regularly filled with mercenaries – Swiss, Irish or German – whose pay was a vital factor. Bankruptcy could lead to a withdrawal of allegiance and a rapid end to hostilities. Prussia and Austria relied heavily on foreign troops, and loans or subsidies were often essential to keep them in a war. The fighting power of most states was often unreliable; evasive manoeuvre, march and counter-march held out better prospects than a bitter fight to the finish.

Weapons were also seldom trustworthy; the musket was notoriously inaccurate while cannon were still mainly used for primitive bombardment in siege warfare or for the occasional blast of grape shot. Transport remained slow and supplies often failed. Russian organization was especially haphazard and even Frederick the Great was sometimes held up by the irregular speed of his baggage train. War was a gamble in the course of which most belligerents sustained a measure both of victory and defeat. Battles were lost or won by small margins of error, numerical advantage or minor failures in communication. Every effort was made to achieve a vital element of surprise on the battlefield though Austria and Russia still relied on massed weight rather than speed and mobility.

Naval warfare was becoming increasingly significant. Ships were few and took time to construct. The British fleet was still the largest and remained a vital factor in colonial expansion. The expulsion of the French from India and Canada was largely a result of British naval superiority which excluded French reinforcements. Spain and France maintained fleets of some size, but the Spanish lacked the support of mercantile or aristocratic enterprise while the French fleet, though well constructed, was handicapped by lack of money and effective officers. These obstacles had been overcome in

Britain as a result of her expanding trade, her commercial aristocracy, her well-trained officer class and an efficient press-gang system designed to fill the ships in wartime. The importance of naval power was clearly recognized even in Russia. Peter the Great had built a fleet on the Baltic and Catherine constructed a second on the Black Sea. The defeat of the Ottoman navy by the Russians in 1770 was to presage a coming struggle for domination between the European powers in the Middle East.

6. Church and State

The Church was, for the vast majority, a vital force binding society on earth and assuring salvation in heaven. Faith remained strong especially in the country areas where life was still dominated by the rites and festivals of religion. In Roman Catholic countries – in Spain, Italy, France and Austria – the village priest was the only link between the isolated poverty of rural life and a wider, more dazzling horizon. He watched over birth, marriage and death, organized charity and education, guided opinion and centred devotion upon a higher authority. In Russia the Church maintained the traditional ritual of its Orthodox faith. The Protestant pastors of northern Europe promoted similar ideals. The literature of the seventeenth century had been profoundly Christian; the criticism of the eighteenth seldom penetrated into the simple regularity of rural life. In Habsburg lands the Catholic Church remained popular, ready to resist encroachment. In Protestant Germany a new Pietist movement encouraged a personal faith that illuminated the soul through revelation and inner light.

Within the upper reaches of the Church, however, a number of weaknesses had become all too apparent. Conflicts for control over ecclesiastical institutions and divisions in doctrine created growing fragmentation. In the Catholic world the Papacy maintained to the full its traditional spiritual claims, but its temporal authority was in obvious decline. Its powers had been attacked by von Hontheim, suffragan bishop of Trêves, writing under the pseudonym of Febronius in a book, *Concerning the Condition of the Church and the Legitimate Power of the Roman Pontif*, published in 1763. Besides urging that papal power be limited

C

by bishops in council, it advocated royal action to reform religion; rulers were above bishops, divinely appointed to protect the Church in their territories. In spite of papal condemnation the work was translated into French, Spanish and Portuguese and encouraged kings to consolidate their control over the Church. In France similar action was fostered by an independent 'Gallican' tradition, and by Jansenism, which spread a desire for simple piety and dedication among the lower clergy. Its doctrines had been condemned and its institutions destroyed, but its traditions lingered to foster the convictions of the penitent and the poor.

Febronians, Gallicans and Jansenists combined to attack the Jesuits – the most powerful advocates of papal supremacy. Their wealth, authority and papal connection made them an obvious target of royal antagonism. Between 1750 and 1770 they were expelled from Austria, France, Portugal and Spain. This encouraged Catholic kings to combine and put pressure on the Pope to force through the long projected dissolution of the order. After considerable delay Clement XIV agreed. To prevent further friction within the Church the Jesuits were dissolved in 1773. Nothing could have revealed more clearly the weakness of the Papacy.

In Protestant states and in the Russian Orthodox Church princes were already supreme. Convinced of their divine rights and their political supremacy they turned religion into a department of state. Ecclesiastical councils and the Holy Synod in Russia were part of a bureaucratic machinery of government responsible for appointments and the definition of doctrine. Rulers recognized the value of religion as a basic element of order, essential for keeping people passive and obedient. Prussian rulers encouraged Pietist introspection which was politically harmless. The Orthodox were set to worship a divine Tsar. Religion became an instrument of politics. Catherine the Great encouraged the Jesuits to pacify the Poles and refused to sanction their dissolution in Russia, thus saving them from extinction. At the same time she used the plight of Orthodox believers in Poland and the Ottoman Empire as an excuse for intervention. Frederick tolerated and encouraged Catholic and Huguenot minorities for military and economic purposes. The Pope expressed himself gratified by such generosity.

Divided in doctrine and tied to the policies of the State, the Church became a prisoner of the social order. In Protestant and Orthodox Europe its highest officials fitted into the rungs of a royal bureaucracy. In Catholic Europe bishops and higher ecclesiastics were generally noble. In southern Germany sees were distributed among the younger sons of ruling Houses. Spain demonstrated a greater flexibility. The Church controlled great wealth and vast estates. Though redundant monasteries had been dissolved, the remaining properties still created an impression of clerical domination in most towns and villages.

By contrast, the lower clergy remained poor and were often reduced to the status of their parishioners. In Russia they were depressed and primitive. In Spain and Austria the clergy worked with enthusiasm, but their life appeared restricted and burdened by poverty when compared to the wealth and grandeur of their superiors. In France the *curé* struggled with a pittance of 500 livres to instil zeal and devotion. He paid most of the *décimes* levied to fulfil the annual free gift to the Crown and began to demand redress of grievances and an increasing voice in the organization of the Church. These attempts were vigorously suppressed by the Court and the ecclesiastical heirarchy. Discontents spread unrecognized, while Jansenist ideals and naturalist philosophies gradually undermined traditional loyalties.

Outwardly, however, the Church appeared rooted in the past. Bishops, aristocratic, wealthy and privileged, relied upon the prince. The Church maintained a vital cohesion that held together the isolated communities in the State. Its belief in a natural order brought security to the privileged and succour to the poor. The prince, the lord, the seigneur were accepted as part of a divine establishment. Disobedience was sin and death; acceptance brought sorrow but salvation. Society was geared to obedience and to a resigned acceptance of an inevitable order of things. Nevertheless, new factors had already begun to exert a corroding influence. These were to shift the foundations of economic and political power and create ideas that were eventually to destroy the established standards of action and belief.

II · THE FACTORS OF CHANGE

1. *Introduction*

THE study of change is of considerable interest to the historian. The growth of new movements, ideas and techniques and their impact upon society, the economy and the life of the state has provided the material for repeated study and research. Some have emphasized a gradual process of growth – a steady rise in population, the incidental accumulation of wealth, a progressive definition of institutions and ideas; others have stressed the revolutionary impact of new discoveries, actions and beliefs. It is part of the fascination of the study of history to try to unravel this sort of problem, even if its finer points may sometimes straggle into obscurity. To do so, however, it is essential to make a preliminary study of what these changes were, how and why they happened, and when their development began to make any impact upon the existing patterns of human behaviour.

Difficulties immediately arise because change is seldom the result of one factor, but the outcome of a cross-fertilization of a number of parallel developments. Thus a growing population, new wealth, new imperial markets, and new scientific and technological discoveries combined to promote agricultural and industrial progress. The use of reason, the discovery of natural scientific laws and the romantic vision of the individual fused in revolutionary action and inspired the highest achievement in music, literature and art. These and other changes were to have a decisive impact upon the social and political framework of Europe. Combination or conflict between the old and the new created varied patterns and unexpected relationships. With shifting emphasis and repeated modifications, states and societies acquired new characteristics and laid the foundations for nineteenth-century developments.

2. *The Agrarian and Industrial Revolution*

A number of factors contributed towards the gradual acceleration of agrarian and industrial growth during the second half of the eighteenth century. The population began to rise more steeply throughout Europe. England, France, Spain and northern Italy seem to have conformed to a general pattern of demographic expansion. The causes are still in dispute but would appear to include both a decline in the death rate, particularly infant mortality, due to medical improvements, hospitals, hygiene and midwives, and a rise in fertility especially in the cities and during wartime. Improvements in diet and living standards also contributed towards the growth of both rural and urban populations. In England and Wales numbers rose from 5·5 to over 8·8 million during the course of the eighteenth century; in France the increase ranged from approximately 19 to 26 million – creating a noticeable pressure of population in the countryside and in many of the towns. Elsewhere the acquisition of new territory or immigration led to further increases. Prussia trebled her total numbers by conquest and settlement. Russia grew from 18 million to nearer 30 million as a result of new territorial gains. The total for Europe has been variously calculated, but a figure of 118 million in 1700, 140 million in 1750 and 187 million in 1800 would not appear unreasonable.

This increase had an inevitable impact upon demand. Prices rose and created additional incentives for investment and reconstruction. New urban development required increasing supplies. London, Paris and the larger cities of Europe became expanding markets for rural produce and industrial goods. In western Europe the expansion of imperial trade stimulated manufactures. Demand for textiles and cottons increased, together with a need for hardware products. Production began to rise; the putting-out system flourished. In Lancashire it was the golden age of the hand-loom weavers. In Prussia the State built new mills and encouraged manufacture. The output of raw materials was also increased. Russia raised her production of iron ore, while in England the iron industry also maintained a steady rate of growth.

Expansion, however, was held up by lack of capital, primitive transport facilities and the immobility of labour. In Russia, Prussia and Austria the State lacked the funds to create conditions for revolutionary change; peasant populations were tied to the soil; the incentives to exploit new techniques were almost entirely lacking. In Germany, tolls and political divisions made any concentration of capital difficult. In France the orientation of society round land, office or the Court focused attention away from economic activity, while internal customs barriers led to the accumulation of capital in towns or isolated provincial regions such as Bordeaux and Toulouse. Only in England with its growing wealth, mercantile society, unified market and scientific development were conditions suitable for a significant breakthrough.

The wealth of England was one of the notable features of the eighteenth century and a source of envious wonder to many Europeans. Profits were derived from aristocratic estates and commercial interests, and provided the basis for further economic growth. A favourable trade balance brought in a steady surplus for most of the century. Financial security was assured by the extension of banking and the stability of the Bank of England. Wealth was promoted by the investments of the aristocracy, gentry and merchant classes who combined in pursuit of profit regardless of social distinctions. Between 1740 and 1800 personal capital rose by perhaps 500 per cent.

England was not restricted by internal tolls or a tied peasant labour force. Communications were free, though hampered by lack of a good road system; rivers and coastal transport were used to facilitate trade. Shipping boomed and canal construction was twice as extensive as in France. The population from the countryside had little difficulty in reaching the towns. Irish labour could easily supplement Lancashire needs. Mobility encouraged concentration, the growth of towns and an upsurge of demand already stimulated by colonial expansion. Bristol rose from 30,000 to 50,000 between 1700 and 1750, Liverpool from 5,000 to 20,000 in the same period. With capital for investment and an active mercantile community, new techniques were soon exploited to increase production and promote higher returns.

New invention was the outcome of a combination of scientific discovery and technological experiment. Progress in agriculture included new cattle breeds, crop rotation, improved mechanization and new chemical fertilizers. These reflected the work of a wide variety of men from practical farmers like Tull, who advanced the design of horse-hoes and seed drills, to chemists like Humphry Davy who advocated the use of liquid manures.

Science in the eighteenth century had concentrated both upon a philosophic examination of natural laws and on practical problems such as pumping, engines, gunnery and navigation. After an initial burst of enthusiasm which had culminated in the foundation of the Royal Society in 1660, the progress of invention had been maintained by generations of practical iron masters and mechanics. Newcomen designed an atmospheric pump which had been adapted for use in coal mines during the century. The Darbys at Coalbrookdale had begun to use coke instead of charcoal for smelting iron, and had added cast-iron rails into their mines. The cotton industry was stimulated by Kay's flying shuttle which accelerated weaving, and by the invention of Hargreaves's Spinning Jenny (1764), and Arkwright's Water Frame (1769), which provided the necessary yarn.

Simultaneously science and technology were promoted by Dr. Black's discoveries in heat and their application by Watt to a modified steam pump. Chemists also explored the properties of sulphuric acid and chlorine for use in bleaching. Learned societies in Manchester, Newcastle and Birmingham discussed every scientific subject from steam engines and clocks, to dyes and paper production. Lecturers toured the country demonstrating apparatus and explaining new discoveries, while a flood of books added to the growing popular interest in scientific invention.

By 1789 these developments had set off a train of revolutionary changes in industry and agriculture. The 'Norfolk system of husbandry' combined soil cultivation, a three-course rotation of cereals, turnips and clover, within a pattern of careful estate management. This gradually brought an end to traditional methods of open field, strip cultivation and led to an increase in enclosure and a rapid decline of smallholdings in favour of long leases and larger farms. Wheat replaced rye as a basic crop and improvements in animal breeding increased the value of meadow. Bakewell doubled the weight of his new Leicester sheep and set the pace with cattle and improved methods of farm management. These changes, however, were slow to spread. Though nearly a million acres were brought into cultivation during the century many areas remained backward and poor.

In Europe the progress of change was even slower. Though Norfolk methods were advocated by many French writers, their adoption was generally prevented by the prevailing pattern of small peasant land tenures. The work of Tull was popularized by Voltaire, and the principles of breeding developed by Bakewell were certainly appreciated in the stables of the aristocracy. But enclosure remained regionalized and aroused bitter opposition. In Germany new techniques were adopted at a still slower pace. English developments were only popularized by Thaer in 1798. Prussian monarchs encouraged land reclamation, but it was only with the greatest difficulty that Frederick the Great was able to persuade a suspicious peasantry of the value of the potato, while opposition to enclosure remained widespread.

Changes in industry were generally more significant. In England a 'take-off into self-sustained growth' was closely associated with cotton. Exports rose ten-fold between 1750 and 1769. By 1789, 20,000 spinning jennies were in operation. New inventions were quickly incorporated into cotton machinery. Crompton's Mule combined the earlier designs of Hargreaves and Arkwright with a spindle carriage to feed in the thread. Water power had been harnessed by 1769, and in 1785 Cartwright's looms were being driven by steam engines in his new cotton mills. Power looms spread rapidly through Lancashire and into the West Riding, where woollen textiles were soon manufactured by similar techniques.

The needs of the cotton industry created a growing demand for coal, iron and new machinery. The number of engines built at the Soho works of Boulton and Watt in Birmingham increased steadily and by 1800 over 300 were in operation. Iron production was able to rise to meet these new demands as a result of the puddling and rolling processes developed by Cort. By 1788 total output had reached some 68,000 tons compared to 25,000 in 1720. The output of coal, vital for steam power and the iron industry, also doubled with the aid of pumps to tackle floods, and rails to speed conveyance to the pit head.

Improvements in transport and communication were the direct outcome of a need to convey raw materials and finished products in bulk. Canals were built to transport coal to Liverpool and Manchester, to carry pottery from Staffordshire, salt from Cheshire and manufactures from the Midlands. A network of canals and navigable rivers gradually covered England and helped to promote the concentration of new industry and the growth of towns. New roads, however, were constructed more slowly. No efforts were made to plan a systematic network. Improvements were limited to isolated experiments in the North and to the individual enterprise of turnpike trusts.

Expansion in cotton, iron and coal brought changes to many other sectors of the economy. The chemical industry, armaments, printing, paper and glass production all responded to rising demands and the application of new techniques. Urban concentrations grew in the Midlands and the North to attract a growing stream of labourers from the countryside where enclosures were gradually restricting employment. These changes helped to promote a social revolution. New generations of mill owners, iron masters and industrialists rose to join the merchants and lawyers of the middle classes. They quickly consolidated their wealth and influence, while their capital and enterprise opened up new horizons in society and politics. As a result the bourgeoisie became established and ready to play a decisive role in nineteenth-century England. But below them the conditions of artisans and smaller craftsmen deteriorated. They were forced to fight for survival or adapt themselves to new competitive conditions. Meanwhile, in the mills and the mines, new factory hands and miners began to form the nucleus of a future proletariat. Drawn to the towns by hope of better work and wages, their conditions were subsequently to decline into the slums of a 'Black Country'.

By 1789 Europe had been little affected by these new developments. Industrial innovations spread slowly, handicapped by lack of capital, labour and free market conditions. Moreover, Britain tried to keep a monopoly in cotton machinery and prohibited its export as early as 1774. The export of metal processes was also banned and European states had to rely on spies or the assistance of defaulting engineers to build up their own industries. In France a textile boom in the 1750s created suitable conditions for mechanization. By 1789 some 900 jennies were in use, and English cotton engineers were building machines in Rouen, Harfleur and Le Havre. The coal mines at Anzin had twelve steam engines in operation and already employed over 4,000 men. Iron output was increased by the expansion of the Le Creusot works with the help of an English engineer, Wilkinson, brother of a Midlands ironmaster. Otherwise changes were few and further growth was retarded by the subsequent outbreak of revolution and war. In Germany and Italy handicrafts remained dominant until well into the nineteenth century; in Russia traditional methods survived even longer – though a form of steam engine may have been used in the Urals as early as 1758.

England was to retain a decisive lead for several decades. This became a factor of vital importance during the Napoleonic wars when the British economy was able to survive severe strain and pour out vast sums to subsidize European coalitions. Naval guns drilled by new techniques at the Carron works displayed decisive superiority at sea. Wealth ensured the final victory and laid the foundations of nineteenth-century prosperity. But at the same time new social tensions were increasingly apparent. Disaffected labourers had to be restrained by ruthless Combination Acts. Artisan Luddites smashed the machines that threatened to deprive them of their livelihood, and their actions were soon echoed by textile workers in Rouen destroying the new *méchaniques*. In England, aristocrats and middle class capitalists combined to defeat the agitation. But in Europe the ambitions of the upper bourgeoisie were generally in conflict with the aristocracy. Thus in France bourgeois agitation encouraged the unrest of artisans, craftsmen and the labouring classes and hastened an eruption of violence that was eventually to break through the weakened framework of the established order.

3. *Science and Scientific Rationalism*

The ideas that were to revolutionize society first developed from the reasoning of the 'scientific' mind rather than from any specific industrial or economic changes. The foundations had been laid by English scientists and thinkers at the end of the previous century. Their work was to infect European thought and spread new attitudes of mind with which to probe the past and replace existing institutions by a more rational framework. Sir Isaac Newton (1642–1727) had combined objective observation and mathematical precision to demonstrate the existence of natural physical laws which could be verified by experiment. His conclusions were as significant as his methods. He appeared to demonstrate the existence of forces which held the universe in a permanent state of equilibrium; he vindicated a process of induction and deduction from observed facts and could claim to prove the absolute validity of a scientific method and of an objective and rational approach.

John Locke (1632–1704) used a similar approach to study the problems of philosophy and politics. Understanding came as a result of applying the reason to the impressions registered upon the mind. By observation and analysis a basic order in society could be determined. This required both freedom for the individual and an authority to preserve that freedom, and the property which guaranteed it, from the predatory demands of less reliable neighbours. The solution lay in a contract by which the people gave consent to government, and a constitution which balanced an executive order and an elected legislature within a framework of law. Similar principles required religious toleration for every man to reach his own understanding of the Creator. Newton and Locke allowed for the existence of God as designer and prime mover, but rejected revelation and any divine intervention into natural law and the workings of a reasonable mind. Dogma was an unjustifiable assertion of an irrational absolute and had no right to contradict empirical evidence or scientific observation.

The rational approach was extended by other writers to both philosophy and religion. John Toland popularized Locke's views on the validity of reason and advocated a deist position. Similar ideas were absorbed into Freemasonry which was founded in England at the beginning of the eighteenth century and spread into France, Germany and Russia. Combining a rational approach with an emphasis on moral behaviour it did much to spead toleration and to undermine dogmatic assumptions. Dogma was criticized with increasing violence by sceptics and agnostics who attacked the validity of religion and criticized everything that could not be proven by tangible evidence.

David Hume (1711–76) took rationalist arguments to their logical conclusion. If the senses determined everything then they alone could decide what did and what did not exist. As the senses could only rely on physical and tangible evidence there could be no certainty where this was lacking. God, miracles and revelation were thereby excluded and sceptics launched an attack on religion that opened a new phase in the spread of rational criticism. Scepticism found no justification for obscurantist religious beliefs and was not prepared to compromise with any form of divine authority.

English ideas accelerated and extended parallel developments on the continent of Europe. The achievements of Newtonian mechanics, the success of the 1688 revolution and the subsequent victories of England in Europe and the New World gave her ideas and institutions a unique influence and prestige. In every country Institutes of Arts and Sciences explored the implications of a rational and scientific approach. Leibniz in Germany developed theories of mechanical evolution, d'Alembert in France systematized mechanics, while Lavoisier constructed the earliest tables of elements by the observation and measurement of chemical change.

Bayle (1647–1706) was among the first to base all his ideas upon observation and criticism. In his *Historical and Critical Dictionary*, 1697, he demanded facts and experimental proofs, and urged that toleration was essential to promote any real understanding. He advocated deist principles and by a comparative criticism of the Bible opened an attack that was to be copied and extended by French writers throughout the eighteenth century. The 'empirical' approach was popularized in the writings of two leading French *philosophes,* Montesquieu (1689–1755) and Voltaire (1694–1778). Both visited England and returned profoundly impressed by its scientific achievements, balanced constitution and tolerant society. Montesquieu tried to systematize his observations in his book, *l'Esprit des lois,* published in 1748. His enthusiasm for a constitution which appeared to separate power within a framework of law was to have a notable influence. Voltaire popularized the work of Newton and Locke and emphasized the need for toleration. With biting wit he ridiculed the futile and intolerant administration of the old order and urged a wider and deeper understanding of society.

French writers spread this rational approach throughout Europe. The age of Louis XIV had witnessed the supremacy of French thought and culture and of her ideals of absolute monarchy and state control. The French language had become universal to all educated men. It now scattered the seeds of a rational and revolutionary criticism. Natural law and the ideals of a tolerant and reasonable mind became the basis of the *Aufklärung,* or 'enlightenment' in Germany. At Leipzig professors advocated rational and systematic criticism of literature and law and the need for order and toleration in the State, as well as new theories of science and mathematics. The vocabulary of criticism became fashionable among the European aristocracy. Frederick the Great joined the Freemasons and advocated toleration; Catherine the Great corresponded with Voltaire, read Montesquieu and, in her early days, encouraged the translation of philosophic books into Russian.

The doubts which developed from the rational mind led to a wave of attacks upon the institutions of church and state. Voltaire had begun with bitter criticism of intolerance, dogma and religious practices. Helvetius popularized the role of the senses, and his ideals, designed to give the greatest happiness to the greatest number, were to be the foundation of a nineteenth-century Utilitarianism. His book *De l'esprit,* which in France was burnt by the hangman, was widely read in Germany and in Russia. D'Holbach moved on to an atheist position and attacked religion as a pretext for keeping society enslaved. These writers combined under the dynamic guidance of Diderot and d'Alembert to publish a notable *Encyclopédie* which redefined art, religion and politics in rational and scientific terms. Church and state were attacked directly or by veiled implication; sceptical and deist views were generally advanced. The first volume was published in 1751 and, after some delay due to censorship and editorial disagreements, the final volume appeared in 1766.

As criticism moved eastwards it became increasingly hostile to the existing social and political framework. Schlozer at Göttingen attacked the tyranny, incompetence and immorality of governments in the petty principalities of the Empire, and advocated the balanced and tolerant constitutions of England and Hanover. Moser criticized the privileges of the nobility, and attacked Divine Right, court flattery and corruption. He demanded political liberty. His books spread to France and Russia where their impact began to undermine authority. Journals attacking tyrant landlords and incompetent governments spread in westernized circles. Novikov in *The Drone* ridiculed the aristocracy and supported the downtrodden peasant.

Thus the rational enlightenment became firmly entrenched in educated minds. Man became the measure of all things. Reason, based upon observation and sense perception, was the guide to understanding. Condorcet in France proclaimed the rule of 'reason, tolerance and humanity', urging the need for social reform and education to hasten the process of evolution. New movements in religion, economics and art were influenced by this rational emancipation. The growth of literary classicism emphasized the perfectability of man, the beauty of the human form as revealed in the statues of ancient Greece and Rome, and the need for individual fulfilment within the framework of a new natural law.

In economic thought the emphasis on observation, reason and natural growth led to the foundation of a new *physiocrat* school which stressed the need to free trade and economic activity from mercantile restrictions. In France, Turgot and Quesnay maintained that wealth was based upon land and increased by the unrestrained action of free and natural laws. Following English methods they advocated enclosure and soil cultivation. Guild restrictions and state tolls hampered expansion and frustrated the stimulating impact of individual and natural competition. Their views were followed up by Adam Smith who, in *The Wealth of Nations*, 1776, advanced the classic liberal arguments in favour of free trade. Division of labour increased output which could be further stimulated by a free exchange between countries. Benefits would be mutual and any differences made up in the long run by new investment and production to restore a natural equilibrium. He stressed the benefits of increased industrial manufacture in the economy and favoured the abolition of tariffs between English goods and French agricultural produce.

4. Pre-Romanticism

The Pre-Romanticism of the late eighteenth century was both a development and a reaction from the reason of the enlightenment. It was but a small step from an emphasis on man to an enthusiastic belief in the individual. Rousseau transformed a rational analysis of natural law and an intellectual contemplation of human rights into a revolutionary cry for liberty. For him academic philosophic discussions were not enough. Man had to achieve a break-through and awaken to a new realization of himself. This led Rousseau to criticize the arid and atheist views of his contemporaries. He proclaimed a new faith in human ideals and in God who 'makes all things good' till 'man meddles with them and they become evil'. He found new hope in man's higher nature which could be liberated by a return to a new order in society.

The new order allowed for no compromise with the established authorities of the eighteenth century. It was a romantic synthesis in which man fulfilled his destiny by a revolutionary surrender to a society in which the will of each became the will of all. This 'general will' fused the rights of the individual into a democratic sovereignty where every man could feel himself to be part of an organic union within the State. This appeal to the mass was received with sceptical alarm by the philosophers and with horror by the aristocracy. Upon illiterate peasants and artisans it had little or no immediate impact. It was easy to point out flaws in Rousseau's argument: that in practice a 'general will' could easily lead to the tyranny of the majority; that it would be difficult to operate in the backward state of contemporary Europe; that its logical conclusions, which allowed society to 'force men to be free' to their true nature, was full of obvious contradictions. Rousseau himself admitted that only in a perfect society could his synthesis become a practical system and allowed for the election of representatives and the balanced constitutional principles of Montesquieu when he came to draw up his own outlines of government.

But in spite of any theoretical or practical contradictions Rousseau's influence on Europe was immense. His books took Germany by storm. *Émile*, in which he advocated a natural education free from restriction and intellectual criticism; *Contrat social*, where he explored the ideal fusion of the self and the State. He attacked the narrow rationalism of the enlightenment, the specialist classification of botanists and chemists, the calculating precision of reason. He exploded into a new enthusiasm for man, for nature, for hope and for individual fulfilment. Herder infused Rousseau's vision with a Germanic intensity. His *Fragmente*, published in 1767, inspired a new introspection, an examination of the individual, a search into the soul. Study of human nature led on to an examination of different peoples, of the *Volk*, and Herder's collection of folk song and poetry did much to stir up the first symptoms of national feeling in Germany and among the Slavs. His studies in history and popular literature were taken up by Poles, Czechs and Slav writers crying out for liberty and struggling for a new identity.

In German literature the influence of Rousseau, Herder, Shakespeare and Macpherson's wild and exaggerated forgeries of Ossian's poetry combined into the *Sturm und Drang*, a movement in which nature and the individual became fused into a romantic climax. The early works of Goethe (1749–1832) and Schiller (1759–1805), two of Germany's greatest writers, were filled with a longing for the natural, for the true self and for the ideal. A rational order in society only brought frustration, despair and ultimate suicide, as in *Werther*, a book by Goethe published in 1774 which rapidly became a European best-seller.

The excess of the *Sturm und Drang*, however, soon burnt itself out and moved on to become fused with a maturer rationalism into a new classicism. This synthesis created some of the greatest achievements of European civilization in the later works of Goethe, Schiller, Beethoven and Schubert. Vision and experience were distilled by rational discipline. The ideals of a balanced framework and a classical perfection became filled with an individual intensity that perhaps found supreme expression in Goethe's *Faust* and Beethoven's symphonies.

No such ideal synthesis was to appear in politics. History was to be a bitter commentary on the failure to reconcile the hopes and ideals of countless individuals within a rational and organized political framework. Rousseau's vision had little bearing upon the practical problems of the State. People could only achieve their ambition through instruments of government. These were in the hands of kings and aristocrats who soon realized the danger of allowing others to go to extremes. Their attempts to keep power in their own hands forced critics to take a revolutionary course and to destroy the entire framework of a traditional order.

But revolt also demonstrated the total ineffectiveness of individuals once the framework had been destroyed. In a lawless and fragmentary society power became vested in possession, in arms and in men. Amid the general confusion the strongest won and imposed his rule upon the remainder. Individual ideals were soon smothered and subjected to the rule of the majority or to the rule of the one. Thus the romantic ideals of Rousseau did inject a new liberating influence into eighteenth-century life. But they also released a wave of conflicting interests and individual ambition. This was to convulse Europe, shatter governments, destroy the established framework of the State and open up new prospects both of dictatorship and democratic development.

5. *Enlightened Despots*

'Enlightenment' was generally attributed to those rulers who claimed to govern their kingdoms by principles based upon the new rationalism of the eighteenth century. Their object was usually to perfect their own autocracy and they showed little real regard for the individual interests of their subjects. Whenever reason threatened to arouse popular agitation they quickly reverted to a rigid authoritarianism. The views of Frederick the Great, 'reason as much as you like and about whatsoever you like – but obey', were typical. In time, thought and obedience were to prove incompatible. Nevertheless, authoritarian reforms did consolidate royal power and delay the growth of revolutionary agitation. It was an attempt to reach a compromise with change, regulated by traditional methods and controlled by the monarch from above. Success or failure was to have a significant influence upon the future.

'Enlightenment' certainly enabled despots to articulate their claims to absolute control with a greater precision. Joseph II proclaimed himself, 'King by profession', and

D

Frederick the Great, 'the first servant of the people', while Catherine expounded upon the value and benefits of authority. The Crown became the mouthpiece of the State, the monarch the visible personification of law and order. Rulers were more consciously aware of the role of monarchy and of the need to retain the initiative and keep control.

Catherine the Great was probably the most spectacular and the least effective of the enlightened despots. In her youth she had read the French *philosophes*, in her early life she had corresponded with Voltaire and dallied with Diderot, anxious to display an affected familiarity with the latest literary fashions. This brought a flurry of praise from her distant admirers – but it was praise for words rather than for actions. At St. Petersburg she maintained a dazzling court amid a spectacular round of artistic, dramatic and musical activity housed in the new palaces and ornate buildings by the banks of the Neva. New Academies of Science and Colleges of Medicine introduced the latest discoveries from the West. The aristocracy adopted French custom and social mannerisms in a degrading round of competitive entertainment.

Government was rationalized round the Tsarina: royal secretaries sent directives, the Senate drafted and checked decrees, ministries carried through executive decisions. The provinces were reorganized under governors and provincial boards which were checked by state bureaucrats under Senate control. Yet much of this remained a veneer. Local authority continued in the hands of the aristocracy. The vast substratum of Russian society remained savage and uncouth.

This social division made most of Catherine's enlightenment illusory – a fact she was to recognize herself. Though swift to secularize church land and reduce the clergy to the rank of state officials, she protected the Jesuits in defiance of papal and diplomatic pressure in order to help assure the obedience of her Polish subjects. An attempt to codify the law, preceded in 1767 by a *Nekaze* of enlightened suggestions urging equality and the abolition of torture, failed once the vested interests of the nobility were threatened. The Pugachev rebellion (1773–5), when peasants murdered landlords and burnt aristocratic property, brought a threat to the whole order. The reaction was swift: an enlargement of the standing army, an increase in noble authority and a more rigid censorship of French and Russian literature. Catherine turned upon her early associates with bitter sarcasm.

Yet both at home and abroad she retained the initiative. In spite of the financial chaos and inflation caused by war deficits and excessive note issues, trade flourished, exports boomed and the frontier continued to expand. After the first partition of Poland (1772) and the Treaty of Kutchuk-Kainardji (1774) the Crimea was annexed in 1784 and Georgia incorporated in the same year. In 1789 Russia reached the Dniester in spite of opposition by Turks and Swedes, and consolidated her frontier in a new advanced position. Thus the Tsarina could indeed proclaim herself the champion of the State, the personification of law, authority and government, the apex of a society enlightened by western thought. But the mass of the Russian people, some 33 millions, remained serfs untouched by the abstract intentions of their ruler.

Frederick the Great was probably the most effective among contemporary rulers. Sharing the conventional correspondence with Voltaire, he nevertheless organized his state on military lines. Society was divided into castes: a nobility to officer the army and administer the State; a middle class for commerce; and a peasantry to work on the land and promote wealth. The King wielded an absolute executive authority from Potsdam. Directives were sent through secretaries and ministerial departments to the local War and Domain Chambers or town administrators. In the provinces officials linked up with the *Landräte*[1] who worked with the central bureaucracy to levy taxes, maintain law and order and conscript peasant quotas for the royal army. Frederick was aware of the need to consolidate and develop his small and divided territories. Berlin was enlarged by immigration, commercial enterprise and extensive public works. Agriculture and industry were encouraged to foster prosperity and guarantee the solvency of the State.

Though Frederick the Great created the framework of a powerful despotism he remained restricted in the range of his enlightenment. At the centre efficiency could be maintained; Prussia was one of the few states to support a stable financial system and a budget surplus; investment in mines,

---

[1] See p. 16.

agriculture and communications encouraged growth; the army was kept at over 150,000 men under the King's immediate command. Enlightened policies were adopted in religion and the law by proclaiming toleration, abolishing torture and promoting speedy and impartial trials. But, as in Russia, little could be done about the vested interests of the aristocracy while they remained an essential prop of the régime. Peasants lived tied to the land, committed to their lords and to the routine of manorial life. The King could tidy up details and intervene in cases of outrage, but efforts to reform the law were only partially successful and a code published in 1786 after Frederick's death was received with little enthusiasm.

Joseph II was alone in tackling some of these basic issues. Though less spectacular and less able to capture the imagination than his contemporaries, he was perhaps the most genuine. Determined to carry rationalization and reform to a logical conclusion he was ready to suffer the consequences. Issuing over 11,000 laws and some 6,000 orders and decrees he attempted to effect a peaceful revolution in church and state. Much of his policy followed a familiar pattern of autocratic pronouncements, a brilliant Viennese court to attract the German and Magyar nobility, and an administrative machine under central departments and local officials. But, in addition, he was not prepared to compromise and carried his reforms into the provinces, the law, the Church and the serf economy with a rigidity and a fanaticism that roused a storm of protest from every sector of the community.

The Habsburg territories were divided into thirteen provincial governments directed by German bureaucrats in the Viennese Chancellery, and subdivided into Circles where Captains were responsible for finance, conscription and law. This machinery was designed to enforce a wide variety of novel legislation. To increase taxation manorial labour services were to be abolished and replaced by a land tax applicable to all regardless of class. To equalize the law new courts were established by codes authorized between 1786 and 1788. These by-passed manorial courts, abolished torture and promised the right of appeal. To control the Church and assure independence a series of edicts guaranteed toleration, restricted papal power, cut down monasteries and nunneries, abolished tithes and vested administration and appointments in the hands of the Crown. Finally Joseph II tackled the problem of serfdom. Manorial obligations were cut, labour services, *robot*, abolished together with tithes, and security of tenure guaranteed, with a system of state loans to purchase property. Other reforms introduced new schools to replace Jesuit colleges and reformed the army to compete with the growing power of Prussia.

The reaction to Joseph's decrees was extremely violent. The Hungarian and Netherlands provinces revolted against Viennese control and demanded the restoration of Magyar privileges and provincial rights. In Brabant and Lombardy resistance was reinforced by opposition to religious reforms. Priests inflamed the mob, while aristocratic nuns demanded the restoration of their comfortable institutions. The aristocracy was outraged by the peasant legislation and the new land tax. In 1790 Joseph died, weighed down by a sense of failure. At home he had roused national provincialism, which was to become an endemic problem in the Habsburg Empire, alienated the Church and angered the aristocracy, while support from a peasantry caught between lord and priest could at best only be half-hearted. Abroad he had failed to acquire Bavaria due to Prussian opposition, and his war against the Turks in 1787 had been undermined by the revolt of Hungary. His brother Leopold II withdrew much of the peasant and administrative legislation. Magyar privileges were guaranteed, labour services restored, the land tax abolished. But the peasants kept their lands and began to commute their services for rent, while the new machinery of state survived to provide the necessary foundation for future action.

The rest of Europe followed varying degrees of enlightenment. Germany ranged from the tolerant régimes of Hanover or Saxe-Weimar to the arbitrary and reactionary states of Bavaria and Hesse. The Spanish Bourbons centralized the administration and extended provincial control, attempted to reform taxation and extended increasing control over the Church. Their relatives in Naples maintained the outline of an enlightened government, a gay court and an opera house. Though scarcely aware of the changes that were to disturb the equilibrium of eighteenth-century life, their activities were sufficient to dazzle, to divert or to evade the economic, political and social problems in their states.

Enlightened despots thus attempted, in varying degrees, to reach a compromise with change. Today it is easy to say this was doomed to failure. Then it did not seem unreasonable. If the experience of Catherine was enough to show her the dangers of enlightenment, the control of Frederick seemed to contemporaries a pinnacle of achievement. It could be considered ironical that in 1789 Joseph was faced with revolt as a result of the very measures which, in the same year, were among the demands of French revolutionaries. It might seem that any attempt to change or reform the institutions of society or government was bound to provoke revolt from some quarter. Yet by concentrating power, by the articulation of a rational policy and by the maintenance of the social framework, monarchy was preserved, despotism enhanced and revolution averted.

Among the states of continental Europe France failed significantly to achieve either 'enlightenment' or 'despotism'. Though almost buried beneath the weight of autocratic precedence the successors of Louis XIV were unable to maintain effective control. Louis XV, handsome and well meaning, lacked drive and preferred hunting or the company of his mistresses. Louis XVI who succeeded in 1774 amid popular acclaim was almost completely inarticulate. Unable to formulate state policy or to take any initiative, his good intentions were exploited on every side. He was unfortunate in his marriage with Marie Antoinette – the outcome of the unpopular Austrian alliance.[1] Vivacious and independent, she failed to blend with the exclusiveness of court life at Versailles and retired to live in a romantic world of idyllic 'dolls houses' in the gardens of the Petit Trianon. She was unlucky to get involved in the 'Scandal of the Queen's necklace', when a down-and-out countess persuaded the Cardinal de Rohan to buy a diamond necklace for delivery to the Queen which never reached its destination. This and the subsequent trial helped to build up a picture of extravagance and immorality which, though largely untrue, split the Court and further isolated the Queen from aristocratic society. Versailles ceased to be the centre of the State. Ambitious nobles, financiers and writers gravitated to Paris. The King lost control over the instruments of government which soon became a prey to rival

[1] See p. 20.

factions struggling for power at court and in the provinces.

As a result the State was neither rationalized nor consolidated. While society became increasingly divided the government was gradually paralysed. The main source of weakness lay in finance; warfare led to repeated bankruptcy which in turn limited the opportunities for reconstruction and for military and naval reform. Efforts to revise the financial structure by a more equitable distribution of taxation were thwarted by bitter opposition from the Church and from Parisian and provincial *parlements*. Attempts to free trade and break down tolls or guild restrictions met with equal hostility. *Parlements* attacked ministerial proposals and the orders of loyal *intendants*.

The aristocratic opposition, not content with its obstruction of the government, sought to monopolize the offices of state and to gain control over the central institutions of government. Nearly all the high church livings were reserved for the nobility. When army reforms were introduced to encourage the advancement of able officers through new military colleges, the *parlements* reacted with a demand that only those who could prove four generations of nobility were to be promoted above the rank of Captain.

The Church, which elsewhere was brought increasingly under royal control, maintained an aloof independence. The expulsion of the Jesuits, which throughout Europe reflected the will of enlightened despots struggling for control, was in France the result of aristocratic opposition in the *parlements* and was forced upon the King against his will. Ecclesiastical wealth remained vast and largely untaxed. The Church could vote a free gift to the Crown – usually an insignificant fraction of its total revenue – and continued to govern itself through its own independent assemblies.

Yet royal prerogatives remained – *lits de justice* to enforce the registration of laws on obstructive *parlements, lettres de cachet* for the arrest of disobedient subjects. But the will to use them was lacking. Some reforms were undertaken to close decayed religious houses, abolish serfdom on royal estates, prevent torture and improve the Paris water supply. Reforms in the navy and the artillery were to have an important influence in the future. Abroad, France acquired Lorraine in 1761 and purchased Corsica seven years later. But these gestures were not enough to justify the claims of a paternal despotism or of a divine royalty. They were only sufficient to irritate the clergy and the nobility who became more and more determined to remove the last remnants of royal authority and to acquire absolute control. The aristocracy little realized that by demolishing the framework of royal government they were also destroying the basis of their own powers, privileges and social status.

6. Revolution

Revolutionary activity remained fragmentary and generally ineffective in countries under royal control. Catherine the Great imposed a rigid censorship that soon eliminated both satirical journals and critical books. Joseph II had little respect for tolerance or for a liberty which threatened to oppose royal policy; he extended the censorship to cover the book trade, the press, education and the theatre. In the German states lack of uniform control encouraged the spread of revolutionary ideas. Writers such as Müller and Schubart wrote of an imminent revolution and a vast transformation in Europe through which a German imperial throne would soon arise.

The main centre of criticism, however, continued to be in France. Rousseau died in 1779 and it was left to his successors to translate his lofty romantic ideals into more concrete political slogans. In 1780 Raynal (and Diderot) attacked despotisms that upheld serfdom, authority without consent, and religious superstition. They declared the majority of nations to be in fetters, the multitude sacrificed to the passions of a few privileged despots. They proclaimed that liberty would be born from the bosom of oppression and that the subject would achieve freedom in the end. Their book was burned, the authors fled the country, but the legacy remained. Copies filtered as far as Russia where Radishchev used extracts to expose the desperate undergrowth of peasant life. Other writers explored and defined ideals that were to have a considerable impact on the future. Mably advocated a utopian Socialism designed to guarantee equality and human rights within a new order of society. Babeuf moved on to advocate the equal division of property under state control. No real efforts were made to reconcile the contradictions between liberty and equality advocated in the writings of revolutionary thinkers. Nevertheless, the French were becoming increasingly familiar with the vocabulary of revolt, with the conflict of ideals and with the limitations of the old order.

A further burst of enthusiasm was occasioned by the revolt of the North American colonies against British rule and the notable contribution of French volunteers in the ultimate victory. The Declaration of Independence with its 'inalienable rights' of 'life, liberty, and the pursuit of happiness' seemed the realization of decades of philosophic speculation and frustrated hope. To Raynal it was a great revolution for freedom, inflaming the imagination. German writers attacked the 'sale' of Hessian troops to assist the British government and praised the United States in its struggle for independence. French officers returning from the war were filled with enthusiasm for the new democracy; in Germany troops returned with tales of promise and new opportunity. Theories of social contract and human rights were suddenly intelligible in terms of individual experience and immediate benefit. Ideals which seemed bound to wither beneath the weight of despotism and aristocratic privilege had been realized. Writers throughout Europe composed Odes to Liberty and to the birth of an example that would live on to reveal their goal.

Nevertheless, it is unlikely that these ideals would have been realized, at any rate for some time, had it not been for the failure of the French monarchy to keep pace with other 'enlightened' rulers and exercise a measure of control over the institutions and the social and economic changes that were creating growing tension and bitterness throughout France. Aristocratic ambition, bourgeois frustration, artisan anxiety and peasant despair were inflamed by economic crises and intellectual criticism. The general inertia and limited activity of government only helped to worsen the situation. The factors of change and the established framework were allowed to drift into explosive conflict and create a chain reaction decisive in the history of Europe and the world.

III · THE FRENCH REVOLUTION

1. Introduction – the Fragmentation of Society

THE French Revolution was perhaps one of the most complicated episodes in the history of Europe. It was, in effect, at least six revolutions combined, each one involving the leadership of a different cross-section of society, all provoked by a variety of economic, social and political grievances. During the period known as the pre-revolution, 1786 to the calling of the Estates General in 1788, the established aristocracy tried to seize power with the apparent intention of limiting the monarchy, but really to secure their own interests. During the second stage, from the meeting of the Estates General in 1789 to the end of the Constituent Assembly in 1791, the reforming aristocracy, clergy and upper bourgeoisie tried to consolidate their authority with the often unwelcome backing of further revolutionary outbreaks in Paris, the provinces and among the peasantry.

The moderate measures and limited reforms of the upper bourgeoisie and their supporters led to a further wave of revolutionary activity during the session of the first Legislative Assembly, October 1791 to September 1792. Middle bourgeois Girondins and Jacobins now tried to gain ascendency by harnessing artisan and lower bourgeois elements to their respective interests. The struggle was maintained during the early days of the Convention, September 1792 to June 1793, and culminated in yet another revolution which ultimately secured Jacobin control. This led into a period known as the Terror, August 1793 to July 1794, during which artisans and extremists tried to seize power in Paris by independent revolutionary action.

Such a confused series of developments was further complicated by the total breakdown of government and by the interaction of economic crises, religious conflicts and foreign war. But perhaps one of the more significant developments in recent research into the French Revolution has been the careful analysis and growing emphasis that has been placed on the social conflicts and the class struggles involved. When all the factors have been weighed up and examined it was the people at every level of society who, when broken up into innumerable and rival fragments, were responsible for the crises and confusion of the revolutionary years.

French society on the eve of the revolution was probably the most divided in Europe. It was severed by class, by privilege, by wealth and by a struggle for power. A 'feudal' aristocracy of about 400,000 was split up between old established *épée* and *robe* families, some 20,000 court followers struggling for pensions and promotion, and a majority of poor provincials still working their estates.[1] All were forced to compete with a rising tide of new men, financiers, merchants and lawyers, and sought by every means to maintain their status at the summit of society and even to increase their influence in state affairs.

This attitude was shared by the highest dignitaries of the Church. Bishops, abbots and monastic orders controlled about one-tenth of France and governed a semi-autonomous Estate of some 100,000 members. They extracted tithes from peasants, often on an arbitrary basis, which they were able to spend lavishly at will. Meanwhile, the *curés* only received a meagre allowance, became increasingly hostile to their lordly superiors, absorbed Jansenist views and felt an ever closer affinity to their exploited parishioners.[2]

The bourgeoisie, increasing in wealth and power, discovered their progress permanently blocked by a barrier of aristocratic opposition and a cascade of noble contempt. They could buy titles, purchase land, serve the Crown and open up empires, but remained outcasts at court and excluded from the *parlements* and from positions of power. Even the bureaucracy had become increasingly hereditary, vested in a few privileged families. Thus though the upper bourgeois financier might 'live nobly' and mingle with the highest in the realm he was denied full recognition of status and the ultimate fruits of his ambition. This inevitably created bitterness and frustration and led to growing demands for equal rights and equal privileges. The more modest bourgeois *avocat* or *commerçant* shared this antagonism towards a privileged and exclusive aristocracy. Though often jealous of

[1] See pp. 5–11.   [2] See pp. 23–5.

his immediate superiors it was easy at first to make common cause against the entrenched positions at the top.

In the countryside the peasant, though often divided between rich and poor, had equal cause for complaint. Whether a freeholder, tenant farmer, share-cropper or labourer he found himself paying a vast burden of dues and taxes. Most direct charges fell on him – *taille, corvée, milice* – while the indirect levies such as the *gabelle* and innumerable regional tolls also inflicted the greatest hardship on the poor. Feudal dues forced him into dependence on the local lord, while tithes stripped a further proportion of his income.[1] Even the taxes levied on the nobility, *vingtième* and *capitation,* were usually extracted from tenants in the end.

During the second half of the eighteenth century economic changes created a notable increase in social tension. Population growth led to rising demand, increased prices and a gradual penetration of new capital into agriculture and industry. While prices rose wages lagged behind.[2] The aristocratic and upper bourgeois landowners raised rents and increased productivity by introducing new agricultural methods from England. These often included the enclosure of common land and added to the distress already felt by the excessive subdivision of peasant plots within larger families. At the same time *seigneurs* began to exploit feudal dues with greater efficiency, employing managers to draw up new maps, *terriers,* of their estates, and noting with legal precision the obligations of their tenants.

In the towns the impact of capitalization brought similar division and discontent. The security of guild regulation was undermined by new entrepreneurs putting out cloth, silk and craft materials to the struggling peasantry, and building up rival trade organizations. The introduction of new textile machinery from England added to the strain. Unemployment kept wages down. To the surplus labour in the towns was added a growing influx of vagrants from the rural areas.

The aristocracy, while taking every advantage of the price rise, tried to exploit the general dissatisfaction in order to launch an attack upon the Court which could conveniently be blamed for all the ills of the nation. Thus the nobles denounced increases in taxation and the follies of court ex-

---

[1] See p. 10.   [2] See p. 13.

travagance. *Parlements* resisted the abolition of regional tolls on the grounds that this would dislocate trade and encourage speculation. They disguised their ambition in constitutional slogans and took over the destructive vocabulary of the *philosophes* and the lawyers in order to promote their own aristocratic interests. A division of power would both limit the Crown and also increase noble authority; guarantees of regional government and the rule of law were quite compatible with aristocratic ambitions as long as *parlements* and Estates continued to exist under the exclusive control of the aristocracy.

When, however, the nobility began to clamour for liberty and freedom from royal authority they shifted on to dangerous ground. Other sectors could easily put forward similar claims and were unlikely to discriminate for long between royal or aristocratic pretensions. The economic crises of the 1780s made many desperate. There is evidence that trade declined affecting the merchants and the ports, thus making tolls appear increasingly intolerable. At Lyons half the silk looms stood idle. In 1785 drought necessitated the mass slaughter of cattle. In 1787 and 1788 bad harvests pushed up the price of bread, while a surplus in the wine trade caused prices to fall and brought increasing hardship to producers. As food prices continued to rise, wages fell, vagrants increased and bandits roamed the countryside and invaded the towns. Unrest seriously threatened the stability of the economy and the social order in which the privileges and increasing exactions of the nobility were an obvious target for attack.

Middle classes, peasants and artisans were unlikely to be deceived by the so-called constitutional claims of an aristocratic élite. The latter, however, remained confident of their power and determined to assert their ultimate authority over the Crown. Their action opened the first phase of the French Revolution which was eventually to engulf every level of society. By splitting the established order at the top they created a fissure through which the accumulated frustrations of every other sector were soon to erupt with unexpected ferocity.

2. *The Revolt of the Aristocracy*

Bankruptcy and the threatened collapse of government gave the aristocracy an opportunity to assert their claims. Necker, an astute banker from Geneva, had financed the American war by extensive borrowing. In 1781 he had published a misleading financial statement, *Comte Rendu*, in which he had estimated that an annual surplus of 10 million *livres* was available for debt repayment when in fact there was an annual deficit of between 40 and 80 millions. Realizing a dangerous discrepancy Necker had demanded urgent financial reforms, had probably provoked his own dismissal and acquired an undeserved popularity. Subsequently the debt continued to grow: by 1786 the deficit had risen to nearly 112 million *livres*, by 1788 to 126 millions. Expenditure was 629 millions, of which 318 went on debt repayment; 165 millions was spent on defence and the foreign service, and 146 on the civil estimates of which 35 millions covered court costs. The debt standing at some 3,400 million *livres* had become an impossible drag upon the government. Drastic financial reforms were needed to reduce it, but these, cutting into the vested interests of the nobility, were bound to rouse bitter opposition.

The first minister to make a genuine attempt at solving the financial crisis was Calonne. In 1786, when the war *vingtième* of 1782 expired, he realized that financial reform was inevitable. His proposals were far-reaching and would have gone a long way towards removing the worst abuses of the old order. The *vingtièmes* were to be replaced by a general land tax, *subvention*, levied on all landowners without exception. This was to be assessed by local assemblies of proprietors elected regardless of their order and presided over by local *intendants* (except in the *Pays d'Etat* where the local Estates were already responsible for taxation). A clerical debt, accumulated to pay the free gifts to the Crown, was to be paid off by the sale of Church property. Other reforms included commuting the *corvée*, abolishing internal tolls, freeing the grain trade, equalizing the salt tax and reforming the *taille*, though the nobility were to retain their privileged exemption.

In spite of these gestures to privilege Calonne could anticipate nothing but bitter hostility from the *parlements*. He therefore decided to by-pass these bastions of the aristocracy and rely on an Assembly of Notables selected by the King. This met in February 1787 and included princes, prelates, councillors, *parlementaires* and representatives of Estates and municipal authorities. They agreed to any reforms which did not affect their own privileges – in the *corvée*, the *taille* or the grain trade. But elsewhere their opposition was violent. They declared the new land tax to be unconstitutional and demanded inspection of all government accounts. They attacked the new local assemblies as a threat to their order, the *intendants* as a danger to their 'liberties' and the redemption of the clerical debt as a threat to property. Calonne took the conflict into the provinces: pamphlets attacking the Notables were read from the pulpits, while the Assembly replied with demands for constitutional liberty, the redress of government abuses and control over taxation. Meanwhile the Court took fright, the Queen worked to undermine so dangerous a minister and in April Calonne was dismissed. By August he had retired to England pursued by the angry denunciations of Notables and *parlementaires*.

Calonne's successor, Brienne, Bishop of Toulouse, tried to meet the opposition half way. Government accounts were opened for inspection, local assemblies were allowed to retain their separate orders, the clerical debt was referred to a Church Assembly, and the new land tax fixed at 80 million *livres* a year. But elsewhere Brienne's proposals were much the same as Calonne's with additional demands for increased stamp duties and a loan of 50 millions. These were rejected by the Notables who now claimed the right to inspect the accounts regularly and insisted that all fiscal proposals required the approval of either the *Parlement* of Paris or of the Estates General, a body representing the three orders of the kingdom, aristocracy, clergy and Third Estate which had not been convened since 1614. Nothing gained, the Notables were dismissed in May.

Brienne now had little choice but to call the *Parlement* of Paris. This body met in June, agreed to the new local assemblies, provided that they met by order, and also to *corvée* and grain tax reforms. But it rejected any form of land tax or stamp duty and also demanded regular inspection of the accounts. By August Brienne had lost patience. He enforced the registration of his proposals by a *lit de justice* and when the *Parlement* declared his action invalid he exiled its members to Troyes. This, however, only spread increased agitation into the provinces where the nobility now prepared to assert their claims to control both the Estates and the *parlements* in the interests of the 'nation'. The government was forced to recall the *Parlement* in September. Wild scenes of popular enthusiasm made it increasingly obstructive. Brienne's proposals to extend the *vingtième*, raise loans of 420 million *livres* over the next five years and then call the Estates General to advise on further measures were all bitterly attacked. Another *lit de justice*, this time to enforce the necessary loans, was furiously denounced and followed in the spring of 1788 by a campaign against loans, *lits de justice*, *lettres de cachet* and all forms of ministerial authority.

In spite of divisions at Court, Brienne pressed on. On May 3rd, 1788, the *Parlement* of Paris formulated its claims in a set of fundamental laws asserting the sacredness of provincial custom and demanding national consent to taxation in the Estates General. An oath to uphold these claims was to become a precedent for future action. Brienne, however, struck back, surrounded the *Parlement* with troops and arrested its leaders. There followed a series of edicts drawn up by Lamoignon, Keeper of the Seals, which abolished the *parlements* and replaced them by new courts of appeal and registration. At the same time Brienne amended the composition of the local assemblies by nominating half the members himself, and by doubling the representation of the Third Estate in order to counter the obstruction of the higher orders.

The reaction of the nobility was violent and widespread. Having split the old order at the top they now proceeded to rouse rebellion from below. The new courts were attacked in Dijon, Grenoble, Toulouse and Bordeaux; at Pau the *Parlement* summoned the aristocracy whose farmers and shepherds descended to intimidate the *Intendant*, while in Brittany the *Parlement* of Rennes organized riots against the edicts. The aristocracy tried to keep control over the revolt by excluding the lower orders from any positions of influence or authority. While the *parlements* claimed to speak for the 'nation' the bourgeoisie were prepared to watch or to follow their lead.

Only in Dauphiné was there a genuine attempt at co-operation between the orders; at Vizille, Mounier, a skilful lawyer,
negotiated a compromise guaranteeing aristocratic privilege
yet establishing fiscal and political equality by doubling the
number of representatives from the Third Estate.

Faced by the collapse of local government, widespread revolt, the failure of taxation and the imminence of bankruptcy, Brienne was forced to give way. The Lamoignon
edicts were suspended, the Estates General called for May 1st,
1789. In August the government admitted bankruptcy, suspended treasury payments, and enforced the circulation of
paper money. The only man left who could restore confidence and float new loans was Necker. When he refused to
serve in the ministry, Brienne fell from office and Necker returned as Controller of Finance. Lamoignon was dismissed,
the *parlements* recalled and attention directed to the forth-
coming meeting of the Estates General.

Thus the Crown had lost the initiative. The aristocracy
had forced the government to admit defeat and to take the
road to reform. On September 23rd the *Parlement* of Paris
returned in triumph to the capital; two days later, however,
it irrevocably split the nation. A declaration proclaimed that
the Estates General were to meet in the form prevailing in
1614. This meant that the three orders were to meet separately, and left the clergy and the aristocracy in a position to
outvote the proposals put forward by the Third Estate. The
effect of the declaration was disastrous. The claims of the
nobility to represent the nation were destroyed overnight.
Their determination to maintain their own privileges at all
costs was exposed. Society was shattered into rival fragments
in which each sector fought to promote its own interests in a
struggle for power.

3. *The Estates General and the Collapse of the Old Order*

In July, Brienne had appealed for precedents to clarify the
procedure for summoning the Estates General and had
suspended the censorship. The declaration of the *Parlement*
now released an avalanche of pamphlets and passionate denunciations. The middle classes demanded equality; petitions
to double the Third Estate poured in from the towns; protest

E

meetings led to riots in the provinces. The aristocracy were swift to reply; the Notables, reconvened by Necker for consultation in November, rejected any suggestions of doubling the Third Estate and demanded voting by order. The princes of the blood attacked the pamphlet war and petitioned that separate orders be maintained. At the same time the claims of the Third Estate were reaffirmed by the Abbé Sieyès in three notable pamphlets which attacked privileges, defined national sovereignty and claimed that the Third Estate, the nation, was the only true representative of the people.

Amid the ensuing turmoil a national or patriotic group emerged. This claimed some support from liberal aristocrats, reforming churchmen, lawyers, bankers and writers. They included Lafayette, the popular leader of the French troops sent to assist the United States, Mirabeau, an aristocrat at once powerful, oratorical, ambitious and dissolute, the bishop of Autun, later to be better known as Talleyrand, the Abbé Sieyès, and Mounier the organizer of the Dauphiné experiment which now became a model for patriotic policy. Many were included in a Committee of Thirty which helped to formulate petitions and stirred the provinces into action. At the same time new clubs and salons promoted debate in Paris. The Duc d'Orléans, a dissident member of the royal family, encouraged popular disaffection from the Palais Royal. The bourgeois youth of Nantes marched to attack the aristocratic *Parlement* of Rennes. Only prompt and vigorous action by the government appeared likely to prevent the imminent outbreak of revolution or civil war.

But Necker, uncertain of the King and faced by a hostile and privileged court, had to play for time and adopt an ambivalent policy. In December 1788 he persuaded the King to agree to double the Third Estate but left the question of whether voting was to be separate or in common undecided. Necker's instructions laid down a different voting procedure for each order and he may have assumed that these distinctions would be retained when the Estates General met. Alternatively he may simply have tried to evade the issue. Whatever the reasons this lack of definition was to have grave repercussions.

Each order elected representatives at separate assemblies where they also drew up *cahiers* or lists of grievances suggesting possible areas for reform. The *cahiers* of the aristocracy revealed the provincial exclusiveness of the nobility. A free press, individual liberties, equal taxation and local and national assemblies would all be accepted provided the privileges of their order were retained. The *cahiers* of the bourgeoisie, however, demanded the destruction of these very distinctions and urged equal rights for all. Led by militant lawyers they attacked aristocratic privilege and concentrated on promoting their own immediate interests. Their demands completely swamped the grievances of the peasants whose complaints about dues, tithes and *terriers* were generally ignored when the *cahiers* of the Third Estate came to be finally drafted under bourgeois leadership.

In spite of these contradictions every class awaited the opening of the Estates General with fervent hope. The peasants expected immediate relief; the middle classes a constitution to assure their rights; the aristocracy increased control. The event turned out to be something of an anti-climax. Ceremonial processions and religious services merely emphasized the distinctions between plumed aristocrats, bejewelled prelates, black robed *curés,* and the sombre colours of members of the Third Estate. On May 5th all assembled for the opening speeches in the great hall behind the Hôtel des Menus Plaisirs at Versailles. The King's address was well meaning but vague; the Keeper of the Seal's colourless and inaudible; while Necker's speech was bitterly disappointing. Frightened to commit himself the Controller merely emphasized the need for tax reform to relieve government debts and appealed for advice. The problems of constitutional reform, voting procedure and privilege were evaded. Rival suspicions were allowed to develop unchecked until smouldering discontent burst into open conflict.

While the nobility and the clergy hastened to verify their election returns separately, the Third Estate refused to do so. Verification in common was a vital preliminary to voting in common which alone would assure the passage of their demands in face of the inevitable opposition from the aristocratic orders. This issue was thus a test case not merely a procedural quibble and was followed with close attention by Parisian and provincial correspondents. For four weeks the Third Estate paralysed activity by rejecting separate verification. Leadership slowly crystallized round a radical Breton Club and the more moderate Dauphiné representatives. Necker's attempts to mediate failed. Both sides were aware of the implications and proved intractable. Eventually Sieyès urged the Third Estate to 'cut the cable' and take the initiative. On June 10th it invited the other orders to verify in common and two days later began to vote on a common roll. On June 17th, after three days of searching debate it declared itself to be the 'National Assembly' and claimed the sole right to authorize taxation.

Faced by these revolutionary claims the nobles, bishops and *parlementaires* now turned about to appeal to the King. A number of *curés* had already joined the Third Estate and the possible defection of the remainder made the privileged orders suddenly aware of their isolation and weakness. A council on June 19th agreed that royal intervention was vital but was divided between the demands of d'Artois and the aristocracy for firm action and Necker's plans for reform, which now included fiscal equality, equal opportunities for public office and recognition of the right to vote by head rather than by order. But two days later, under pressure from the Queen and the Court, the King's views hardened. Necker's proposals were rejected. The King was prepared to grant the Estates control over taxation, to abolish the *corvée* and *taille*, reform tolls and taxes and allow a free press. But the separation of the orders was to be preserved and with it the privileges and social structure of the past.

Meanwhile rumours of aristocratic plots inflamed opinion. On June 20th these were increased when the great hall was closed without any apparent warning to prepare for the royal session. The presence of troops seemed to confirm fears of another forcible dissolution. Led by Mounier the deputies moved to a nearby tennis court where they took an oath never to dissolve until a constitution had been won. Joined by the *curés* and the moderate Dauphiné nobility they awaited the royal session with anxiety. Surrounded by some 4,000 troops the King gave his instructions quashing the decrees of June 17th, conceding the agreed reforms and insisting upon the separation of the orders. At the end the aristocracy and the bishops left the hall; the Third Estate refused to move. Mirabeau gave voice to the collective defiance of members with his cry that they would only move at the point of a bayonet. The tennis court oath was reaffirmed together with the June decrees. Members were declared inviolable from arrest. A revolution had become explicit.

Louis XVI wavered; Paris was in ferment; addresses of solidarity favouring the union of the orders poured in from the provinces; clergy and aristocracy appeared divided; rumours of a march on Versailles spread at court. Petulantly he allowed the Third Estate to stay. On June 27th he ordered the nobility to join them. The revolution appeared to be over. The King and Queen were cheered by the crowds while the Assembly settled into committees to draft a Constitution and draw up a Declaration of the Rights of Man.

On July 9th members had assumed the title Constituent Assembly to emphasize their authority and official status. But Louis' action had only been a temporary expedient. As early as June 28th six regiments had been ordered to Versailles. Efforts were made to regain control of Paris. Disobedient French Guards were arrested and ten regiments posted outside the city. At the same time the aristocracy began to withdraw from the Assembly and to reaffirm the separation of the orders. Plans for a royalist counter-revolution appeared imminent. On July 11th Necker was suddenly dismissed and ordered to leave the country. Aristocratic government was restored. The Assembly expected immediate arrest. They were saved by the revolt of the capital.

Paris had followed events at Versailles with keen anticipation. The electors had continued to meet and had maintained regular contact with their deputies. They had also taken over the administration of the city and occupied the Hôtel de Ville. Bankers anxious to safeguard their government bonds watched the fortunes of Necker with anxiety. Bourgeois orators demanded equality and attacked aristocratic plots. Artisans expected relief from the growing economic crisis. This had already led to rioting in April. During the summer the situation grew steadily worse following the failure of the 1788 harvest. Bread, basic to the diet, more than doubled in price. In the country, conditions deteriorated and beggars and vagabonds streamed into the towns. The situation was already explosive when news of Necker's dismissal reached the city. Fears of an aristocratic conspiracy to prevent reform, maintain prices, and ruin credit seemed confirmed. Paris exploded into violence.

On July 12th orators took up the cry 'to arms'. Incited by the bourgeoisie and with the connivance of bankers, electors and Orléanist agents, artisans rose to burn the toll gates round Paris and to search for food and arms. The convent of Saint-Lazare was pillaged; law and order in the city collapsed. Next day the electors themselves took command of the situation. Each electoral district was instructed to provide 200 men to form a town militia wearing the city colours – red and blue – ready to maintain order. On July 14th the search for arms led to the Bastille, an ancient fortress symbolic of royal despotism but containing only seven nondescript prisoners and a garrison of 110 under a governor – de Launay. Alarmed by the riots he had prepared his defence and delayed when called upon to surrender arms. This roused the suspicion of the mob which began to climb in. When de Launay fired on the crowd bitter fighting broke out. As a result the town militia and French Guards were sent with cannon and soon forced the fortress to surrender. The infuriated mob stormed in. The governor was lynched while under escort and the Bastille demolished.

The fall of the Bastille signalled the final collapse of royal authority and the disintegration of the country into regional fragments. On July 15th the electors reorganized Paris under a new Common Council elected by the districts, and formed the militia into a National Guard of reliable bourgeois under Lafayette to maintain order. Other municipalities quickly followed the lead of the capital. In Lyons, Rouen and Marseilles electors had already been admitted to office in June. In Bordeaux the established authorities disintegrated. But elsewhere aristocratic corporations were only dislodged by violent means, as in Rennes, Dijon and Strasbourg, where Arthur Young witnessed the sack of the Hôtel de Ville. The new authorities soon set up national guards to maintain order and uphold the interests of the bourgeoisie, now suddenly elevated to power. As these varied from place to place so France became a mosaic of independent municipalities.

The impact of events upon the peasantry was even more violent. Their great hopes in the Estates General had remained unfulfilled. Their grievances against taxes, tithes, feudal dues and *terriers* had been generally ignored. Inactivity was attributed to aristocratic plots. Rioting had already broken out in May; the events of July 14th were to prove decisive. Throughout northern and eastern France châteaux were attacked, archives burnt and fences demolished. Violence created panic. Fear of aristocrats, brigands and vagabonds combined to create a 'great fear' which swept through wide areas of the countryside in July and August. When title deeds had been burnt and obligations abolished the peasants were left with their land secure. Once in an entrenched position they soon lost interest in any further changes and only acted in defence of their newly won gains. They refused to pay compensation and failed to distinguish between the claims of aristocrats, bourgeois or wealthy peasant proprietors. The paralysis in government gave them time to consolidate their holdings. By the end of the revolutionary years much of the French countryside had become the property of a broad class of peasant smallholder.

The immediate effect of urban and rural revolt upon the Court was decisive. Louis recalled Necker and withdrew the troops. Rejecting flight he visited the capital on July 17th and accepted the Tricolour Cockade – Bourbon white flanked by the colours of Paris – from Lafayette who was confirmed as Commander-in-Chief of the national Guard. Many aristocrats, however, led by d'Artois and the Polignacs, fled abroad in a first wave of emigration and tried to rally the European powers to their cause. This helped to promote fears of a counter-revolution and generated further violence.

Meanwhile the Constituent Assembly was given time to draft a Constitution. Determined to proclaim basic principles by drawing up a Declaration of the Rights of Man and the Citizen, it was faced with the problem of reconciling the legal and property rights of the aristocracy with the fact that these rights had largely disappeared as a result of municipal and peasant revolts. On August 4th the Breton Club persuaded the liberal nobility to come half way by surrendering all their feudal privileges. Then, carried away by fear and fervour, the Assembly passed the August Decrees which abolished the feudal régime with all its exemptions, services and tithes, but upheld that 'real' fees due on property should be redeemed. The way was now clear for the Declaration which was passed on August 26th: men were born free and equal in rights; liberty, property, security and equality of opportunity were guaranteed; limitation and restraints could only be imposed by the law which was an expression of the 'general will'.

As the law was in fact determined by an assembly which was essentially bourgeois, any assumption of a 'general will' presumed their peculiar right to represent the nation. This may have reflected the supreme self confidence of the Assembly but it did not fully reflect the facts. The provincial aristocracy bitterly opposed the August decrees; the *curés* attacked the abolition of tithes; in Paris, district assemblies and artisans demanded control of prices and grain in defiance of any free trade principles; moreover the peasants refused to pay compensation merely to preserve property rights. As a result a split developed between the moderate patriots led by Mounier, who wanted to guarantee their interests by creating an upper chamber and preserving a royal veto, and the more radical members led by Barnave who were anxious to consolidate their power in a single chamber and hoped to rally support from middle bourgeois elements to re-enforce their claims.

These early divisions soon encouraged Louis and the aristocracy to attempt a come-back. Urged on by the fury of the clergy and the Court and prompted by secret support from the moderate patriots the King refused to give his consent to the Declaration and to the August decrees. On September 15th he summoned the Flanders regiment to Versailles. At a banquet on October 1st the Tricolour was trampled underfoot and royalist toasts drunk amid signs of enthusiasm. But this action soon provoked renewed intervention by the Paris mob. The harvest was not yet in; bread remained scarce and prices high. In the districts orators attacked aristocratic plots and the royal veto which appeared responsible for holding up reform. Radical deputies at Versailles added fuel to the fire with tales of an imminent counter-revolution. On October 5th groups of women assembled at the Hôtel de Ville demanding bread and began to march to Versailles. The National Guard soon forced Lafayette to follow.

At Versailles, Mounier led the women to Louis who agreed to send bread to Paris. The arrival of the National Guard caused some panic at court, but Louis refused to flee and now accepted the August decrees unconditionally. Next morning, however, a number of women tried to break into the palace to attack the Queen who was considered the main obstacle to reform. She was forced to flee to the King's apartments where both were rescued by Lafayette and the National Guard. Helpless, the royal family were brought to Paris and housed in the Tuileries. The victory of the revolution had been confirmed by violence. This was to add a new disturbing factor to the situation and became even more significant when the Constituent Assembly followed the King to the capital in order to continue the work of constitutional reconstruction.

4. *The Failure of Compromise*

The October days were a defeat not only for the Crown and the aristocracy but also for the moderate patriots who had hoped to maintain their interests by setting up a balanced constitution based on English examples. Mounier withdrew in protest at the intervention of the mob to lead a second wave of exiles. The way was left clear for a radical wing of the patriots led by Barnave to draw up a unitary model in which sovereignty could be vested in a single chamber under their immediate control. Louis was now proclaimed King of the French in order to emphasize the unity and sovereignty of the nation and was granted a 'suspensive veto' of four years which could do little more than annoy. In November members of the Assembly passed a law which debarred them from holding any ministerial office. This move, which was partially designed to frustrate the ambitions of Mirabeau, gravely weakened the possibility of effective government. Though the sovereignty of the people was now clearly vested in an Assembly untainted by the corrupting influence of royal or executive power, it was difficult to determine how this sovereignty was to be put into effect.

Another weakness lay in the fact that sovereignty was restricted to a very small section of the bourgeoisie. This became all too clear from the very limited franchise which was to determine the election of members. Citizens were divided into the 'passive' who paid no direct taxes or a sum less than the value of three days wages, and the 'active' who paid at least three days wages in tax. The 'passive', though enjoying full civil rights, could not vote; the 'active' might vote in the primary elections held at local and national level for electors who would subsequently choose the deputies for the Assembly. In order to become an elector and vote at the secondary stage, or to hold any local government office, a ten days' tax qualification was required. To become a deputy a qualification of one silver mark was proposed. Thus some four and a half million 'active' citizens could vote for about 50,000 electors whose interests in effect determined the 'general will'.

These interests, however, were essentially bourgeois and emphasized the maintenance of order, the protection of property and the promotion of a free, 'natural' economy. In October a law was hurried through the Assembly to allow municipal authorities to declare martial law and use troops, after raising a red warning flag, in order to suppress disorders. In Paris and the provinces national guards took action to restore control and protect bourgeois property from artisan or peasant attack.

During the winter of 1789-90 the Assembly reorganized the provincial administration upon a rational and uniform foundation. Aware of the complete fragmentation of the country it accepted the 40,000 communes as the basic units of local government. Here the mayors and the councils were to be elected by all 'active' citizens. Superimposed, however, was a pattern of districts and 83 departments based upon roughly equal geographical areas where councils and officials responsible for the supervision of administration and law were controlled by the electors.

The infinite variations of the feudal régime were replaced by a new legal system. Justices of the Peace were to act as conciliators in groups of communes known as cantons. District courts were to deal with civil and departmental courts with criminal cases. The appointment of judges was once again placed in the hands of the electors who thus assumed complete responsibility for the maintenance of law and order. As this, however, was still undefined each unit was allowed to drift into an almost complete autonomy.

Meanwhile the deputies were faced by the problem of a mounting financial crisis. Taxes could not be collected;

attempts to raise loans had failed in spite of Necker's appeals; the deficit continued to mount. A solution was eventually found by the appropriation of all ecclesiastical property and by the issue of *assignats* or paper money which was subsequently to be redeemed by the acquisition of church land. As long as the *assignats* were limited to the real value of the land the new issue was an unqualified success and brought the country two years of relative financial stability.

Attempts to carry through a complete reorganization of the Church were, however, to prove disastrous. The clergy accepted the loss of their property with resignation once the State undertook to pay their stipends. But in July 1790 a new Civil Constitution of the Clergy planned to bring the entire administration of the Church under state control. Priests were to be elected by district and bishops by departmental assemblies. New dioceses were to coincide with the departments. The Pope was to be informed but denied any opportunity to interfere, thus losing his jurisdiction over the French Church. This attempt to combine the ecclesiastical and the secular was to provoke violent conflict and civil war.

Nevertheless the summer of 1790 still appeared a time for optimism. The great events of the previous year were commemorated in a round of feasts and pageants. The Jacobin Club, the centre of Breton and radical bourgeois opinion in Paris, corresponded with its affiliated branches throughout the provinces and gathered representatives from every region for rallies in the capital. On August 24th the King took the oath and signed the Civil Constitution. In Paris the Assembly continued patiently with the work of constitutional definition. But below the surface the divisions that were to undermine and eventually destroy any moderate settlement were already apparent. 'Passive' citizens, artisans and peasants were becoming increasingly resentful of the arrogant claims and political assumptions of the *haute bourgeoisie*.

In Paris the district assemblies had continued to meet. Orators of the lower bourgeoisie denounced the exclusiveness of electors and of the respectable members of the Jacobin Club. The Cordeliers Club became a rival centre for shopkeepers, students and artisans where Danton pressed the demands of 'passive' citizens while Dr. Marat attacked the new aristocracy of wealth in his journal, *l'Ami du peuple*. The

Assembly tried to curb the districts by passing a law which divided Paris into 48 sections, limited meetings to 'active' citizens and placed all national guards under municipal control. But the new sections were not to be so easily intimidated. Meetings continued, 'passive' citizens were soon admitted, while the policies of the municipal council were repeatedly attacked.

Similar conflicts developed in the countryside where peasants found themselves expected to pay large sums in compensation for their newly won property. It seemed as if the feudalism of the past were being replaced by a new economic slavery and peasant opposition to enclosures or title deeds did not distinguish between bourgeois or aristocratic ownership. The country became the scene of a violent struggle between the peasantry and the town bourgeoisie who appeared to be taking away with one hand what they had previously given with the other.

These divisions were intensified by the growing religious crisis. The Assembly, impatient of opposition and papal evasion, demanded an oath of loyalty to the Civil Constitution from every public servant, including members of the clergy. This, however, was rejected by all but seven bishops and by over half the priests. Non-jurors were thereupon deprived of office and joined their peasant parishioners in denouncing the activities of the Assembly and attacking the work of godless, greedy men. Agitation in Britanny and the Vendée became increasingly violent and France drifted to the brink of civil war.

The situation might have been saved had the moderates in the Assembly found leaders capable of co-ordinating these conflicting elements and able to secure some working relationship with the King who was still, in theory at least, responsible for executive action. But Mirabeau, though inspired in speech and broad in vision, was suspected by the Assembly for his constitutional views, his ministerial ambitions and his personal vice. In 1790 he opened secret negotiations with the Court and, in return for a pension and the payment of his debts, promised to advocate constitutional revision in order to strengthen the hand of the royal executive. But Louis and Marie Antoinette were never prepared to trust so unreliable a character and his death in April 1791 probably saved him from imminent exposure. Lafayette, once the hero of the moderates, never displayed the courage or the convictions needed for leadership. He followed events but was unable to control them, and the revolution drifted on leaderless while every sector generated fresh grounds for confusion and violence.

After some months of agonising indecision the King eventually determined to escape. The Pope's official condemnation of the Civil Constitution, the increasing violence of the sectional clubs and the growing divisions between moderates and extremists persuaded him to appeal directly to the crowned heads of Europe for assistance against the claims of the Assembly. On June 20th, 1791, an ill-organized flight ended at Varennes where, once recognized, Louis made no further efforts to escape.

Completely discredited, the King was brought back virtually a prisoner to the capital. The effect was to intensify the conflict between the radical patriots and the new revolutionary groups in the clubs and sectional assemblies. The former, suddenly aware of the growing confusion and of a potential threat to their own position, now adopted the policies previously advocated by Mounier and the moderates. Anxious to preserve the monarchy as a symbol of order they suspended the King but refused to depose him, and tried too late to establish the second chamber and the ministerial responsibility which they had themselves rejected in the previous year.

These moves, however, only succeeded in arousing the fury of the more extreme radicals who demanded the deposition of the King and began to agitate for a republican constitution. Their influence became increasingly dominant even in the once moderate Jacobin Club. Rejecting arguments that the King had been 'kidnapped' they organized a monster petition on July 17th on the Champ de Mars demanding that a referendum be held to determine the King's fate. When the crowd lynched two spectators the municipal authorities declared martial law. Lafayette and the National Guard appeared, preceded by the red flag. Renewed provocation led to shooting and the death of some fifty petitioners.

Open conflict between moderate constitutionalists and republicans was now inevitable. For three weeks the municipal authorities hounded down republican and sectional leaders.

Danton fled, Marat was arrested and radical papers were suppressed. But the moderate and constitutionalist cause was discredited and all faith in the Constituent Assembly destroyed. The Jacobin Club split between moderate 'Feuillants' anxious to revise the constitution and strengthen executive control, and democratic republicans who hoped to gain influence by broadening the franchise to bring in their lower bourgeois supporters.

During the summer of 1791 the Feuillants failed to revise the constitution in their favour. Attempts to restrict the franchise and set up a second chamber were defeated. The King and Queen refused to co-operate with their former enemies and now placed increasing hopes in foreign and *émigré* aid. Meanwhile radicals and republicans had begun to harness popular support to their cause. When the King signed the constitution on September 14th few Frenchmen had any confidence in its provisions. The country was hopelessly divided; the authority of government had largely collapsed. The elections to the Legislative Assembly only attracted an indifferent response and less than fifty per cent of the 'active' citizens bothered to vote. Royalists, moderates, radicals and republicans prepared to renew the struggle for power and to extend revolutionary action in Paris, in France and eventually throughout much of Europe.

5. *The Struggle for Power*

The first Legislative Assembly which met on October 1st 1791 was quite unable to control events. Elected on a restricted franchise it lacked popular support and was further weakened by a decree of the previous May which had excluded all members of the old Constituent Assembly from the new legislature. As a result the moderate Feuillant majority was weak and inexperienced while the radical opposition was determined and vigorous. The latter soon took over the organization of the Jacobin Club with its affiliated provincial societies and began to agitate for action against the Queen, the *émigrés* and all their foreign allies. Led by Brissot and a group of lawyers, merchants and journalists they reflected middle bourgeois elements and viewed courtiers, moderates and lower bourgeois artisans with equal mistrust. Loosely labelled Girondins, they were to suffer the same fate as the moderate and radical patriots before them. Isolated from the Court and frightened of the artisans and the crowd below they were to come into sharp conflict with the growing demands of the Paris sections and were eventually to be swept away in a further wave of revolutionary violence.

During the coming winter the Paris sections emerged as a powerful centre of revolutionary activity. The return of Danton, Marat and other radical leaders after an amnesty was overshadowed by the emergence of Robespierre. Cool, clear and detached, he appealed to a wider democratic ideal designed to embrace every citizen. By November he had come to dominate the Jacobin Club and had begun to win powerful support in the Paris sections. During the coming winter, however, opposition to war placed his career in temporary eclipse.

War seemed an immediate solution to many of France's difficulties. It would rally the nation against *émigré* and foreign intrigue, mask the conflicts between priests, peasants and republicans in the provinces, and spread the Declaration of Rights throughout Europe on a wave of popular revolt. As enthusiasm for war increased so every class and faction hoped to profit from it. The King expected to be restored by foreign intervention or moderate intrigue; the Feuillants hoped to restore their position; the Girondins planned to seize control. Throughout the winter Brissot worked for war, inflaming the press, denouncing the Feuillants, demanding the confiscation of *émigré* property and urging that a new oath be imposed upon all priests. When Louis vetoed these demands on Feuillant advice new passions were roused; the King and Court were accused of counter-revolutionary sympathy and forced to take belligerent action.

The spring of 1792 witnessed a gradual drift to war. In reply to French protests the Elector of Trêves agreed to expel the *émigré* court from Coblenz. But Leopold, now Emperor,[1] refused to respond to pressure and in February concluded a defensive alliance with Prussia. The accession of Francis II in March added new vigour to a war party in Vienna increasingly determined to humiliate France and to curb the Revolution. Meanwhile Brissot continued to denounce the duplicity of the Court and the indifference of Feuillant ministers. In

[1] See p. 43.

March the ministry eventually collapsed and was replaced by Girondin candidates. On April 20th the Assembly declared war.

The war was to precipitate a new wave of extremism and violence. Popular hopes of an early victory were not realized. France was totally unprepared for a major conflict: the army was disrupted by the desertion of *émigré* officers, supplies were paralysed by conflicts in the provinces and recruiting was ill planned and un-co-ordinated. Shortage of cash led to an over-issue of *assignats* which rapidly depreciated to 50 per cent. When French armies fled before superior Austrian forces the effect upon the political situation in Paris was immediate. Robespierre re-emerged to censure court treachery, the generals and the Girondin politicians. Not to be outdone the latter attacked the traitors in the Tuileries and passed decrees to disband the King's guard and to deport any refractory priest denounced by twenty 'active' citizens. A further decree summoned to Paris the provincial national guards – *fédérés* – both to reinforce the frontier and to consolidate Girondin control. This provoked Louis into a last desperate move to preserve his authority. On June 12th the ministry was dismissed and the Feuillants restored; the decrees summoning the *fédérés* and deporting refractory priests were vetoed.

The effect was to provoke a new series of revolutionary uprisings. The deposed Girondins quickly turned to the republican elements in the capital for support. On June 20th they rallied the sectional assemblies, 'active' citizens were armed and the 'passive' allowed to carry pikes. The Assembly was presented with a petition denouncing the veto and the Feuillant ministry. The Tuileries was invaded and the King forced to drink the health of the nation. Three days later Louis agreed to a *fédéré* camp at Soissons which would necessitate volunteers passing through the capital. On July 11th a decree proclaimed 'the fatherland in danger' and called up all Frenchmen capable of bearing arms.

These actions, however, were not enough to satisfy the Girondins, who were still excluded from power, or the radical republicans and section agitators who were determined to destroy the monarchy at all costs. These were soon joined by the *fédérés* who now reached Paris and included a detachment from Marseilles determined to dethrone the King and singing the 'Chant de l'armée du Rhin' soon to be known as the 'Marseillaise'. Feuillant attempts, abetted by Lafayette, to restore royal authority were denounced together with possible Girondin moves to save the monarchy. A committee of five was set up to plan further insurrection. 'Passive' citizens were officially admitted to section debates. Petitions were organized demanding the deposition of the King and the summoning of a National Convention. Popular passions were finally roused by the ill-timed manifesto of the Duke of Brunswick[1] which reached Paris on July 28th and threatened to restore the King and exact exemplary vengeance if any harm were done to his person.

By August 9th the sections had united to demand deposition. Their representatives had formed a new revolutionary Commune and taken over the Hôtel de Ville. On the 10th fédérés and radical guards marched on the Tuileries. Louis and his family fled for refuge to the Legislative Assembly while 600 of the loyal Swiss Guard were massacred and the palace set alight. The Assembly now agreed to summon a National Convention elected by universal suffrage and to suspend the King. The Commune agreed to spare his life but imprisoned him in the Temple. The Feuillants disintegrated and fled; Lafayette deserted to the Austrians; radicals and republicans had seized control.

The victory of the republicans was, however, by no means assured. Though the Girondins had clearly lost their hold on the capital, they still assumed the lead in the Legislative Assembly and clung to power with considerable tenacity. Realizing the need for popular allies they added Danton to the ministry. His tireless energy rallied the capital against foreign invaders and acted as a link between the remnants in the Assembly and the Commune. The government was saved by the demands of war. To gain popularity 'passive' citizenship was abolished, feudal dues were finally suppressed without compensation and émigré property sold on easy terms. Refractory priests were seized for deportation and a new Vigilance Committee set up to search houses and make arrests. But in spite of these actions it was difficult to hide the fact that real power in Paris lay in the hands of the Commune. The re-organization of the National Guard under sectional

---

[1] See p. 83.

F

control consolidated its powers. Agents sent to the provinces claimed responsibility for the August revolution and the reforms of the Assembly and set up a new network of popular cells.

Meanwhile the advance of Prussian and Austrian armies created mounting panic. Searches and arrests increased and the prisons became filled with refractory priests. News of the loss of Longwy reached Paris on August 23rd. By September 1st the fall of Verdun appeared imminent. A fresh rising in the Vendée and rumours of a prison plot to break out and massacre the inhabitants of the capital led to fierce denunciations of counter-revolutionary conspiracies. The result was an upsurge of frenzy and the massacre of some 1,200 in the Paris prisons. Similar outrages occurred in the provinces, the outcome of an accumulation of bitterness and fear.

The elections for the National Convention took place at the height of the crisis. Feuillants and all those who had refused the new civic oath were deprived of the vote. The general confusion led to widespread abstentions but the moderate bourgeoisie, afraid of the excesses of the capital, rallied to support the Girondins who won an uncomfortable majority. In opposition were grouped the popular radical elements led by the extreme Jacobin deputies from Paris who sat on the high benches at the back of the hall and were thus known as the Mountain. These had behind them the Commune and many of the Paris sections, as well as a network of Jacobin clubs throughout France. Led by Marat, Danton and Robespierre they proceeded to launch a bitter personal attack on their Girondin opponents whom they suspected of royalist sympathies and excessive tolerance.

The Girondins countered with equal ferocity, blaming the Commune and the Jacobin members for the September massacres and the growth of violence in the countryside. They were determined to maintain moderate bourgeois control and to exclude lower middle class and violent artisan influence. Their vague policies and ambivalent attitudes were, however, easily exposed as duplicity by their more ruthless opponents. Though republican in their desire to abolish royal symbols and rename the Paris streets, they hesitated to eliminate the King himself. The monarchy was officially abolished on September 21st, but the King was not brought to trial until December. The discovery of incriminating papers in an iron chest in the Tuileries led to an almost unanimous verdict against Louis. But the death sentence was only passed by a small majority and while the Jacobins were unanimous the Girondins appeared divided and discredited. Their constitutional proposals roused equal dissatisfaction. A new calendar which began the year I on September 22nd was agreed, but plans to set up a balanced constitution with a complex system of proportional representation to maintain bourgeois control were withdrawn under severe Jacobin criticism.

The Girondins were soon exposed to even greater attack by their conduct of the war. On September 20th Dumouriez had halted the slow advance of the Duke of Brunswick at Valmy.[1] When the Prussians retired, he moved north and decisively defeated the Austrians at Jemappes. The results filled the Convention with enthusiasm. Hoping to unleash a crusade of liberation the Girondins issued an 'Edict of Fraternity' appealing to all peoples to rise against their governments. In December they promised to abolish tithes, feudal dues and to establish free institutions throughout Europe. Belgium and Savoy were annexed and the Scheldt opened up to navigation in defiance of the Treaty of Utrecht.

This precipitate action led to war with England, Piedmont and Spain. French armies were not yet able to take on the whole of Europe. Dumouriez was defeated at Neerwinden and, exasperated by the political quarrels of the capital, deserted to the Austrians in April. This gave the Jacobins added opportunity for hurling accusations of treachery against their opponents. Robespierre became increasingly prominent in his attacks on the war and again began to appeal to the sections with their *sans-culotte* committees for support. These represented the interests of the lower bourgeois artisans and working men. They demanded price controls and deplored the depreciation of the *assignats* due to speculation and war profiteers.

The Girondins now took desperate measures to save the situation. But a new Committee of General Defence failed to promote the war. General conscription stirred up an open revolt in the Vendée. The increasing circulation of *assignats* led

[1] See p. 83.

to further depreciation, while the price rise was aggravated by widespread shortages of bread, sugar and soap. As a result the sectional movements in Paris became even more violent and were soon provoked by extreme agitators or *enragés*. To co-ordinate the war effort and break down opposition Commissioners of the Convention were sent into the provinces. A Committee of General Security was created to supervise the police. Revolutionary tribunals were established with absolute powers to deal with anyone convicted of crimes against the State. Finally, on April 6th, the Committee of General Defence was transformed into a Committee of Public Safety with Danton to direct the war.

But these measures were not enough to satisfy the Jacobins and *sans-culottes* who now worked actively for yet another revolt to expel their opponents. The Girondins tried to forestall their rivals. Marat was brought to trial only to be acquitted amid scenes of enthusiasm. A commission was appointed to investigate the conduct of the Commune and the sections. Hébert, a leading *enragé*, was arrested together with some of his supporters. But such action only increased the agitation. The sections were mobilized, the Convention was invaded and the Hébertist prisoners freed. Twenty-nine Girondins were placed under house arrest. The remainder drew up petitions of protest and fled to the provinces to organize resistance against the new Jacobin dictatorship in Paris.

6. *Terror and Reaction*

During the summer of 1793 the Jacobins consolidated their position. A new constitution with provision for direct elections based on universal suffrage and for social reforms was drawn up to rally support but shelved due to the critical situation on the frontier. In July, English and Austrian troops occupied Valenciennes, while the Prussians invaded Alsace and the Spanish attacked in the South. Troops had to be diverted to suppress the Vendéen revolt and to curb Girondin risings in Marseilles, Toulon, Bordeaux and Lyons. As a result of this train of confusion and disaster Danton and his supporters were replaced on the Committee of Public Safety by Robespierre who soon imparted fresh energy into military operations against rebels and invaders. In August the

Vendée was systematically devastated and troops were sent to recapture rebel towns. Carnot and Prieur were elected to the Committee to reorganize the army and its supplies. On August 23rd a *levée en masse* was decreed. The entire nation was mobilized, some to fight, some to make arms, ammunition, bandages and provisions. All were to contribute to the national war effort.

In Paris, however, the *sans-culottes* and *enragés* still remained dissatisfied. Repeated risings to save the revolution called first by Girondin and then by Jacobin leaders had not led to the gratification of any of their immediate demands. While the peasants had been pacified with *émigré* estates and the complete abolition of compensatory dues, nothing had been done to control prices and wages or to save the *assignats* which had meanwhile depreciated to 25 per cent. Throughout the summer *sans-culotte* leaders struggled to gain control over the sectional committees and to eliminate moderate influences. Inflamed by the murder of Marat and the renewed bread shortage, led on by Hébert, Chaumette and unscrupulous fanatics, they pressed their demands to the point of planning yet another revolt. News of the surrender of Toulon to the British on September 2nd and rumours of a plot to free the Queen roused a surge of protest in the Commune. Petitions presented to the Convention demanded the arrest of suspects, a new revolutionary tribunal, price controls and a popular revolutionary army. Robespierre and the Jacobins gave way to their radical supporters; they had little alternative.

The demands of war and of the extremist elements in the capital fused into the 'Terror'. Economic controls froze prices and wages at a 'general maximum', organized the distribution of bread and essential supplies and requisitioned food and equipment. The new revolutionary tribunal now brought the Queen, Girondins and other suspects specified in a law of September 17th to trial and execution. In the provinces new *'représentants en mission'* instituted varying degrees of terror: at Nantes some 4,000 were executed or drowned in barges, at Lyons 2,000 were mown down by gunfire. Hébert, Chaumette and Fouché led an attack on organized religion. Crosses were demolished, churches closed and Christian ceremonies replaced by new cults of reason. A new calendar abolished old established usage, rearranged weeks and months into *décades* of ten days each, and replaced saints' days by festivals of plants, fruits and flowers.

By the end of 1793, however, more moderate elements once again began to assert themselves. Robespierre, while believing in democracy and a 'general will', remained hostile to economic controls and to the independent claims of the sections. He opposed the attack on religion and considered that some form of belief was an essential foundation of any social order. Moreover, the Jacobins were still essentially bourgeois in attitude and resented the intervention of the *sans-culottes* under their independent leadership. An improvement in the war, the containment of the Vendéen revolt and the recapture of Toulon encouraged Jacobin moves. Revolutionary government was gradually co-ordinated. A decree of December 4th gave the Committee of Public Safety control over policy decisions and over the activities of local authorities. New agents were sent to districts and communes with orders to suppress the excessive activities of the *représentants en mission*. In Paris the sections were placed under the direct authority of the Committee of Public Safety; their meetings were limited and the Commune deprived of its power to send independent representatives to the provinces.

Robespierre now proceeded to attack the dechristianization campaign of Chaumette and Fouché. With the assistance of Danton, who probably hoped to exploit subsequent divisions between Robespierre and the *sans-culottes* to his own advantage, the leading Hébertists were arrested in December. But a sudden wave of opposition forced Robespierre to pause and to agree to their release. Warily the factions circled to establish supremacy. Realizing their danger the Hébertists revolted in March. But by this time the government was prepared. Hébert, Chaumette and their associates were guillotined. The Dantonists soon followed. Robespierre remained supreme.

For three months Robespierre was left free to mould his ideals into a 'Republic of Virtue'. Equality, moderation and control were proclaimed the basis of true liberty and patriotism. Simple clothes, smallholdings and a virtuous family life became the hallmarks of loyalty to the Republic. Classical ritual was fused with Rousseau's romantic synthesis to formulate a new religion – the worship of the Supreme Being. Education and art were encouraged to foster understanding and a balanced appreciation of line and form. The Republic was to be the agent of a new social and cultural revolution. Men were to be elevated to a new realization of their own potential. Society and the state were to become one.

Robespierre's ideals did not, however, correspond to the facts. Society was essentially divided and hostile. The Republic was only supported by a small group of Jacobins. The majority would only be persuaded by force. Carried away by the intoxication of his own vision Robespierre became increasingly isolated. The execution of Hébertist leaders and the curbs imposed on the sections left the *sans-culottes* bitter and indifferent. Social and economic reform ceased to rouse any enthusiasm. The enforcement of the wages maximum in July raised a storm of protest. The new religion had no appeal for the majority who began to resent the intolerance of their puritanical Jacobin rulers. Robespierre's lofty claims aroused increasing hostility and alarm. He proclaimed himself the arbiter of good and evil, the virtual high priest of the Republic. A decree of 22 Prairial (June 10th) hastened the procedure at trials in the revolutionary tribunal. The defence was deprived of counsel, and death made the only punishment. In the next two months over 1,500 were executed. Ideals had turned into dictatorship. The Terror threatened to become universal.

Opposition slowly crystallized. Dantonist, Girondin and Hébertist sympathizers combined in the Convention with disgraced '*représentants en mission*' like Fouché and the remaining moderates in the centre. The Committee of General Security became increasingly hostile to Robespierre's independent authority. Eventually the members of the Committee of Public Safety split over the conduct of the war. Carnot's reforms had led to victory; Alsace had been cleared, Belgium reoccupied and Spanish troops expelled in the South. Opinion now split between those who favoured consolidation and those who demanded further advance. Robespierre retired from the discussion into a remote and threatening isolation. His opponents rallied and reassured by victory abroad met his vague denunciations of 8 Thermidor (July 26th) with a volley of recrimination. Next day, Barras, appointed to defend the Convention, raised troops from the moderate sections only. When the *sans-culotte* sections failed to rally, Robespierre was seized and guillotined together with eighty-seven of his supporters. Confident in his own beliefs he had failed to translate them into that 'general will' which he had so often claimed to represent. Nevertheless he was the outstanding personality of his time, the personification of much that was both noble and savage in the history of the Revolution.

The fall of Robespierre was followed by a slow reaction. The Revolution had played itself out. Each class and every interest had tried to harness it to their own cause only to be swept away by elements too powerful to control. The revolutionaries were now discredited and France struggled to restore some form of social and political equilibrium. The institutions of the Terror were abolished. The dictatorship of the committees was destroyed as the surviving members of the Convention gradually regained control. The trials law was repealed and the revolutionary tribunal reorganized and eventually eliminated. *Sans-culotte* committees were evicted in the provinces and Jacobin terrorists arrested by new representatives. The Jacobin clubs were closed to prevent any radical revival. Economic controls were also allowed to lapse. The 'maximum' was repealed, and the apparatus of food distribution dismantled. Relief and exhaustion combined to introduce a gradual thaw. Suspects were freed, Girondins restored to the Convention and moderate authority revived. Negotiations were opened with the Vendéen rebels and religious toleration agreed. The ideals of a civic religion lapsed together with the virtues and the intolerance of the Robespierre régime.

By 1795, however, a new wave of intolerance had begun to replace the Terror. Freed suspects and Girondin exiles demanded revenge for their imprisonment and humiliation. At Marseilles, Lyons and Toulon, Jacobins were lynched. In the south-east restored priests led the reaction. 'Companions of Jesus' massacred terrorists dragged from the prisons. The Thermidoreans, as the successors to Robespierre were called, followed the climate of opinion. Jacobin leaders were expelled from the committees. Carrier, the 'butcher of Nantes', was guillotined. Counter-terror spread into the provinces.

The ending of controls led to mounting economic dislocation. The *assignats* fell to 3 per cent of their face value, prices
rose wildly as the bread ration failed in the towns. Near
starvation the urban artisans organized fresh revolts. *Enragés*,
Hébertists and Babouvists rioted in April (Prairial) and demanded bread and the lost constitution of 1793. In May they
invaded the Convention only to be expelled by the National
Guards drawn from the bourgeois sections. Further reaction
followed. Jacobins were disarmed, the Commune was abolished, police control tightened. The remaining members of
the Committee of Public Safety were executed or deported to
Guiana. Only Carnot 'the organizer of victory' was spared.

Abroad, 1795 witnessed an easing of tension. France had
reached her 'natural' boundaries: Belgium had been reoccupied; the Rhine frontier had been consolidated; the
occupation of Savoy and Nice had brought France to the
watershed of the Alps. Prussia made peace in April anxious to
free herself for the final partition of Poland; Spain followed
in July. Only England and Austria remained, the former isolated by the Channel, the latter preoccupied in the East. In
July an English naval force landed a group of *émigrés* at
Quiberon Bay in an attempt to link up with the Vendéen
rebels. But it was defeated with little difficulty. Stronger
measures would be required to destroy the established power
of the Revolution.

At home, France seemed to have reached an exhausted if
temporary equilibrium. A new constitution consolidated
the power of the moderate and upper bourgeoisie. The Convention was replaced by an executive Directory of five members and a legislature of two chambers – a Council of Elders
and a Council of Five Hundred. Voting remained indirect
and, though the basic franchise was high and included most
taxpayers, the electoral assemblies continued under wealthy
bourgeois control. Priests and *émigrés* were still disenfranchized. Urban and rural workers continued without a vote. But
the administrative achievements of the Revolution were retained. The communes were preserved as the basis of local
government. Departments were linked to Paris by new agents
of the Directory.

To preserve continuity and exclude their Jacobin and
royalist rivals the Convention had concluded by declaring the

automatic re-election of two-thirds of its own members. On August 10th (13 Vendemiaire) the disenfranchized rallied for a last desperate revolt. Supporters from 33 sections converged on the Convention. They included respectable bourgeois, royalists and aristocrats. But the occasion for successful revolutionary action had passed. The defence, organized by Barras, had been entrusted to a young artillery officer, Napoleon Bonaparte. His guns quickly scattered the crowd leaving 300 dead; the future of the Revolution was to lie with the army.

IV · THE REVOLUTIONARY WAR AND THE RISE OF NAPOLEON

1. *Europe and the Revolution*

THE French Revolution has become a vital formative influence in European history. Its doctrines of political rights, human freedoms, equality of opportunity and justice have been accepted in many parts of the world and remain the ideal objectives of many more. But this has been the outcome of a great deal of subsequent conflict and experience. In 1789 its future was still uncertain and its impact confused.

Romantics, intellectuals and liberals welcomed the fall of the Bastille with varying degrees of enthusiasm. For Goethe, for Rhineland romantics, for Wordsworth it was a new dawn. Bourgeois writers, teachers, idealist aristocrats meeting in secret societies in Turin, Naples, Vienna or Berlin looked to France with vague and instinctive optimism. French revolutionary literature was translated into Russian and smuggled round European capitals; French ideals and actions were watched in hopeful anticipation. Only in England, however, were such influences to have any political importance. Moderate reformers revived the Society for Constitutional Information; radicals like Tom Paine and Thomas Hardy formed Corresponding Societies in the towns; Fox felt free to champion liberty against Pitt's government in a 'Society of Friends of the People'. Burke, however, in his *Reflections on the French Revolution*, published in 1790, warned of inevitable anarchy and dictatorship, and the threat to property and order soon brought disillusion and hostility.

European governments watched events with mounting alarm. Crowned heads were universally hostile. Catherine fulminated against mob rule, 'the fermentation of the scum', banned French books and sent suspect Jacobins to Siberia. In Prussia, Frederick William II, though mystical and ineffective, had little difficulty in eliminating the few bourgeois societies inclined to dabble in idealism. In Spain and Italy the authority of Church and Inquisition helped to maintain a close censorship. In Habsburg territories Francis II soon inaugurated a complete reaction. Reformers and Jacobins were easily identified and eliminated in dramatized trials.

In spite of aristocratic pressure and ecclesiastical alarm European sovereigns saw no reasons at first for intervening in French affairs. Few showed any sympathy for the early plight of Louis XVI; the majority displayed an obvious pleasure at France's collapse. Prussia, Russia and Austria were fully engaged in dismembering Poland or the Ottoman Empire. Events in France were a tiresome diversion only to be exploited. In England, Pitt remained cautious and aloof. He welcomed the initial stages of the Revolution which set up a constitutional monarchy, but reacted with horror at mob excess. Nevertheless, he hoped to avoid war and continued to declare for peace. In 1790 he was preoccupied with Spanish claims to Nootka Sound in western Canada and strengthened the fleet. In 1791 he was prepared to protest against the Russian occupation of Orchakov only to find the Prussians indifferent and engrossed in the Polish question. In 1790 the Poles had begun to reform their constitution and institute a national revival in defiance of Russian threats. But by 1791 Catherine had consolidated her Ottoman acquisitions and turned to invade her obstinate neighbour. Pitt recognized his impotence and cut the naval estimates.

The situation was, however, gradually transformed by the agitation of *émigrés* and the growth of revolutionary violence. In 1790 the revolt in Avignon and the Civil Constitution of the Clergy added clerical opposition. By 1791 d'Artois had set up his *émigré* court at Coblenz and sent agents to most European capitals to create panic and undermine French policy. After the failure of Louis XVI's flight to Varennes, Leopold II and Frederick William were persuaded to make a gesture. In August 1791 a Declaration at Pillnitz stated that French affairs were of common interest to all Europe, and threatened to intervene to protect the King if common agreement were obtained from all the European powers. As this was unlikely intervention seemed highly improbable. Within France, however, the danger of counterrevolution appeared imminent. The Girondins hoped to win popularity and gain control by rallying the nation to attack the growing threat on France's eastern frontier.[1] Leopold

[1] See p. 69.

tactlessly increased tension by ratifying the claims of the German princes in Alsace. In December, Louis was forced to demand the expulsion of *émigrés* from Coblenz. Though the Elector of Trèves agreed, Leopold deliberately sent imperial troops to protect him. When the French Assembly became increasingly hostile he negotiated an alliance with Prussia. In March the accession of Francis II, who was determined to protect the Pope and the rights of the German princes, led to complete deadlock. On April 20th 1792 France declared war.

2. *The Revolutionary War*

France had been propelled into war on a wave of revolutionary enthusiasm. But her military resources were by no means prepared for a major conflict with the great powers. By 1791 discipline in the army had largely collapsed, nearly half the officers had deserted to *émigré* detachments and new volunteers had still to be trained. Communications and supplies were hampered by civil war and widespread dislocation. Generals were unreliable and divided by political intrigue. Narbonne who had rallied the army throughout the winter was replaced in March by Dumouriez, a Girondin candidate. Ordered to advance at all costs he marched north to attack the Austrians in the Netherlands but was forced to retreat in confusion. Lafayette in Metz refused to move to his assistance. In July the Duke of Brunswick, Commander-in-Chief of the Austrian and Prussian forces, began to advance slowly from the Rhine. Under *émigré* guidance he drew up the manifesto threatening vengeance on Paris which precipitated the August revolution.[1] On August 20th he reached Longwy without encountering any effective resistance and marched on to Verdun. The desertion of Lafayette, the fall of Verdun and the September massacres seemed to herald the imminent collapse of France.

But the advance of Austrian and Prussian troops was unexpectedly held at Valmy. Dumouriez, now in command at the front, concentrated French troops in defence and called up Kellerman with the artillery to join him. Reformed by Gribeauval in the last years of the old order, the artillery was the best in Europe. Its officers were drawn from the poorer nobility and less inclined to emigrate than the aristocrats in

[1] See p. 71.

the infantry. When, on the foggy morning of September 20th, the French guns were brought to bear on Brunswick's forces their progress was brought to a sudden halt. Unable to advance, isolated on foreign soil, dampened by torrential rain, Prussian and Austrian armies retreated to the frontier. Dumouriez now turned to attack the Austrian Netherlands. In November he won a decisive victory at Jemappes and entered Brussels in triumph. Meanwhile newly invigorated republican armies invaded Savoy and Nice and crossed the Rhine in pursuit of the Austrians to occupy Frankfurt and Mainz.

Success encouraged the Convention to issue its Edict of Fraternity on November 19th offering assistance to all peoples wishing to recover their liberty. In December the abolition of feudal dues, tithes and ecclesiastical property in all occupied territories was declared official policy. This was followed up by action which became a pattern repeated after every French invasion: Jacobin Clubs of agents, sympathizers and army officers were set up to take over the local administration; the abolition of feudal dues and privileged corporations was decreed; security of tenure was guaranteed to peasants, and official posts thrown open to the bourgeoisie; noble and ecclesiastical property was confiscated and sold; wholesale requisitioning, law and order were imposed by military backing. Finally petitions for annexation were drawn up and the territory incorporated into the Republic and partitioned into new departments and districts. Savoy, Mainz and other Rhineland areas were annexed in this way with some show of popular support.

In Belgium, however, French action roused the bitter opposition of the Church and bourgeois corporations which had but recently recovered their liberties from Joseph II. Annexation was nevertheless decreed, the doctrine of France's 'natural' frontiers proclaimed, and the Scheldt opened to navigation regardless of any treaty obligations.[1] This inevitably roused the hostility of Holland and Great Britain. Since the execution of Louis XVI diplomatic relations had already been suspended. The threat to Holland and to her mercantile interests was bound to bring England into opposition. On February 1st 1793, France declared war.

[1] See p. 73.

The war led to an intensification of the deep hatred felt for revolution by all the established orders in Europe, and to a rapid identification of all reform with revolutionary action. The execution of the King was greeted with outraged indignation. Jacobin Clubs in Italy and the Empire were hounded into oblivion. In Vienna, court panic and press denunciations extinguished the reforming policies of the 'enlightenment'. Performances of Mozart's 'Magic Flute' were banned as an alleged revolutionary allegory. In England, Pitt was forced to take measures against radicals and reformers. Corresponding societies were suppressed. Tom Paine was prosecuted for publishing his *Rights of Man* and leading Jacobin sympathizers were arrested and imprisoned. Merchants, bankers and squires supported Pitt to safeguard their position and curb any revolutionary unrest. In 1794 the Whig opposition split; Burke and Portland joined Pitt to close the ranks against subversion, while Fox maintained an isolated and unpopular stand in favour of liberty and moderate reform.

England's entry into the war made little immediate impression. Pitt, like most of his contemporaries, anticipated a speedy end to the conflict. A small expeditionary force of some 6,500 under the Duke of York was sent to aid the Austrians and assist in the defence of Holland. Hessians and Hanoverians were as usual taken into British service. Greater reliance, however, was placed upon the navy through which Pitt hoped to revive the imperial strategy of the Seven Years' War.[1] Simultaneous expeditions were sent to the Britanny coast, to the Mediterranean and the West Indies. With a total army of only 20,000 and a fleet of 113 ships of the line, British efforts were hopelessly dispersed.

French reverses were due more to internal dissension than to enemy strength. Dumouriez quarrelled with the Girondin Convention about the reorganization of Belgium and created bitter divisions which helped to contribute to his defeat at Neerwinden in March. His subsequent desertion left the north-east frontier exposed, and the Anglo-Austrian armies were able to reoccupy Belgium during the summer in a war of slow and leisurely sieges. The civil war also weakened the French forces and precipitated the rapid withdrawal and expulsion of French troops from Mainz and the Rhineland. The

[1] See p. 20.

French navy, with eighty ships of the line and heavier broadsides, was weakened by the collapse of discipline and the desertion of half its officers. Promotion from the lower decks by election and the enlistment of merchant seamen antagonized the remained. In September, Admiral Comte de Trogoff surrendered Toulon to the British fleet together with thirty ships.

Pitt slowly built up the First Coalition with a liberal distribution of loans and subsidies. In March a subsidy treaty was negotiated with Russia; by the end of August Britain had agreed to help finance Prussia, Austria, Sardinia, Spain and Naples in a war against France. The 'allies', however, remained divided. In January, Prussia had invaded Poland; her intervention in Alsace seemed half-hearted and her subsidies were soon withdrawn. The Austrian advance moved at a slow pace and soon halted at Valenciennes, while an English diversion to capture Dunkirk was defeated. Piedmontese and Austrian reinforcements failed to arrive at Toulon; Spanish raids over the Pyrenees were of little significance.

Meanwhile the Terror revitalized and co-ordinated the French war effort.[1] In August, Carnot and Prieur de la Côte d'Or were elected to the Committee of Public Safety which authorized the *levée en masse*:[1] total mobilization of the country's human and material resources. While Carnot reorganized the army Prieur mobilized supplies. Scientists were brought in to help expand war production and France produced seven thousand cannon in 1793. Workmen were conscripted into munitions factories. In Paris 258 forges were erected in the open air, constructing some thousand gun barrels a day. Shoes, uniforms and medical supplies were obtained by mass organization. Old professionals, volunteers and conscripts were amalgamated into new regiments. Discipline was restored and the army supervised by *réprésentants en mission*. In September the advance of the Austrians was halted. By December the revolts in the Vendée had been contained and Lyons, Marseilles and Toulon recaptured.

In 1794 France had some 850,000 men under arms. The allies were hurled back on every front. In May the Anglo-Austrian troops were defeated at Tourcoing. In June the French won a decisive victory at Fleurus and reoccupied Bel-

[1] See p. 75.

gium. British and Austrian troops separated, the former strag-
gling back through Holland to Bremen, the latter diverted to
join Russian and Prussian intervention in Poland. Here the
partition of 1793 had roused bitter resistance. Led by
Kosciuszko, who had fought for the American army in the
War of Independence, the Poles defeated the Russians in
April 1794. But by September Polish resistance had been
broken and in the following year a final partition eliminated
Poland from the map.

The French had meanwhile again occupied the left bank of
the Rhine, annexed Belgium and consolidated their positions
in the Alps. Pitt's coalition slowly disintegrated; Prussia
made peace in April, Spain followed in July. Holland had
been overrun during the winter and her fleet captured while
frozen in the ice. In 1795 her liberators set up a satellite
'Batavian' republic. In England agitation increased as a result
of the bad harvest of 1794. In 1795 the price of wheat rose by
50 per cent, the King was mobbed on his way to open Parliament and the windows in Downing Street broken by a rabble
shouting 'No war! No famine! No Pitt'. The minister found
small consolation in the victories of the navy and in imperial
gains overseas. The Glorious 1st of June 1794 was a victory for
the fleet, but allowed the grain ships to escape and relieve the
French food shortage. In 1795 Britain took advantage of the
surrender of Holland and Spain to occupy the Cape of Good
Hope, seize Ceylon and rival trading stations in the East.
Failure in Europe, however, seemed complete and was only
confirmed by the fiasco at Quiberon Bay.[1]

France had reached her 'natural' frontiers on the Rhine
and in the Alps. 1795 seemed to afford a breathing space, a
moment of temporary saturation. Only Britain and Austria
remained in effective opposition, divided and mutually suspicious. Many hoped for peace. Pitt made tentative overtures
but France insisted on keeping all her conquests. These,
however, could only be safeguarded by the decisive defeat of
Austria. The year 1796 was to see a new push to defeat the
Austrians on the Rhine. There was to be a diversionary attack
through Lombardy in the South. The command of the
Italian army was given to General Buonaparte whose spec-

[1] See p. 79.

tacular rise was to bring a new dynamic factor into the war and into the history of Europe.

3. The Rise of Napoleon and the Italian Campaign

Napoleon Buonaparte was born on August 15th, 1769. Like many great men his background and early life combined a variety of formative influences. The Buona Partes were one of the leading families of Ajaccio; 200 years of nobility had been officially registered in 1771, three years after the island had been purchased by France.[1] Napoleon was the second of eight surviving children brought up under a sensible and matronly mother. The family tie, characteristic of a close mountain people, was to remain strong all his life, and he was often conscious of a hot southern blood in his veins. Through the influence of the local *Intendant* he was admitted to the royal military school at Brienne, founded for the sons of nobles, where distinction in mathematics led to a choice of career in the artillery. He was the first Corsican to pass through the *Ecole militaire* in Paris and seems to have suffered from the aristocratic snobbery of some of his fellows. In 1785 he was commissioned Lieutenant in the artillery and continued his specialist training in the new techniques and tactics developed in the last years of the old order. Familiarity with Gribeauval's light artillery, Bourcet's *Principles of Mountain Warfare*, Guibert's flexible methods of attack and du Teil's concentrated use of gunfire were to provide the groundwork for his future action and success.

But the young Napoleon was more than a soldier. He read widely in the classics, in history and in politics. He was familiar with the writings of eighteenth-century philosophers, and often wrote his own somewhat romantic tracts. A man of independence and action he already resented subordination to church or state. At the outbreak of the Revolution he helped to rouse Corsica and welcomed back Paoli who had been forced to flee to England twenty years earlier. The flight to Varennes converted Napoleon to republicanism and, when Paoli refused to fall into line, he led a rising against his former hero. Some indiscriminate shooting resulted in widespread criticism. In 1792 he returned to Paris and witnessed the struggle of the factions and the sack of the Tuileries. This left

[1] See p. 45.

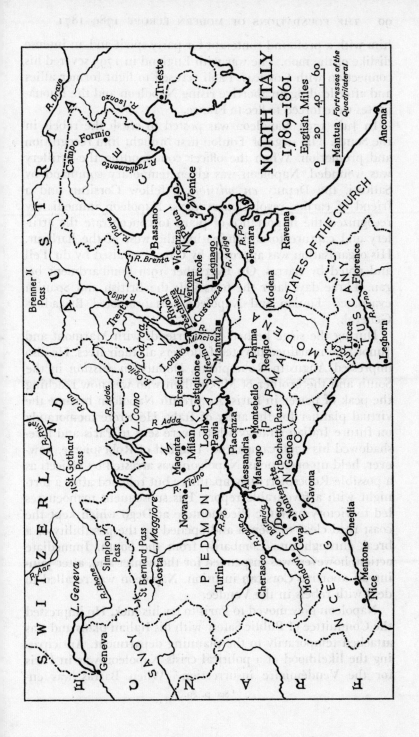

NORTH ITALY
1789–1861

English Miles

0   20   40   60

■ Mantua   *Fortresses of the Quadrilateral*

him with a profound contempt for party spirit and an intense dislike of the mob. The war with England in 1793 severed his connection with Corsica: Paoli refused to fight former allies and after leading an abortive rising Napoleon and the Buona-partes were forced to flee to France.

In July 1793 Napoleon was posted to crush the rebels in the South. The siege of Toulon first brought him recognition and promotion. When the officer commanding the artillery was wounded, Napoleon was given temporary command by Saliceti, the Deputy *en mission*, a fellow Corsican and a friend of earlier revolutionary days. Napoleon immediately recognized the importance of plans to concentrate the artil-lery and capture forts dominating the west of the harbour. His organisation was approved by Carnot, praised by du Teil and noted by Barras. On December 19th bombardment be-gan. Three days later the forts fell; the British and Spanish evacuated Toulon and Napoleon was promoted Brigadier-General.

During the siege he had made friends with Marmont and Junot who remained devoted followers all their lives. He also impressed Augustin Robespierre, Deputy *en mission* in the South and the brother of Maximilien who was now reaching the peak of power in Paris. As a result Napoleon became the virtual planner for the army of Italy. He wrote memoranda on future Italian strategy which were sent to Paris and fore-shadowed his 1796 campaigns. The fall of Robespierre, how-ever, held up operations. Napoleon was arrested by Saliceti as a possible Robespierrist sympathizer but released after a fort-night with a favourable report. His subsequent manoeuvres led to victory over the Piedmontese at Dego which kept the coast road clear to Genoa and opened up the possibility of a break through into Lombardy from the South. Immediate action, however, was suspended for the winter and, after join-ing an abortive Corsican invasion, Napoleon was recalled to deal with rebels in the Vendée.

Napoleon now moved to Paris to try his luck. He impressed the Committee of Public Safety with his Italian plans and was attached temporarily to the planning department. Anticipat-ing the likelihood of a political crisis Napoleon was in Paris for the Vendémiaire insurrection.[1] When Barras was en-

[1] See p. 80.

trusted with the defence of the Convention, Napoleon was placed second in command and scattered the advancing columns with gunfire. He was now promoted Major-General, succeeded Barras as Commander of the army of the interior, and married Josephine de Beauharnais, an elegant and aristocratic widow. When the Commander of the army of Italy failed to take the initiative in the spring of 1796 Napoleon was given command by a unanimous vote of the directors. On March 11th, two days after his marriage, he left Paris for the frontier.

Napoleon's victories in Italy took Europe by surprise. The ingredients of success were, however, already at hand: equipment had been improved, tactics redefined and the strategy anticipated. The armies of the Republic had been reconstructed; the French were poised on the crest of the Alps. Napoleon was familiar with the ground and well known as a brilliant theorist and strategist; his co-ordination of the elements of war and the impact of his personality were to be decisive. He rapidly removed any suspicions on account of his youth and won the confidence of his commanders by dignity, precision and indefatigable energy. After nearly a month of careful preparation, reorganizing supplies, arranging loans, restoring discipline and shooting deserters and brigands, Napoleon was ready to attack.

With 38,000 men in the field against 30,000 Austrians and 12,000 Piedmontese victory depended on separating his opponents and defeating each in turn. This characteristic manoeuvre required careful organization and control. When the Austrians moved south to capture Voltri, anticipating a French advance along the coast, Napoleon attacked their right wing in the mountains and defeated separate units at Dego and Montenotte. An Austrian retreat to Alessandria left the Piedmontese exposed to superior French numbers. Defeated at Ceva and Mondovi, Piedmont sued for peace and by the Truce of Cherasco on April 28th opened the route into Lombardy.

Napoleon immediately gave chase to the retreating Austrian armies. Advancing with spectacular speed on the south bank of the Po, he outflanked his opponents at every defensible point on the northern side. Crossing the river at Piacenza he struck north, defeated the Austrian rearguard at

Lodi and occupied Milan. By the end of May Napoleon had cleared the Austrians from Lombardy, besieged Mantua and taken up a commanding position in the area of the Quadrilateral fortresses south of Lake Garda.

Victory brought increasing confidence and allowed Napoleon to consolidate his position at home. After Lodi he had premonitions of greatness and realized he was a 'superior being'. When the Directory proposed to divide command between Kellerman in the North and Napoleon in the South he protested vigorously and retained complete control. He ignored demands to march south to plunder Rome and Naples, and continually urged an attack against Austria through the Tyrol. His independence may have caused anxiety but this was soon calmed by vast quantities of loot, art treasures and cash sent to Paris to support the dwindling state finances. In June a swift expedition through Bologna and Florence forced Naples, Tuscany and the Papacy to make terms and pay tribute to the French Republic. By July some 60 million francs had already been levied from Italy. Napoleon began to pay his troops in cash instead of in *assignats*. Opposition from government *commissaires* with the army was criticized for undermining the campaign: by the end of the year their office had been abolished.

Napoleon's treatment of the Italians was equally independent and arbitrary. The Directory, who hoped to restore Lombardy to the Austrians in return for guarantees on the Rhine, urged pacification and a limit to republican agitation. Napoleon, however, was more concerned to preserve the position of his diminishing forces. To ensure security he was prepared to exploit every means and any argument. Loyal republicans in Milan were encouraged with promises of independence; a rising in Pavia was ruthlessly crushed. Opponents were flattered, ignored, praised or shot according to the demands of the moment. As the military situation deteriorated in the autumn, the northern states were urged to take up republicanism and to prepare plans for national unity. In October deputies met at Modena to lay the foundations of a new Cispadane[1] Republic.

Meanwhile Napoleon was forced into a series of defensive campaigns. The failure of French armies on the Rhine en-

[1] South of the Po.

abled the Austrians to reinforce their Italian front and march
to the relief of Mantua. Napoleon with some 32,000 men
faced Austrian armies of over 47,000. While the Austrians divided into three columns and marched through the Alpine
foothills down different valleys, Napoleon concentrated his
men and in a series of swift and brilliant moves defeated each
column in turn, the right wing at Lonato, and the centre two
days later at Castiglione. When the Austrians retired to regroup near Padua, Napoleon struck north, captured Trent,
and attacked them in the rear at Bassano, forcing them to
retreat into Mantua. Two campaigns in November and
January followed a similar pattern. When fresh Austrian
columns converged on Napoleon's weary troops near Verona,
he forced one to retire by turning its flank after a desperate
three-days battle at Arcola, and then moved north to defeat a
second column at Rivoli. In January relieving columns were
again defeated at Rivoli, and three days later at Mantua. The
fortress surrendered at the end of the month. The road to
Vienna was clear. By March Napoleon had reached Klagen-
furt, his army reinforced by 40,000 men. At Leoben, less than
100 miles from Vienna, the Austrians agreed to a truce.
France was to keep Belgium and Lombardy while Austria
was to be compensated with the mainland territories of
Venice.

The Truce of Leoben had been negotiated without reference to the Directory. A treaty imposed upon the Pope in
February had also ignored demands to destroy papal government and to erase the Roman religion. Napoleon realized the
hold of religion upon the masses and preferred, where possible, to temporize with so dangerous a rival. He forced the
Pope to surrender claims to Avignon, close his ports to hostile
navies, pay an indemnity of 30 millions, and cede Bologna,
Ferrara and the Romagna to the new Cispadane Republic.
Here he attempted to maintain a balance between priests and
aristocrats on the one hand and republican democrats on the
other, encouraging both moderate and Jacobin journals. By
May 1797 there were indications of a clerical revival, and
Napoleon joined Lombardy and the Cispadane into a new
Cisalpine Republic with a French constitution of five
Directors and two Councils. Napoleon himself nominated
all the members of both the executive and the legislature,

and it was difficult to disguise the fact that the constitution
had been imposed by force with the support of a small
minority of bourgeois intellectuals and radical agitators.
Napoleon soon came to despise the Italians for rejecting
their enforced liberation. The Italians reciprocated with
mounting opposition. An attempt to completely revolutionize Italy in 1798 was to lead to the sudden collapse of French
rule.

Meanwhile Napoleon was building up and consolidating
his influence in France. In 1797 moderates and royalists tried
to stage a come-back and elected a royalist President of the
Five Hundred and a pacifist director. Peace negotiations were
begun with England and Austria, ratification of the Truce
of Leoben delayed. Napoleon was determined to maintain his
interests and sent General Augereau to Paris. On September
4th 1797 (18 Fructidor) he surrounded the Tuileries with
troops, invaded the Councils, arrested the offending Directors, who included Carnot, and quashed the election of 200
deputies. Austria was now forced to recognize that only Napoleon could make peace. He had invaded Venice after a
massacre of the French in Verona. The Doge was forced to
accept a democratic constitution and a government which
immediately called in French troops. Napoleon could now
use the whole of Venetian territory as a bargaining counter.
At the Treaty of Campo Formio Austria ceded Belgium,
recognized the Cisalpine Republic and received Venice with
most of its mainland territories and the Dalmatian Coast,
while France took the Ionian Islands and Venetian Albania.
In addition, Austria agreed to support French claims to the
left bank of the Rhine in return for French help in gaining
Salzburg at a congress to be held at Rastadt. Napoleon was
appointed the delegate of the French Republic; he had become arbiter of Europe.

4. *The Naval War and the Egyptian Campaign*

In 1797 the European powers appeared quite incapable of
resisting Napoleon's increasing influence. Catherine the
Great had died the previous year. Her son, Paul I, though
remotely idealistic, was widely eccentric and verging on
madness. Hating his mother and her policies he freed critics

like Novikov and Radishchev, but continued to attack every symptom of revolution. He attempted to restrict the working days of serfs but continued to distribute lands to the nobility. A succession law of 1797 defined the hereditary claims of the Romanovs. Attempts to impose additional obligations on the nobility led to increasing opposition. Overcome by fear and suspicion Paul introduced a régime of terror. Noble ladies were sent to be lashed, all had to kneel prostrate in the snow on sighting the Tsar's coach. Abroad he reversed Catherine's policy and sought to protect the Ottoman Empire, while coveting with increasing passion the Grand Mastership of the Knights of Malta.

In Prussia the death of Frederick William II in 1797 and the accession of his son Frederick William III only hastened the decline of the State. Though pious and well-meaning he was feeble and irresolute, and unable to co-ordinate and direct the many departments dependent upon royal initiative. The army continued to stagnate; foreign mercenaries and officers replaced national levies; manoeuvres were limited to save expense. The social caste system excluded any bourgeois officers or new blood; strategy and tactics were fossilized in Frederickian patterns and upheld by aged and inflexible generals. Few noted the changes which had taken place in France, or drew profitable lessons from the experiences of the 1792-4 campaigns. Self-confident and complacent the Prussians turned to digest their new acquisitions in Poland.

In November, Prussia, Austria and the German States assembled at Rastadt to meet Napoleon's demands for a German settlement. While France gained the left bank of the Rhine, Prussian and Austrian compensation created bitter feuds and debates which lasted for over a year. The myth of a 'Holy Roman Empire' was shattered, a weak and divided Germany lay exposed to attack. But Napoleon now turned his attention to the problem of England. In 1797 he had been appointed commander of the 'Army of England' and directed to attack the last country to remain in active opposition to France's European claims.

The year 1797 had been a bleak year for Pitt. Spain and Holland, angered by their colonial losses, had declared war on Great Britain in the previous year. Corsica and the Mediterranean had become untenable and the fleet had been withdrawn. In April the navy mutinied at Spithead and the Nore, complaining of rotten food, bad pay and brutal discipline. Genuine grievances were put right, the Spithead mutineers pardoned, political agitators hanged. A financial crisis due to the cost of the war, loans and subsidies led to the suspension of cash payments. A rebellion in Ireland appeared imminent. In the summer Pitt agreed to offer generous terms in the peace negotiations: France was to keep all her continental conquests while Britain was willing to return all her colonial gains with the exception of Trinidad and the Cape of Good Hope. The Fructidor coup, however, put a rapid end to the discussions. Britain was left to continue the fight alone.

British naval strength was able, in spite of the mutinies, to play a significant role. In February, Jervis and Nelson scattered the Spanish fleet at Cape St. Vincent and prevented further enemy moves in the Channel. In October the Nore fleet regained confidence and destroyed the Dutch at Camperdown. When Napoleon came to inspect the Channel ports in February 1798 he realized that an invasion of England was impracticable. His mind had already turned to the idea of an expedition to Egypt. Venice had been marked out as a gateway to the East with the French occupation of Corfu as a further stepping stone. Such an expedition would open up a new front against England, threaten her position in India and eventually bring her to her knees.

Napoleon's plans won the support of Talleyrand, now Minister of Foreign Affairs, and were approved by the Directory. An expedition to Egypt would be less costly in men and money than the vast expenditure needed for a cross-channel invasion. Moreover, the Mediterranean was for the moment free of English ships. The secret of the expedition was well kept. It sailed on May 19th, 1798, with a landing force of 35,000 men, nearly 400 transports, 13 ships of the line and 150 scientific experts to civilize and explore the area. On May 4th Nelson had arrived at Gibraltar, ordered into the Mediterranean on the vaguest premonition that Napoleon intended to sail to the East. On the 17th he was off Toulon, but Napoleon slipped out unnoticed and sailed with a fresh north-west wind down the east coast of Corsica, while the British fleet was nearly wrecked during a fierce gale on the western side.

While Nelson turned north to search out his enemy at Toulon, Napoleon captured Malta. He stayed only six days to water and provision the fleet, expel the Knights and establish a new republican constitution. Meanwhile Nelson, informed of the general direction of the French fleet, was sailing down the Italian coast in swift pursuit. Delayed by contrary winds the French sailed on June 19th and crossed Nelson's course off the east coast of Sicily one day ahead. While Napoleon sailed slowly up the central Mediterranean, the British on a southerly tack reached Alexandria on June 28th – two days ahead – and finding the harbour empty moved north in a vain sweep. Napoleon was able to land unopposed. On July 2nd Alexandria was captured by storm with little loss. After two weeks gruelling march across desert wastes the French army massacred the Mameluke Beys, the aristrocracy of Egypt, at a battle near the pyramids and made a triumphant entry into Cairo.

Napoleon immediately set to work to reorganize the government and administration of the country. He employed the usual combination of promises and threats to win over the native population: promises to restore rights, establish equality, expel the Mamelukes and respect Mohammed; threats to burn down and destroy opposing villages. The government was a mixture of sound administrative organization and military force. A central council, or Diwan of Nine was made responsible, with provincial diwans, for the maintenance of law and taxation, while new French regulations covered anything from sanitation to metric reform. An Assembly of Notables nominated by French governors was to advise on affairs of state. Simultaneously obedience was maintained by directives from Napoleon himself and a regular batch of daily executions.

Napoleon was aware of the vital significance of religion. He professed himself an admirer of Allah and the Koran, and won official approval from the muftis and the authorities in Mecca. The birth of Mohammed was celebrated by the French army with military parades and fireworks. Rumours of mass conversion were widespread. At the same time scientific and archaeological exploration was hurried on. An Institute of Egypt was officially established on August 22nd and its research formed the basis of modern Egyptian studies.

Napoleon himself led an expedition to investigate Suez and the remains of the ancient canal joining the Red Sea to the Mediterranean.

Meanwhile, however, Nelson had at last caught up with the French fleet anchored behind the shallows at Aboukir Bay. Confident that the shoals at the western end afforded complete protection, the ships had been anchored in line and most of the guns moved to the seaward side. Nelson and his captains, with a following wind, were in a favourable position to manoeuvre and, slipping round the edge of the shoals, steered half their ships behind the French line and half in front. Caught in a crossfire the French fleet was annihilated and all but two ships of the line and two frigates captured or destroyed. The battle altered the prospects both of the expedition and of the European powers. Napoleon made light of the disaster and blamed the French admiral for taking up a position he had himself proposed. Nevertheless, cut off in Egypt by a British blockade, his position was critical and soon became worse.

In Egypt unrest began to grow as the French imposed forced loans and new taxes to replace the bullion sunk in their flagship. In October a major rising took place in Cairo which took two days to crush. As soon as the news of Aboukir reached Constantinople the Turks declared war on France and began to organize their forces in Syria. Napoleon, reassured by news that the European powers had not yet moved to the attack, invaded Syria with the intention of making the whole coast friendly 'by negotiation and war'. At the time he regarded the Syrian campaign as a limited diversion and only added the wider prospects of an eastern campaign in retrospect. Taking some 13,000 men he captured Jaffa by assault and besieged Acre. Here, he was frustrated by the British naval squadron under Sir Sidney Smith which helped to rake the repeated French assaults with accurate gunfire. Having thrown back a Turkish relieving army at Mount Tabor on April 16th, Napoleon abandoned the siege and returned to Cairo.

By now Napoleon had heard that Russia and Austria had declared war and invaded Italy. In July the annihilation of a Turkish invasion force at Aboukir seemed to guarantee the French position in Egypt. When he learned from newspapers provided by Sir Sidney Smith that the French had been defeated in Italy and on the Rhine, he decided on an immediate return and ordered two fast frigates to be prepared in the greatest secrecy. To his second in command, Kléber, he left promises of reinforcements and the prospects of ultimate relief. He sailed on August 24th with a handful of generals and scientists and landed safely in France on October 9th.

5. The Second Coalition

Throughout 1798 Pitt had laboriously built up a Second Coalition. The French occupation of Malta had incensed the Tsar, whose dreams of suzerainty over the Knights of St. John had been shattered! His anger at the occupation of Egypt and the threatened attack on the Ottoman Empire led to the completion of an alliance in December. Russia agreed to send an army into Italy under Suvorov and another into Switzerland, which had been occupied by the French earlier in the year. The Austrians, though still embroiled in German negotiations at Rastadt, were drawn by the hope of regaining Lombardy in exchange for Belgium, and angered by the ruthless expansion of French activities in Italy.

Action in the Italian peninsula had led to a bitter reaction against French rule. Napoleon's departure in 1797 allowed extreme Jacobin and irresponsible military agents increased license. In Rome the French envoy Joseph Bonaparte encouraged local agitators. After a riot in which a visiting general was shot, the French army occupied Rome, deposed the Pope and despoiled the city. Pius VI was moved north under French surveillance and Rome turned into a new Republic ruled by a host of French commissioners and puppet Italian 'consuls'. This action was viewed with considerable alarm in Naples. When Nelson returned, having destroyed the French fleet at Aboukir Bay, excitement led to an immediate decision to destroy the Roman Republic. An ill-disciplined invasion was easily defeated by the French, north of Rome. Naples was now invaded in turn and Ferdinand forced to flee with his family and the royal treasure on to Nelson's flagship in which he escaped to Sicily.

French attacks upon the Church and the systematic looting of Italian cities provoked bitter reprisals. In Naples priests led the peasants in guerilla warfare. Trees of liberty were uprooted, crosses restored and the government of the new 'Parthenopean' Republic harassed throughout the countryside. Gradually opposition developed into a Holy War led by the *Sanfedisti*, Congregations of the Holy Faith. Peasants, poor and unemployed were harnessed to attack the French, destroy the unbeliever and save the Pope.

In the North, French pressure led to conflict with the Swiss. Pretexts for intervention were easily found in disturbances engineered by French agents. After invasion, a Helvetian Republic was set up with the aid of Swiss Jacobins like Laharpe and a constitution with a Directory and councils on standard French lines established. When the cantons rebelled against enforced unification the Austrians were given another cause for renewed action. By March 1799 they had agreed to join Russia, Britain, Naples, Portugal and the Ottoman Empire in the new coalition.

Russian and Austrian armies invaded northern Italy in April. A victory at Cassano destroyed the Cisalpine Republic, and a decisive battle at Novi on August 15th expelled the French from Italy. As French garrisons withdrew from the peninsula they were followed by a rising tide of violence. Ferdinand reoccupied Naples, executed eighty-four republicans and exiled some thousand liberals. *Sanfedisti* risings helped to expel the enemy from Rome, Florence and the Papal States. In the North, however, Austrian intervention led to early signs of a growing opposition to all foreign action and a rising demand for an independent Italy. When Pius VI died in captivity at Valence, the Austrians hoped to manipulate the election of a subservient Pope. A conclave called at Venice in November, however, elected a compromise candidate, Chiaramonti, who had been prepared to work with Napoleon in the early days of the Cisalpine Republic and now took the title of Pius VII.

Austrian ambitions in north Italy were but one of many causes of friction which soon undermined the Coalition. Austria resented Russian intervention in Italy and Switzerland and failed to co-operate. Masséna defeated the Russians at Zürich in September and Suvorov, who came to their aid after a spectacular march over the Alps, narrowly escaped encirclement. But the Austrians, having driven the French from the Danube to the Rhine earlier in the year, withdrew leaving the

Russians exposed. As a result volleys of bitter recrimination threatened to break up the alliance.

In Holland an Anglo-Russian expedition was a lamentable fiasco. Pitt's failure to draw the Prussians into the war had already made intervention on the continent precarious. Although he had paid out over £1 million in subsidies for Russian troops, he himself only embarked 12,000 men – half the agreed number. After a slow advance in the rain the armies stuck in the mud and sickened. Faced by Dutch indifference and increasing French resistance, the expedition was forced to withdraw on October 18th. Paul I, already disgusted by Austrian duplicity, recalled his armies in open resentment.

6. *The Triumph of Napoleon*

By the time Napoleon landed in France the armies of the Second Coalition had already been defeated in Holland and Switzerland and the alliance appeared on the verge of disintegration. But Italy had been re-occupied by Austrian troops and the last French armies were encircled and hard pressed in Genoa. News of the defeat of the Turks at Aboukir had been received the previous week. This wiped out the dismal impression created by the Syrian campaign. Everywhere Napoleon was received with popular enthusiasm and acclaim.

The Directory was already showing obvious signs of collapse. Ever since the attempted rising of Vendémiaire it had been forced to rely upon the army to hold down a mounting wave of royalist and Jacobin criticism. In 1796 a Babouvist 'conspiracy of equals' demanding communal property and economic control had been uncovered and crushed. The following year had witnessed a royalist revival in the elections, monarchist intrigue and the opening of peace negotiations, which had only been frustrated by the intervention of General Augereau.

In 1798 the Directors had attempted to maintain control by purging the Councils and controlling the press. Official lists of candidates were drawn up for the elections, but in spite of this over a hundred elected deputies had to be excluded for being too Jacobin. The press was placed under police supervision for a year. Suspected journalists and politicians were deported to Guinea. In 1799 the elections in May produced another round of crises. Defeat abroad and economic unrest at home led to a new Jacobin revival linked to dissident elements in the army led by Bernadotte. Changes in the Directorate brought in Sieyès, determined to play once again the role of constitutional reformer. Having escaped the Terror he hoped to establish a new moderate balance in which he could play a key role. He had, however, to find someone with enough power to put his plans into operation.

In spite of permanent crises and constant attacks from Jacobin and royalist factions, the Directory had much to its credit. The administrative framework of the Revolution with its communes, districts and departments had been consolidated; some co-ordination through agents of the Directors had been retained. The outlines of a bureaucracy had been created. A statistical bureau had begun the vast problem of tax reassessment. Communications, poor relief and education had gradually been improved. The currency had been stabilised, the *assignats* fixed at one thirtieth of their face value and a new metallic currency introduced. In 1798 universal conscription had become law and the military machine had been brought under increasing control. Vast problems remained: lack of effective authority to enforce law and collect taxation; a budget deficit of 400 million francs; the continued resistance of the Church. The Directors appeared ludicrous in their plumes, while the Councils seldom commanded respect in their togas. Nevertheless the Directory might well have survived had not Napoleon deliberately joined up with factions working to destroy it.

The situation throughout the summer of 1799 remained critical. When the Jacobins in the Council passed a Law of Hostages, which authorized the imprisonment of *émigré* families, and ordered a new tax on incomes the days of the Terror were recalled. The moderates struck back. Lucien Bonaparte was elected President of the Five Hundred and another moderate President of the Elders. Bernadotte was dismissed from the Ministry of War. Sieyès, looking round for a general to organize the usual coup, approached Moreau. When, however, the latter heard that Napoleon had landed, he replied, 'There is your man, he will make your *coup d'état* better than I.'

Napoleon rapidly weighed up the prospects. He clearly had no intention of working for anyone but himself. The only problem was how best to exploit the situation. Having rejected the advances of Barras and the Jacobin faction, who would have tied his hands, Napoleon agreed to work with Sieyès, whose involved constitutional proposals no doubt gave the best chance of acquiring complete control. The coup was carefully planned with the aid of Fouché, Minister of Police, Talleyrand, anxious to increase his influence and Sieyès, who considered himself the master-mind. Napoleon, however, had already made it clear that he expected to become one of the consuls in any provisional government. Mutual suspicions nearly wrecked the whole affair.

On November 9th (18 Brumaire), the Elders were persuaded by rumours of a conspiracy to vote for the Councils to meet next day at St. Cloud, well away from Paris. To ensure their protection Napoleon was appointed to the command of the Paris garrison. But he altered the decree to give himself command of the guards of the Councils and of the Directory as well. Barras was persuaded to resign, and, when the other Directors refused to follow suit, they were placed under house arrest. On the following day, when the Councils met at St. Cloud, the Jacobin opposition launched a bitter attack on the proceedings. Enraged by Napoleon's military preparations and obvious contempt for the Directory, they demanded details of the alleged conspiracy. Losing patience Napoleon harangued the Elders in an incoherent speech which ended with a threat of force. Moving on to the Five Hundred he was greeted with cries of anger and threats of outlawry. Forced out of the hall, Napoleon appealed to the guards, but it was only when his brother Lucien called for aid that they agreed to move. Rumours of attempted assassination and blood on Napoleon's face roused the ranks. The guards marched into the hall; the deputies fled.

In the evening the Elders and some one hundred remaining members of the Five Hundred nominated a provisional executive of three consuls – Sieyès, Ducos and Napoleon – and two commissions of 25 from each Council to draw up a new constitution. During the discussions Napoleon imposed his will upon the remainder. Paris had watched the collapse of the Directory with indifference; the loyalty of the army and the hopes of Frenchmen in 'victory and peace' gave Napoleon overwhelming support. Sieyès had drawn up elaborate constitutional plans, but Napoleon soon shaped the unwieldy proposals to suit himself. Having vested complete executive power in a First Consul, who was to hold office for ten years, he persuaded Sieyès to nominate him for the post in return for the Presidency of the Senate. Together they now nominated the remaining members of a Senate and Legislature. When Sieyès was persuaded to retire, rewarded by a large estate, Napoleon retained undisputed authority.

Within a year Napoleon had consolidated his position at home and abroad. A plebiscite resulted in a vote of three million in favour of the constitution and 1,500 against. Napoleon nominated officials at central and local level. A Council of State to draft laws and advise the First Consul was established with sub-committees to examine every aspect of government. Moderates and experts of all parties were brought in to establish a sound and well balanced administration: Gaudin at the Treasury had been a royalist; Fouché a Jacobin; Talleyrand a man of all parties. Napoleon appealed above faction to national unity. After Brumaire there were few deportations, protests were reasonably considered, the Law of Hostages repealed. Efforts were made to pacify the Vendée by guarantees of free worship. The army was rewarded with pensions and praise. Napoleon impressed all who came in contact with him by his moderation, breadth of view and grasp of facts. After ten years of revolution and terror, France accepted his proclamation that the Revolution was 'complete' with gratitude and relief.

Napoleon realized, however, that the settlement would remain provisional until confirmed by victory abroad. In December 1799 he had made peace offers to George III and Francis II. By February in the following year, however, he was again demanding the terms of Campo Formio. Already a reserve force was being assembled at Dijon. In May the French army of 50,000 crossed the Alps to attack the Austrians, who were still besieging Genoa, in the rear. Milan was occupied on June 2nd and by the time Genoa surrendered on the 8th Napoleon was marching to capture the Austrian base at Alessandria. The deciding battle was fought at Marengo. For once the Austrian army remained united while Napoleon, anxious to trap the enemy, split up his troops. His main force was being driven back relentlessly by superior numbers when some dispersed divisions returned just in time to attack the Austrians in the flank. Taken by surprise they fled in confusion and subsequently agreed to evacuate the whole of Lombardy. Napoleon had assured the survival of the Consulate by victory in the field.

When the Emperor refused to make peace and abandon the English alliance French armies broke through on the Rhine and captured Munich. Negotiations were opened at Lunéville in the summer but dragged on due to Austrian evasion. While Napoleon opened friendly discussions with Russia, Prussia and Spain, five French armies advanced to the attack on a front stretching from the Danube to the Arno. On December 3rd Moreau crushed the Austrians at Hohenlinden and pushed on to within 50 miles of Vienna. The Emperor accepted an armistice. On February 9th, 1801, by the Treaty of Lunéville, France received the left-bank of the Rhine from Switzerland to Holland, while Austria retained her Venetian gains. The Dutch, Swiss, Cisalpine and Ligurian Republics were again recognized. France was supreme on the continent.

The war against England continued for another year and confirmed Britain's naval supremacy. Her seizure of Malta in September 1800 had enraged the Tsar, who now built up an Armed Neutrality to exclude English shipping from the Baltic. This, however, only angered Russian merchants and roused increasing opposition to Paul's lunatic excesses. On March 23rd he was assassinated and his policy reversed by his successor Alexander I. On April 2nd Parker destroyed the Danish fleet at the battle of Copenhagen. Meanwhile the French expedition remained cut off in Egypt. Kléber had maintained his position on land by defeating a Turkish invasion at Heliopolis and recovering Cairo. But he was murdered in June 1800 and a demoralized French army was defeated by a British expeditionary force in March 1801. Napoleon was now anxious to repatriate the remnants of his army and was thus more inclined to consider the possibility of peace.

In the meantime Pitt had resigned and war weariness in England brought moves for a settlement. Addington's peace policy won general support: preliminaries were signed in

London on October 1st and finally ratified at Amiens on March 2nd, 1802. The French regained their West Indian islands but withdrew from Naples and the Papal States. England restored the Cape of Good Hope to Holland, and Malta to the Knights of St. John, but retained Trinidad and Ceylon. She accepted French possessions in Europe and recognized the satellite republics. Peace was welcomed with wild enthusiasm and Englishmen, with customary magnanimity, swarmed over the Channel to study their former enemy with curiosity and not without a certain admiration.

V · THE NAPOLEONIC EMPIRE

1. *The Consulate and the Codes*

PEACE gave Napoleon time to complete the work of reconstruction in France. His appeals to the 'nation' had already helped to pacify opposition. *Emigrés* had been assisted by a partial amnesty, the bourgeoisic gratified by the repeal of the incomes tax; the army had been loaded with pensions and disaffected generals banished to remote commands. Sieyès and the senators were provided with estates in Italy and France. Catholics, Protestants and Jews were guaranteed freedom of worship. The new constitution had introduced universal suffrage, though only at the first stage of a lengthy election procedure. Every Frenchman could take a pride in the conquests and achievements of the Consulate.

Napoleon took quick advantage of the victory of Marengo to consolidate his position. As First Consul he already held complete executive authority. The Council of State, filled with experts in every field and personally appointed, was now free to draft laws and edicts. Napoleon presided over a round of sub-committees covering finance, justice, war, the police and the interior. In thirteen years the Council covered 58,435 separate items of agenda. The ministries were subordinate to the Council and all ministers were appointed by the First Consul who kept control by frequent interviews and a stream of directives. Talleyrand at the Foreign Office, Fouché at the Police, Lucien Bonaparte, Gaudin and Berthier were examples of men brought together from every political background into the service of the State.

Nevertheless, it was not for a few years that Napoleon's control over the Senate and legislative councils became complete. Sieyès had initially selected many who were opposed to Bonaparte's claims. The Senate's powers, which included interpreting the constitution, appointing judges, electing future consuls and selecting members of the legislature, left room for considerable obstruction. Napoleon, however, soon bribed senators and appointed men loyal to himself. The legislatures were designed to discourage possible criticism. Members were to be selected by the Senate from 'notables' who had filtered to the top in a three-stage election process. A Tribunate was permitted to speak but not vote, while a Legislative Corps was given powers to vote but not talk.

This complex structure did, somewhat surprisingly, begin by providing limited opposition. In 1799 Sieyès and Napoleon had by-passed the election procedure to appoint members. The Tribunate contained many ex-Jacobins and Councillors of the Directory hostile to the government and ready to obstruct the actions of the Council of State. Opposition, was, however, soon intimidated; a plot to assassinate Napoleon at the opera in December 1800 led to the shooting, guillotining or deportation of more than a hundred Jacobins. In 1802, when one fifth of the Tribunate was up for re-election, the Senate was persuaded to specify those due to retire and thus eliminate twenty of the most prominent members of the opposition.

Government, however, could only become effective if linked to the remotest provinces by a tight administrative framework. Napoleon accepted the fundamental changes of the Revolution but cast the 40,000 individual communes into a mould more rigid than anything experienced under the old order. Departments and districts were placed under the control of Prefects and sub-Prefects who together with their councils were appointed by the Minister of the Interior and confirmed by Napoleon himself./ They were responsible for law and order, taxation, conscription and the supervision of the communes. They appointed the communal mayors and their councils who administered departmental business at local level. An elected council was only allowed to meet for fifteen days to agree to tax allocations. All communal accounts and reports were checked by the Prefect before being forwarded to Paris. Napoleon never selected local men and relied upon a wide but loyal cross-section of notables, ranging from ex-royalists like Mounier to ex-Jacobins like St. André. Nothing was to inhibit their dependence upon Paris, and throughout the nineteenth century the Prefect remained one of the key agents of government influence and control.

Authority was strengthened by the re-organization of justice and the action of the police. Here, again, the reforms of the

Revolution were clarified, extended and redefined. With the law courts Napoleon did little more than confirm the structure established by previous revolutionary reforms. He took care, however, to appoint the Justices of the Peace in the *cantons* and the judges in the departmental courts and to nominate judges of appeal in the Senate. At the same time the jury system was largely done away with and punishments increased in ferocity. The police, under the direction of Fouché, kept up a constant watch over all suspected persons and sent in regular reports about the state of public opinion and conditions in the provinces. Napoleon was able to cross-check the information forwarded to Prefects, senators and spies in order to assure the security of the State. He was equally prepared to rely on special courts and tribunals when necessary – to curb the Vendée and to clear the South of brigands. In 1810 a decree permitted the Council to arrest and detain suspects without trial, thus virtually restoring the *lettre de cachet* of the old order.

The unity of the French nation was emphasized by the completion of a new Civil Code. In 1789 some 366 local codes combined Roman law, Teutonic custom, feudal dues, ecclesiastical and royal decrees in a maze of conflicting rights and relationships. The Revolution had added to the confusion, destroying feudal rights, redistributing property and introducing new concepts of equality and justice. A redefinition of the law was obviously needed. In 1792 the Convention had begun to draft a code which underlined individual liberties and the equality of the sexes. By 1796 a reaction had begun and the Directory introduced modifications in favour of Roman and authoritarian principles. In the final draft, efforts were made to reach a compromise and to co-ordinate the achievements of the Revolution within the fabric of a new order. Napoleon, who presided over 36 sessions of the Council, provided not only a driving force but often tilted the balance in favour of authority and tradition.

The Civil Code guaranteed equality before the law and religious toleration. Feudal privileges were abolished and property rights assured. The equal division of property among heirs was reaffirmed, but the testator did now acquire the right to distribute one quarter of his estate at will. The importance of the family and of paternal control was emphasized. Grounds for divorce were limited and the rights of women both within the family and over property severely curtailed. This subordination of women was partly due to the personal intervention of Napoleon and remained one of the less satisfactory features of the Code. In other fields it provided a unique synthesis of law, established a permanent foundation for the French legal system of today, and influenced, through French enterprise and conquest, most of Europe and much of the world.

Additional committees were set up to draft a Communal Code, a Commercial Code, a Rural Code and a Code of Civil Procedure. Every aspect of judicial action was carefully detailed and defined. France acquired a new legal uniformity, a national identity that was fundamental to the working and development of a popular sovereign state.

2. Religion and Education

Napoleon realized that there could be no final pacification without a solution of the religious conflict. By 1799 a degree of tolerance had been achieved. Catholics, Protestants and civil authorities were able to share in the use of the Cathedral of Nôtre Dame. Nevertheless many fundamental divisions remained: a state recognized church in conflict with hostile non-jurors; priests loyal to the Pope in open revolt throughout Brittany and the Vendée. While the Pope refused to recognize the sale of ecclesiastical property neither the bourgeoisie nor the peasantry could feel secure. While the vital significance of the Roman Catholic faith in France continued to be ignored there could be no peace and little hope of unity.

Napoleon was fully aware of the importance of religion in everyday life as a result of his Italian experiences. In France, prefectorial reports confirmed the attachment of the peasantry to their priests. A *Société catholique* had for three years been rebuilding altars and sowing the seeds of a powerful Catholic revival in the countryside. The election of Cardinal Chiaramonti as Pius VII in 1799[1] encouraged hopes of reaching agreement with a Pope who had been prepared to work with the French in the Cisalpine Republic. Napoleon made the first moves in 1800 during the Italian campaign.

[1] See p. 100.

After some hesitation the Pope agreed to negotiate and a Concordat was completed within a year.

The Concordat recognized the Roman Catholic religion as 'the religion of the great majority of the citizens', not the 'established' or 'dominant' religion as the Pope had wished. Constitutional and non-juring bishops were all to resign; new bishops were to be nominated by the First Consul and instituted by the Pope. As the bishops were also to appoint the *curés*, thus replacing the private patronage of the old order, the authority of the Catholic Church was in fact enormously increased. The State agreed to pay all clerical salaries, and the Church accepted the nationalization of ecclesiastical property. Religious practice was declared free as long as it conformed to such police regulations as were required to keep the public peace.

This last clause gave Napoleon a pretext to add another 77 Organic Articles which were issued together with the Concordat in 1802. His belief that the people required a religion and that it should be in the hands of the government were now fully realized. Papal bulls, decrees and church councils were placed under government control. Clerical dress and church services were regulated. Permission was needed to ring bells or hold special meetings. Regular prayers for the Republic and the Consuls were decreed. The Pope protested against the articles in vain; grateful for the restoration of the altars, he was not prepared to re-open the schism in the Catholic Church. Napoleon was allowed to impose upon the Church a Gallican control more rigid than anything experienced in previous centuries.

Appearances, however, were to prove deceptive. The reconstitution of the episcopacy restored papal control. Pius VII refused to institute twelve former 'constitutional' bishops nominated by Napoleon. Some divisions remained as thirty-eight of the ninety-three non-juror bishops refused to recognize the Concordat and maintained their independent congregations in what became known as the *Petite Église*. The Catholic Church was re-established as a powerful influence in the country; church festivals and Sundays were restored. Though under the supervision of the State, clerical power steadily increased as permanence led to continuity and brought control in the parishes. A reaction in favour of the Pope and

against secular restrictions was to create frequent conflicts between clerical supporters and their anti-clerical opponents
throughout the nineteenth century.

The Concordat had only been passed against powerful
opposition from Jacobins, generals and a scattering of
rationalists and agnostics in the Tribunate. (It could only be
passed after the elections of 1802 had purged the opposition.) Though the Organic Articles satisfied some of the critics
a powerful anti-clerical element remained to attack the
growing authority of the Church and to limit its influence.
This conflict was soon to focus upon the problem of education where Napoleon's reforms were already sowing the seeds
of future discord.

Napoleon repeatedly stressed the importance of education.
It could provide the experts needed to serve the State, spread
the new ethic of national unity, and add a 'source of power'
which could be harnessed to condition popular opinion. The
Revolution had proclaimed the principle of compulsory free
state education, but in a decade of confusion little had been
achieved. A hundred central schools provided a progressive
and modern secondary education; an *Institut de France* and
an *Ecole polytechnique* encouraged advanced research. But
their influence was small and lacked a broad foundation as
primary schooling, which had been in the hands of the
Church, had largely disintegrated.

Napoleon replaced the central schools, whose liberal cur-
riculum he mistrusted, by *lycées* where strict control, military
type uniform and boarding routine could inculcate the necessary discipline. Classical studies were the groundwork for
logical analysis and an appreciation of order. Here an élite,
drawn from all sections of the community by over 6,000
scholarships, could be trained. Further study was encouraged
at specialist schools of law, medicine or the *Ecole normale
supérieure*. Technical experts and civil servants were absorbed into the administrative machinery and trained for
responsibility. Napoleon took groups of potential candidates
as *auditeurs* to work with the committees of the Council of
State.

The influence of the *lycées*, however, remained limited.
Primary education was largely ignored and left in the hands
of the Church, now rehabilitated by the Concordat. This

created dangerous divisions. Local secondary schools set up by the communes or by private interests soon restored religious instruction. Many of the bourgeoisie preferred a more parochial approach and encouraged the consolidation of a Catholic tradition. A dualism was thus slowly created in French education.

Few signs of opposition appeared while Napoleon retained control; the censorship was applied with vigour. In 1800 sixty of the seventy-three newspapers in Paris were closed down. Books, plays and publications were carefully scrutinized for any criticism of the government. Control over public opinion was a vital guarantee of power. 'If the press is not bridled I shall not remain in power three days,' were Napoleon's words. In 1803 the section of the *Institut* devoted to Moral and Political Science was suppressed. Madame de Staël, the daughter of Necker, who ran a salon that was both critical and romantic was banished from France.

Napoleon attempted to harness literature and art for the purposes of state propaganda. In David he found a painter able to portray his achievements with a combination of classical dignity and romantic vigour. Most of the painting, however, remained lifeless, the architecture heavy and the writing mediocre. Art and literature would not respond to order nor flourish within the straitjacket of a Napoleonic bureaucracy.

3. *Finance and the Economy*

Achievements in the economy and in finance were both less controversial and less spectacular. The Directory had left a legacy of debt and financial confusion. Reassessments of taxation, begun in 1798, remained both incomplete and unenforced.[1] Th Revolution created a tradition of hostility to both direct and indirect taxes and it was only with the reorganization of local government that tax collection could be effectively restored. With Gaudin at the Ministry of Finance the administrative machinery was soon overhauled. Officials assessed every department, *arrondissement* and commune, where the mayor and his council were responsible for individual estimates. Collectors were required to make deposits in advance of receipt and their accounts were checked by

[1] See p. 102.

regular inspectors. By the end of 1800 the tax returns were up to date.

In 1800 Napoleon set up the Bank of France to help raise loans for the government. In spite of its privileges and its monopoly in issuing notes it remained in essence a private bank with a limited number of shareholders. By controlling the money market and co-ordinating government borrowing it was able to exert a considerable influence. But it never extended its activities to include the public loans with which Britain financed the war. Failure to understand the significance of a national debt, and lack of confidence in credit finance led to a growing reliance upon restrictive monetary policies, and Napoleon had increasingly to depend upon mercantile exactions and the tributes of European satellites.

Economic policy was directed towards making France a self-sufficient power and subordinating the rest of Europe to her interests. Napoleon was aware of England's industrial lead and made determined efforts to promote French industry and to exclude British goods from the continent. With a subsequent excess of imports over exports Britain would no longer receive the bullion to finance her continental allies, while a favourable trade balance would build up increasing gold reserves in France. Technical schools were encouraged to promote inventions; prizes were offered for scientific achievements. Spinning and weaving machinery was imported from Britain and adapted for French use: spinning jennies reached Alsace by 1803 and the flying shuttle followed two years later. The French chemical and dyeing industries, already in the lead through the work of Lavoisier, were encouraged. As a member of the *Institut* Napoleon did much to foster science, even allowing the distinguished English scientist Sir Humphry Davy to tour France in wartime to examine extinct volcanos!

The government furthered economic expansion by vast road building schemes, largely designed to speed up the movement of troops. In 1804 roads and bridges were the biggest item of departmental expenditure. The loss of the West Indies sugar trade, due to the English blockade, led to the rapid development of beet sugar especially in northern France. Though often ridiculed in caricatures across the Channel, this did provide a valuable alternative. Elsewhere lack of raw materials remained a fundamental weakness of the economy. New silk and cotton imports from Italy could not make up for the loss of France's imperial possessions. Attempts to exploit the European economy provoked growing opposition in neighbouring states where Piedmontese silk, Ruhr manufactures and Italian cotton were cut off from their regular markets and diverted to France by the deliberate manipulation of tariff barriers.

In spite of these efforts the economy was slow to respond. Government action failed to stimulate private enterprise. Lack of labour and capital, due to the demands of the war, restricted growth. The small partnership with its limited liability and legal guarantees remained the basic unit of business activity. The peasantry also stuck to its traditional crops, tools and techniques. The subdivision of estates enforced by the Civil Code maintained a general pattern of smallholdings. An agrarian survey of 1814 noted the general prevalence of open fields, especially in the North.

Though government action may have failed in the long run to stimulate an industrial revolution the majority of Frenchmen remained more than satisfied. The peasantry now felt secure in their holdings, gratified by the Concordat and assured of their influence in the commune. Fears of Jacobin intervention or a Bourbon restoration maintained their loyalty to the régime. Workers and artisans were kept fully occupied by programmes of government works, the building of canals, roads and quays and the reconstruction of Paris. Napoleon, who retained a permanent fear of mobs and food riots, made certain of the Paris bread supply and guaranteed full employment. Crowds were entertained by fêtes, flag presentations and fireworks. The achievements of the French were magnified and the victories of historic campaigns, like those of Joan of Arc, regularly commemorated.

For the middle classes the rule of Napoleon consolidated some of the fundamental achievements of the Revolution. Equality in law had been recognized in the Codes. Feudalism and privilege had been abolished; the right to property guaranteed. Careers were now open to talent and all could compete for promotion and honour on equal terms. The confusion caused by religious conflicts and revolutionary excess had been curbed. The police, the roads, new buildings and the Bank added hopes of a permanent settlement. Lawyers, doctors, financiers and bureaucrats had all acquired lands and titles during the revolutionary years. Napoleon's interest in law, science, industry and wealth seemed to guarantee the security of middle class interests.

Critics remained, but their influence faded amid a general sense of well-being. Aristocracy and clergy, though sometimes hostile, were prepared to weather their objections to the régime. Many *émigrés* took advantage of an amnesty to return to France, regain part of their estates and serve the new government. The new élite of senators, generals and notables was liberally provided with estates and subsequently with honours. Their immediate loyalty was generally secure, though in the long run they were often more anxious to save their acquisitions than to support their benefactor. The bishops were prepared to operate the Concordat and consolidate their authority. Many were not opposed to the Gallican articles which gave them independence from papal control and found co-operation with the Prefects the best way to avoid regimentation by the State.

Thus, though Napoleon was in many respects a dictator, he retained for at least a decade the overwhelming support of the French nation. The Consulate secured the main social and material gains of the Revolution which seemed, in the short run, more important than political liberty. Liberty could be seen merely as a means to an end – equality, fraternity and economic well-being. In so far as these objectives were indeed achieved, Napoleon's claims that he was the true heir to the Revolution were at least partially justified.

4. *The Empire*

Popular enthusiasm for the peace and the Concordat gave Napoleon an opportunity to secure the Consulate for life. When the Senate proposed that the Consulate be extended for a further ten years, Napoleon referred the matter to the Council of State who prepared a plebiscite which asked for a vote on a Life-Consulship. This was approved by three and a half million as against eight thousand votes. Napoleon now acquired powers to nominate a successor, select senators and preside over the Senate. A new Privy Council of eleven men could draft decrees by a process which did not require the approval of the Legislature. Powers to grant estates to only one-third of the Senate enormously increased his powers of 'persuasion'. The reorganization of election procedure, as a result of which primary colleges could only choose candidates from among the six hundred most highly taxed citizens of the department, tightened still further Napoleon's hold at the top.

The constitution of the Life-Consulate gave Napoleon practically the powers of an absolute monarch. The uncertainty of war and the dangers of royalist plots soon led to the institution of a permanent, hereditary Empire. In 1804 English agents, Jacobin generals and royalists combined in the Cadoudal conspiracy. When the plot was betrayed to Fouché, Napoleon struck back with vigour: the leaders were exiled or executed; the Duc d'Enghien was kidnapped from Baden and shot in spite of evidence that he had nothing to do with the plot. This reversion to the methods of the Corsican vendetta was to remain a lasting blemish on Napoleon's character. It nevertheless succeeded in its purpose as Bourbon agents and foreign governments ceased conspiring against his life. It identified Napoleon with the Revolution and ended the immediate likelihood of a Bourbon restoration. It also prepared all shades of French opinion for the establishment of an Empire.

In May 1804 the Senate declared 'the government of the Republic is confided to a hereditary Emperor'. The plebiscite brought the usual overwhelming support. The powers of the Emperor were completed by his right to appoint all senators and govern by decree, and by the eventual elimination of the Tribunate in 1807. The fiction of a republic was retained upon the coinage until 1808; otherwise the liberties of the French were to be guaranteed in the person of Napoleon. The coronation brought clerical approval and the papal blessing. Pius VII agreed to travel from Rome to crown the Emperor. Anger against the Articles was balanced by gratitude for Napoleon's lone struggle to restore the Church and by hopes of obtaining concessions in Italy. In the event the Pope only annointed, and Napoleon crowned himself – a compromise in the struggle for symbolic supremacy which had been agreed beforehand. Pius failed to gain any concessions, but was gratified by the widespread signs of affection and respect with which he was received both in Paris and upon the journey.

Signs of a growing religious revival were one reason for the increasing rigidity of imperial control. Gradually the machinery of government began to permeate the very fabric of the State. Napoleon himself worked up to eighteen hours a day writing some 80,000 letters during his fifteen years of office. Imperial instructions covered almost every sector of French life. This led to a steady swing towards authoritarian principles. The Penal and Commercial Codes had already emphasized the practice of Roman law and curtailed the influence of juries. In 1807 the Civil Code was renamed the Code Napoléon. The role of the police became increasingly prominent. The censorship was gradually extended: in 1810 Paris was only allowed four newspapers and the departments one each. The personnel of government also changed; independent critics like Talleyrand and Fouché were replaced by others who knew better how to obey.

The control of education was vested in a new University of France. Established in 1808 under a Grand Master appointed by Napoleon, it was to co-ordinate syllabuses at every level and control the training of teachers and the building of schools. This new authority set a rigid pattern which survived for over a century. Under Fontanes, the first Grand Master, clerical and classical studies were given increased weight and the discussion of politics suppressed.

The rigid controls of the Empire, however, were to defeat their own purpose. When the renewal of war and the blockade restricted mercantile revenue Napoleon was forced to revert to the taxes of the old order. In 1804 the taxes on salt, wine and tobacco were revived and brought in an increasing proportion of revenue. Napoleon also relied more and more upon the flow of tribute from European satellites. By 1811 his *Domaine extraordinaire* had collected some two milliard francs. Regulation failed, however, to stimulate the economy and, though workers in the cotton mills doubled between 1788 and 1812, estimates put the level of French industrial output in 1815 at the English figure for 1780. By 1810 the almost complete strangulation of trade had done much to destroy earlier gains. An economic crisis alarmed the middle class, who began to lose faith in the policies of the Empire.

Napoleon covered up criticism by an increasing emphasis on glory and imperial prestige. Paris was decorated with columns and triumphal arches. A role of national honours had already been instituted in 1802 with the *Légion d'honneur*. The establishment of an imperial court led to the creation of a new nobility graded from dukes to barons. Napoleon was anxious to replace an aristocracy of birth by one based upon service and merit. He hoped to bind the old with the new. The accumulation of wealth and estates in Italy soon, however, exerted a corrupting influence and weakened the solidarity of the army and the administration. The revival of court etiquette and ritual brought back many relics of the old order and *émigrés* anxious to serve the Emperor in fortune but prepared to abandon him in case of failure.

Efforts to consolidate the dynasty led to a continued extension of imperial claims. A new catechism of 1806 proclaimed the Emperor to be 'God's image on earth'. God had given Napoleon the will and the force to overcome all obstacles. Divine right, however, was not enough. Napoleon realized that he ruled only through fear; that it was his destiny to be fighting almost continuously. A monstrous egoist who claimed no friends and cared for no one, he would stand or fall as he had risen – by war: 'Conquests have made me what I am, conquest alone can maintain me.'

5. *The Renewal of War and the Third Coalition*

The peace of 1802 was little more than a suspension of active warfare. Though all sides were anxious to prevent war in principle, Napoleon could not contain himself in Europe and England refused to tolerate any further French expansion. In 1802 Napoleon consolidated his influence in southern Germany, redistributing the ecclesiastical principalities and free cities among the states to compensate them for French acquisitions on the left bank of the Rhine. In Italy the creation of an Italian Republic in the North with Napoleon as President ensured control. Melzi d'Eril, the Vice-President, introduced religious articles allowing civil marriage, divorce and the election of the clergy. Papal protests caught Napoleon at a favourable moment and a Concordat was negotiated in Milan in 1803, which retained clerical mar-

I

riage and safeguarded Church property. Melzi, however, merely copied his master and evaded the Concordat with additional articles. Napoleon had no use for imitators and the Italian Republic soon came to an end when the Kingdom of Italy was proclaimed two years later.

Napoleon was quick to subordinate any plans for his republics to the strategic requirements of France. Piedmont was annexed in 1802 and split into departments under prefectorial control. The introduction of the Civil Code permitted civil marriage and divorce in spite of bitter clerical opposition. Secularization was imposed and Piedmont absorbed into the French Republic. Napoleon's treatment of Italy followed no real principles but was dictated by personal ambitions and the needs of the moment. Control over the Alpine passes necessitated the subjection of the Helvetian Republic. An Act of Mediation in 1803 enforced a new centralized constitution and gave the French a freer hand to build a new road over the Simplon Pass.

Napoleon's colonial policy was equally opportunist. In 1801 Louisiana was acquired from Spain and its ports closed to foreign shipping. Difficulties of communication and exploitation resulted in its sale two years later to the United States. Meanwhile efforts were made to conquer the new native republic of San Domingo which had been ceded by Spain in 1795. Napoleon sent suspect generals and Jacobins, most of whom died of yellow fever, to capture the island. This created widespread alarm about his intentions but achieved little. In Europe a report by Sebastiani, who had been sent in 1802 to study the Middle East, created a sensation. He commented unfavourably on the activities of the British and estimated that 6,000 men would be enough to reconquer Egypt for France.

All shades of English opinion were soon exasperated by Napoleon's steady encroachments and repeated sallies. The closure of European ports affected British trade, annexations in Italy appeared deliberately provocative, while France's refusal to evacuate Holland directly threatened security. Temperamentally there seemed to be something incompatible between the self-confident Corsican and the negligent superiority of the English. While the British press showered abuse Napoleon became enraged by the arrogant assumptions of a 'nation of shopkeepers'. The British government demanded the immediate evacuation of Holland and Switzerland and determined to retain Malta to balance French gains. This was in breach of the Peace of Amiens and put England in the wrong on a point of law. Napoleon's anger, which he discharged into the face of the British ambassador, was answered in May 1803 by a final ultimatum and declaration of war.

Napoleon immediately put into operation plans for a blockade and an invasion of England: all French ports were closed to British or British-borne colonial goods; an army of 100,000 men was assembled at Boulogne to prepare for an attack across the Channel, which Napoleon contemptuously described as a 'mere ditch'. Naval supremacy was, however, essential and against 189 British ships of the line and some 200 frigates the French could only raise 77 capital ships and less than 100 smaller vessels. Of these the majority were anyway shut up in the harbours of Toulon, Brest, Ferrol and Rochefort as a result of the British blockade. Failure to break out and concentrate the fleet in 1804 led to the postponement of Napoleon's plans. Next year, however, fresh designs were drawn up to assemble the fleet in the West Indies, disperse the British squadrons sent in pursuit and return to control the Channel for the few vital hours needed to cover a French landing.

Villeneuve successfully broke out of Toulon at the end of March 1805 and sailed for the West Indies, while Nelson obsessed by a possible threat to Egypt, Malta and Sicily, concentrated in the eastern Mediterranean. By the time that Nelson had joined in pursuit the Toulon squadron had reached Martinique. The French fleet at Brest was, however, unable to break through the British blockade and Villeneuve returned to France alone only to be driven by the blockading fleet into Corunna. When instructed by Napoleon in July to join the Brest squadron, Villeneuve panicked at the sight of some unidentified French ships and sailed into Cadiz where he remained immobile throughout the summer while the army waited at Boulogne. On August 24th Napoleon broke camp and marched to the Danube to deal with a new Austrian initiative.

The Battle of Trafalgar provided a dramatic epilogue to the naval war. Ordered on October 21st to sail for Naples 'at all costs' Villeneuve's line was forced to turn about to meet the British fleet. Nelson attacked in two columns demonstrating at sea the same devastating tactics that Napoleon employed on land. The French and Spanish line was broken at two points, superior seamanship and gunnery did the rest. Eighteen French and Spanish ships were sunk or subsequently surrendered; no English ships were lost. British casualties were amazingly light compared to those of their opponents, though the death of Lord Nelson at the moment of victory tended to cloud the celebrations. As a result of the battle Napoleon was never again seriously able to consider the possibilities of an invasion. Trafalgar, however, had no immediate effect upon his strategy. On the previous day he had forced the capitulation of the Austrian army at Ulm.

Austria had been provoked to intervene as a result of continued French action in Italy. Italian ports had been occupied in 1803, Genoa incorporated into France a year later, and a new Kingdom of Italy proclaimed in 1805. Napoleon's imperial designs left little room for rival powers. An ostentatious coronation in Milan was followed by the introduction of the Italian Concordat, Organic Articles and the Civil Code. Italy was to be remodelled in France's image. Behind Austrian hostility lay the growing opposition of Russia to French action in Germany, Naples and the Ottoman Empire. The Tsar had been outraged by the execution of Enghien and had ordered official court mourning besides vigorously protesting to France. In 1804 Alexander signed an agreement with Austria and Prussia to limit French expansion in the Middle East, and opened negotiations with Pitt who had returned to power in May. This led to an Anglo-Russian Convention in April 1805 whereby Pitt agreed to pay £1,250,000 for every 100,000 men put into the field by her allies. Austria joined in August and began to prepare for war. Only Prussia wavered, waiting for the outcome to secure her spoils.

Napoleon was, as usual, fully aware of Austrian plans. When a series of probing ultimatums brought no reply he rapidly moved his armies to the Rhine ready for action and secured Prussian neutrality by vague promises of Hanover. Spies and generals disguised as tourists were sent to map out Bavaria and the Black Forest. When 60,000 Austrians under Mack invaded Bavaria in September, Napoleon marched some 172,000 men in seven columns from the Rhine to the Danube. While Mack moved westwards to Ulm, Napoleon passed him to the north, dropped south to the Danube at Donauwörth, and completely surrounded the Austrian army. After an assault on the town Mack and his entire army surrendered on October 20th. Due to miscalculation about Napoleon's intentions the main Austrian force of 80,000 under the Archduke Charles was still in Italy. The road to Vienna lay open; Napoleon demanded immediate surrender.

Francis II, however, prevaricated and waited for Russian aid. Alexander's arrival from Berlin with guarantees of a Prussian alliance led to immediate action. Advancing to Austerlitz they made contact with Napoleon's army, seemingly in retreat, on December 2nd. Stretching their line to encircle the French they fatally weakened their centre. Napoleon immediately attacked, cut the opposition in two and routed his enemies. Francis sued for peace, Alexander retreated in tears and Frederick William of Prussia hastened to convert an ultimatum, due to expire on December 15th, into a treaty which offered him Hanover in return for Anspach.

The battle of Austerlitz was decisive. Pitt might well remark, 'Roll up the map of Europe; it will not be wanted these ten years.' On January 23rd, 1806, he died prematurely, worn out by years of ill health and European warfare. At the Peace of Pressburg Austria was humiliated, losing Venice, the Tyrol and the Dalmatian coast and paying an indemnity of £2 million. Napoleon, determined to eliminate Austrian influence, created a Confederation of the Rhine under French protection. The German princes agreed to help France with men, money and supplies. In return they acquired new territories and titles under Napoleonic mandate. In August 1806, one month after the formation of the Confederation, Francis II formally renounced his imperial dignity as head of a German Empire and remained Emperor of Austria, a title he had assumed in 1804. The Holy Roman Empire had collapsed before a new Empire of the Bonapartes.

In the summer of 1806 Russia and England made overtures for peace. The death of Pitt brought Fox back into power after twenty years in opposition. Anxious to test Napoleonic reactions he was prepared to negotiate. Alexander, shaken by defeat, was prepared to accept a French occupation of Naples and Sicily in return for the Ionian Isles and a free hand in the Balkans. Napoleon successfully played off Britain against Russia, but in offering to restore Hanover he antagonized Prussia. A calculated leak enraged Frederick William who began preparations for war. Britain and Russia abandoned the negotiations; Prussia delivered an ultimatum in October.

Napoleon had been informed of Prussian mobilization in August; orders for the withdrawal of the Grand Army from Germany were cancelled in September. When the Prussian army lumbered slowly westwards without waiting for Russian reinforcements, Napoleon moved round to attack from the rear. As the Prussians wheeled to retire the French came upon their divided armies at Jena and Auerstädt on October 14th. The Prussians were routed and disintegrated under the impact of a ruthless cavalry pursuit. By October 25th the French were in Berlin; in November the Prussian fortresses surrendered; Frederick William fled to Königsberg for safety and, having failed to gain terms from Napoleon, placed himself under the protection of Alexander.

When the Tsar prepared to continue the fight in Poland, Napoleon appealed to the Poles with hints of renewed independence and was able to raise a Polish contingent of 30,000 men. After indecisive battles at Pultusk and Eylau, fought in appalling conditions of snow and mud, Napoleon won a decisive battle in June 1807 at Friedland. Alexander, angered by the lack of English assistance and anxious to divert troops to attack Persia and the Ottoman Empire, accepted an armistice. Napoleon and Alexander met on a raft in the river Niemen and agreed to partition the Continent into spheres of influence. Magnetized by Napoleon's personality the Tsar was converted to a complete diplomatic revolution. Russia was to force England to make peace, close her ports to English shipping and recognize a Grand Duchy of Warsaw. In return she was left free to deal with Finland, Sweden and the Ottoman Empire where she was offered French support. By the published Treaty of Tilsit Prussia lost her western and Polish provinces, recognized a new Kingdom of Westphalia under Napoleon's younger brother Jerome, and agreed to remain occupied until the payment of war indemnities had been completed.

6. *Imperial Watershed*

Napoleon was now free to complete his plans for the re-organization of Italy. A new imperialism had already been proclaimed in 1805 at his coronation in Milan and a new Kingdom established under a viceroy, Eugène de Beau-harnais. Venice had been acquired by the Peace of Pressburg and the remainder of northern Italy incorporated into France. Naples, which had received an Anglo-Russian fleet after Trafalgar, was occupied in February 1806 and given to Napoleon's elder brother, Joseph. All Italy was to come under imperial control, the Civil Code and the authority of France. Such a policy did not, however, imply the unification of the peninsula. Napoleon was quick to realize the dangers of establishing new powers on the French frontier. His plans in Germany and Italy favoured confederations of satellite states which he could play off against each other and dis-tribute among his relations. Unity was stimulated more by the frustrations imposed by the Napoleonic system than by any positive encouragement.

Napoleon's claims were bound to lead to a growing conflict with the Pope. Disturbed by the coronation and by the new catechism, Pius VII could never accept the introduction of the Civil Code which cut at the roots of Catholic teaching on divorce. He felt deceived by Napoleon's ruthless exploita-tion of the Concordats, and by his refusal to restore papal territory or Catholic control. When Napoleon occupied Ancona and marched through the Papal States to attack Naples, Pius began to protest. Napoleon's assumption that the Papacy was for ever tied to French imperial interests brought a firm reply affirming papal independence, an author-ity above the rule of princes, a universality which could not be tied down to any one secular power. Napoleon was in-furiated and only prevented from immediate action by his involvement in the North. Negotiations were resumed in 1807 but the Pope refused to abandon the temporal in-dependence which he considered indispensable for spiritual authority, and rejected plans to incorporate the Papal States into an Italian confederation.

The need to overcome England added new urgency to Napoleon's action. Unable to invade by sea he was deter-

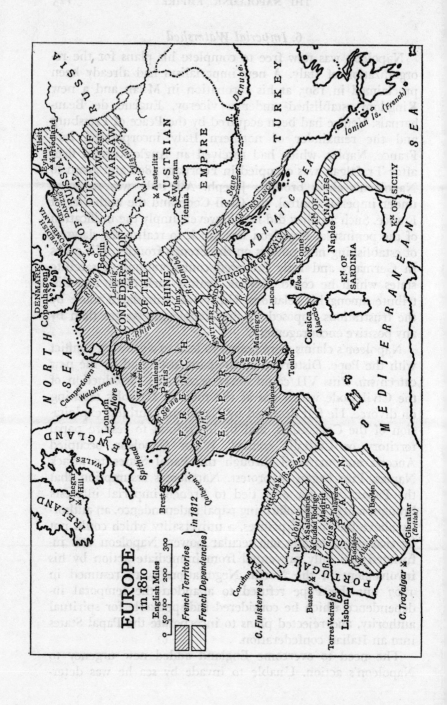

EUROPE
in 1810

English Miles
0 50 100 200 300

☒☒ French Territories

☒ French Dependencies in 1812

RUSSIA

DUCHY OF
WARSAW

✕ Austerlitz
✕ Wagram
Vienna
AUSTRIAN EMPIRE

R. Danube
R. Vistula

TURKEY

Ionian Is. (French)

ADRIATIC SEA

ILLYRIAN PROVINCES
R. Save

KM OF NAPLES
Rome
Naples

KM OF SICILY

MEDITERRANEAN SEA

KM OF SARDINIA

Corsica
Ajaccio

Elba
Lucca
KINGDOM OF ITALY

SWITZERLAND
Marengo ✕

R. Po

CONFEDERATION
OF THE
RHINE

Leipzig
Jena ✕
Ulm ✕
R. Danube

DENMARK
Copenhagen

Trilsit
✕ Friedland
✕ Eylau

DUCHY OF PRUSSIA
SWEDISH POMERANIA
DEP. OF
DANZIG

KM OF
PRUSSIA

R. Elbe
Berlin

NORTH
SEA

ENGLAND

London

WALES

IRELAND

Vinegar ✕
Hill

Camperdown ✕
Walcheren I.
✕ Nore

Spithead
Brest ✕

WATERLOO ✕
Amiens
Paris

R. Seine
R. Rhine
R. Rhone
R. Loire

FRENCH

EMPIRE

Toulon ○

✕ Toulouse

Quiberon B.

R. Ebro
R. Douro

C. Finisterre ✕
Coruña ✕

Busaco ✕
Torres Vedras ✕
Lisbon

PORTUGAL

SPAIN

Vittoria ✕
✕ Salamanca
✕ Ciudad Rodrigo
Madrid
Talavera ✕
R. Tagus

Badajos ✕
✕ Albuera

✕ Baylen

Gibraltar
(British)

C. Trafalgar ✕

mined to 'conquer the sea by the land'. In November 1806 he had issued the Berlin Decrees declaring the British Isles to be in a state of blockade and closing every port on the Continent to vessels coming from or calling at any port in England or her colonies. The Treaty of Tilsit had brought Russia into the blockade and the Milan Decrees regulated and extended the system in 1807. Napoleon hoped by blockading the continent to exclude British goods, ruin British credit and stimulate social unrest. Unable to sell, Britain would still be forced to buy, her gold reserves would drain away preferably towards France, and her economy would ultimately collapse. This system, however, demanded watertight control over all European ports and assumed, quite wrongly, that Britain would be unable to acquire alternative markets. Napoleon therefore took rapid action to remove any remaining free enclaves in southern Europe.

When the Pope continued to reject federation, papal ports were taken over and Rome itself occupied in 1808. For a year the Pope remained shut up in his palace deprived of advisers and the instruments of government. Refusing to flee he managed with the aid of a few remaining cardinals to organize an underground opposition, and was able secretly to publish a Bull of Excommunication against all those who violated papal rights. Napoleon's anger led to hasty remarks that the Pope was a raving madman who ought to be shut up. The generals in Rome took him at his word and without specific instructions stormed the Quirinal and arrested the Pope. Taken in a closed coach and in great discomfort he was hastened by night across northern Italy. Pushed on by embarrassed officials from state to state he had reached Grenoble before Napoleon caught up with events and ordered him to stay in exile in Savona. Napoleon protested that the seizure of the Pope was utter folly and his responsibility for the action has remained in dispute. Though his excommunication was carefully disguised in France, it soon added to the rising clerical reaction in southern Europe.

Napoleon's determination to control the continental coastline brought additional involvement in Spain and Portugal. The Portuguese had refused to close their ports to British shipping; the Spanish government dominated by Godoy, though allied to France, had become alarmed by colonial losses and evasive in the payment of its monthly subsidy of a million livres. In October 1807 Napoleon agreed to partition Portugal with Spain at the Treaty of Fontainebleau. In November, Junot invaded Portugal and French troops occupied many of the fortresses of northern Spain. French intervention, however, created bitter division within the Spanish royal family. Ferdinand, heir to the throne, appealed for French support against the Godoy régime. A revolt in Madrid forced Charles IV to abdicate. Napoleon, impatient and anxious to settle Spanish affairs, summoned all the leading characters to Bayonne. Charles and Ferdinand were both persuaded to abdicate, Godoy was imprisoned and the Spanish throne given to Joseph whose experience in Naples appeared to suit him for dealing with the Spanish problem.

Napoleon's actions, however, provoked a general revolt throughout Spain. Risings in Madrid were crushed by Murat in May. But throughout the summer provincial committees of priests and aristocrats stirred up the peasants into bitter guerilla warfare. Though official Spanish armies were easily defeated, a combined force of troops and local levies forced 20,000 French to capitulate at Baylen in July, a victory which rippled with increasing exaggeration across Europe. The British took immediate advantage of the rising to send an expedition to Portugal under Sir Arthur Wellesley. Landing with 10,000 men he defeated the French under Junot on August 21st at Vimiero and forced the French to evacuate Portugal by the Convention of Cintra. In November Napoleon decided to intervene with a new army of veterans and conscripts. Brushing aside Spanish opposition he forced Sir John Moore, commander of the main British force to retreat towards Corunna. But his edicts abolishing feudal rights, tolls and the Inquisition only aroused increasing hostility. The ideals of a French revolution imposed by an imperial army were incompatible with the social and religious background of the Spanish people. When Napoleon left the peninsula in December to deal with yet another Austrian initiative, he left behind a morass of smouldering discontent.

Austria, too, had been roused by a revival of patriotic enthusiasm. In 1808 Napoleon had urged the introduction of his Code at the Erfurt Congress. He had talked of people longing for equality, liberalism and law; he had visited Goethe and decorated him with the *Légion d'honneur*. German opinion, however, was becoming increasingly hostile towards an Empire which had to impose its own terms before introducing any of its so-called reforms. Austrian military reorganization had also created renewed confidence. France's Spanish entanglement appeared to offer an ideal opportunity for action. But by the time war was declared in April, Napoleon was back on the Rhine ready to attack. The Austrians were out-manoeuvred and forced to abandon Vienna. Nevertheless the French were held at Aspern and Essling, and Napoleon was forced to retreat to Lobau, an island in the Danube, to await reinforcements. New detachments from Italy soon brought his army up to 180,000 men. On July 5th he defeated the Austrians at Wagram, but there was no rout and the Archduke Charles was able to withdraw with an army of 80,000 still intact. Though Austria was defeated and lost Salzburg, Illyria and Galicia at the Peace of Schönbrunn in October, Napoleon had met renewed and formidable opposition and was made to realize for the first time the infinite costs of constant warfare.

As opposition increased so Napoleon made concentrated efforts to secure his position. Lack of an heir made for continued uncertainty. He divorced Josephine with regret and married, after Wagram, Marie-Louise, Archduchess of Austria. In 1811 his son was called the King of Rome to emphasize the universal claims of the Empire. But the claims remained unrecognized for, indeed, they were impossibly contradictory: ideals of equality imposed by invading troops; fraternity based on foreign codes, economic controls and the rule of innumerable alien Bonapartes; liberty based on obedience to one man. Only within the ambition, vision, and character of an exceptional personality could such paradoxes be reconciled. Napoleon synthesized everything within his own omnipotent ego. Herein lay his greatness, his fascination, and the causes of his ultimate collapse.

VI · EUROPE AND THE DEFEAT OF NAPOLEON

1. *The Continental System*

By the end of 1807 Great Britain remained the last major obstacle to the consolidation of French hegemony in Europe. Napoleon realized that without a navy any invasion of England was quite impracticable. Even before Trafalgar he had calculated that it would take ten years to bring the French fleet up to British strength. As an alternative he had decreed a blockade in 1806, closing the continent to any ships sailing from British ports. The mercantile rivalry of centuries was transformed into a new weapon of economic warfare. Napoleon hoped that by cutting off Britain's exports her industry would be ruined, her subsidies exhausted and her society undermined by unemployment and unrest.

This 'Continental System', in spite of early ridicule in the British press, caused hardship, anxiety, and a certain amount of panic in official circles. After Tilsit the Baltic was closed to trade; timber and hemp imports fell by half and, until the effective reversal of Russian policy in 1811, England was hard pressed to obtain adequate naval supplies. The British Orders in Council and Napoleon's Milan Decrees of 1807 intensified the conflict: Britain ordered a counter-blockade of European ports and required neutral shipping to buy special licences, while Napoleon declared all licence holders enemies and liable to confiscation of goods. By 1808 the blockades began to have a noticeable effect on British trade: exports to northern Europe were cut by over 50 per cent, though the overall figure fell by only a fractional amount. Losses were offset by an increase of exports to other markets – Latin America, the United States, and southern Europe where export values doubled. It was not for nothing that Napoleon determined to close every port and independent enclave in the Mediterranean.

The next two years, however, witnessed a complete breakdown of the system: the war against Austria meant a loss of

control over northern ports. Britain's markets in southern
Europe and America boomed. In 1810 her exports reached a
record height of £48 million. European opposition to Napoleonic controls encouraged widespread smuggling. Resistance
in Holland led to an open breach and assisted the entry of
neutral shipping. Napoleon himself was forced to give official
approval by agreeing to licences for essential goods; his
armies were supplied with British boots and overcoats. In
1810 French peasants were allowed to sell their surplus wheat
and wine to Britain; although it was one part of Napoleon's
policy to sell his goods for gold, the sale of food to England
was hardly consistent with a policy designed to provoke social
unrest.

Nevertheless, 1811 was a critical year for Britain. In the
previous October Napoleon's Fontainebleau Decrees had re-
sorted to desperate measures and ordered the destruction of
all British goods. In addition, the boom of the previous two
years was followed by a slump in both South America and
Europe, now drained of currency and strangled by regulations. Exports dropped to their lowest level for over ten years
and trade with northern Europe fell by 80 per cent. A wave of
bankruptcies created financial panic while a 50 per cent fall
in cotton exports brought widespread unemployment and
provoked Luddite riots which wrecked the new machines.
Had Napoleon been able to consolidate his power the position could have become even more serious. But the Spanish
markets remained open, and in 1811 Russia suddenly abandoned a system which, by cutting off trade with Britain, was
progressively ruining her own economy.[1]

But meanwhile the length and frustration of the war had
led to increasing strain. The death of both Pitt and Fox in
1806 had removed leaders of real stature. Their followers
broke up into factions and often seemed to place private interests before national needs. Attempts to open up more markets
in South America in 1807 had failed when a British expedition
was defeated at Buenos Aires. Efforts to extend control in the
Mediterranean had been equally unsuccessful. An expedition
directed against the Turks had been split between Constantinople and Egypt and had failed in both areas. Enthusiasm
was roused by a raid on Naples which encouraged the peasants

[1] See p. 140.

to revolt and defeated a French detachment at Maida. This individual effort by the British commander had, however, no official support, and ended in an inevitable withdrawal to Sicily.

The Treaty of Tilsit had once again focused attention on the Baltic where the Danish fleet now appeared an easy prey for Russia and France. In 1807 the British government took swift action to forestall any French intervention and organized an expedition to bombard Copenhagen and seize the fleet. The destruction of the town led to widespread criticism at home and abroad and could only be justified in terms of the mounting requirements of warfare. Attempts to help Sweden, now exposed to direct Russian attack, created further confusion and misunderstanding. When Sir John Moore was sent with 12,000 men to help King Gustavus the crazed monarch sought to divert them to conquer Norway and Moore had to flee in disguise without even landing his troops.

Yet in spite of indecisive policies at home and abroad Britain was able to build up increasing military reserves. The economy continued to boom; the Industrial Revolution gradually accelerated under the stimulus of war. A continued growth of population in both rural and urban areas brought a rise in demand and an increase in the labour force. The rapid expansion of government war expenditure and the increase of loans and credit led to a steep rise in prices and a growing incentive to invest in new industries and techniques. By 1811 over 100,000 power looms were employed in cotton factories; raw cotton imports trebled in twenty years. The output of pig iron doubled in the decade before 1806 and by 1811 Birmingham iron wares were worth some £2 million a year.[1]

The significance of the steam engine became increasingly obvious. By 1800 at least 300 of Watt's models were in use and mechanical hammers, drills, pumps and looms soon speeded up mechanization in almost every sector of British industry. Coal output doubled, while the production of bar iron more than made up for the loss of Baltic imports. When Watt died in 1819 Lord Liverpool acknowledged that England could not have survived the war without the steam engine. It heralded a surge in production which Napoleon

[1] See pp. 30-1.

never grasped. With new markets abroad and investment in iron works, bridges, canals and armaments at home it created an industrial complex ready to withstand the threats of any continental system.

Meanwhile, Britain's position was assured by her naval supremacy. After Trafalgar the blockade was relaxed and French ships encouraged to emerge for destruction. This move, however, had a disastrous effect upon British merchant shipping now suddenly exposed to enemy privateers and naval squadrons. In twelve years of war, losses averaged 444 ships a year. These were made up, however, by the seizure of neutral and enemy vessels. Throughout the war the registered number of British ships rose steadily, while enemy fleets were gradually eliminated and control over supply routes assured.

At the same time military reforms were laying the foundations for ultimate victories on land. The Duke of York's administration established a new military academy and a staff college to train officers. Promotion was to be based on merit, encouragement given to initiative. New tactics were developed by Sir John Moore based on speed, mobility and the use of cover to surprise the enemy. A new Baker rifle guaranteed accuracy up to 300 yards and provided the essential weapon for a light brigade trained in marksmanship, rapid manoeuvre and disciplined withdrawal. Independence was emphasized by self-supporting supply lines and the use of maps. A new army was gradually built up which, with European experience, was to prove more than a match for even Napoleon's veterans.

In 1808 it seemed at first unlikely that any landing upon the continent of Europe could ever be undertaken. The Spanish revolt, however, suddenly changed the entire situation. After appeals from the revolutionary Junta in Seville, an expedition due to sail for Mexico, was hastily diverted to Portugal to be followed by Sir John Moore's army from Sweden. Wellesley, in command of the advance party, demonstrated the value of British tactics by decisively repelling Junot at Vimiero. The Convention of Cintra, imposed by more cautious commanders, allowed the French to evacuate Portugal in British ships together with all their loot. The outcry in England led to the recall of all concerned including Wellesley. Moore was left in command, but the arrival of Napoleon brought new drive to the French army. Moore was driven to the sea at Corunna and only escaped with the aid of the British fleet and some desperate rearguard fighting.

Wellesley's experiences, however, convinced him that the peninsula was not a lost cause. In March 1809 he wrote a report which claimed that Portugal could be defended by a force of 30,000 against an enemy numbering anything up to 100,000. Powerful family connections and the friendship of Castlereagh brought him command of a new expedition which landed at Lisbon in April. The presence of British troops added new enthusiasm to the Spaniards and Portuguese, dejected after a year of division and defeat. Together they now began to erode the power of the Napoleonic Empire.

2. *The Peninsular War*

The revolt in Spain was a rising of aristocrats, *hidalgos*, priests and peasants against the intervention of despised and atheist foreigners. It thus included almost every section of the population in a violent reaction in favour of the Crown, the Church and the liberties of each separate province. Only a few court nobles, merchants, lawyers or intellectuals could find any advantage in a French administrative system or in uniform Napoleonic codes; denounced by the Church and hounded by the mob, they were soon lynched or reduced to silence. Throughout the provinces committees or Juntas of priests and gentry incited attacks on governors and *corregidors*. In Portugal, the Bishop of Oporto led a rising in the town. Throughout the peninsula *hidalgos* organized bands of brigands to attack the French and rob or murder possible sympathizers.

The extent of the revolt was both its strength and its weakness. The local Juntas represented provincial interests and lacked any co-ordination. Seville appealed to Gibraltar, Oviedo, in the North, to London, yet when Wellesley first landed at Corunna he could get no information of any action in other parts of the peninsula. A supreme Junta in Madrid lacked effective power, quarrelled with its subordinates and spent much of the war besieged in Cadiz drafting the moderate liberal constitution proclaimed in 1812. Spanish armies were equally isolated and ignorant. Untrained and ill-disciplined they appeared in hordes with medieval weapons and primitive uniforms. Blindly confident of victory they were no match for French armies and fled before the impact of enemy columns. After early defeats at Medina del Rio Seco and Cordoba, an unprecedented French defeat at Baylen gave the Spaniards an unjustifiable self-confidence. Napoleon himself easily swept them all aside on his brief visit to the area.[1]

Spanish armies were equally unreliable in co-operating with the British forces. Failure to link up with Moore's plans or even keep him informed was at least partially responsible for his defeat. Wellesley soon found co-ordination impossible and after bitter experiences refused to rely on Spanish promises. Nevertheless, Spanish resistance played a vital part in the war, if only in a negative way. The activities of brigand armies over wide wastes of mountainous countryside kept a quarter of a million French troops tied down. Galicia in the North remained in a permanent state of revolt. Valencia was never pacified while the southern mountainous provinces threw up an unending series of brigand and peasant armies. In addition, every priest was on the side of the British, and every peasant was a potential ally. French communications were harassed, supplies seized and stragglers eliminated. The French were left completely in the dark about British movements. Their armies were isolated in a hostile wilderness where frustration and hunger brought an increasing harvest of bitterness, brutality, horror and despair.

Wellesley's plans were based upon a combination of native resistance and a small British force of some 30,000 men. While the French remained divided he could deal with their armies separately; if they combined, Spanish opposition would flare up in the rear. Portugal, with but three frontier passes in the East, could be established as a base, supplied by sea and guarded by well placed fortresses. In 1809 Soult was driven from Oporto and Victor forced to retreat to Talavera. Here, however, the failure of Spanish armies to co-ordinate their attacks from the East enabled the French to concentrate their troops. In a desperate battle Wellesley held their attack by taking up strong defensive positions and using devastating

---

[1] See p. 128.

K

fire-power. A new threat from Soult in the North then forced him to retreat to the frontier fortress of Badajoz. His forces were never a match for the combined French armies in the peninsula.

The following winter was spent in building up reserves, and constructing impregnable lines of defence covering the Lisbon peninsula round Torres Vedras. A Portuguese army of 20,000 was trained under Beresford and 10,000 reinforcements were sent out from England. Confidence slowly grew in Wellesley's plans and after Talavera he was raised to the peerage as Viscount Wellington. Meanwhile the French again split up to cover regional resistance, Soult moving south defeated the Spaniards at Ocaña and besieged Cadiz, while Joseph moved east to deal with the revolts stirred up by the British in Valencia. In 1810, the French launched a combined attack with some 140,000 men under Masséna, the most experienced of Napoleon's marshals. After capturing the border fortresses of Ciudad Rodrigo and Almeida he moved relentlessly forward to drive the British into the sea. Wellington retreated cautiously, scorched the land, and, having given his British and Portuguese troops fresh confidence by defeating the French on a ridge at Busaco, retired behind his lines.

Masséna was surprised by the walls and bastions which reared out of the hillsides at Torres Vedras. Informers in Spain had left him completely in the dark. He could only sit down and wait for his enemy to come out – which Wellington refused to do. French troops starved and died in thousands; as they became increasingly desperate and savage, the guerillas took even more brutal reprisals. Frenchmen were seized, clubbed, tortured and nailed alive to trees while in return native priests were hacked to pieces and women raped and torn apart. Soult, jealous of Masséna's command, was slow in coming to his support. By the time Soult had captured the southern fortress of Badajoz, Masséna's armies were in full retreat after a four months fruitless siege of Wellington's positions.

In 1811 the French were finally expelled from Portugal. The British followed the tail of Masséna's retreating armies, besieged Almeida and repulsed a relieving force at Fuentes d'Onõro. The battle was again desperately close and Mas-

séna's effort to turn the British right wing was only defeated
by rapid manoeuvre and unshakeable discipline. 'If Boney
had been there,' Wellington wrote, 'we should have been
beat.' But Napoleon, tied down at the centre of power in
Paris, refused to risk his reputation in Spain. Instead he replaced Masséna by Marmont, diverted troops to aid Soult in
the South and rejected Joseph's pleas for pacification and
compromise. The Emperor would not admit defeat even
when he could not win victory.

Wellington, however, remained too weak to break into
Spain. Though Almeida surrendered he lacked a siege train
to capture the Spanish fortresses of Ciudad Rodrigo and
Badajoz. In the South, Beresford only just held Soult at the
battle of Albuera and Wellington had to build up strong
defences on the Caya to prevent a new invasion of Portugal.
In the autumn, however, Napoleon withdrew 50,000 veterans
to prepare for the Russian campaign. Soult had again turned
South and Marmont North to deal with further revolts in
Galicia. Wellington had meanwhile received reinforcements
including a siege train, which brought his army up to 38,000
men. In the winter he launched a campaign against Ciudad
Rodrigo. In January 1812 the fortress fell after a surprise
night attack. By April, Badajoz had fallen. Wellington drove
on between the French armies, defeated Marmont at Salamanca and entered Madrid on August 12th.

The French, however, were able to regroup. Soult again
moved up from the South, abandoning the siege of Cadiz.
Wellington's lines were extended and his supplies uncertain.
Once again he was forced to retreat to Portugal for the
winter. But in 1813 he planned a surprise campaign in the
North, where he could rely on supplies by sea. Appointed
Commander-in-Chief of the Spanish armies he was at last able
to rely on some support from rebel detachments. With 84,000
men Wellington surprised the French by breaking out of
northern Portugal and threatening their communications
across the Ebro. At Vittoria, on June 21st, with a clear
supremacy in numbers, he routed the French and drove them
from Spain without their artillery or baggage. Counter-
attacks were defeated at the battle of the Pyrenees. In
October, Wellington crossed the French frontier. Reinforced

and supplied through the Biscay ports he prepared to besiege Bayonne.

Meanwhile Napoleon's Empire had begun to crumble in the East. Russian disasters and Prussian revolt had opened wide gaps in his dominions. The news of Vittoria removed the last chance of Austrian neutrality. Ten days after Wellington's invasion of France Napoleon himself was decisively defeated at Leipzig. The future of Europe was once again to be decided on the plains of Germany where Napoleon's armies had won some of their greatest victories and were now to experience their worst defeats. Nevertheless, the Peninsular War, though often considered a mere sideshow, was a dangerous sore which, allowed to fester, contributed both to the resistance of Europe and to the ultimate collapse of the Empire.

3. Russia and the 1812 Campaigns

The accession of Alexander I as Tsar in 1801 was welcomed as a merciful escape from the rule of his maniac depressive father, Paul. Educated by the Swiss Jacobin Laharpe, he was known to hold liberal views and to associate with moderate reformers in a Confidential Committee. Exiles were recalled, foreign travel restored, the Secret Chancellery disbanded and torture abolished. Printing presses were again allowed and property purchase opened to all classes. But Alexander's liberalism remained elusive and vague. The murder of his father haunted him and left a legacy of insecurity and fear. In practice he was forced to compromise with the need to uphold an absolute autocracy.

A number of reforms were, however, introduced. The majority followed the eighteenth-century pattern or copied the ideas of Napoleonic France. Ministers were made responsible for departments of state and their work co-ordinated under the Tsar. A Ministry of Education established new universities at St. Petersburg, Kharkov and Kasan and set up some forty-two gymnasia for secondary education which included many features of the new French schools. Efforts were made to hasten the drafting of a new legal code; the Senate was restored to its administrative functions. Reform, however, did not go far: in the provinces the powers of the nobles and the towns were revived and their charters restored; efforts to relieve serfdom were unspectacular. At the instigation of Stroganov, an ex-Jacobin in the Confidential Committee, a decree of 1803 allowed owners to free their serfs if provision for the transfer of land could also be arranged. The measure was unpopular with landowners, who needed cheap labour, and with serfs who lacked capital to buy up their plots; only some 40,000 were freed in the course of Alexander's reign. Nevertheless, advertisements for sale were banned, the landowner's power to sentence serfs to penal servitude restricted, and the distribution of royal peasants to the aristocracy terminated.

All attempts at constitutional reform, however, foundered on the bedrock of Tsarist absolutism. Speranski, son of a country priest, was ordered to draw up a plan to remodel the administration of the Empire. Using French precedents he outlined schemes which divided powers between local *dumas*, elected on a narrow property franchise and responsible for the election of a national *duma*, and an independent judiciary all under the absolute prerogative of the Tsar and a Council of State. Such revolutionary proposals, however, were too much for both Alexander and the aristocracy. Only the Council of State was established to advise and draft decrees. Speranski was left to improve the efficiency of the administration and speed up the collection of taxes. His French methods made him the target of bitter aristocratic attack. In 1812 Alexander's growing sense of insecurity and isolation led him to abandon Speranski and his proposals.

By then the threat from Napoleon had obliterated all thoughts of reform and forced the Tsar into complete dependence upon the army and the aristocracy. Opposed to both social and administrative change, they were equally hostile to Alexander's dealings with the upstart and atheist Bonaparte. At Tilsit the Tsar had been flattered and favoured by Napoleon's most persuasive personality. Having failed to split Russia from Britain in 1803 and 1805 the Emperor was determined to convert Alexander to the Continental System and draw the impressionable Tsar into his orbit. The Treaty seemed to confirm a complete reconciliation, with Europe divided into spheres of influence and joint action against the British. Appearances, however, were deceptive. The Treaty of Tilsit was regarded by the Russian

Court as a league with the devil. The army, humiliated at Austerlitz and Friedland, resented their enforced sub-servience to France. Alexander had to counter opposition at home by undertaking new foreign initiatives that were bound to lead to a revival of tension.

The Russian occupation of Finland and the defeat of Sweden in 1808–9 created little difficulty. Intervention in the Ottoman Empire, however, was viewed by Napoleon with considerable suspicion. At a meeting at Erfurt in 1808 Tsar and Emperor had tried to settle their differences. But Alexander had refused to become embroiled in India or intervene against Austria merely to satisfy Napoleon, and had con-tinued to advance Russia's boundaries in Moldavia and Wallachia. In 1809 relations deteriorated when the Tsar re-fused to assist Napoleon during the Wagram campaign. When eventually the Emperor decided to enlarge the Grand Duchy of Warsaw by adding to it Austria's share of the third partition, and threatened to restore a code, a constitution and an army to a new Polish State, Alexander was forced to pre-pare counter-measures.

Equally disturbing was the effect of the Continental Sys-tem upon the Russian economy. Exports slumped, the bal-ance of payments became increasingly unfavourable and the revenue of both the government and the nobility fell disastrously. The issue of paper money led to wild inflation, the rouble dropped to 20 per cent and the State faced bank-ruptcy. Landowners lost their best markets and attacked the Tsar and his policies. In December 1810 restrictions were re-laxed, the ports opened to neutral shipping and duties placed on French luxury goods; the blockade had become intoler-able, inflicting excessive hardships on every class, and the Tsar was well aware that conditions in France were little better. Irritated by Napoleon's abrupt rejection of a Romanov bride and by the annexation of his brother-in-law's duchy of Oldenburg, Alexander prepared for war. His strategy had already been planned: following Wellington's example he would retreat, starve out the enemy and wait for the winter.

By 1811 Napoleon was also determined on war. His mon-strous egoism could tolerate no rivals. Austria had been humiliated and bound to France by marriage, Prussia had been occupied, the Pope intimidated and forced to agree to the appointment of Bonaparte's bishops, the whole of France and much of the Continent seemed bent to the will of one man; it was intolerable that Russia should dare to show independence and encourage the British in their continued defiance. Napoleon was warned by his ambassador, Caulaincourt, of the horrors of the Russian winter. He studied carefully the problems of a campaign and admitted it to be the most difficult enterprise in his career. The confidence that made him bold made him blind to the possibilities of defeat. With an army of over half a million men, half French and half subservient allies, unwieldy to manoeuvre and impossible to supply, he crossed the Niemen on June 25th, 1812.

The campaign was a long series of miscalculations and mistakes. The size of the army involved repeated delays to allow for its provisioning. Subordinates were slow to manoeuvre and the Russians were allowed to escape at Vilna and Smolensk. Napoleon was racked by moments of indecision when his marshals urged retreat. He failed to rally the Lithuanians and Poles by guaranteeing their independence. He roused the bitter hostility of the peasantry by the looting and ill-discipline of his famished troops. Yet he was unable to stop; the die was cast; victory would save him.

Alexander, however, was never prepared to admit defeat. His Ottoman war had been terminated by the Treaty of Bucharest in May 1812 whereby he restored the Danubian provinces but retained Bessarabia. Meanwhile the Swedes, stung by the continental blockade, made an alliance with Russia and prepared to attack Norway. The Tsar could devote all his attention to Napoleon. When the interminable retreat and the quarrels among his generals caused unrest, Kutusov was appointed Commander-in-Chief. He maintained a policy of retreat, burning villages, destroying supplies and luring the French army into the wasted plains of Russia. He had no alternative while Napoleon's armies retained their vast numerical superiority. Beyond Smolensk, however, the French striking force had already fallen to 160,000 men. With 130,000 men Kutusov was forced by the pressure of opinion at court to fight a battle for Moscow at Borodino.

The ensuing battle, the only major engagement of the campaign, was probably the bloodiest in all Napoleon's wars. The Russians, entrenched on a ridge with superior artillery cover, were in a strong position. The French with 160,000 men and 600 guns remained a massive force. Napoleon, however, lacked the troops to turn the Russian positions and determined on a frontal assault. Column after column was hurled straight at the Russian guns, and the positions were only captured after a whole day of fighting. The casualty figure was enormous with 30,000 French and over 50,000 Russian losses. Kutusov abandoned Moscow but withdrew in good order, determined to avoid another battle.

On September 14th Napoleon entered Moscow to find it deserted. That day fires began and raged for five days; the fire pumps had been removed and it is clear that the governor gave orders to destroy the city. When Napoleon returned to the Kremlin he waited in vain for Alexander to negotiate. The Tsar had neither the inclination nor the power to do so; Russia was united in its hatred of the invader. Ignoring warnings about the onset of the Russian winter Napoleon stayed on until mid-October. On the 19th he left Moscow with an army still 100,000 strong but encumbered with its loot, its sick and wounded and its 600 guns.

The weather remained fine as far as Smolensk, but already losses were heavy due to lack of supplies and the harassing tactics of Cossacks and partisans. Thereafter the winter slowly set in and devastated the army: 60,000 just escaped encirclement when crossing the Beresina. By the time the last troops re-crossed the Niemen on December 14th less than 40,000 men of the Grand Army survived. Of the 40,000 veterans of the Guard only some 500 remained. Guns, baggage and treasure had all been abandoned: 'General Famine and General Winter' had conquered.

Four days later Napoleon reached Paris. He had left the army on December 6th and set out with speed to ensure his position at home. He seemed unmoved by the magnitude of the disaster and prepared to withdraw troops from Spain and raise fresh conscripts in France. He blamed the weather for his defeat and attempted to disguise his losses. Opposition in France grew, however, with the first army plot to seize the government and a mounting wave of hostility to the new call-up. In Europe the retreat from Moscow was hailed with enthusiasm, and led to fresh efforts to organize the powers into combined action against Napoleonic domination.

4. *The Emergence of Prussia*

On December 30th, 1812, General Yorck, Commander of the Prussian auxiliaries covering the northern flank of the French armies during the retreat from Moscow, concluded the Convention of Tauroggen with the Russians and declared his neutrality. Though Frederick William quickly repudiated this independent initiative, the reformers at court put increasing pressure on the King to take action. For six years Prussia had been stirred up by a small group of dynamic men determined to restore the State after the shock and humiliation of Jena.[1] The French retreat from Moscow appeared to provide an opportune moment to launch a war of Prussian liberation.

By 1813 Prussia had an army of only 65,000 effective troops, but the officers had been trained in the latest tactics, foreign mercenaries had been dismissed and plans for reserve regiments and a national militia prepared. Reforms had begun as a result of the Commission of Military Reorganization set up by the King in 1807 to enquire into the Jena disaster. The Commission was dominated by Scharnhorst and his disciples, Gneisenau, Boyen and Grolman. The King laid down terms of reference which, besides the punishment of defaulters, implied a wide field of enquiry and showed that he was well aware of the failings of the rigid, aristocratic officer caste. The Commission only cashiered some 208 officers; from the beginning its members recognized that the collapse of Prussia had not merely been military, but had also been due to fundamental social and political weaknesses. They recognized the need to harness all the elements in the State; to unite the army and the nation; to create from a divided and apathetic people a new enthusiastic union. Aware of the spirit generated in revolutionary France they hoped to match its achievements by copying some of its methods.

A new officer corps was built up, based on education and ability rather than on class distinction. The old military schools were abolished and new ones established to provide basic short-term courses. A new Military Academy in Berlin trained selected officers and a new general staff in the latest strategic and tactical developments. Among its instructors,

[1] See p. 124.

von Clausewitz was to become one of the classic exponents of the art of warfare. An order of 1808 opened prospects of a military career to the middle class and based entry upon examinations, much to the anger of reactionaries like General Yorck who maintained that an excessive emphasis upon examinations would kill character. The new officer class, however, proved a vital factor in Prussia's rapid military and political recovery.

The extension of reform and the creation of a new army presented greater difficulties. Prussia remained under close French surveillance and in 1808 Napoleon had imposed a limit of 42,000 men on the Prussian army. Lack of money and the loss of half her former population added further obstacles to expansion. Nevertheless, reforms were introduced: foreign troops were eliminated and discipline humanized by new articles of war; the principle of universal conscription was decreed; service was determined by lot and exemption restricted; plans for a national militia, *Landwehr*, were drawn up to rally the middle classes to the service of the State. The opposition delayed many of these reforms. The King suspected a popular militia; the generals decried French methods; the aristocracy continued to press for their privileges. But by 1813 the plans had been drafted and Prussia was ready to arm.

Military reform had been but part of a wider programme. Von Stein carried out the social and political reforms implicit in the work of the military commission. Trained in the administration of the Prussian Rhineland he had long been critical of the rigid distinctions maintained by the aristocracy and the Junkers of the eastern provinces. In 1807 his outspoken criticism had led to his dismissal. But when Napoleon required the removal of the Chancellor, Hardenberg, Stein was named as a suitable alternative. At home he immediately set out to 'arouse a moral, religious and patriotic spirit in the nation.' Edicts of 1807 and 1808 abolished hereditary serfdom and all personal servitude. But, though the older peasant copyholders were able to acquire their holdings, most of the serfs were not guaranteed any security of tenure, and, losing their communal rights, were forced to become landless labourers.

Stein followed up his plans for national reform by giving

greater freedom and authority to the bourgeoisie. Land purchase was freed and class appropriation abolished. In November 1808 municipal reforms introduced elected mayors and
councils in which the middle classes were encouraged to
acquire office. By 1813 they were ready to enlist in the new
Landwehr and rally with enthusiasm to support the resurg-
ence of the Prussian State.

Stein planned to follow up these measures by the reorganization of central government. The division of power
between the King's inner cabinet and the state secretaries was
to be replaced by the appointment of five ministers of state
directly responsible to the King for their separate departments. Their work was to be co-ordinated in a *Kabinets-
ministerium* under royal control. The new structure was,
however, slow to take shape. The King did not appoint a
Minister of War till 1814, preferring to maintain a division of
responsibility in order to keep control in his own hands. Stein
was unable to complete his work. In 1808 he was carried away
by enthusiasm at the news of the French capitulation at
Baylen and urged immediate intervention. His correspondence fell into the hands of Napoleon who demanded his dismissal. After three years retirement in Bohemia he became
adviser on German affairs to the Tsar and in 1812 helped to
prepare plans for Russian intervention in Europe.

Meanwhile Prussian policy drifted in the hesitant hands of
Frederick William. The Austrian declaration of war against
Napoleon in 1809 was greeted with enthusiasm and Archduke Charles's call for aid echoed through the country. The
French withdrawal after Aspern led to renewed demands for
action and independent expeditions marched to expel the
enemy from Westphalia. Frederick William, however, refused to make any official moves; Gneisenau resigned from
the army while Grolman departed for England to join a
newly formed foreign legion in Spain. In 1810 Napoleon's
demand for the immediate repayment of the indemnity led to
the recall of Hardenberg. His income and property taxes
were increasingly unpopular; his legislation of 1811 brought
security of tenure to the wealthier peasants, but only on condition that one-third to one-half of the land reverted to the
lord in compensation. Hardenberg was not cast in a heroic
mould and preferred subtle diplomatic methods to any bold

imaginative measures. By 1812 the King had become further demoralized by the death of his popular and heroic wife, Marie Louise, and agreed to accept a treaty with France, allow the passage of French troops and supply 40,000 men to cover the Russian campaign. Scharnhorst and Gneisenau retired in disgust. Prussia appeared sunk in humiliation and despair.

The work of the reformers, however, continued to spread. The philosophy of Fichte and the educational reforms of von Humbolt fostered new ideas and aroused national enthusiasm. Fichte's thought was hardly original but his teaching did much to inspire the work of the reformers. He had observed and analysed the French experience: the enthusiasm generated by equality, the power harnessed within the State. To this he added the romantic ideals of Herder, the spirit of a nation, and the destinies of the *Volk*. In his memorable 'Addresses to the German Nation' delivered in an enemy-occupied Berlin during the winter of 1807-8 he applied these principles to Germany. The individual would be liberated by education to find freedom in the nation; the separate states would be united to fulfil their destiny within a wider national union. Von Humbolt, head of the Department for Instruction, built up the educational framework required to put these ideals into effect. Primary schools were followed up by new gymnasia modelled on the French pattern. New universities at Berlin and Breslau made up for the loss of Halle and the western provinces.

In December 1812 the advance of the Russian armies precipitated immediate action. Stein arrived in East Prussia as emissary of the Tsar and arranged with Yorck for the summoning of the East Prussian *Landtag*. Prussian harbours were opened to foreign ships and the *Landwehr* hurriedly mobilized. The King fled from Berlin to Breslau and on February 28th signed a treaty of alliance with the Russians at Kalisch. Prussia was to be restored to the equivalent of her 1806 territories. Any loss of lands to Russia in the East was to be made up by compensation in northern Germany. A proclamation prepared by Stein heralded the revival of a German nation. By March 4th the allied powers were in Berlin; on the 17th Frederick William officially declared war and in a dramatic appeal to the nation called for volunteers. After some initial confusion the country rallied and the militia regiments formed up. By the end of March French troops had withdrawn beyond the Elbe. Prussian liberation appeared in sight.

5. *The Defeat of Napoleon*

In the spring of 1813 the diplomatic scene was still confused. Napoleon had not yet been eliminated. Metternich, who had guided Austrian diplomacy since the disasters of 1809, continued to follow an ambivalent course. Austrian auxiliaries had been withdrawn from the retreating French armies in December 1812, but Metternich had little desire to ally with the Russians and was indeed openly suspicious of Prussian and Russian aims. Austria seemed in danger of losing her position as arbiter in central Europe. Talk of German union, wars of liberation and nation states threatened her very existence as an Empire in which different nationalities were combined under a single crown.

Metternich was, from the start, anxious to maintain an equilibrium in Europe by balancing a possible Habsburg–Bonaparte dynasty in France against the increasing power of Russia and Prussia. He opened negotiations with Napoleon in February, urged moderation, and offered to mediate in favour of a French Rhine frontier in return for the suppression of both the Grand Duchy of Warsaw and the Confederation of the Rhine, and the restoration of the Illyrian provinces to Austria. Only after Napoleon's refusal to moderate his wider imperial claims was Metternich forced to join the allies. Meanwhile the Russian and Prussian advance was delayed and Napoleon was given time to muster reinforcements.

In the early months of 1813 French cadres were recalled from Spain, the 1814 age group was summoned to the colours and 100,000 national guardsmen diverted into the army. By April Napoleon was able to march back to the Elbe with 200,000 effective troops. Only in the cavalry was he noticeably weaker; the loss of nearly 80,000 horses on the retreat from Moscow was irreparable. The Prussian and Russian armies, however, were both exhausted and divided, hesitant to move while Austria continued to waver on their left flank. Kutusov, who did not share the Tsar's passion for liberating Germany, remained at Kalisch, and his death in April only added to the difficulties of the Russian army. Alexander was only able to advance with some 40,000 men. The Prussian armies were not yet fully mobilized; the new *Landwehr* was slow to form up and Blücher, the Prussian Commander, had little more than 65,000 effective men at his disposal.

Napoleon was therefore able to return to the attack with a decisive numerical advantage. When Blücher struck the right wing of the French army at Lützen on May 2nd, Napoleon was able to bring up massive reinforcements and force his opponents to retreat. On May 20th the allies once again engaged Napoleon at Bautzen, but were forced to retire. Marshal Ney with a supporting French army failed, however, to drive in the allied right flank due to lack of clear instructions and the battle was again indecisive. Elsewhere, however, the new spirit of the Prussian army was responsible for the defeat of several French detachments. Even in the major engagements allied troops had appeared better able to withstand the onslaught of superior forces. Alarmed by his lack of cavalry and heavy wastage Napoleon at last accepted offers of Austrian mediation at the Armistice of Pläsnitz on June 4th. He did not realize that the allies were equally demoralized and might have been defeated by a decisive blow.

The armistice allowed both sides time to consolidate and indulge in diplomatic manoeuvre. The uncertainty created by Austrian mediation aroused widespread alarm in Britain where it seemed as if the allies were about to abandon the war. Lord Castlereagh, Foreign Secretary in the Liverpool administration, was determined to construct a new coalition to destroy Napoleon's power. In March 1813 he negotiated a subsidy treaty with Sweden, offering £1 million and recognizing Swedish claims to Norway. In April he began to negotiate similar treaties with Russia and Prussia in order to keep the allies in action. On June 14th these were eventually signed at Reichenbach. Prussia was to be restored to the equivalent of her 1806 position and keep 80,000 men in the field: Russia was to provide 150,000 troops; £2 million was to be divided between them on condition that none of the signatories made a separate peace.

Meanwhile, however, Metternich had been following a completely different line in order to create a European settlement which would exclude Britain whose intervention he resented. Britain's maritime and colonial monopoly was attacked and her relentless determination to eliminate Napoleon openly criticized. On June 24th he negotiated at Reichenbach a treaty with Russia and Prussia which set out conditions for peace: the restoration of Prussia, the dissolution of the Grand Duchy of Warsaw and the expulsion of France from north Germany and Illyria. British interests in the Netherlands, Spain and the colonial territories were ignored; British envoys were left completely in the dark.

The powers were saved from the consequence of these contradictory policies by the obstinacy of Napoleon. At a meeting with Metternich at Dresden on June 26th he rejected the Reichenbach proposals and refused to evacuate Germany. He agreed to extend the armistice and call a peace conference at Prague to gain time to build up his armies. Throughout the summer he combed France for reserves and exempted conscripts. By August his army again stood at over 400,000 men including 40,000 cavalry and a Guard of 50,000. But many were raw recruits, untrained, lacking in stamina and unable to survive the rapid movement that Napoleonic strategy required.

The allies also used the armistice to build up their own forces. The Prussians brought in their reserves and reorganized the *Landwehr* into new infantry and cavalry regiments numbering 123,000 men. Prussia was now able to contribute over 280,000 to the allied cause. The Russians also increased their field army to over 180,000 and began to co-ordinate plans to defeat Napoleon's lieutenants in detail before attempting to engage with Napoleon himself. Castlereagh meanwhile hastened Swedish intervention and urged Bernadotte, now Crown Prince of Sweden,[1] to move from the Baltic to the theatre of war on the Bohemian frontier. As allied activity intensified Metternich was forced to show his hand. Napoleon's rejection of the Reichenbach proposals meant an inevitable end to the negotiations. Convinced that allied armies were adequate to stem another French invasion, Metternich declared war on August 12th.

The allied armies – Bernadotte in the North, Blücher in the East and Schwarzenberg, the Austrian Commander, in the South, now totalled over 500,000 men. Napoleon was outnumbered at last but his situation was not entirely hopeless – no more so than in his earlier Italian campaigns. The

[1] See p. 448.

strategic position, indeed, presented certain similarities, but he failed to take advantage of them. He appeared tired and worn by the rigours of the Russian campaign; his generals were inflexible and easily exhausted. Napoleon advanced to Dresden to threaten the allied armies from a central position, but was forced to retreat by wary allied encircling movements. On October 17th the three allied armies began to converge simultaneously on the French at Leipzig. Outnumbered two to one Napoleon was forced to retreat. Lack of co-ordination created confusion and defeat. After a three day battle the French withdrew; only 60,000 remained to cross the Rhine. Leipzig, 'the battle of the nations', had led to the destruction of yet another French army.

But Napoleon's will to survive appeared indomitable. When he reached Paris in November his Empire seemed in ruins. Bavaria had joined the allies, followed by the other German states. The Saxons, who had changed sides too late, had been occupied by Prussia. Bernadotte had moved north to free Hanover and attack the Danes to make good his claims to Norway. Holland revolted in November, expelled the French and restored the House of Orange. The Emperors reached Frankfurt and seemed poised to invade France. Metternich, however, fearful of Russian and Prussian advance, was again prepared to negotiate. The Frankfurt Proposals of November 9th offered France her 'natural' frontiers and 'maritime rights', and guaranteed the independence of Holland. These terms, which ignored some basic British interests, were nevertheless accepted by Lord Aberdeen who had largely fallen under Metternich's persuasive influence.

Napoleon's evasions and delays, however, once again held up negotiations. He may have doubted Britain's willingness to accept the proposals; at any rate he only agreed to accede to the terms at the end of November, in spite of criticisms at his delay in the Senate and the Legislature. Meanwhile, the Tsar, prompted by Stein, had become much less disposed to peace. In December Castlereagh himself set out for Bâle to represent Great Britain and take personal charge of the negotiations. The allies waited for clarification of the British case: no discussion of maritime rights; Antwerp and Belgium to be included in a barrier against France; as much of the Rhine as possible to be freed from French control; Italy and the Iberian peninsula to be liberated. In return Britain agreed to barter some colonial gains and offered subsidies of up to £5 million.

In 1814 Napoleon tried to rouse France against these new demands. He called up 600,000 men, mobilized the National Guard, appealed to 'the spirit of 1793'. But only 120,000 came to serve; desertion was widespread. France was exhausted. Napoleon had destroyed the spirit which in desperation he now attempted to rally to his support. The allies with increasing confidence demanded the 1792 frontier and after a victory at La Rothière prepared to march on Paris. In reckless haste, however, they divided their armies and Napoleon was able to defeat Blücher and Schwarzenberg in separate engagements. The alliance again seemed about to disintegrate. When Schwarzenberg offered an armistice, Napoleon demanded the Frankfurt proposals.

Castlereagh's presence at headquarters steadied the alliance. He instituted a series of round table conferences to iron out disagreements. In March, Britain, Prussia, Austria and Russia signed the Treaty of Chaumont: the allied powers each agreed to keep 150,000 men in active service, undertook not to make a separate peace and pledged themselves to continue the alliance to protect Europe against French aggression for twenty years. This opened a new phase in allied co-operation; in return Britain was prepared to restore some colonial gains and release her promised subsidies.

Meanwhile the allies had become increasingly exasperated with Napoleon. When Bordeaux raised the Bourbon flag, Castlereagh urged the restoration of Louis, brother of the late King. While Napoleon moved South to harass allied communications, Talleyrand in Paris corresponded with the Tsar. Convinced that the capital would surrender, the allies concentrated and moved forward. Paris capitulated on March 30th after the flight of the Empress and Regency Council. On the following day the allied sovereigns made their formal entry into the capital. When Napoleon reached Fontainebleau and tried to rally an army his marshals finally refused to fight. On April 6th Napoleon abdicated. On the same day the Senate, led by Talleyrand, voted the recall of Louis XVIII and unanimously passed a new constitution, to be known as the Charter, which reflected many of the features of the Constitution of 1791.

L

The Treaty of Fontainebleau on April 11th guaranteed to Napoleon an imperial title, the sovereignty of the island of Elba and a revenue of two million francs. The Empress was offered Parma and the Bonaparte family generously endowed with pensions. After attempting suicide Napoleon departed for his new kingdom. Travelling through the South in fear and disguise he sailed from Fréjus, the port at which he had landed from Egypt some fourteen years previously.

6. *The Hundred Days*

The hundred days added a dramatic sequel to Napoleon's tempestuous career. He was persuaded to return to France by renewed quarrels among the allies, the unpopularity of the Bourbon restoration and the frustration of rule on the island of Elba. In October 1814 the great powers had assembled in Vienna to determine the settlement of Europe. By February they were already at loggerheads over the problems of Saxony and Poland.[1] Napoleon's informers led him to expect an imminent dissolution of the alliance. In France, meanwhile, Bourbon actions, had alienated most sections of the community. The return of *émigrés* and Ultramontanes[2] threatened peasant and bourgeois property. The maintenance of imperial taxation and the retirement of some 15,000 civil servants alienated the bourgeoisie. The army felt insulted by the pensioning off of 11,000 officers on half pay and their replacement by former enemy aristocrats. The nation's pride was stung when the Tricolour flag was replaced by the white colours of the Bourbons.

On Elba, Napoleon's life was dull and restricted. His devotion to the people's happiness was short lived, and the administration of his petty principality no substitute for the wider canvas of a European empire. An attempt to create an imperial court with its palace, estate, hunting lodge and social whirl could only crumble into a routine of disgruntled etiquette. Moreover, the Bourbons refused to pay his pension and the allies did not allow Napoleon's wife or son to join him. Marie-Louise was brought to Vienna where she fell victim to one of Metternich's officers. Napoleon certainly felt her absence and this added one more incentive to restore his fortunes in France.

[1] See p. 166.   [2] See p. 219.

He sailed at a favourable moment on February 26th 1815 and landed with nearly 1,000 men three days later. Moving north through the mountains towards Grenoble, he appealed to the army and the nation, renounced the Grand Empire, and proclaimed his rule to be founded on the achievements of the Revolution and the will of the people. At Grenoble he stepped before an infantry battalion sent to arrest him and invited them 'to kill their Emperor'. The men cheered and joined his standard. Opposition melted away. D'Artois fled from Lyons. Ney, who had promised 'to bring Napoleon back in an iron cage', joined his former master. The march to Paris became a triumphant progress. On March 20th a cheering mob bore him up the steps of the Tuileries.

Napoleon's position, however, remained precarious. The allies at Vienna had not separated and rapidly made up their differences. On March 7th Napoleon was declared an outlaw and the alliance renewed. Moreover, opinion in France was by no means unanimous. Men were tired of war and half-hearted in their renewal of allegiance to a fallen idol. There was sporadic opposition in the Vendée and from royalists, prefects and many of the clergy. Napoleon's attempts to establish a new constitutional régime were received with scepticism and failed to rally support. An 'Additional Act', which introduced some of the features of the Charter to the imperial constitution and established an elected Lower Chamber, a hereditary peerage, a free press and a responsible ministry was judged to be no more than a temporary expedient. When the Chambers met in June they were openly hostile. Napoleon himself admitted that once he had secured his position he would have abandoned them.

Everything depended, once again, upon the outcome of war. For Napoleon speed was essential. With 123,000 effectives he struck into Belgium and found the allies divided and unprepared. Wellington with a mixed force of some 93,000 was still regrouping to cover Brussels; Blücher with 117,000 Prussians had not yet concentrated his troops. While the allied armies were gathering some ten miles apart at Ligny and Quatre-Bras Napoleon had a chance of defeating them separately. But his armies failed to move with their former speed and his orders went astray. While Ney sent the reserve to hold Wellington at Quatre-Bras, Napoleon lacked the manpower to encircle and defeat the Prussians at Ligny.

When the allies retreated Napoleon failed to maintain contact with the Prussians. Wellington moved north to take up new positions before Waterloo and Napoleon brought up his main force to the attack having assumed that the Prussians would retreat eastwards towards their lines of communication. In fact Blücher had also moved north in a line parallel to Wellington and was able to assure him of Prussian support. Thus when the battle opened on June 18th it was inevitable that Napoleon would eventually be faced by the combined strength of the allies.

Nevertheless, the battle of Waterloo was, in the words of Wellington, 'a damned nice thing'. The Prussians advanced slowly and only reached the field in the early evening. Meanwhile, Napoleon had launched his columns against the British line which was carefully placed along the crest of a ridge. Four densely massed infantry columns were mown down with heavy loss. The French cavalry suffered similar destruction. When the infantry nearly broke the British centre, Napoleon refused to release the last reserves. By the time he launched the Guard in a final assault the breach had been repaired. When this failed and Wellington sent in his cavalry the French, now hard-pressed by the Prussians on their right flank, broke in panic and fled.

Napoleon hastened to Paris to rally support. Fouché, however, was already organizing opposition to the Empire and the continuation of war. Lafayette carried a resolution in the Chamber declaring that any attempted dissolution would be treason to the nation. It was followed by a demand for Napoleon's abdication. Napoleon agreed on condition that his son be proclaimed Napoleon II, but this was brushed aside and he was ordered away to Rochefort. On July 8th Louis XVIII re-entered Paris 'in the baggage train of the allies'. On July 14th Napoleon surrendered to the captain of the British frigate *Bellerophon* hoping to be offered a comfortable place of retirement in England. But the government was not prepared to take the risk and Napoleon was ordered to St. Helena where he spent the last six years of his life in bitter exile reflecting upon his life and re-interpreting it in the most favourable light, for the benefit of posterity and for his own future glory.

VII · EUROPE AND THE PEACE 1814–1824

1. *Europe in 1814*

IN Europe, 1814 was a year of reappraisal. The old order had triumphed; the seeds of revolution remained. Traditional ties had been broken; new social and political barriers had emerged. The weapons of war had been sharpened; government control through the bureaucracy and the police had also become increasingly effective. At the same time much of the pattern of daily life appeared almost unchanged. Society was still essentially divided, the economy slow to advance. Crowned heads were again supreme in government, and the Church upheld as the essential mediator between God and man. Nevertheless new classes had grown up to challenge the old. New ideas and new industries had been scattered across Europe in the wake of rival armies and revolutionary administrators. The impact, though sometimes small, could never be entirely eradicated.

For fifteen years the frontiers of Europe had been determined by the ambitions of Napoleon. In 1814 it was the turn of the victors to redraw the map. The majority looked back to the social and political ideals of the eighteenth century. Some were inspired by a new pietist and mystical vision. Today, they are often condemned as short sighted; then, however, their attitude did not appear so unreasonable.

The war had been won by kings and aristocrats; by statesmen and generals who held office through patronage and by birth. They naturally tended to restore a pattern of politics with which they were themselves familiar. Bourbons were restored in France, Naples and Spain. Princes reclaimed their patrimony in central Europe. In the East the aristocracy probably increased their powers. In Austria they took over much of the bureaucratic administration and continued to maintain legal jurisdiction over their estates. In Russia, serfdom remained practically universal and the nobility rejected any plans for social or political reform. In Prussia, the Junker gentry, recovering from the Jena catastrophe, reasserted their claims and tried to limit the impact of the Stein-Hardenberg reforms.[1] *Émigrés* returned to France with similar hopes: victory had restored their pride, peace might consolidate their power and even their privileges.

By contrast the middle classes appeared weak and divided. Liberal ideals had been shattered by the effects of the French Revolution and the impact of Napoleon. Liberty had turned into anarchy; equality had bred dictatorship; a career open to talent had degenerated into a trial of strength. In England the middle classes joined with the aristocracy to curb agitation. In eastern Europe their isolation forced them into dependence upon the Crown. The Prussian bourgeoisie, though now officially recognized by the State, faced growing hostility from both aristocratic and artisan elements. In the Rhineland and in Italy or Spain any lingering admiration for French liberty and law was smothered by hatred of the French occupation and French economic controls.

In France itself, however, the upper bourgeoisie were able to consolidate their status. Many had profited out of the revolutionary land settlement. Promotion remained open to talent and offered hopeful prospects to bankers, lawyers and industrialists. A new class of notables demanded control over taxation, liberty within the law, a free press and a new constitution. The Charter,[2] drawn up in 1814, restricted the vote to an exclusive section of the middle class. Even the constitution of 1791 was considered too generous, and a high property qualification cut down the total electorate to some 100,000. Thus the vast majority – bourgeois, artisans and workers – were excluded from political action and denied even the right to protest. The Le Chapelier Law of 1791 had prohibited combinations and the Napoleonic Codes attacked guilds and unions for restricting free economic enterprise.

The rest of Europe followed a similar pattern. Where middle class influence remained, as in the Rhineland, Holland, Switzerland and Sweden, it was reserved for an exclusive few. The majority remained unrepresented; guilds were gradually abolished and artisans exposed to the disruptive influences of capitalist investment. Thus the Revolution brought freedom, but only to a few; the majority remained dependent and generally exploited.

[1] See p. 145.   [2] See p. 220.

The state of the peasantry was still subject to great variation between East and West. In France, the Rhineland and
neighbouring regions peasants had been able to consolidate
their holdings. Feudal dues had been abolished and lands
redistributed by invading French armies. Napoleonic Codes
and Papal Concordats had guaranteed the property of a
permanent class of independent smallholders. In France they
represented 75 per cent of the population, jealously guarded
traditional rights, and carried on the practice of *métayage*
and a primitive peasant agriculture into the twentieth
century.

East of the Elbe and in southern Europe, however, the
peasantry remained servile and tied down to a traditional
manorial society. In Naples and Spain the consolidation of
aristocratic estates led to frequent eviction. In Austria,
though personal freedoms and guarantees of tenure had been
established by law, the *robot* remained.[1] In Prussia serfs
could only obtain release under the emancipation decrees by
surrendering a proportion of their property in compensation
to the lord.[2] Tenants thus often lost their subsistence
margins, sold out to the aristocracy and became landless
labourers. In Russia, less than one per cent of the serfs were
freed in the twenty-two years which followed the Tsar's
proclamation allowing voluntary emancipation.[3]

Economic changes seemed equally marginal. A shift of emphasis from landed wealth to middle-class trade and industry
could be detected in the West. But the revolutionary changes
which were to transform Europe during the century had
hardly begun to operate. In agriculture, traditional field
systems prevailed. Isolated model estates had introduced English methods into France, Prussia, northern Italy and Austria,
but even the largest estates often lacked the capital needed
for extensive investment, while the smaller proprietor had
neither the money nor the incentive to change. Only the
introduction of sugar beet, potatoes and some improved
breeds of cattle and sheep added any variation into the established pattern of rural life.

In industry, traditional craft methods and the 'putting out'
system of the previous century still predominated. Textiles
had flourished under protection of the blockade and new

---

[1] See p. 43.   [2] See p. 145.   [3] See p. 139.

machinery had penetrated as far as Austria and Russia. In France over three hundred spinning machines were in operation; the French occupation had led to the introduction of new techniques in the Netherlands and the Rhineland. Coal and iron had, however, hardly been affected. Attempts to introduce coke furnaces had generally failed; coal responded but slowly to new methods. France had exploited the Netherlands coal and iron mines rather than develop her own resources. Only in Silesia had new smelting techniques been successfully applied. Elsewhere, lack of capital, the isolation of markets, obstacles to communication and the apparent failure to understand the technological implications of new discoveries slowed up the rate of growth and militated against change.

Trade had become increasingly paralysed towards the end of the war. Though the French market absorbed most of the textile and mineral products of northern Italy and the Rhineland, this was only at the expense of native markets and regional trade patterns. France's exports had been crippled by the blockade and her western ports lay derelict and idle. In eastern Europe lack of competition stimulated local manufacture, but provided little incentive for investment. The peace did nothing to improve the situation. The market was flooded by cheap goods dumped from accumulated stocks in Britain. Textile production in Austria and the Netherlands collapsed. Output of industrial goods in the Ruhr and the Rhineland fell. Lack of credit and unstable finances added further causes of dislocation. When the inflationary policies of the war years were replaced by tighter economic controls, the combination of high prices and falling demand brought an inevitable slump.

Amid the general confusion governments tried to restore order and regain an element of control. The value of competent administrators, codes, police methods and central direction had been clearly demonstrated by the French example. Austrian, Prussian and Russian monarchs soon tried to adopt similar methods. They also came to rely increasingly on the Church and the aristocracy, both somewhat chastened after their experiences in revolution and in war. The nobility had in adversity suddenly discovered a new enthusiasm for 'throne and altar' They now recognized that a monarchy was an essential element in a hierarchy which justified their own particular status. They realized that religion, by advocating a divine order of society, provided both a justification for their own position and a consolation for everyone else. Thus Metternich could promote a devout Catholic aristocracy into positions of influence. Other monarchs and statesmen hastened to follow his example.

The action of kings and ministers did partially reflect a widespread disillusionment with liberal and radical principles, and a genuine reaction in favour of a more stable authoritarian system of government. Bourgeois ideals were discredited as 'Jacobin' and destructive. Rationalism created doubt and generated confusion. Burke, who had anticipated the whole outcome of the Revolution,[1] urged a return to a natural law in which God and property were sacred. His views were taken up by Bonald and de Maistre in France who both upheld religion as the very cornerstone of any social order. Their views eventually crystallized into a romantic movement which discovered its noblest ideals in the past, in Gothic splendour and in the continuity of the Catholic Church. Writers like Saint-Martin, Novalis and Baader urged rulers to act in the spirit of these ideals and to embrace both their subjects and the State in a wider mystical union.

Romanticism, however, also had a more revolutionary impact. It was felt among nationalists and idealists fired by the propaganda of Napoleon and roused by the passions of war. Their loyalties might be to the Church, like the *Sanfedisti* in Naples who pursued the retreating French armies with bitter and barbarous fury. But this was not always the case. Dalmatians, Greeks and Slavs were stirred by hopes of possible liberation. In Germany, the war inspired a romantic upsurge of folk songs and collective passion. Medieval sagas like the *Niebelungenlied* turned, under the impact of a French occupation, into songs of patriotism and defiance. Arndt praised the heroism of the German race and his songs, *Was ist des Deutschen Vaterland?* and *Wacht am Rhein* roused the first expressions of a new nationalism. Jahn glorified the *Volk* and appealed to the young to fight the French and build up the foundations of a united Germany.

These romantic hopes were an obvious threat to the

[1] See p. 81.

restoration of any traditional order. In addition they provided cover for further agitation. Republicanism, planted in northern Italy by the armies of Napoleon, could not be so easily erased. Though returning monarchs uprooted 'trees of liberty' and discarded French furniture and Napoleonic Codes, a residue remained to fertilize discontent and stir up the minds of dispossessed officials and frustrated bourgeois. The *Carbonari*, a secret society with branches throughout Italy, combined disaffected elements. Buonarroti, relying on French experience, spread doctrines of revolt through a maze of secret revolutionary organizations.

Agitation, however, remained isolated and generally ineffective. Its romantic and conspiratorial nature defeated its very purpose. Rejection of a rational organization weakened its impact and undermined any practical political programme. The majority, peasants and bourgeois, remained resigned to peace and passive obedience. Many were prepared to compromise with an established government for the sake of security and the promise of some constitutional guarantees. A few monarchs and statesmen were prepared to accept such a solution. The majority, however, overcome by alarm at reports of continuing conspiracy and revolt, united in opposition to change and to any modification in the established order of things.

2. *Personalities and Powers*

The monarchs and statesmen who assembled at Vienna in 1814 to determine a European settlement represented a wide variety of attitudes and interests. Their calibre was in many respects as impressive as at comparable conferences after recent wars. Their solutions were often equally effective; their errors, as on subsequent occasions, were often the outcome of guarantees and commitments undertaken in the heat of war to forge an alliance against the common enemy. They were obviously conditioned by their age and their collective experience. It is, however, incorrect to brand them all as reactionaries, and unfair to blame them for not being clairvoyant.

The ruler who was at once the most powerful and the most paradoxical was probably Alexander I, Tsar of Russia. Autocratic in temperament he appeared in turn liberal, paternal, mystical and ambitious. His power was based on absolute principles and was reinforced by an army of some 600,000 men scattered across Europe. His liberalism had led to a charter for Finland and talk of a new Polish constitution. Alexander saw himself as the father of peoples struggling for liberation and as guardian of a wider European federation. He failed to detect the contradictions implicit in such policies. The burning of Moscow had 'lit up his soul' and under the influence of pietists and mystics like Baader, Saint-Martin and the Baroness von Krüdener he was determined to fulfil his role as both liberator and divine arbiter of Europe. He was unable, however, to distinguish between theory and practice, between myth and reality and his actions did not therefore always appear compatible with his ideals. Often impulsive, unreliable and tactless, he was judged by many to have inherited some part of his father's madness.

Alexander brought with him a group of advisers to gratify any of his seemingly contradictory policies. Laharpe, ex-Jacobin, Rousseaunian, some-time Swiss revolutionary, expounded principles of federation and national development. Pozzo di Borgo, appointed French ambassador, planted agents and contacted sympathizers. Czartoryski advised on Poland, while Stein re-emerged to advocate plans for a united Germany. Nesselrode, the Foreign Minister, and Capo d'Istria, an expert on Balkan nationalities, fitted into the Tsar's varying moods. It was hardly surprising that allied powers viewed the advent of Russian intervention in European politics with some alarm. Alexander's open determination to keep Finland, Poland and Bessarabia seemed to confirm their worst suspicions.

Prussia, who had most to lose from a Russian advance, was, however, in no position to protest. Her recovery had been largely due to Russian intervention. Her ability to acquire territorial compensation for losses in Poland depended upon the support of the Tsar. While Frederick William III clung to Alexander's coat-tails, Hardenberg manoeuvred to ensure the restoration of Prussia by a series of unscrupulous and conflicting agreements. At Kalisch, Russia had promised to restore Prussia to the equivalent of her 1806 position and compensate her for the loss of any of her Polish territories. Britain had accepted a similar undertaking at Reichenbach.[1] The Prussian general staff, however, were determined to acquire Saxony, and Hardenberg also negotiated with Metternich to this effect agreeing, in return, to oppose a Russian occupation of Poland! Such contradictory policies soon became untenable and Frederick William eventually chose the Russian alliance as the most advantageous for immediate purposes.

Hardenberg was also influenced by the military reformers like Gneisenau, Blücher and Boyen who urged plans for Prussian hegemony in northern Germany, championed schemes for unity and demanded the annexation of Saxony. Von Humbolt, though a liberal and a follower of Fichte, also urged the promotion of purely national ideals. Frederick William and the Court, however, remained reserved, deplored violent plans and were already moving towards policies of cautious conservatism.

Metternich, the Austrian Minister for Foreign Affairs, regarded Russian and Prussian policies with alarm. By nature conservative and cynical he had dedicated his life to the destruction of revolution, the preservation of the Habsburg Empire and the maintenance of the existing order in society and the State. He regarded liberals as dangerous agitators ready to release anarchy and confusion. Constitutions were equally unsound, promoted selfish and sectarian interests and would lead to the disintegration of Habsburg territories.

Metternich's policy was to maintain a balance of power, an equilibrium of authority, 'that which is.' This meant holding back any Russian or Prussian advance, preventing the spread of national and liberal ideas, curbing constitutions and resisting change. Such objectives also required the control of universities, schools, books and journals, the suppression of agitation and the sterilization of bourgeois aspirations. Metternich held himself up to be the supreme realist who took everything into account and could thus master the dangers which threatened society. He had little faith in religion, held most kings, courts and aristocrats in contempt and claimed to govern not by any system but by varied and appropriate combinations of influence and action in conformity with natural and inevitable laws. He perpetually wrote and talked about himself, and his opinions displayed the characteristics

[1] See p. 148.

of a complete egoism. Self-confidence and undoubted ability helped to keep him in power for nearly forty years. His policies were indeed able to slow down the rate of change for a time even if they could not in the end stifle the factors that were making change inevitable.

Metternich was backed up by the Emperor Francis I, who was yet more conservative, and assisted by Gentz who became his secretary and was even more cynical. Francis opposed every novelty and all reform in principle. He refused to acknowledge the existence of peoples and only recognized subjects. Gentz, witty and venal, believed in exploiting anything in religion and politics in the interests of his own and Austrian security. Metternich had also, however, to take into account the military men like Stadion and Schwarzenberg who wished to emphasize Austrian ascendency in Germany and were bitterly opposed to any extension of Prussian influence and determined to resist her plans for the annexation of Saxony.

Castlereagh, the British plenipotentiary, was perhaps the most reasonable. His aloof detachment, though invaluable in solving immediate problems, was not in the long run calculated to inspire European co-operation. His policies were designed to destroy and contain the revolutionary power of France, to safeguard British trade and maritime rights and to establish a just equilibrium in Europe. In pursuit of these policies Britain had poured millions into Europe by means of subsidies, Sweden had been tempted into war by a promise of Norway and Prussia's restoration had been guaranteed. Castlereagh had refused to allow any discussion of maritime rights but had agreed to restore non-strategic colonial gains on condition that British demands for ensuring the security of Europe against future French aggression were met. These included the independence of Portugal and Spain, the strengthening of Piedmont as a barrier in northern Italy and the transfer of Belgium to Holland in order to exclude France from the Scheldt and block any future French advance. In addition he suggested proposals to further allied understanding, guarantee the security of Europe, and promote action 'in concert' to maintain the peace.

Castlereagh's proposals won quick support from Metternich who soon realized 'that ideas about the reconstruction of

France in a manner compatible with the general interests of Europe' did not materially differ from his own. Austria had little interest in the Netherlands and was willing to exchange her remoter territories for adjoining provinces in north Italy. Castlereagh was willing to consolidate an Austrian presence in Italy in order to promote stability and exclude France. He was also anxious to strengthen the central powers as a counter-weight to both France and Russia, and his plans to bring Prussia into contact with the French frontier on the Rhine, first suggested by Pitt in 1804, appeared to Metternich a use-ful way of deflecting Prussian attention from Saxony.

With this measure of preliminary agreement Castlereagh hoped for a rapid conclusion to the negotiations. The settle-ment, however, created more difficulties than he had anti-cipated. Early discussions in Paris revealed fundamental disagreements between Russia, Prussia and Austria over the problems of Poland, Saxony and German reconstruction. Castlereagh's mediation proved of no avail. When the sove-reigns and statesmen assembled in London for a round of festivities there was no time to get down to business. The Tsar merely roused general opposition by his rudeness and tactless behaviour while Metternich ingratiated himself with judicious flattery. When the Congress assembled in Vienna in September 1814 a settlement for central and eastern Europe had still to be determined.

3. *The Vienna Settlement*

At Vienna discussion was generally unmethodical and con-fused. The Emperor Francis I was host and Metternich acted as president, but no plan of procedure or agenda had been formulated. The four major powers had invited not only the remaining signatories of the Peace of Paris – France, Spain, Portugal and Sweden – but delegations from nearly every European state, all of whom now expected to participate in the negotiations. The Big Four, however, were determined to keep the major issues under their own immediate control. A secret clause in the Peace Treaty had agreed that the disposal of territory and 'the relations from which a system of real and permanent balance of power in Europe is to be derived' were to be decided by the four major powers. Thus the smaller delegations found themselves frustrated and powerless. A vast

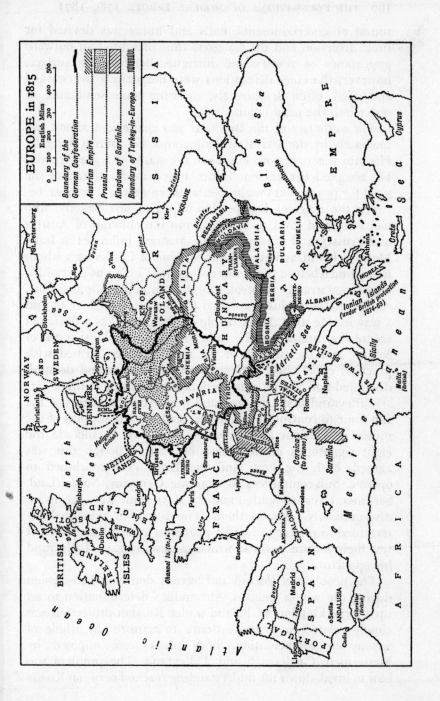

round of entertainments, balls and hunts was devised for
their diversion and the Congress thus presented an outward
appearance of revelry and intrigue. Beneath the surface,
however, the chief delegations were desperately overworked
and tried, often despairingly, to bring some semblance of
order into the negotiations.

The authority of the Big Four was challenged almost immediately by the arrival of Talleyrand, the French delegate.
His aim was to restore France to the status of a great power.
He accepted her ancient limits, urged moderation and the
need for peace, and sought to establish a practical balance between the states of Europe. He hoped to save Saxony, who
had remained loyal to France, from the clutches of Austria
and Prussia, and wanted to limit Austrian influence in Italy.
Many of his ideas were similar to those of Castlereagh whom
he had met before the Congress opened. This was part of his
long-range strategy to break into the counsels of the Big Four.
At Vienna he rapidly exploited the lack of procedure to find
a way in. He used the principle of 'legitimacy' as a device to
secure the interests of the Bourbons in Italy, the survival of
Saxony and the support of the smaller states. Armed with
practical experience, patience and skill Talleyrand delayed,
disrupted and almost came to dominate the proceedings.

Talleyrand first criticized and destroyed the claims of the
Big Four to control the Congress. Rallying the support of the
minor delegations he demanded a council to include the
eight signatories of the Peace of Paris. Though this was
agreed, both the Four and the Eight now continued to
operate. Sub-committees to examine Germany, Switzerland,
Sardinia, river navigation and the slave trade were set up indiscriminately between them. The Big Four remained determined to resolve the major problems among themselves. It
was their failure to do so which eventually gave Talleyrand
his opportunity.

The problem of Poland and Saxony dominated discussion
during the winter months. Alexander's determination to set
up a large kingdom of Poland under Russian protection was
closely related to Prussia's desire to acquire the whole of
Saxony in compensation. Both plans were opposed by
Metternich, Castlereagh and Talleyrand. The problem was
how to break down the understanding reached between Russia

and Prussia and force each one to cut down her demands. Castlereagh first tried persuasion, which failed. His second move was to line up Austria, Prussia and Britain against the Tsar. Prussia would be guaranteed Saxony in return for joining in opposition to Alexander's Polish plans. This, however, also failed. The Tsar flew into a rage, Frederick William collapsed, and Talleyrand denounced the seizure of Saxony. Hardenberg, however, persuaded Alexander to give up his claims to Thorn and Cracow and accept reductions in the size of his new Polish kingdom.

The deadlock was eventually broken by the intervention of Talleyrand. Denouncing Prussian ambitions he proposed a secret treaty between Austria, Britain and France to frustrate her designs on Saxony. Castlereagh, hoping to mediate, agreed to this revolutionary proposal. The Prussian general staff exploded in rage and threatened to fight. Neither the Tsar nor Frederick William were, however, prepared to do so. By the end of January a compromise had been reached. A new kingdom of Poland was to be created with a diet and a constitution, but Prussia was to keep Posen and Austria was to regain Galicia. Prussia received only two-thirds of Saxony and acquired alternative territory in Swedish Pomerania and Rhineland Westphalia. Austria acquired the Tyrol, Salzburg, Illyria and Italian territory. Talleyrand had gained admittance to the Big Four who now became Five; he had saved Saxony, but the arrival of Prussian power on the Rhine was to prove, in the long run, a very mixed blessing.

Once the problem of Poland and Saxony had been settled the remaining items soon fell into place. In Italy, Genoa and Savoy were added to the kingdom of Sardinia in spite of Genoese protests. 'The Congress of Vienna,' observed Castlereagh, 'was not assembled for the discussion of moral principles but for great practical purposes, to establish effectual provisions for the general security.' Italy was thus handed over to Austria for preservation. Venetia and Lombardy were annexed to strengthen the Austrian presence and to compensate for her losses in the Netherlands. Austrian claimants were restored in Modena and Tuscany, while Marie-Louise was given Parma for life! Further south, the Papal States were reconstituted together with their northern Legations. Naples had originally been left to Murat but Metternich had already

M

begun to plot his overthrow when a rash effort to rally Italy for Napoleon during the Hundred Days led to his defeat at Tolentino. Ferdinand was restored as King of the Two Sicilies in 1815. Thus Italy was to remain divided and, in the mind of Metternich, no more than 'a geographical expression'. The preservation of this order was, he believed, a matter of life and death.

The independence of France's neighbours was ensured. Spain and Portugal were to be independent; Switzerland was established as a confederation of twenty-two cantons, her neutrality guaranteed by a declaration of the five powers. Belgium was united to Holland in accordance with Castlereagh's principles and the demands of British policy. An Act of Union guaranteed religious toleration and commercial equality but failed to pacify the Belgians, who remained bitterly dissatisfied. Having established a balance in Europe, Britain restored her Dutch, French and Spanish colonies, retaining only Malta, Mauritius, Ceylon, Guinea and the Cape of Good Hope for strategic and mercantile purposes.

The settlement of Germany was, in many respects, the least satisfactory. Attempts to reach a compromise in the German committee between provincial interests and a federal constitution failed. A final scheme provided that a federal diet be constituted at Frankfurt under the presidency of Austria to draft the fundamental laws of a Confederation. These required each sovereign to grant a constitution to his subjects, and set up a central diet at Frankfurt – a *Bundestag*, which could act in an advisory capacity but lacked the power to put anything into effect. The German Confederation thus remained a loose union of thirty-nine states in which Austria and Prussia played a dominant role. Metternich was confident that provincial patriotism and sober reflection were the basic features of the German character. These could easily be harnessed to maintain the existing order and frustrate the plans of isolated bourgeois revolutionaries. Over-confidence led him to underestimate the powerful passions and ideals stirred up by the Napoleonic wars, and to overrate his own capacity for controlling events.

The Congress concluded by condemning the slave trade and advocating freedom of navigation on international rivers and waterways. Both these principles were only gradually put into effect. Nevertheless, they did indicate a genuine desire to increase human happiness and well-being. Even the less satisfactory redistribution of territory assumed similar intentions. While security was considered the corner-stone of social and political survival, its needs had obviously to take priority over local, regional or racial considerations. The settlement, by establishing an equilibrium which satisfied the existing powers, set up a balance which preserved peace in western Europe for almost half a century. In the end it failed to survive when the factors of change operating in society and the economy made its provisions appear intolerable. But these developments could hardly have been anticipated, let alone assessed, in 1814.

4. The Holy Alliance and the Concert of Europe

The outcome of the Congress of Vienna left the Tsar vaguely dissatisfied. His Polish plans had been defeated, his reputation tarnished, his influence reduced. Plans for a wider universal framework under his personal guidance still haunted his mind. These combined the liberal ideas of his youth, the proposals for a system of universal guarantee first raised in 1804, with the mystical and Christian images stirred up under the influence of Baader, Saint-Martin and the exotic Baroness von Krüdener. On May 25th he suddenly brought out the draft of his 'Holy Alliance'. The previous course which powers had taken in their reciprocal relations 'must be fundamentally changed and replaced by an order of things based on the sublime truths which the holy religion of our Saviour teaches'. The subjects of the contracting parties were 'to lend each other aid and assistance', and their armies were to consider themselves 'as belonging to the same army for the protection of religion, peace, and justice'.

This declaration of intent was judged by Metternich to have dangerous implications. He made some 'verbal alterations' which eliminated all references to the need for change, to subjects and to armies, and emphasized the fraternity and leadership of monarchs. Metternich called the Holy Alliance a 'loud-sounding nothing', but agreed to sign it to please the Tsar whose mind, he thought, had become affected. Eventually the Alliance was signed by most European states with the notable exception of the Pope, the Ottoman Empire and

Great Britain. For the former its implications were too political, while to Castlereagh it appeared a 'piece of sublime mysticism and nonsense'. Whether either of these contradictory criticisms was fully justified it is difficult to determine. It may have been no more than 'the expression of the mystical sentiments of the Emperor Alexander and the application of Christian principles to politics'; on the other hand it went further than most defensive or closely defined treaties by advocating a more general need for positive action and leadership. When later some of the contracting powers took steps to suppress agitation and revolt it was assumed that the original aims of the Alliance had been reactionary and repressive.

But the need for some form of wider guarantee was emphasized by the escape of Napoleon and the Hundred Days. The allies were aware that they had defeated both Bonaparte and 'the revolutionary system threatening Europe'. Castlereagh was prepared to follow up Pitt's proposals of 1804 for territorial security and the establishment of 'a general system of public law in Europe'. When, however, the Tsar demanded sweeping guarantees to underwrite the Bourbons, support Russian claims for territory round the Black Sea and for the protection of Christians in the Ottoman Empire, Castlereagh determined to limit any treaty to carefully specified objectives. A Quadruple Alliance was signed on November 20th, 1815. It guaranteed the territorial arrangements determined at Chaumont, Vienna and Paris and excluded Bonaparte's heirs from the French throne. In order to maintain allied understanding it was agreed that the Powers would renew their meetings at fixed periods to discuss measures most 'salutory for the repose and prosperity of nations and for the maintenance of peace in Europe'.

The Quadruple Alliance thus set out the principle that concerted action should be taken after due deliberation in order to maintain the general security. In practice, however, the full scope of such a principle was open to varied interpretations. While Castlereagh maintained that it was strictly limited to a guarantee of existing frontiers and to the containment of France, he also believed the concert to be 'the only perfect security against the revolutionary embers more or less still existing in every state of Europe'. As Britain, however, was not prepared to commit herself to taking a lead in continental affairs and preferred to exert a 'conciliatory influence' from outside, it was hardly surprising that the limited objectives of the Quadruple Alliance were soon confused with the wider implications of the Holy Alliance.

The Second Peace of Paris, signed on the same day as the Quadruple Alliance, restored the Bourbons but imposed an occupation force of 150,000 men for five years under the direction of an ambassadorial committee. Castlereagh, whose influence was dominant after Waterloo, frustrated Prussian demands for Alsace-Lorraine, the Saar, Luxembourg and Savoy. With the aid of Alexander, he negotiated moderate compromise proposals which modified the French frontier to its 1790 position, restored the works of art seized by French armies and imposed an indemnity of 700 million francs. When Alexander tried to guarantee Bourbon rights Castlereagh objected that such interference was unwarranted. The ambassadors, who met weekly in Paris, nevertheless continually interfered. Laws and regulations were checked, the payment of reparations hastened and efforts made to bolster up the authority of Louis XVIII.

Allied intervention in France tended to obscure the growing rifts between the major powers. The British position was ambiguous. Though anxious to maintain the *status quo,* she was not prepared to take action beyond the commitments specified in the Quadruple Alliance. Nor was parliament willing to take action against their commercial or constitutional interests. But while Britain drifted into isolation preoccupied with maritime and colonial expansion, Russian agents competed for influence in Paris, Madrid, Naples and Constantinople. Alexander advocated plans for world-wide mediation and general guarantees covering the smaller powers and the Spanish colonies. These plans brought him into frequent conflict with Metternich and Castlereagh, who thus found renewed occasion for agreement. When Pozzo di Borgo urged the reduction and ultimate evacuation of the army of French occupation, they agreed that a congress should be summoned in 1818 to meet at Aix in order to consider the problems of France and iron out the differences in the alliance.

The Congress of Aix accepted the evacuation of France

once her debts had been repaid. This was completed with the aid of loans from the London bankers, Baring and Hope, and allied troops were withdrawn by the end of the year. France was also admitted to the councils of the major powers, though not without reservations on the part of the British government. These, however, were resolved by a renewal of the Quadruple Alliance which catered for any specific revival of French aggression. Russian plans for a general alliance and wider guarantees to curb revolution and support legitimate sovereigns were evaded as a result of careful preparatory work by Britain and Austria. Metternich had never seen 'a prettier little congress', and Castlereagh extolled the virtues of his 'new discovery in European government'.

Appearances, however, were again deceptive. The Congress had only papered over the cracks. The admission of France into the inner circle of powers had, as Metternich later observed, removed the only practical objectives of the Quadruple Alliance. It now contrived to exist only in a 'negative manner'. Positive action came to be increasingly associated with the 'Holy Allies', while the British cabinet became more and more absorbed in domestic matters and less inclined than ever for any European commitments. Castlereagh, himself, became increasingly aware of the growing rift. The Congress of Aix was in many respects the brief climax of his short-lived 'system'. Thereafter the policies of the powers soon split apart. It only needed a momentary upsurge of agitation and unrest to make these divisions explicit.

5. *Agitation and Revolt*

Agitation after the Napoleonic wars was varied and widespread, provoked by a whole range of social, economic and political grievances. But it was generally isolated and reflected the disappointments and disruption of the past rather than the pressures and problems of the future. Embittered aristocrats, intellectuals, bureaucrats, students and military men conspired but seldom combined into any consistent pattern or for any constructive purpose. Whenever revolutionary agitation flared up sovereigns had little difficulty in suppressing it. Though affected by an element of panic, established monarchs had little to fear from the sporadic and isolated outbursts of the immediate post-war years.

The post-war decade was a period of economic dislocation and readjustment. In 1816 the harvest in western Europe failed almost completely. Prices in Britain and France nearly doubled. By the summer of 1817 Savoyard peasants were eating grass while German labourers made bread out of the bark of trees. Potatoes were equally short and many regions suffered from acute starvation. In France there was rioting and widespread looting of bread-shops; over 20,000 Germans emigrated to the United States. Industry was restricted by the loss of credit, and a decline in demand. Unemployment was widespread especially in Britain where the textile industry was unable to find foreign buyers for its products. Germany and Italy suffered from a general recession due to the abandonment of Napoleon's public works and a decline in war manufactures. Trade was disrupted by new alignments on the continent: Italy was severed from France and joined to the Austrian market; southern ports were again opened to competition from the Baltic and the North Sea. Spain lost her markets due to the revolt of her colonies in the New World, while her agriculture and industry were devastated by years of warfare and destruction.

Government policies were rigid and unenlightened. Britain protected her corn market, but demanded free entry for her exports in other fields. In France, the government made a 'liberal' economic policy the excuse for inactivity and for buying the minimum quantity of wheat to relieve the food shortage. In Germany and Italy high tolls prevented the distribution of surpluses and the free circulation of trade. Article 19 of the Constitution of the German Confederation had anticipated the creation of a 'customs union'. No such action had, however, been taken. Francis I and Metternich were horrified at thoughts of change and at any possible infringement of state sovereignty.

Metternich, indeed, was soon preoccupied with a wave of discontent released once the worst of the famine had been overcome. Besides bourgeois merchants and manufacturers, angered by the incompetence of reactionary governments, disaffected elements could be found at every level of society. Even among the aristocracy there were many who viewed the restoration with alarm: new men with church property, Muratists in Naples, Bonapartists in Spain, barons of the

Napoleonic Empire. Bourgeois liberals contemplated Europe with increasing dismay: in Frankfurt Görres denounced the Confederation; Cavour described Piedmont as an 'intellectual hell'; French republicans and intellectuals attacked the reactionary activities of the restored nobility and their clerical accomplices.

Europe was also filled with many whose careers had collapsed with the fall of Napoleon. Administrators, officers and advisers were driven into exile or premature retirement. In Italy an army of some 50,000 had been disbanded; in Spain collaborators had been hounded down, imprisoned or executed. Armies provided a permanent centre of unrest. Conditioned to action, promotion and respect by twenty years of war, they did not take kindly to the routines of peace-time living. In Naples many looked back to the days of Murat with regret and grew disaffected under their new Austrian Commander-in-Chief. In Spain regiments resented exile in the New World to fight in a seemingly endless and profitless colonial war.

Meanwhile idealists and agitators remained in the universities and in cells dotted over Europe. In Germany the students' unions organized by Jahn, *Burschenschaften*, kept alive ideals of unity and freedom, and demanded constitutions to implement Article 13 of the Federal Act. Widely travelled and cosmopolitan they flocked to liberal professors and denounced Metternich's repressive measures. In 1817 they organized a combined rally at the Wartburg Castle to celebrate the fourth anniversary of the battle of Leipzig and the tercentenary of Luther's 95 theses. Reactionary books, together with the Code Napoléon, were burnt on a great bonfire while speeches attacked the existing authorities. Metternich was alarmed and when, two years later, a union fanatic murdered the dramatist Kotzebue, he was determined 'to take as much advantage of it as possible'. Representatives of the nine principle German states were summoned to Carlsbad and drew up decrees to dissolve the *Burschenschaften*, inspect universities and schools, and censor the press.

The Carlsbad Decrees were the first of Metternich's measures designed to smother the opposition. In 1820 a Final Act limited the topics open for discussion in the few constitutional chambers which had been established in the German states. In Prussia Frederick William, now increasingly under Metternich's influence, refused to grant a constitution and relied increasingly on reactionary advice. Jahn was imprisoned, Arndt expelled and Görres forced to flee from Frankfurt. Students and professors were indeed powerless to resist the spies and police employed by Metternich's refined methods. While peasants, aristocrats and many bourgeois remained loyal to the establishment, intellectuals and agitators were no great threat. Gneisenau considered it all 'twaddle', and thought the entire episode had been highly exaggerated.

In southern Europe greater danger appeared to come from a proliferation of secret societies. They were not, however, co-ordinated, as Metternich feared, but isolated and regional, each one attracting a varied combination of malcontents. In Naples the *Carbonari* brought together dissident officers, intellectuals, doctors, lawyers and landlords. Membership was essentially bourgeois, though some effort was made to attract a cross-section of peasants and *lazzaroni* from the Naples water-front. These, however, remained largely under the influence of the Church, and were often organized by the police and the aristocracy into rival *Calderari* societies or into *squadres* to counter *Carbonari* and bourgeois activities. The country thus degenerated into gang warfare with *banditti* groups selling themselves to the highest bidder. Similar societies existed throughout the peninsula together with religious fanatics and visionary settlements. Most combined ideals and ambition with some sense of grievance at the restoration of church property, censorship and government control. It was only with military backing that such an opposition could ever be made effective.

The revolutions which broke out in 1820 were everywhere begun by army mutinies and generally led by senior officers. In Spain the restoration of Ferdinand in 1814 had led to a period of arid reaction. The Constitution of 1812 had been abolished; the Jesuits, Inquisition and ecclesiastical property had been restored; liberals and intellectuals had been imprisoned or expelled. The country was devastated and the ports ruined. Nevertheless the Church and the peasantry remained loyal to their liberator King and the bourgeoisie, though dissatisfied, were generally cowed and divided. On January 1st, 1820, a mutiny broke out at Cadiz led by

Colonel Riego. It was essentially a protest against poor conditions, lack of pay and promotion, and a posting to the American Colonial war. Nevertheless the 1812 Constitution was again proclaimed in an effort to rally support, and Riego marched into Andalusia to rouse enthusiasm among the peasants. His efforts were, however, totally unsuccessful and the majority of the population remained apathetic and hostile.

The revolt was revived by garrison mutinies in the northern provinces. Ferdinand gave way and accepted the Constitution with its provisions for a *Cortes* elected on a limited bourgeois franchise, ministerial responsibility, a free press and legal personal and property rights. This, however, was only a temporary expedient. The Court and clergy remained bitterly hostile and soon rallied support. The abolition of entails and the confiscation of ecclesiastical property roused conservative anger. The peasantry, excluded from the franchise and denied property rights, were generally indifferent to bourgeois reforms.

Moderate ministers who tried to promote toleration and curb the excesses of the press and the new patriotic societies roused both radicals and reactionaries to fury. The *Cortes* split into factions with a moderate centre struggling against attacks from extremes on both the left and the right. The *Exaltados,* on the left, demanded the abolition of religious houses, unrestricted press freedom and increasing constitutional powers. They relied increasingly on Riego, the army and a network of new masonic *Communeros* to extend their influence in the provinces. Here a civil war soon broke out between *bandidos*, clergy and *Communeros* which threatened to reduce the country to anarchy. In 1822 the moderates eventually lost control. When the *Exaltados* in the *Cortes* pressed on with plans to control religion, education and the administration of justice, Ferdinand began to rally support from even moderate sections and appealed to the French Bourbons to free him from extremist control.

In August 1820 garrisons in Oporto and Lisbon led a revolt in Portugal. The royal family had remained in Brazil since 1807 and a regency had governed the country under the direction of General Beresford. But by 1820 the aristocracy resented foreign control, the army opposed British officers and the bourgeoisie protested at increased taxation. A *Cortes* drew up a constitution based on the 1812 pattern, abolished feudalism and the Inquisition, and guaranteed a free press and equal rights. British officers were deprived of their commissions and the royal family urged to return. In 1822 John VI left Brazil to his eldest son, Dom Pedro, and returned to take an oath to the Constitution. His wife and younger son, Dom Miguel, however, had no use for liberal governments and soon plotted to restore absolute control.

Meanwhile, revolutions had broken out in Naples and Piedmont. When news of the Cadiz coup reached Italy in July, two sub-lieutenants led a mutiny in part of the Neapolitan army, proclaimed the 1812 Constitution and raised the *Carbonari* colours. They were joined by other mutineers and by General Pepe, a Muratist general, who now put himself at the head of the revolt. Ferdinand in panic proclaimed the Constitution without even being aware of its contents. A cheering mob hailed the victory. Prisoners were released, the press freed and a new chamber elected. Here the same divisions that had undermined the Spanish revolt were soon apparent. While a moderate ministry attempted gradual reform, extremists led by a radical press urged violent methods. At the same time a popular revolution in Palermo threatened to break up the union between Naples and Sicily. Exploiting the divisions on the island, the government rallied the aristocrats with their *squadres* of *banditti* and sent a fleet to bombard the port. Neapolitan authority was restored; Ferdinand, however, no doubt profiting by this example, meanwhile appealed to Metternich for aid against his own discredited revolutionaries.

In March 1821 revolt spread to Piedmont. Agitation had been growing for over a year: the *Carbonari* appealed to officers, artisans and the lower bourgeoisie; the aristocracy and moderate bourgeois created a focal point for anti-Austrian propaganda in the *Adelfi*, another secret society. Victor Emmanuel attempted to compromise and evade action. Army intervention, however, again forced the issue. Mutinies at Alessandria and Turin persuaded the King to abdicate in favour of his brother Charles Felix. The 1812 Constitution was proclaimed and efforts made to rouse the population against Austria. But as usual the peasants remained indifferent, many bourgeois appeared timid and the rebels were soon isolated. Charles Felix, returning from a meeting with Ferdinand of Naples, realized the imminent danger of Austrian intervention. Denouncing the Constitution he prepared to reassert royal authority.

As *Carbonari* activity spread from Italy into France, and as revolutions broke out in Spain and Portugal, the Tsar and Metternich became increasingly alarmed. The murder of Kotzebue had impressed Alexander, who was also becoming aware of increasing unrest inside Russia. Here the army had been demobilised into military colonies designed to establish a permanent national reserve. This had, however, roused the opposition of displaced peasants and aristocrats fearful for their estates and their independence. The brutal discipline in the colonies was a further cause for complaint. The Tsar's liberal autocracy seemed on the point of collapse. Gradually he veered to the side of Metternich and began to advocate tighter and more effective control. In France, where displaced officers and bourgeois organized protest marches and café conspiracies, the government was equally alarmed at the spread of disaffection. Royalists hoped to divert discontent and win prestige by military intervention in Spain which would both occupy the army and baptize the Bourbon colours in a victorious campaign.

6. *The Collapse of the Concert of Europe*

Intervention to curb revolutionary agitation soon exposed the contradictions within the 'Concert of Europe'. The diplomacy of the major powers became increasingly two-faced as they tried to maintain both their separate interests and an appearance of corporate action. Each state identified the security of Europe with its own particular advantage and repeatedly assumed the good of all to be intimately connected with the good of its own cause. This led to the growth of recrimination and eventual disruption.

The Spanish rising roused the Tsar to violent activity. Obsessed by fears of military revolt, he urged immediate action and threatened to march 150,000 men across Europe to quell the disturbance. Prussia supported the Russian move and urged intervention by the Holy Alliance. Metternich, however, anxious to avoid both Russian penetration and any action by a Holy Alliance, which to him was no more than a 'moral union', attempted to draw Britain in first. Castlereagh, however, had no intention of intervening in Spain and in a decisive paper of May 5th, 1820, amplified his earlier statements at Aix and denied that the alliance 'was a union for the government of the world or the superintendance of the internal affairs of other states'. His action, however, was also influenced by a belief that the spread of constitutional government was in Britain's interests. He was under strong pressure from critics in the cabinet led by Canning, and from a powerful Latin America trade lobby in the House of Commons. Nevertheless his memorandum did persuade the powers not to intervene in Spain and managed to keep the alliance 'asleep'.

The revolution which broke out soon afterwards in Naples rapidly hardened Metternich's attitude. The danger of 'conflagrations, torrents and earthquakes' as he put it appeared imminent and immediate action was vital to meet 'the evils which threatened to break out all over Europe'. Castlereagh immediately recognized that Austria had special interests and responsibilities in Italy and urged her to crush the revolt alone. He refused, however, to involve Britain or commit the Quadruple Alliance. When Metternich anxiously turned to the Tsar for support, Alexander, detecting a chance for a come-back, demanded a congress to impose a European settlement. Caught between the conflicting demands of Britain and Russia, Metternich was forced to agree to the Tsar's fraternal proposals for a meeting at Troppau.

Alexander arrived at Troppau determined to crush revolution and destroy liberalism. He was alarmed and incensed by reports that his agents had stirred up revolt, and even more shaken by news of a mutiny among his personal Semenovsky Guards in Russia. He identified himself completely with Metternich and urged immediate action to make up for lost time. On November 19th, 1820, a protocol issued by Russia, Austria and Prussia, consecrated the principles of intervention. If alterations in any one state threatened any other states, then 'the powers bind themselves, by peaceful means, or if need be by arms to bring back the guilty state into the bosom of the Great Alliance'. Castlereagh, who had eventually been persuaded to send an observer to Troppau, issued a strong protest on January 19th, 1821, in which he admitted that Austria had a special right to intervene in Italy but denied categorically any claims that the Alliance had a general right to put down revolutions or intervene in the affairs of any state.

Metternich, having won support for his Italian plans, now moved the conference to Laibach to prepare for action. Ferdinand was invited to attend and, having first sworn loyalty to the Constitution, was allowed to leave Naples. At Laibach he immediately denounced the rebels and appealed for aid. In March an Austrian force defeated a disorganized Neapolitan army under General Pepe at Rieti. Naples was rapidly reoccupied, liberals exiled or shot, and Ferdinand restored to the throne as absolute sovereign. In April an Austrian force helped Charles Felix defeat the Piedmontese mutineers at Novara. The leaders fled to Spain, while liberal sympathizers throughout Piedmont and north Italy were expelled or imprisoned in Austrian fortresses. Liberals, secret societies and mutinous troops were no match for the combined forces of the Holy Alliance.

The unity of the Troppau monarchs was itself, however, suddenly threatened by the outbreak of a new revolt in Greece. Alexander regarded the Greek question as one within his special sphere of influence and advocated immediate intervention in favour of the rebels. His inconsistency, however, was too obvious and Metternich exploited the Tsar's embarrassment to dissuade him from taking any action. Castlereagh had also been persuaded to bring some pressure to bear on Russia and to help delay intervention by an appeal to the Sultan for urgent reforms. Metternich now hoped to restore the alliance and settle the Greek and Spanish problems at a conference at Verona in 1822.

But before the opening of the congress, Castlereagh had committed suicide, worn out by over-work and personal anxiety. Canning, the new foreign secretary, was far more explicit, opportunist and concerned with Britain's commercial and maritime interests. At Verona, Wellington, the British delegate, was instructed to reject any military intervention in Spain. Having delivered a protest he therefore withdrew and finally severed Britain's connections with the continental powers. Metternich, meanwhile, successfully parried Alexander's demands for a European army to crush the Spanish rebels. This responsibility was delegated to France where the royalists were anxious to display their military prowess on behalf of their Bourbon cousins. In April 1823 a French army invaded Spain in spite of British protests. The untrained Spanish levies were defeated and the King finally liberated after the storming of the last rebel stronghold at Cadiz. The savage reaction which followed with mass executions and the public quartering of Riego revealed a spectacular return to the methods of medieval barbarism.

Canning took revenge by increasing arms exports to the rebellious Spanish colonies, recognizing their independence and loudly declaring in 1825 that he had 'called the New World into existence to redress the balance of the Old'. In fact President Monroe of the United States had already warned European powers against intervention in the Americas two years previously. His doctrine, though welcomed in Britain, was probably directed against her as much as against Spain or Russia. The Tsar had continued to extend his influence from Greece to the Bering Straits. By 1824 Alexander had become increasingly impatient with Metternich and was under growing pressure to come to the aid of the Greeks. After an abortive conference in St. Petersburg he opened direct negotiations with Britain in 1825.

Meanwhile Canning had intervened to restore the Constitution in Portugal. The revolt in 1820 had ended the British regency and John VI had returned from Brazil in 1822 and granted an '1812' Constitution. Events in Spain, however, persuaded the reactionary party led by his younger son, Dom Miguel, to seize power. In 1824 John escaped to a British frigate in the Tagus and appealed for aid. Britain and the powers restored the King and the Constitution, while Dom Miguel went into exile at Vienna. Britain had vindicated her policy 'to be no party to a general interference in the concerns of other states; though prepared to intervene on special concerns in her opinion justifying such interference.' As Canning remarked it was, 'every nation for itself, and God for us all'.

By 1824 it was clear that the Concert of Europe had collapsed. Britain's withdrawal emphasized the split between her constitutional and mercantile interests and the policies of the Holy Alliance. The Greek revolt brought out the growing rivalry between Russia and her allies in the Balkans and in the Ottoman Empire. Metternich felt isolated and despondent. At the very moment that he had successfully smothered revolutionary unrest, the growing rivalry between the powers threatened the established order and encouraged the extension of future revolt. 'I was a rock of order,' Metternich repeatedly remarked at the end of his life. He was to become increasingly isolated from his allies as they struggled to promote their individual power and prestige.

At the same time new factors, submerged beneath the postwar reaction, were steadily eroding the foundations of the restoration. Changes in society, in the economy and in thought were to strengthen revolution and weaken resistance. When division and rivalry at the top undermined the effectiveness of governments and broke up the cohesion of the major powers, the champions of the restoration were no longer able to damp down the groundswell of change and the old order was once again to collapse. Metternich was able to congratulate himself upon his foresight. It is unlikely, however, that he would have been able, in the long run, to halt the progress of events.

VIII · THE TEMPO OF CHANGE

1. *Science and Technology*

THE growing needs of nineteenth-century society and the spread of new ideas and techniques led to a gradual acceleration in the tempo of change. A rising population and improvements in the standard of living created new demands. Discoveries in agriculture and industry were exploited to meet them. The whole problem of the relationship between man and his environment was examined with greater clarity and precision. Increasing emphasis was placed on the methods of science which appeared to bring a new insight into the problems of growth, behaviour and natural development.

Observation became increasingly accurate with the use of better equipment. Giant telescopes probed into space. New microscopes examined nerves, cells and micro-organisms. The spectroscope brought a clearer understanding of light, and improved balances a finer degree of measurement. These developments led to discoveries which seemed to confirm the superiority of scientific methods. Calculations and observation which revealed the planet Neptune vindicated the prophetic powers of natural law and the principles of Newtonian mechanics. The mathematical formulae of Gauss added a new degree of precision to scientific and statistical calculation.

Scientific analysis led on to a clarification and redefinition of established concepts. Traditional chronology was replaced by ages that seemed to extend back beyond definable limits. Matter appeared to consist of indestructible atoms which were formed into compounds according to fixed properties of volume and weight. Work on thermodynamics was carried forward by Joule, Helmholtz and Kelvin who related work to heat and established theories of conservation and kinetic energy. Discoveries in electromagnetism included the works of Volta, Ampère and Faraday. J. Clerk Maxwell synthesized the theories of magnetism and electricity into a mathematical relationship that seemed to offer a new understanding of the nature of the universe.

It was inevitable that similar techniques should be extended to examine both natural and human behaviour. Species were first classified and related by Lamarck. The geology of the earth was outlined by Lyell as a gradual and lengthy process of evolution. Human behaviour was also explained in terms of physical characteristics and natural environment. The study of glands, nerves, tissues and body functions appeared to reveal the mainsprings of thought and action. The physical basis of growth and vision seemed to justify the view that man was conditioned by his surroundings and had developed as a result of purely physical processes.

Darwin gathered together many of these ideas in his book *The Origin of Species,* published in 1859. Theories of evolution, classification, and environmental influence were linked to data from fossils, breeding and animal behaviour to outline a clear pattern of development. Progress was the result of natural selection working on random mutations: species had evolved from more primitive organisms by accidental variation; some had survived and others had been eliminated in a struggle which favoured those best able to adapt themselves to a changing environment. These ideas were widely publicized by Huxley and created a considerable impact. It provoked criticism from many who saw in it a denial of creation and free will. To popular minds it associated man and apes; thus many preferred to retain a belief in a traditional biblical order.

Nevertheless, as the application of science became more widespread so its principles appeared increasingly irrefutable. The spread of research to medicine, chemistry and communications was eventually to condition much of everyday life. The growing study of organic chemistry hastened the development of new dyes, chemical fertilizers and carbolic acid. As the importance of nitrates and phosphates became recognized, so artificial fertilization spread and food production rose. The increasing use of soap, and the introduction of chloroform and antiseptics improved hygiene and cut the death rate. Louis Pasteur, who began his career as a chemist, started to investigate the role of bacteria in fermentation before moving on to apply his findings to animal and ultimately human diseases. Lister, working on similar lines, used carbolic acid to destroy germs on the surface of wounds and established the principles of antiseptic surgery.

The effects of these changes were not immediately apparent but they did lead to a gradual shift towards better hygiene and planned sanitation. Drainage schemes were introduced into the larger cities. Water supplies were improved and houses designed with adequate washing facilities. Nursing and medical practice were given increased attention and were further stimulated by the needs of the Crimean and Franco-Prussian wars. In all, the number of epidemics slowly declined while the population of Europe rapidly increased. By 1850 it had risen to over 270 millions and continued to grow dramatically, reaching a figure of some 400 millions by the end of the century.

Progress in medicine and food production were paralleled by rapid developments in communication. The electric telegraph (1844) was followed by the invention of the telephone (1861). In 1851 the first submarine cable was laid between Calais and Dover and the first effective transatlantic line followed in 1866. The introduction of the dynamo in 1867 heralded the commercial exploitation of electricity which was to become a major source of power during the next hundred years. The telegraph hastened the spread of news and the speed of action. Governments became better informed in diplomacy and negotiation; newspapers were able to report rumours of war or stock-exchange quotations with a new and startling rapidity.

Nevertheless, the most obvious progress in the middle of the century was made in the fields of technology and engineering. Advance depended largely on the mechanization of the textile, mining and metallurgical industries rather than on the finer discoveries of dyes and alloys. Bessemer worked out his new steel process from the shop floor; the steam engine preceded the mechanical calculations of the scientists. Transport was dominated by the spread of railways and the growth of shipping. The invention of the screw propeller established the supremacy of steam over sail. The introduction of wood pulp in the 1860s encouraged the development of newsprint and mass publications. The Great Exhibition in London in 1851 illustrated Britain's lead in technological invention; twenty years later most of western Europe was in a race to catch up with her achievements.

At the same time the implications of natural science were becoming equally apparent in philosophy and the social studies. Scientific methods claimed universal validity and a process of classification and analysis was applied in almost every field. Auguste Compte advocated 'positive' theories which would establish laws of 'political science'. These could be used to build a new social order based on scientific principles and were soon elevated into a new science of society – sociology. Jeremy Bentham and John Stuart Mill applied aspects of Compte's teaching to political and economic theory. Their 'Utilitarian' philosophy advocated 'the greatest happiness for the greatest number' and attempted to reach a measured compromise between 'liberty' and 'utility'.

Scientific principles were soon used by every social and political class to justify their arguments and further their own ends. While liberal historians found evidence to prove the inevitable advance of constitutional government, Darwinians and Marxists discovered laws to predict national and class warfare. While bourgeois economists emphasized principles of free trade and free association, the new sociologists discovered laws of inevitable determinism. Neither examined the means by which these changes were to come about; if laws were natural and inevitable there was no reason to do so. Social studies, however, did not have the same standards of objective proof as was available to the natural sciences. This became only too clear when their 'scientific' principles failed to work out in practice. Though influenced by scientific attitudes, political theorists were also conditioned by social and economic factors about which they often chose to remain unaware. These added an element of 'subjective' prejudice to their 'objective' principles and often led to a breakdown in their social and economic plans.

The majority of writers tended to assume that the economic and social changes of the first half of the nineteenth century were taking place on a universal scale. In fact these changes remained isolated and limited, and only developed a decisive momentum in the second half of the nineteenth and the first half of the twentieth centuries. Nevertheless their eventual significance has tended to reinforce assumptions about their earlier importance. This has coloured many of the judgements of the period and nineteenth-century politics have often been assessed in the light of subesquent twentieth-century developments.

2. *Economic Growth*

Though scientific research was to make a growing impact during the second half of the nineteenth century, the economic changes of the first half were largely the result of a gradual extension of eighteenth-century discovery. The new methods and materials of the agrarian and industrial revolution, spread slowly eastwards across Europe, and gradually modified the structure of society and the activities of government. These changes were of special significance in the West where economic advance hastened the disintegration of the feudal order. In Russia, eastern Prussia and the Austrian Empire development was less rapid and a traditional framework often survived.

A continued rise in population[1] was one but by no means the only factor which promoted growth. In the first half of the century the overall increase was some 40 per cent. Distribution, however, was very uneven: while numbers in England and Russia nearly doubled, numbers in Prussia rose by 75 per cent, in Austria and Belgium by 50, in Italy and south-west Germany by 35 and in France by only 30. Several explanations have been suggested for these variations. In the first half of the century the rate of increase was generally higher in the countryside, and the large manorial estates of Prussia and eastern Europe promoted bigger peasant families while the subdivided smallholdings in the West did not. During the second half of the century, however, industrial urbanization and improved sanitation swung the increase in favour of the towns. Here Britain and Belgium were already well in the lead. France, Italy and south-west Germany, on the other hand, were handicapped on both counts: security of small peasant tenures cut down expansion in the countryside, while the slow speed of industrialization failed to create a sufficient demand for urban labour.

A notable feature of the period was the dramatic growth of capital cities and new industrial towns; these attracted sur-

[1] See Appendix 3.

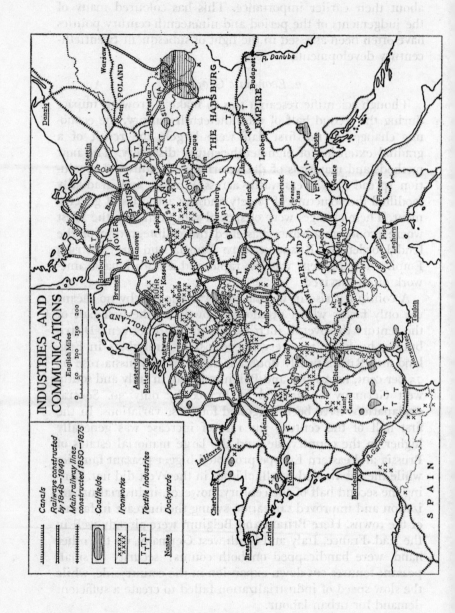

plus labour from the countryside and encouraged further expansion. London, Paris, Berlin and Vienna all more than doubled during the first half of the century. Towns with a new or expanding industry like Essen, Lyons or St. Etienne followed a similar pattern. Traditional centres, such as Milan, Munich and the majority of German cities, however, only just kept ahead of the average rate of population growth. Nevertheless, their overall development was to act as a powerful stimulus to economic enterprise, creating increased demand, new investment, and promoting improved techniques and new methods of transport.

During the fifty years after the Napoleonic Wars the introduction of new crops, cattle, fertilizers and machinery, though laboriously slow, had begun to have a noticeable effect on the agriculture of several regions. Cultivation of potatoes, sugar beet and clover became increasingly widespread across the central plains of Europe. Productivity was increased by cutting out fallow and by the spread of scientific breeding and the use of winter feed. New iron ploughs, threshing machines and beet extractors encouraged deeper ploughing and cut wastage. The use of fertilizers and the rise of Chilean guano imports led to a steady growth in crop yields. In Prussia the cultivated acreage rose by 20 per cent and an increase in productivity of nearly 50 per cent during the first half of the century enabled output to keep up with a rising population.

Progress was encouraged by the development of communications, the growth of training colleges and the spread of agricultural societies and journals. The development of canal and river traffic was vital on the Po and the Danube. The introduction of steamboats and tugs accelerated the distribution of produce. Hungarian food exports doubled in the second quarter of the century, due largely to the development of Danubian navigation. The construction of secondary roads was also of importance and opened up prospects of wider regional markets. In France an Act of 1836 hastened road development. In Prussia the government embarked on a building programme that quadrupled the mileage. In the Habsburg Empire the State and private enterprise opened up the country through a comprehensive road network. In Italy and western Germany, however, innumerable state boundaries held up major construction and frustrated economic enterprise.

Agricultural colleges were established by the French and Prussian governments and were also built on the vast estates of the Habsburg aristocracy. New methods of stall feeding, scientific fertilization and estate management were taught, together with the latest discoveries in physics, chemistry and medicine from the universities. Thus the research of Thaer, Liebig and other scientists was gradually applied to farming practice. Agrarian societies and journals also encouraged new development. In France and Prussia, fairs, cattle shows and congresses gradually spread new ideas. In north Italy and the Habsburg Empire they often took on a political flavour and added demands for reform, easier credit or the removal of obstructive tolls to their agricultural or scientific discussions.

Lack of credit was one of the major obstacles to rapid growth. Though the large landowners of Lombardy and eastern Europe could borrow from private mortgage banks in Milan, Berlin or Vienna, there were no facilities for the smallholder until the French Crédit Foncier in the second half of the century. Thus while the large or wealthy landowners were able to take advantage of new techniques to increase the output of their estates, the smaller peasantry were unable to do so and found even subsistence difficult under increasingly competitive conditions.

Nevertheless, the general picture was one of growing investment and rising output, especially on the larger estates. Marshes were drained and new areas of waste brought under cultivation. The production of cereals rose, cattle breeding flourished and the widespread introduction of merinos increased wool output and improved sheep strains. In France and Italy the expansion of mulberry plantations more than doubled the output of silk. In eastern Europe the spread of sugar beet, oil seed and clover brought new sources of wealth to the proprietor.

In industry the spread of new methods and the impact of new inventions also led to a gradual acceleration of economic growth and a progressive increase in output. Development, however, was isolated and uneven. During the first half of the century only a quarter of the population of western Europe was directly connected to some form of industrial enterprise, and of these not more than a quarter had become tied to any large-scale factory or plant. Only in Belgium were the pro portions notably higher. Elsewhere – in Lombardy, Alsace, the Nord, the Ruhr, Silesia or Bohemia – pockets of industrial development were the exception in what remained an essentially rural landscape.

Industrialization was encouraged by the introduction of British inventions in the coal, iron and cotton industries, and by the subsequent expansion of mining, engineering and textile manufacture. Development was also stimulated by the spread of railways, and by the growth of banking and joint-stock companies. States, however, developed at different speeds. Belgium led the continent during the first half of the century and, after achieving independence in 1830, soon established an industrial economy. France and Germany followed in close correlation. In France the foundations were laid during the restoration period, in spite of the fact that capital development was often frustrated by government policy. After the 1830 revolution, however, bankers, merchants and businessmen acquired a leading role in the state and progress became increasingly rapid, though still discouraged by lack of raw materials, capital and skilled labour. Germany was handicapped by political divisions and Metternich's general indifference to economic problems. But Prussia's acquisition of the Ruhr and Saar brought her a new concentration of economic wealth. By 1834 she had united much of Germany in a customs union, *Zollverein*,[1] which laid the foundations of her future political power. In neither Germany nor France, however, did a take-off into self-sustained industrial development occur until the second half of the century.

Elsewhere, progress was even slower. Northern Italy, Bohemia and Sweden showed some signs of industrial growth during the first half of the nineteenth century, but only developed into fully industrial regions in the twentieth. In Russia and Austria the preliminary build-up lasted for the whole of this period while in the Iberian peninsula industrial activity remained isolated and largely dependant on foreign capital and enterprise.

These general differences were part of a vast mosaic of de-

[1] See p. 195.

tailed variation. New inventions were slow to penetrate the established coal, iron and textile industries. The introduction of British pumps and winding gear allowed deeper mine shafts to be sunk in the Belgian and Ruhr coalfields, but the French failed to adopt new techniques and in Austria and eastern Europe the mines on aristocratic estates remained small and generally static. Coke furnaces and the puddling process spread irregularly across Europe. Belgium led the way with the development of the Cockerill works, named after an English mechanic, William Cockerill, who founded the firm at Liége and introduced both inventions in the early 1820s.

Elsewhere progress was less spectacular. The French failed to adapt the size of their furnaces to meet the increased heat emitted by coke and in the 1840s nine-tenths of their iron was still smelted using charcoal burners. In Prussia, Silesia was unique with some thirty coke furnaces by the middle of the century. In the Ruhr, however, charcoal was in general use until 1848, and by 1855 only twenty-five coke ovens had been built. The puddling process, on the other hand, spread with greater rapidity. By 1827 France had 129 puddling furnaces and the Ruhr, Saar and Saxony began construction at much the same time. Bohemia and Moravia followed in the 1830s and some sixty-three furnaces were in operation by 1846.

Textiles were promoted by the introduction of spinning jennies and power looms. In general, spinning was mechanized before weaving. Worsted spinneries had been established by the middle of the century in France, Germany and Bohemia – where some fourteen plants employed nearly 15,000 operatives. Looms driven by water had been built in Lombardy, Vienna and the Rhineland, but handweaving remained fundamental during the first half of the century. Except in Belgium, cottage industry and the putting-out system still prevailed. In the linen trade traditional methods were almost universal. From Sligo to Silesia the spinning and weaving of linen continued to be the preserve of peasants and artisans.

Mechanization, one of the key factors in the Industrial Revolution, spread more rapidly in the silk and cotton industries. In France, the Jacquard loom was developed during the first half of the century and by 1847 some 60,000 mechanical looms were in operation in the Lyons silk industry alone.

New machinery was also installed in Vienna, Milan, Como and Lecco towards the middle of the century. Concentration, however, had only just begun. Most silk looms in Milan were of a traditional pattern and weaving remained essentially a domestic activity. Developments in cotton were more far-reaching. During the second quarter of the century imports of raw cotton in Austria, Germany and France doubled every decade. The number of spinning jennies in Alsace, Austria and Bohemia trebled during the same period. By the mid 1840s the Prussian *Zollverein* had some three hundred mills with 750,000 spindles in operation. Weaving, however, was again largely domestic. Though power looms had been introduced into France and Germany in the 1820s these were generally concentrated in Alsace and the Rhineland where water was plentiful. Elsewhere handweaving was again the rule. In 1846 the *Zollverein* had only 7,750 mechanical looms compared to over 99,000 handlooms. Nevertheless the growth of a new cotton industry was enough to undermine long-established spinning and weaving centres. In Silesia, Saxony and France artisan enterprise and peasant industries were gradually deprived of an essential part of their livelihood.

The rising demand for machinery in textiles and mining, together with the growing need of the railways, led to new concentrations of engineering works in western and central Europe. The Liége area made pumps, power looms and steam engines. In France textile machinery and locomotives were built at St. Etienne, Mulhouse and Lille. At Essen, Krupp made his first significant break-through, producing railway springs and axles. New engineering workshops became a familiar feature in the suburbs of state capitals. Paris built printing machines and became the focal point of a complex railway network. Beyond the city boundaries of Berlin and Vienna new factories constructed locomotives, presses and textile machinery. These industrial plants, together with the isolated cotton and silk mills of Lombardy, Alsace, Bohemia and the Rhineland were the first examples of a factory system that was to spread across Europe during the next hundred years.[1] In 1850, however, they were still isolated examples amid a mass of small artisans or peasant operatives struggling

[1] For Russian development see p. 418.

to survive against the menacing advance of a new machine age.

After the Napoleonic wars work had been maintained on the canals and rivers of France, Germany and the Habsburg Empire. French canals were developed extensively under the Restoration. In Germany river traffic doubled and by 1847 50 per cent was towed by steam tugs. Railways were first laid down in the 1830s and spread rapidly in a wave of speculative construction during the following decade. Methods of promotion varied but usually combined state action and private enterprise. Belgium led after 1830 with a national framework and private branch lines. In France the State laid the foundations and independent companies added rails and rolling stock. In Germany development was left in private hands, though the Prussian government agreed to underwrite railway shares in 1842. By 1848 Berlin had been linked to the Baltic, Silesia and the Ruhr; Paris was connected to Bordeaux, Bâle, Brest and Verdun; Vienna had been joined to Trieste on the Adriatic. Isolated lines were under construction in Piedmont and Spain. In 1851 a line was opened between Moscow and St. Petersburg.

Expansion was frequently restricted by lack of capital and credit facilities. The Bank of France was the first of a number of state banks. These were subsequently established in Belgium, Austria and Prussia during the first half of the century. But their lending powers were limited and paper money remained suspect after the inflationary issues of the Napoleonic wars. Government finance continued to be based on tolls, land sales and loans from individual bankers. Private banks spread rapidly during this period and made extensive investments in land and industry. Berlin had some thirty mortgage banks by 1850 and others were active in Lombardy and Galicia. Paris was the centre of a network that came to dominate French finance with banking houses run by Laffitte, Casimir-Périer and the Rothschilds. They illustrated the rising influence of the banking community and reflected the growing power of credit in the economy.

The development of joint-stock and limited liability companies encouraged investment and stimulated growth. These *sociétés anonymes* excited small savers with the prospect of easy returns and limited liability. Their activities covered banking, insurance and industrial development. Belgium had twenty-three by 1830. In France they promoted iron, coal and textiles, and speculated in the railway boom of the 1840s. Their interests extended to Austria, Italy and Spain where their activities were regarded with some suspicion. Prussian railways, Paris savings banks and Lombard insurance companies were all promoted by the growth of these capitalist organizations. Chambers of commerce, professional journals and easier communications created a growing realization of economic problems and the possibilities of new enterprise and expansion throughout Europe.

Trade thus increased with rapidity and French exports and imports more than doubled between 1814 and 1848. Commercial growth, however, was obstructed by medieval tolls, tariffs and innumerable currenices. Tolls were maintained between German states and on the Rhine and Po in spite of the Vienna Convention.[1] Tariffs were raised to protect Belgian, French and Russian industries from British competition. In Germany and Switzerland rival currencies added to the confusion and hampered development. The establishment of the Prussian *Zollverein* was designed to remove these obstructions. It was based on the Prussian tariff of 1818 which freed the import of raw materials, levied low transit fees and imposed a tariff of only 10 per cent on imported manufactures. When a petition urging action by the German Confederation failed to persuade Metternich and the Diet, Prussia opened direct negotiations with other German states to create a customs union. By 1828 the separate enclaves within Prussia had been joined, but meanwhile two rival unions had been formed by the southern and central states which divided Prussian territories. Prussia, however, played off one against the other and by 1831, when Hesse-Cassel joined the union, a link between east and west had been established. By 1834 a customs union, *Zollverein*, had been set up which soon included all the German states except Hanover and Brunswick. In 1838 a currency agreement regulated exchange rates. *Zollverein* congresses were organized to discuss tariffs and trade regulation. As a result a new economic organization was built up under Prussian leadership which was to have a decisive influence upon German development.

[1] See p. 168.

Austria, now excluded from the *Zollverein,* France, Piedmont and other European states now had to look elsewhere for markets. The Habsburgs opened up Trieste and the Danube valley rousing opposition from Piedmont and Russia. France with a stable and well backed currency invested heavily in Spain, southern Germany and the Italian states. Bremen and Hamburg opened up trade with Africa and South America. Britain had a considerable lead in imperial trade with her Indian and American Empire. The French, however, soon launched out into North Africa and the Pacific where they roused opposition from British and Dutch interests. Meanwhile, traditional entrepôts like Milan, Stettin and Lübeck found themselves bypassed. While the former looked to Piedmont, the latter came into conflict with Denmark and urged the construction of a Kiel Canal through Schleswig-Holstein.

Economic expansion, however, still remained haphazard and uncontrolled. Development was often interrupted by natural disasters, and by slumps which followed periods of boom and excessive speculation. In 1816 bad harvests had led to recession, riots and general uncertainty. In 1825 the collapse of the South American market brought a slump which continued in France until 1830. In 1846 a combination of drought in Germany, rain in France and blight in Britain led to a collapse of credit which spread over most of Europe. Railway shares slumped, banks closed, demand fell and unemployment mounted. Though many crises were of a purely regional and temporary nature, they were also the first symptoms of the trade cycles and economic disturbance that were to threaten the growth of prosperity during the next hundred years.

3. *Social Change*

Economic developments had a significant influence upon the changing pattern of European society. Increasing wealth and a rising population led to new accumulations of property and a redistribution of capital. This process gradually widened the distinctions between social classes. It also, however, increased the differences within each class. While some members were able to exploit developments in agriculture, industry or finance, others were left behind, swamped or stranded in a surrounding tide of affluence. The 'haves' and the 'have-nots' came into competition and into conflict at every level. They often made common cause with others in similar circumstances outside their own class. While historians in the past have generally stressed inter-class rivalry, recent research has placed an increasing emphasis upon the divisions within each category.

As the aristocracy struggled to secure their status, the various avenues to wealth and advancement began steadily to diverge. While the well established tried to maintain their position at court or in the provinces, others concentrated on improving their estates or engaged in new industrial enterprise. In France, the returning *émigrés* hoped to restore the exclusive distinctions of the old order while in Prussia, Austria and Spain court circles continued to maintain influence and patronage. Simultaneously, however, in northern Italy, Austria and Poland a new aristocracy was reclaiming the land, building roads and introducing new methods of breeding and cultivation. They found their advance repeatedly frustrated by frontier restrictions and government regulations and became increasingly hostile to Metternich whose policies rejected banking and upheld uneconomic guild and manorial obligations. In East Prussia and Hungary a Junker and Magyar nobility cultivated their estates and kept away from court society, which they came to regard with indifference or contempt. Though loyal to the Crown, their sense of duty was frequently qualified by a growing awareness of their own independence.

The bourgeoisie also became divided between an exclusive element at the top, a rising middle section, and a lower artisan class. Financiers and industrialists were able to buy their way into the aristocracy through land purchase, or acquire influence as a separate caste. In France they rose to supremacy in 1830 and maintained control by retaining high electoral tax qualifications which favoured capitalists and landowners. In northern Italy and central Europe they bought estates or agitated for a constitution to ensure their growing political influence. By 1848 the Prussian bourgeoisie had purchased almost a third of the Junker estates. In Italy the merchant banker became a powerful agent for agricultural improvement and invested in new silk and cotton mills.

The rising class of doctors, lawyers, officers and teachers of the middle bourgeoisie were often, however, to play a more significant role during this period. Their advance to influence and wealth was usually frustrated by both aristocratic and *haut bourgeois* elements. In France their income, though gradually rising, failed to reach the minimum electoral qualifications. Both here and in central Europe lack of capital to purchase property forced them to concentrate on political agitation. When the July monarchy refused to widen the franchise they began to support a republican opposition. In Italy, Germany and Austria they led demands for a liberal constitution, a free press, and a representative government. Only then would the barriers of a feudal society be eliminated and the influence of a new commercial and intellectual class be made secure.

While the middle bourgeois concentrated on advancing their status and acquiring new wealth, the lower *bourgeoisie populaire* struggled, sometimes desperately, for survival. Numerically, these craftsmen, handweavers, cobblers, carpenters and artisans still made up a large majority of those involved in industrial production. In France, some 75 per cent worked in *ateliers* of less than five men, and Paris was dominated by such small family units. Elsewhere in Europe, with the notable exception of Belgium, the proportion was much the same. In Germany over two-thirds were still employed in small workshops in 1875. Their standards of living had, however, already become relatively depressed by the middle of the century. The collapse of guild organization, both as a result of official hostility and internal fragmentation, allowed the numbers of craft and textile workers to rise at a time when new industrial machinery was tending to reduce the demand for their labour. Thus printers, handweavers and metal workers were undercut by mechanical techniques, while shoemakers, carpenters and masons were undermined by an influx of unskilled or semi-skilled workers. Artisans in the towns found increasing difficulty in earning a living wage and it was these depressed master craftsmen, their apprentices and dependants who were to make up the proletariat in the revolutionary movements of the nineteenth century.

They were often given massed, if somewhat inarticulate, support by growing numbers of unskilled or unemployed who began to accumulate in the larger cities. Numbers were swollen by a flood of workers from the countryside, where the capitalization of land and the competition of industry had destroyed their traditional means of livelihood.[1] Some tried to restore their fortune in the towns only to be forced out again by new manufacturers. The majority became part of a growing body of the despised and disinherited, and were to remain a permanent scar on the conscience of subsequent generations. In 1847 nearly a third of Rome lived on crime or charity. In Berlin a tenth survived on crime and prostitution. In Paris the police calculated on a *classe dangereuse* of some 55,000. The majority lived in single rooms, in cellars or slum tenements. In Paris, Lyons, Lille and other industrial towns their labour was exploited and their wages generally remained below subsistence level. Women and children were employed relentlessly wherever governments failed to take vigorous action for their protection.

The fate of the unskilled and the unemployed appeared as a ghastly warning to artisans who fought to preserve their status above a faceless mass. Suspended between the affluent bourgeois and the indigent rabble, they felt their security crumbling and their future insecure. They were anxious to maintain the solid bourgeois virtues of the past and felt betrayed by changes in the economy which were denying them similar benefits for the future. Though they combined with other rebellious elements to attack their superiors they quickly disengaged whenever co-operation threatened their own identity and associated their conduct too closely with that of the inarticulate mob below.

As yet only a small proportion could be employed in the new mines and factories of the Industrial Revolution. Belgium was an exception with over half its workers in large industrial plants – notably cotton, woollens and mining. In France, Germany and Lombardy not more than a quarter were similarly employed by the middle of the century. Nevertheless, they were already an élite among the working classes. In Germany, a mill operative could earn ten marks a day where a handloom weaver might earn only two. In Paris and

[1] See p. 193.

O

in the industrial cities of Europe, the wages of the new skilled workers were generally rising. Printers, miners and engineers benefited from new machinery and new locomotive works, and often protected them against hostile mobs of artisans and unemployed. During the 1848 revolution their actions followed no consistent class pattern. While some joined in the attack, others, like the Paris printers or Viennese locomotive men, helped to protect the works. Elsewhere millhands and miners took advantage of the crisis to strike for higher pay, but did not join in any attempt to destroy machines, tear up railway lines or undermine their own industrial future.

Similar social fragmentation was apparent in the countryside. The wealthy peasants were able to consolidate and increase their holdings. In France, Germany and Lombardy larger proprietors gained at the expense of the small. In Prussia some 160,000 of the wealthier serfs had been emancipated on payment of half or a third of the value of their land.[1] Many were able to survive. Others, however, joined the rising mass of displaced and landless labourers who by 1848 numbered nearly two million. These either drifted into towns or sought escape in a growing wave of emigration to the New World. Elsewhere government policy guaranteed security of tenure – as under the Habsburgs, or maintained a serf economy – as in Russia. Though open to economic and ethical objections these did at least provide a limited security in times of economic uncertainty and social dislocation.

It was the modest smallholder who, like the artisan, was often hit the hardest. In France, subdivision and *métayage* often meant survival at bare subsistence level. In 1847 blight and bad harvests led to widespread riots. Revolutionary attacks on landlords and moneylenders broke out during the following year, especially in the poorer areas. In western Prussia and south-west Germany the peasantry, already strangled by a 'dwarf' economy, struggled to pay off emancipation debts, often by the renewal of earlier manorial dues. The failure of cottage industry and lack of capital brought repeated threats of bankruptcy and a landless insecurity. The agrarian crisis made many desperate, and in 1848 the poorer peasants were to revolt in a mass attempt to cancel outstanding

[1] See p. 145.

obligations. Few, however, came to their support and they were eventually defeated by the combined efforts of established proprietors and the obedient tenants of the aristocracy.

4. Rational Creeds

The political and economic ideas of the first half of the nineteenth century may appear at first sight like some kaleidoscope of creeds covering almost every conceivable attitude and belief. Three broad divisions may, however, be detected from the start. The first grew out of the scientific rationalism of the eighteenth century.[1] Writers of every class tried to present a rational explanation of their own social, economic and political predicament and to outline theories that would ensure their own future interests. The second inherited the passion and poetry of a romantic and revolutionary age and extended its objectives to proclaim a new ideal and a new social order. This had a powerful appeal to subject races and those minority groups at every social level who were trying to liberate themselves from foreign powers or from new or alien influences. The third tried to combine all these elements into an ideal synthesis and to fuse the individual into a new organic whole. These idealists, however, though often admirable in intention, tended to obscure more immediate and practical issues in a fog of remote abstractions.

As a rule each group tended to believe in the supreme virtue of its own ideals and assumed that others would inevitably benefit by incorporation into their particular system. These claims, however, were often widely exaggerated. By assuming that the interests of others were similar to their own, most intellectuals failed to observe how very different, in fact, other people were. They were repeatedly surprised by the lack of support for their seemingly admirable proposals. Few realized that in the last resort they represented the interests and attitude of only a small section and that it was only at rare and revolutionary moments that these could be united with the interests of other groups whose own particular objectives were normally very different.

The aristocracy had discovered their apologists during the French Revolution and the Napoleonic wars.[2] Burke had de-

[1] See pp. 32–6.   [2] See p. 159.

fended the sanctity of property and the need for a social and political equilibrium which guaranteed the permanence of an established hierarchy within the gradual evolution of a natural order. Similar ideas had been spread in France by Bonald and de Maistre, who reinforced the process by adding a divine sanction. Gentz[1] followed with a rational diagnosis of the ingredients of order and the sources of revolution. His ideas were echoed in the conservative policies of his master, Metternich.

Nevertheless, though united in their social and political conservatism the European aristocracy became increasingly divided over economic principles. Metternich and court circles considered that a traditional manorial and guild economy was an essential bulwark against a rising tide of selfish bourgeois capitalism which threatened to undermine established institutions. His paternalism, however, cut across the interests of the newer aristocracy who needed capital to invest on their estates, a free labour force in order to cut out peasant holdings, and freer trade to guarantee the export of their produce. Even the East Prussian Junkers advocated free trade, and writers in the Habsburg Empire were soon pointing out the virtues of a freer capitalist system.

The middle classes were equally divided by social status and economic interest. Political attitudes varied accordingly. When the upper bourgeoisie in France found themselves excluded from power by restoration governments they formulated constitutional demands to meet the situation. Benjamin Constant, Royer-Collard and Guizot became leaders of a group of doctrinaires who rejected the divine right of Bonald and de Maistre and replaced it by the claims of a rational bourgeoisie. While in opposition they agitated for a constitution based upon the liberal values of the previous century. Though temporarily discredited by the excesses of the French Revolution, the writings of Montesquieu, Voltaire and Rousseau were soon again in vogue. Demands for constitutional guarantees, limited government, a free press and individual rights within the rule of law quickly revived to rally the middle classes against arbitrary authority. The selective nature of their attitude, however, became apparent once they themselves had acquired power. Guizot then emphasized that

[1] See p. 163.

only a limited number were indeed reasonable, and, as they alone were capable of ensuring the benefits of the enlightenment, political power should be restricted only to them. This meant limiting the electoral franchise to a small section of the propertied and wealthy bourgeoisie who could monopolize the positions of power in the state.

The remainder naturally continued to agitate for a wider extension of the same liberal principles. When the doctrinaires used the monarchy to cover the legitimacy and continuity of their own system, the disenfranchized were forced to adopt republican slogans. These urged all the same liberal ideas but on a wider social front, adding a demand for universal suffrage to broaden the base of their supporters. Once in office, however, their liberal policies turned out to be very similar and little attention was ever paid to artisan or proletarian demands. Liberals had, indeed, little but contempt for the crowd whom they tended to class as failures on the road to a fuller individual development. This attitude was widely held in intellectual circles throughout Europe. Dahlmann and Hansemann in Germany and Sismondi, exiled in Switzerland, all advocated a popular sovereignty restricted to the intelligent bourgeoisie.

While all the middle classes were indiscriminately excluded from power these divisions were seldom apparent. Once any limited constitutional experiment was tried out, however, the same pattern of exclusiveness soon emerged. In Germany new radical and democratic groups were formed in order to advocate the wider interests of the middle bourgeoisie. They in their turn, however, paid scant regard to the needs of others below them. The small businessmen, lawyers and teachers in their republican clubs had as little time for the proletarian as for the privileged.

On economic policies, however, bourgeois principles were in general agreement. The classical liberal theories had been formulated by Adam Smith, who maintained that the individual could maximize his potential in an environment that encouraged free competition and eliminated all restrictive guild practices.[1] He thus advocated free trade and deplored government interference with the natural laws of the economy. His theories were spread in France by J. B. Say and

[1] See p. 36.

in Germany by Prince Smith, a naturalized Englishman. They made an obvious appeal to bankers and merchants who could maximize their profits by the operations of a free market. Industrialists, however, were less unanimous. Those unable to compete with British manufacturers demanded protective tariffs against foreign competition. In Germany their cause was vigorously supported by F. List who made this one of the main arguments in favour of a *Zollverein*. In France governments wavered but generally came down in favour of protection. This, however, was considered to be the limit of legitimate action. Though divided over tariffs, all were agreed on the need to promote free economic enterprise within the state and to eliminate obstruction from tolls or guild regulation.

Such policies, however, did nothing to relieve the hardship of millions of artisans struggling to survive in cottage industries or traditional corporations. For them liberalism meant the destruction of protective institutions and the exploitation of their labour by a growing capitalist class. Ricardo's labour theory of value led economists to conclude that profit was merely surplus accumulated by paying low wages. His ideas influenced Marx and Sismondi who, in his economic writing, noted as early as 1819 that workers were losing a proportion of their wealth to the entrepreneur. Solutions, however, were not easy to formulate. There was as usual a split between the small proprietor, anxious to cling to the security of the past and the propertyless proletarian who saw little to justify the possessions of others. While the former advocated a return to a traditional guild structure and appealed to princes for support, the latter were prepared to advocate far more radical, communal solutions.

In both France and Germany artisans tried to retain their guild organizations or to guarantee work by the creation of collective communities. The *Atelier,* a journal founded in 1840 by a working printer attempted to encourage association among the workers. In Germany pamphlets and petitions urged the cause of protection against the insidious advance of liberalism. Their appeals, however, were limited to a few intelligent artisan groups and remained virtually unknown among unskilled labourers and unemployed. These soon turned to more radical leaders. Louis Blanc hoped to use the institutions of capitalism for the benefit of the worker by nationalizing railways, banks, mines, insurance companies, and setting up state-subsidized national workshops on a co-operative basis. Proudhon, however, argued that property was theft and that only an ideal anarchy in which all would be freely associated could destroy the stranglehold of capital.

Such theories were, however, far too abstruse for the majority who preferred to escape into utopian communities or join more violent and revolutionary associations. Divided and often confused, the early socialist or communist movements made little effective impact during the first half of the century. Economic hardship would provoke violent action. The alternatives offered, however, all too often tended to drift into a romantic and obscure idealism which lacked both the organization and appeal to challenge the development of a capitalist society.

5. Romantic Philosophies

The revolutionary movements at the end of the eighteenth century had released a wave of idealism and passion which had infected nearly every social class. At the giddy climaxes of revolt, when liberty, equality and fraternity had become a rallying cry there were indeed moments of genuine co-operation. Even enlightened despots and romantic monarchs tried at times to promote the well-being of their subjects. In practice, however, few were able to cut through the ties of rational self-interest. Thus in the last resort, however genuine their beliefs may have been at the time, many romantics have inevitably left an impression of naïve, almost wilful self-deception.

Utopian socialists looked back to medieval guild communities to provide a pattern for the new co-operatives of an industrial society. Robert Owen, who had set up a model factory in New Lanark based on Christian and socialist principles, influenced Fourier and Cabet, who tried to establish similar associations in France. Their efforts failed, however, though their influence survived to promote further experiments in Europe and in the New World.

Meanwhile, conspiratorial groups hoped to build up new societies by revolution and violence. They followed the teachings of Babeuf[1] and Buonarroti[2] and hatched romantic plans for the future in innumerable *Carbonari* and visionary sects. Their ritual was often obscure and somewhat melo-dramatic, disguised by cabalistic signs or a naturalist nomen-clature. In France, Blanqui and Barbès disguised their plots under the cover of societies of 'Families' or 'Seasons'. Even so, however, they were unsuccessful. While artisans and workers remained divided between Christian idealists, passive in-tellectuals and isolated conspirators success remained im-probable.

The Romantic movement also had a significant influence upon the middle bourgeoisie who were able to extend their interest into a higher, nobler purpose. Liberal freedom did indeed bring some notable triumphs of the spirit. There was sensitivity and longing as well as a feeling for heroism and drama in the music of Schumann, Chopin or Berlioz, in the poetry of Byron or Victor Hugo. In politics much of this was absorbed into republican ideals. Heine, Hugo and Lamartine favoured a moderate republicanism which would give free play to the aspirations of individuals. But not, as it turned out, at every level. Lamartine having used his purple prose to rouse revolution in 1848 shrank back before the claims of a proletarian mob. His passion could for a brief moment em-brace every interest in a surge of republican enthusiasm. But once sectional ties re-emerged he could only watch in agony as his ideals dissolved into bitterness and conflict.

For the aristocracy and the upper bourgeoisie the Romantic movement also brought reassurance. Though disturbed by the strident tones of Berlioz and the passionate poetry of Lamartine, they found consolation in the historic novels of Walter Scott and the heroic operas of Weber or Meyerbeer. Here the past was recreated in terms of tragedy and passion, yet in a society of aristocrats and peasants that made it all seem vaguely comforting and nostalgic. German princes hastened to reconstruct the past by building gothic palaces and improvising ruins. Historians led by Ranke began a lengthy examination of medieval times and a careful recon-struction of the Holy Roman Empire. Schlegel in Vienna and Novalis in Prussia found in the past the basis of a European order and the source of a fundamental natural law. This

[1] See p. 46.   [2] See p. 160.

added new conviction to kings and their advisers who hoped
to maintain the prerogatives of monarchy within the framework of an ancient tradition.

Though the impact of the Romantic movement was contradictory and varied, it did achieve a universal appeal at one
significant point – in its attraction to nationalism. Every class
saw in the nation an extension of its own interests and a realization of its hopes. Each one, of course, gave it a very
different meaning but this fact could be easily obscured by
the woolly comprehensiveness of a romantic vocabulary.
Thus to kings the nation was a form of medieval corporation
with its estates each kept subordinate under a divine natural
law. For aristocrats the position was very similar only with
the estates elevated to a more significant role. Liberals saw
in the nation a constitutional unit dedicated to liberty, law
and a free economy. Republicans hoped to promote equality
of opportunity and individual freedom. Socialists, like
Lassalle in Germany, hoped that a strengthening of national
institutions would bring added protection to working-class
interests. All found in the nation a suitable vehicle for their
own ideals.

Nationalism thus became probably the most powerful
ideological influence in nineteenth-century Europe. It was
the common factor in nearly every political philosophy and
could be used to harness support on a wide front. Liberals in
England and France exploited it to promote constitutional
governments throughout Europe. Republicans in France
used it to encourage agitation in Italy and independence in
Poland. It received, however, its most powerful support in
countries divided by foreign occupation, alien control or
artificial political barriers. In Germany, Italy, Poland and
among the Slavs, Magyars and Greeks, an appeal to nationalism was to unite social divisions and cover up vested interests
in a wave of romantic intoxication.

A wide variety of ingredients combined to make up the
nationalist elixir. In Italy it was fostered by romantic poets
and historians such as Alfieri and Foscolo, by liberal intellectuals like Sismondi, Gioberti and d'Azeglio, by liberal
economists, aristocrats and bourgeois and by romantic sects
and societies such as the *Carbonari* and *Adelfi*. Together
they formed the basis of the Italian *Risorgimento* which was

to be given a new and ideal impetus by Mazzini. Coming from a middle class Genoese family he inherited a combination of French republican, liberal and romantic influences. These he combined into a passionate determination to work and sacrifice his life for a free, united and purified Italy. He joined the *Carbonari* at an early age but after the failure of the 1830 revolutions set up his own movement, Young Italy, in exile at Marseilles. Here at great personal sacrifice he gathered a group of friends, published his journal *La Giovine Italia* and sowed conspiracy throughout the Italian peninsula. But his plans failed. An invasion of Savoy in 1834 was a fiasco. Mazzini blamed the selfishness and particularism of the Italians. Liberals and even the *Carbonari,* however, considered his plans hopelessly ambitious, impracticable and romantic. Yet though his journal failed and he was himself forced to live in exile in London, his ideals were a powerful force in the Italian *Risorgimento* and his name has outlived that of most of his critics.

Liberal ideals and romantic passions also fused to rouse new feelings of nationalism among the Slavs. Herder's study of folk literature had a profound influence on scholars who began to redefine the elements of Europe's vernacular languages. This created new interest in Czech, Slovak, Croatian and Slovene literature, and led to research into the historic background of the many Slav communities within the Austrian Empire. The Romantic movement soon encouraged poets and historians to write about their legendary past. In Bohemia, Palacky led a Czech revival, which was echoed by the work of Kopitar and Gaj among the South-Slavs. As elsewhere, however, these national or romantic tendencies soon encouraged particular and contradictory interests. Some, like Palacky and Gaj, emphasized the unique significance of each community. Others, including Kollar and Safarik, urged the creation of a wider pan-Slav union. All became obsessed by fears of Russian, German or Hungarian domination.

These fears and rivalries were exploited by the government in Vienna which was able to ensure its own survival by arbitrating between the many nationalities within the Empire. Of these the Magyars gradually became increasingly aggressive. Roused by scholars, poets and dramatists they acquired a growing influence due to their powerful economic and military resources. In 1825 the Hungarian Diet was restored and Magyar made the official language of the southern and eastern provinces. This roused the bitter opposition of the Slavs who began to see Magyar control as a greater threat than the remote and benevolent authority of an Austrian Emperor. Romanticism brought a new passion into politics. Academic compromise was thrust aside and every class surged forward to grasp at hopes of union and the realization of their own individual interests within the framework of some greater all-embracing ideal.

6. *Idealists and Realists*

In spite of the fragmentation and particularism of liberal, romantic and national ideals, they did have a powerful, almost hypnotic, influence during the first half of the nineteenth century. Many represented a high level of ideal and philosophical speculation, and tried to set standards which society is still struggling to realize. In poetry and prose German writers attempted to create a synthesis between the individual and society. Heine and the Young Germans hoped the State could provide the framework within which the freedom of each citizen would develop. The French Revolution had exploded the ideals of an unlimited individualism. Standards had to be set, if only to act as a fixed scale against which the achievements of every man could be measured. They were indeed essential if anything was to be measured at all; thus Kant and the German idealists developed the concept of the whole as an essential instrument for the realisation of individual development.

Hegel, however, attempted to define the idealist position with a new logical precision. The whole thus became the measure of all things, even of understanding itself. Society, the State or the Nation were of greater significance than the individuals who lived in it. Real freedom could only be discovered by identifying the self with the whole, which thus became an end in itself with an independent and separate identity. The State could acquire a totally arbitrary justification and impose its own standards upon its citizens. This philosophy, though originally grounded in an idealist premise, was quickly exploited by all those who believed that their vision of society or of the State was of overriding significance and able to absorb the beliefs of everyone else. It became the basis of extreme nationalist movements and was taken up by Prussia as its official doctrine.

Other writers and thinkers tried to combine their philosophy with science. One of the most influential was the Comte de St. Simon, an enlightened and somewhat eccentric aristocrat of the old order who survived the Revolution to proclaim ideals of a new industrial society where the community would develop on scientific lines for the benefit of all its members. The community would become responsible for planning production, for the distribution of wealth 'to each according to his capacity', and for the general direction of labour. Here again it was clear that such a state might easily develop on dictatorial lines even assuming it had the welfare of individuals at heart. Nevertheless St. Simon had considerable influence on socialists, utilitarians and notably on Karl Marx.

Marx, who was born in Trier in 1818 of bourgeois Jewish parents synthesized much of the scientific and philosophical work of the period. He was influenced by German idealists, Hegelian logic, scientific evolution and his own penetrating but sometimes limited observations. Noting the growing divisions in society he outlined a process of social evolution in which the accumulation of wealth led to a pattern of class war. This would continue until the final victory of the proletariat, which would lead to the creation of an ideal communist state. Marx believed his progression to be part of an inevitable law and thus did not set up any revolutionary organization to put his views into effect. He was a spectator of the 1848 revolution in Paris and his Communist Manifesto, published in great haste in February, did not have the impact for which he had hoped. In fact the revolutions did not entirely fit into a Marxist pattern. There were more divisions in society than Marx had catered for. Both bourgeoisie and proletariat were split into social and national groups whose rivalry destroyed much of their effectiveness. Human behaviour did not, in fact, conform to an idealist or scientific pattern.

Thus the revolutions of 1848 were to shatter the illusions of idealists, theorists and liberal philosophers. The behaviour of almost every level of society conformed to little beyond a fanatical dedication to immediate economic and political interests. The fog of good intentions was suddenly lifted, leaving every sector nakedly selfish and unashamed. Only the aristocracy retained a measure of unanimity in its determination to preserve its status and authority. Using the army with its exclusive and united officer corps and its obedient peasant levies, it demonstrated conclusively that, after the collapse of established authority and the break up of social ties, might once again became right.

In their determination to suppress revolution, courts and aristocrats could generally rely upon the support of the Catholic Church. The Napoleonic experience had left it with few illusions about the opportunism and indulgence of human behaviour. Papal claims retained their absolute implications and appeared to stand for continuity and order in a maze of conflicting argument. In France, Bonald, Chateaubriand and de Maistre praised the continuity of the Catholic Church and lauded its traditions with a new romantic enthusiasm. It, too, however, had its liberal idealists. In France, Lamennais and Montalembert attempted to create a new liberal Catholicism dedicated to social reform and the slogan 'God and Liberty'. Gregory XVI, who became Pope in 1831 just after a wave of revolution, realized all too clearly the ambiguities of such liberal doctrines. The liberal Catholics were condemned and the Papacy maintained its authoritarian control. In 1847 his successor Pius IX was momentarily persuaded to grant liberal concessions. The revolution, however, soon changed his mind. In 1848 a Syllabus of Errors condemned liberalism, socialism and the scientific reasoning that created doubt and destroyed the equilibrium of society.

The lessons of 1848 were not to be lost upon others. In the second half of the nineteenth century the study of idealist philosophy declined and liberals and socialists turned to more realistic ways of achieving their ambition. While the bourgeoisie accumulated wealth, the workers formed unions and political parties to challenge its distribution. Politicians and statesmen no longer relied on principles but accumulated power. By exploiting the divisions in society, by relying on the army, by harnessing classes and creeds they were able to reshape Europe to their own purpose. But it was at a certain cost. Idealism, liberalism and the individual had usually to take second place in an aggregate of vested interests that made up the basis of a new *realpolitik*.

IX · REVOLUTION AND REACTION

1. *The Greek Revolt and the Eastern Question*

THE Ottoman Empire had for over a century suffered from a gradual process of disintegration. Its rulers had been quite unable to reform the administration or to solve an accumulation of economic and regional problems. Its territories had become a prey to vested interests and rival factions which had created a state of almost permanent uncertainty and unrest. Revolts soon led to increasing agitation and encouraged the intervention of foreign powers. This raised vital issues of security and prestige and elevated the 'Eastern Question' from an intricate maze of petty squabbles into a major issue of European diplomacy.

The Ottoman aristocracy was divided between administrative overlords, feudal landowners and a military caste of Janissaries. The *pashas* who ruled over dependent provinces were generally selected from among the local nobility and maintained order by ruthlessly exploiting the area in their own interests. The Janissaries, once a picked corps, had become a closed corporation of some 112,000 guards who lived in exclusive barracks at the expense of the surrounding countryside. The Sultan had been forced to use phanariot Greeks, those resident in Constantinople, to administer the Empire with the aid of the Orthodox Church. These governors, or *hospodars*, soon took to the general pattern of violence which prevailed throughout Ottoman territory.

Greek merchants had, however, been able to establish reasonably prosperous and cultured communities on the islands of the Aegean. Cut off from the anarchy on the mainland they had built up a network of trading connections that spread from Marseilles to Odessa. In 1774 they had been allowed to sail under the Russian flag and had carried a growing proportion of the grain trade during the war years. They had also been granted limited local autonomy by the Sultan and were able to set up schools, establish a university at Chios and develop close ties with the intellectual movements in

France and the rest of Europe. The ambitious could buy offices in the Ottoman administration and spread Greek influence on the mainland.

The majority of the peasantry were poor, ignorant and often bitterly hostile to their own national aristocracy and to any Greek administration. The Serbs in the North retained their own clergy and customs in sullen opposition to Turkish land-owners and Janissary garrisons. Bulgars and Rumanians still maintained a primitive identity and resented the exactions of *boyar* nobles and rapacious Greeks. Their life was brutal and bitter, based on an agriculture of rough cereals, goats, sheep, raisins and oil; its routine was feudal, with taxes, dues, and services to the State, the Church and the landlord. When crops failed the peasants took to the hills and joined the bands of brigands who survived by regular raids on neighbouring territory.

The Sultans appeared quite incapable of putting a stop to the growing fragmentation of their Empire. They were, in theory, autocratic with supreme authority over a central council, *diwan,* and the army, the administration and the Church. In practice, however, their decrees were generally ignored and they were reduced by frustration and rage to use massacre or murder as their most effective instrument of policy. Local *pashas,* like Ali of Janina and Mehemet Ali of Egypt, had established a virtual autonomy. Each area enjoyed some degree of regional independence, religious tolerance and local organization. But if this were a virtue it was only born of necessity and exposed the countryside to an endless round of brutality and violence.

Selim III (1789-1807) had attempted to introduce reforms. He had reorganized the ministries of the *diwan,* improved the collection of the poll-tax and tried to increase military efficiency. His actions, however, had roused the opposition of vested interests in the council, the army and the aristocracy. In 1807 he was deposed by a palace revolution led by a Janissary revolt and replaced by Mustapha IV. A counter-revolution in the following year led to the murder of both previous sultans and the accession of Mahmoud II. It was hardly surprising that government collapsed and revolt became increasingly widespread.

... The Serbs were the first to rebel. Their poverty and isolation were combined with a sturdy peasant independence; their determination was encouraged by Serb writers living in exile in the neighbouring provinces of Hungary. In 1804 Kara (Black) George led an attack on the murderous Janissary garrisons and besieged them in Belgrade. When the Serbs demanded regional autonomy the Sultan, previously sympathetic, became alarmed and determined to reduce them to obedience. Years of confused mountain warfare ended in an Ottoman victory when, after the Treaty of Bucharest (1812), Turkish troops were freed from the Russian front. In 1815 the barbarous repression provoked a new revolt led by M. Obrenovich. During the next two years the Serbs defeated the Sultan's troops and were able to ward off further attack until the outbreak of the Greek revolt fatally weakened Ottoman power. Their future survival subsequently came to depend on the wider struggles which began to consume the Empire.

In 1821 three revolts broke out almost simultaneously in the European provinces. Although there was a certain amount of mutual encouragement there were few signs of co-ordination, and the Sultan would almost certainly have destroyed his divided opponents but for the ultimate intervention of the major powers. Ali Pasha, the lion of Janina and governor of Albania, led the first revolt. Ruthless and turbulent, he had consolidated his power, improved administration and trade, and come into contact with Napoleonic methods in the Adriatic. Determined to gain complete independence, he quarrelled with the Sultan and claimed sovereign rights. Mahmoud, however, was resolved to prevent the continued disintegration of his territory and sent a force to curb Ali Pasha's activities. After a year of fighting he was able, with the aid of bribery and treachery, to corner his rebel vizier and have him murdered with all his family.

Meanwhile a second rebellion had broken out in the provinces of Moldavia and Wallachia led by Alexander Ypsilanti, son of a Greek *hospodar* and a general in the Russian army. This revolt was partly the work of students and malcontents and partly the result of a network of secret societies called the *Hetairia Philiké*. This had been refounded after the Napoleonic wars by Greek merchants in Odessa and on the islands in order to spread Greek trade and culture

P

throughout the Ottoman Empire. Its aims, however, soon became more militant. By 1818 it had moved to Constantinople; in 1820 it had acquired a membership of nearly
100,000 including many leading Greeks. Capo d'Istria, an
Ionian, had been associated with its foundation and this
aroused in many members vague hopes of Russian aid.
Romantic ideals were further stimulated by writers like
Rhigas and Koreas who revived the poetry of a heroic age
and rewrote the chronicles of the past in contemporary
language.

The *Hetairia Philiké* had planned a revolt for 1825 but the
news of Ali Pasha's rebellion persuaded Ypsilanti, a romantic
and unbalanced man, to cross the Pruth with the minimum
of preparation and appeal for aid. He was rapidly disillusioned. The peasants, still living under feudal conditions, had
little use for Greeks and merely turned to attack their *boyar*
landlords. The latter, who regarded the *hospodars* as rivals,
refused to lend any assistance, negotiated with the Sultan and
attempted to turn the peasants against Ypsilanti's army. At
Bucharest, Ypsilanti fell out with the peasant leadership,
executed an obstructive commander and finally alienated all
popular support. Meanwhile the island Greeks, cut off from
the North and fearful of economic reprisals, refused to move.
The Tsar was persuaded by Metternich to denounce the
whole enterprise[1] and in June, Ypsilanti, now completely isolated, was defeated and fled whereupon the revolt collapsed.

Meanwhile, however, a spectacular and bloody peasant
rising had broken out in the Morea on the Greek mainland.
Here peasant grievances and religious hatred fused in
a violent attack against alien and aristocratic rule. Turkish
landlords were massacred; towns were stormed and Turks
and Jews hanged, impaled, ripped open or roasted alive. By
the end of 1822 the Morea had been cleared, but the struggle
moved North and continued on the islands. Here many merchants regarded the atrocities of their fellow nationals with
horror and hoped to stay aloof. The post-war recession had,
however, hit many traders; ships remained in port, seamen
were unemployed and captains took to piracy. When the
Sultan placed restrictions on Russian commerce in the Straits,
largely to cut down Greek profits, the advantages of neutral-

[1] See p. 180.

ity diminished. Threatened by assault from all sides, the islands slowly joined the mainland revolt.

The Turks, however, were quick to take reprisals. On Easter day, 1821, the Patriarch of Constantinople and three of his bishops were hanged in their sacred vestments and then flung into the Bosphorus. In 1822 the island of Chios was attacked, three weeks after a piratical invasion, and over half the population slaughtered or sold into slavery. Europe was outraged and roused to give aid to the Greek cause. Philhellenic societies in Britain, France and the United States, stirred by the glories of ancient Greece and the struggles of a Christian people against barbaric Turks, sent money, gifts and clothing, most of which, however, was embezzled by brigands. Lord Byron, who in England had written heroically on Greek independence, found when he got there nothing but dissension and squalor. Attempts to form an organized government failed: a constitution was proclaimed in 1822 but conflicts between bourgeois and brigands, merchants and peasants made it unworkable. Only the total paralysis of the Ottoman government and its preoccupation with Ali Pasha enabled the Greek revolt to survive.

The governments of Europe watched events in Greece with cautious alarm. Few were taken in by popular myths and the majority, including Alexander, considered the Greeks far too barbarous to work a constitution. Metternich hoped events 'would burn themselves out', and urged the Tsar not to intervene. Britain and Russia, both wishing to avoid any action by the other, remained watchful and detached. Nevertheless Alexander and Canning came under increasing pressure from mercantile interests at home. In Russia, merchants, Slavophiles and Orthodox churchmen urged intervention. In Britain, traders, financiers and philhellenes demanded support. The Tsar, however, accepted Metternich's advice, defied all criticism and only began to consider a new policy in 1825 shortly before his death. Canning, who was both more outspoken and more sensitive to mercantile opinion, recognized the Greeks in 1823 as belligerents largely to protect British shipping from piratical attack and to back up the loans to the new Greek government. Britain, in customary fashion, was now able to sell arms to both sides: while philhellenes continued to pour money and supplies into Greece, the Levant Company maintained its traditional trade with the Ottoman Empire.

In 1825 the situation took a new turn. The Sultan, driven to despair, invited Mehemet Ali to crush the Greeks. He agreed, in return for Crete, and sent his son Ibrahim Pasha with an Egyptian military expedition. Having reduced the islands, Ibrahim turned to the mainland where he began systematically to wipe out the entire population. It appeared that he intended to resettle the Morea with colonists from North Africa. In March 1826 Nicholas I, who had meanwhile succeeded his brother Alexander as Tsar,[1] demanded the withdrawal of Turkish troops from the Danubian principalities of Moldavia and Wallachia. Eager to ignore Metternich and intervene in the Greek and Serb revolts he signed a protocol at St. Petersburg in April with the Duke of Wellington advocating Greek self-government. Canning, under growing pressure at home and alarmed by Russian intentions in the Near East, agreed to join in a united front 'to prevent mischief'.

The Sultan, hoping to split the new alliance, accepted the Danubian proposals but refused to reply to the protocol. A convention at Akkerman agreed to the withdrawal of Turkish troops from Serbia and the Principalities. This, however, only strengthened the determination of the allies. In April 1827 a treaty signed in London between Russia, Britain and France reaffirmed the need for mediation and threatened action to prevent collision between the parties, 'without, however, taking any part in the hostilities'. When the Sultan rejected this ambiguous threat the allied fleets were instructed to intervene, 'when all other means are exhausted, by cannon shot'. The result was a battle at Navarino where on October 20th the Turco-Egyptian fleet was sunk.

Navarino caused considerable confusion in the alliance. The sudden death of Canning led to the formation of a new ministry under Wellington. The Duke, who had come to hate violence and was a firm believer in Castlereagh's policies of non-intervention, immediately withdrew the British fleet and apologized to the Sultan. Nicholas I, however, had no such qualms. In April 1828 Russia declared war on the Turks and,

[1] See p. 298.

after overcoming fanatical Ottoman resistance, broke through to Adrianople in the following year. On September 14th, 1829, the Treaty of Adrianople gave Russia control over the mouths of the Danube, forced the Turks to evacuate the Principalities and recognized Serbian autonomy under Russian protection. Greece, which had meanwhile been cleared by French troops, was to be considered at a conference to be held in London in the following year. Here a protocol recognized Greek independence under a three-power guarantee. In 1833, Otto, the son of the romantic Ludwig of Bavaria, accepted the throne and began to try to reduce a violent and faction ridden state into some semblance of order.

2. *The Restoration and Reaction in France*

In France, the restoration of the Bourbons brought with it all the ingredients of future revolt. Bitter social divisions were accentuated by economic rivalry and inflamed by conflicting creeds. The aristocracy was split between *émigrés*, who returned with a fanatical devotion to 'throne and altar', moderates prepared to compromise, and Napoleonic barons anxious to maintain their status and the benefits of an imperial administration. The former, led by the Comte d'Artois and the Polignacs, were determined to restore the traditions and spirit of the old order. Their extreme views earned them the title of Ultras; their return to France was heralded by a 'white terror' and a campaign of retribution in the provinces.

The bourgeoisie were, as usual, divided by both class and conviction. The wealthy – bankers, industrialists, merchants and administrators – were determined to retain their status and to guarantee their interests. Some favoured a moderate royalist constitution, some remained independent, a few retained Bonapartist sympathies. The lower bourgeoisie, exhausted by years of war, wanted peace and profit; but intellectuals, artisans and army officers were not prepared to allow the achievements of the Empire and the Revolution to go by default. Moreover, no class was willing to restore any of the national property seized or purchased since 1791; peasants and bourgeois were both equally determined to retain their newly won rights.

The Church was divided between returning Ultramontanes and moderate Gallicans. The restoration of the

Jesuits, of religious orders and episcopal control roused the hostility of liberals and national reformers. Conflicts between rival creeds and romantic philosophies added to the confusion. While Bonald, de Maistre and Chateaubriand launched out with claims for a divine or rational Catholic order, liberals, led by Constant, urged the need to limit absolutism by a constitution.[1] Simultaneously republicans like Lafayette and Cavaignac maintained an undercurrent of opposition to any restoration of the old order.

The Charter of 1814 was designed to reach a compromise between these conflicting elements. The land settlement of the Revolution was guaranteed, together with equality of opportunity, freedom of conscience, a free press and legal rights. Catholicism was declared the religion of state, but the Concordat and the Organic Articles were also preserved. The Napoleonic administrative system, the Codes and the educational framework were all retained. The interests of the upper bourgeoisie were guaranteed by a constitution which provided for two chambers, a responsible ministry and a limited electorate. The Upper Chamber contained hereditary peers nominated by the King (though in the first instance they were selected by Talleyrand who chose a broad cross-section of moderate dignitaries.) The Lower Chamber contained deputies elected for five years on a very restricted franchise: electors were to be aged at least thirty and taxed at 300 francs a year, and the deputies at least forty and taxed at 1,000 francs. The King was declared head of the executive with sole right to initiate legislation and to veto laws. Ministers were nevertheless responsible and had to get bills and budgets passed through the chambers.

The constitution was attacked almost at once from every side. Louis himself insisted that it be granted as an act of grace from the throne and not as a popular right. Ultra pressure demanded reference to 'the nineteenth year of our reign'. The franchise was restricted to some 80,000; scarcely 10,000 qualified as candidates, and these could only represent the exclusive heights of the bourgeoisie and of the landed aristocracy. Louis, however, made determined efforts to make the compromise work. Tested in adversity and tempered by experience he realized the need to reduce fanaticism, heal

[1] See p. 202.

bitterness and strengthen the moderate centre. His aim of 'nationalizing the monarchy and royalizing the nation' might have succeeded had he been of heroic stature and won wider support from royalists and independents. The Ultras, however, deplored his moderation and attacked his measures, while the bourgeoisie, anxious to promote their wealth and security, soon lost confidence in their gouty, lumbering monarch.

In 1815 the ultra royalists, 'who had learnt nothing and forgotten nothing', launched a reign of terror in the provinces. Napoleonic officers were lynched, opposition officials purged, garrisons massacred. The elections, held in an atmosphere of alarm and under the control of new royalist prefects, brought an ultra landslide.[1] Louis XVIII, gratified by what he called a *Chambre introuvable,* was able to dismiss Talleyrand and appoint the Duc de Richelieu head of a moderate ministry with Decazes, a royal favourite, responsible for the police. Richelieu, who had already achieved distinction as governor of Odessa, selected middle-of-the-road constitutionalists or doctrinaires to form a government dedicated to pacification and financial reconstruction.

The ultra Chamber, however, had no intention of supporting moderation. They now transferred the terror to the capital. Bonapartists were exiled and some 50,000 officials dismissed. Artists and actors were expelled from the Academy. Attempts to issue an amnesty failed: eighteen Bonapartist generals, including Marshal Ney, were tried and shot. New press laws treated as sedition any attack on the government, the succession or the royal authority. Summary courts were restored with powers to carry out death sentences within twenty-four hours. Simultaneously the Church began a campaign for the restoration of Catholic control. Divorce was abolished in 1816, and religious instruction restored in schools and universities. Revivalist missions and *Congrégations de la Vierge* were set up to organize ceremonies of repentance and rally the faithful.

Ultra action soon provoked republican counter-attacks. In July 1816 a 'patriots plot' created further bitterness. Meanwhile the allied powers had become more and more alarmed

[1] Only 48,478 out of 72,112 had been able to vote.

by the excesses of *émigré* action and urged the dissolution of the Chamber. When the Ultras attacked the budget for selling off 'sacred woods' to pay for the national debt, and began to demand that ministers be made responsible to the Chamber, Louis XVIII dissolved the *introuvables*. New elections were conducted under the careful supervision of government prefects and the restrictions of a new Electoral Law which cut the number of seats in the Chamber to 258. As a result a ministerial majority was returned and the ultra representation cut to 90. The latter, however, were increasingly embittered and determined to destroy Decazes whom they considered responsible for their defeat.

Nevertheless, for the next four years the moderate ministry continued to hold its own and steer a middle course. With the backing of the constitutionalists led by Royer-Collard, Guizot and Cousin, and the support of financiers like Laffitte, the government was able to pay the indemnity, join the Concert of Europe and follow policies of cautious reconstruction. By 1818, with the aid of negotiations between Baring of London, Hope of Amsterdam and Laffitte, the reparations debt was repaid and France was able to join the allies at Aix.[1] In the same year Saint-Cyr's Army Bill created a new national force of some 200,000 men selected by ballot and promoted by merit. In 1819 a Press Law relaxed restrictions and established trial by jury. Attempts to draft a new concordat with the Papacy failed owing to the irreconcilable doctrines of Gallicans and Ultramontanes. As a result the settlement of 1801 was retained and Louis satisfied himself by increasing the number of dioceses to eighty.

Meanwhile France had weathered the famine of 1817[2] and appeared set on a course of economic recovery. High tariffs encouraged agriculture and industry. Protection for cereals and cattle brought a rise in wheat and wool production. Coal and iron output gradually increased, steam engines were installed in the mines and textile machinery brought into operation. An ambitious programme of canal construction was launched by a combination of private enterprise and government loans. The Bank of France was able to build up increasing reserves, pay off the national debt and invest in an expanding economy. It is now generally agreed that it was

[1] See p. 172.   [2] See p. 173.

during the restoration period that the foundations of the French industrial revolution were laid.

All this, however, was of little interest to the Ultras. They denounced the Army Bill as unconstitutional, attacked the religious settlement, exploited the food shortage to criticize the ministry and even opposed the allied evacuation of France in order to embarrass the government. Led by Bonald, d'Artois and Villèle, they attacked every compromise and demanded the full restoration of the old order. The ministry tried to reduce their effectiveness by changes in the Electoral Law. In 1817 the age of voters was cut to twenty-five, and one-fifth of the Chamber was made eligible for re-election each year; new procedures introduced a direct vote by *arrondissement* and cut out electoral colleges. As a result only about 80 Ultras were elected, opposed to some 150 moderates and 25 independents. With each subsequent election the latter element increased until by 1819 there were nearly 90 independent and left wing members including Lafayette, Constant and Manuel. As a result Richelieu, who deplored the advance of the left, resigned and Decazes became head of the ministry.

Decazes continued to steer a middle course between left and right, relying on moderate and doctrinaire support against the ultra and left-wing elements who repeatedly attacked the ministry. The increase of agitation and the spread of revolutionary activity in Europe persuaded him to try to strengthen the moderate right by yet another electoral law which restored electoral colleges, suspended annual elections and gave the most highly taxed class the right to elect an extra 172 deputies. In 1820, however, all hopes of a balanced compromise were shattered by the murder of the Duc de Berry, second son of d'Artois and third in line of succession, by a fanatic outside the Paris Opera House.

Louis XVIII never forgave the murder of his nephew and fell increasingly under ultra influence. The royalists howled for Decazes' blood, accused him of being an accomplice and forced him to resign. Richelieu returned to office and government policy swung further to the right. A temporary Press Law restored a general censorship. Villèle, a firm believer in the moderate right, entered the ministry and began to control education and encourage clerical influence. The new Electoral Law brought an overwhelming royalist majority. In 1821, corn laws and higher tariffs provided increasing protection for the landed interest.

The swing to the right provoked increased opposition from the left. Lafayette, Constant and Laffitte attacked the Electoral Law and encouraged popular disturbances. In Paris, army officers and republican exiles promoted protest marches. These, however, were easily suppressed as were *Carbonari* risings organized in 1821 by liberals and Bonapartists. Mutinies in Belfort and Saumur were put down and rebellious officers at Toulon and La Rochelle shot. More significant however was the disintegration of the centre. Torn between a desire for security and the preservation of their constitutional liberties, they were unable to support either right or left-wing parties. Guizot and Royer-Collard were expelled from the Council of State but remained opposed to the growing violence of the left.

Meanwhile the royalist right renewed the initiative. Villèle became President of the ministry in 1822 and introduced press laws to curb anything injurious to public peace, religion, the King or the constitution. Chateaubriand, who became Foreign Secretary, hoped to win support from the disaffected elements and rally enthusiasm for the throne by intervention in Spain.[1] In 1823 the army marched to restore Ferdinand and the royalist cause seemed assured. Louis XVIII, now exhausted and sick, delegated authority to d'Artois and Villèle. In 1824 the elections returned a decisive ultra majority. The *Chambre retrouvée,* as it was called, demanded the full application of all right-wing policies. The death of Louis XVIII appeared to remove a final obstacle to any ultra ambition. Moderation and compromise were abandoned, the centre disintegrated, and left and right turned once again to face each other in a bitter struggle for power.

3. *Charles X and the 1830 Revolution*

The accession of the Comte d'Artois as Charles X encouraged the realization of ultra ambition. Control of the Chamber was assured; Villèle appeared firmly attached to the Court. Royalist mayors and prefects were placed in control of the provinces and ordered to curb the press. Agriculture flourish-

[1] See p. 181.

ed, industry boomed and the successful intervention of French arms in Spain added new prestige to the monarchy. The King, though chivalrous and not without charm, was a dreamer who still lived in the temper and traditions of the old order. Unintelligent, impracticable and ultra at heart, he allowed himself to be pushed into a situation which was incompatible with the ambitions of the new bourgeoisie and their interpretation of the Charter.

Villèle, though leader of the right, still believed in the importance of working within the constitution. He hoped to satisfy ultra and aristocratic demands and yet maintain the basic framework of the Charter. Such a policy, however, only increased the violence of liberal attacks, while the Ultras became more and more outraged by the slow realization of their hopes. When Villèle attempted to pacify the *émigrés* and heal revolutionary scars by introducing an indemnity for lost lands, he was attacked from left and right. Plans to raise a capital loan of 1,000 million francs by cutting the interest on government bonds from 5 per cent to 3 per cent were attacked as a 'fine on the nation'. The money distributed among 67,250 persons of almost every class was denounced as inadequate! The indemnity was nevertheless passed, after amendments in the Upper House, and did much to pacify lingering resentment.

The ministry also tried to strengthen the landed interest by a law of primogeniture which amended the Legal Code and allowed property to be handed down intact. Though only applicable to those above the 300–franc tax level, it was criticized as an attack on equality and rejected by the peers amid popular enthusiasm. The Upper Chamber, which still retained a moderate majority, was able to act as a brake on official ultra policies. It was unable, however, to prevent the gradual spread of religious influence throughout the country.

The obvious advance of Ultramontane and Catholic institutions provoked mounting agitation. Charles's coronation at Rheims cathedral amid all the pageantry and ritual of a medieval tradition aroused both anxiety and ridicule. The spread of Jesuits, *Congrégations* and missions into the provinces appeared to threaten bourgeois interests and values. Both primary and secondary schools were placed under episcopal control; by 1828, one hundred and thirty-four church schools had been established. In 1822 Mgr. Frayssinous was appointed Grand Master of the University of France. Guizot, Cousin and liberal teachers were suspended; twelve medical professors were expelled. In 1825 a law of sacrilege prescribed the death penalty for the theft of church plate; the official celebrations of the papal jubilee in the following year appeared to identify the Court with Jesuit and Ultramontane policies.

Clerical action roused increasing opposition from the moderate left and also forced the constitutionalists of the right into opposition. The press launched a bitter series of attacks against the Jesuits and the *Congrégations*. The *Globe,* which represented the views of the new liberal doctrinaires like Guizot and Cousin, became more and more political in tone while popular papers such as *le Constitutionnel* and *le Journal des Débats* attacked the clergy and organized a campaign in defence of the Charter. Efforts to curb press action generally failed as moderate and Gallican judges often refused to convict. The circulation of liberal newspapers increased to some 50,000 and, when handed round in cafés and reading rooms, must have reached a far wider public.

Ultra extremism even led to a split within the Catholic Church. The violent views of Bonald were countered by the moderate Gallicanism of Montlosier who attacked the Jesuits and vindicated press criticism. In 1824 Villèle dismissed Chateaubriand from the ministry and provoked his lasting enmity. For the next six years he led a group of liberal Catholics in violent attacks against the government and the threatened revival of a Bourbon despotism. Meanwhile the Ultras themselves were by no means satisfied by the slow pace of change and took every opportunity to undermine Villèle's position at court.

By 1827 it was clear that the ministry had become desperately unpopular and the monarch dangerously isolated. When Charles inspected the National Guard he was met by cries attacking the government. The Guard was thereupon disbanded, much to the anger of the liberal bourgeoisie. In 1826 the failure of South American loans had begun a financial panic which spread dissatisfaction and led to a gradual decline in industrial expansion. Villèle's attempts to control the press were unpopular and totally unsuccessful. A law to increase stamp duties and enforce registration was met by a flood of petitions from the provinces and defeated in the Upper House. When the government created seventy-six new peers and called new elections, moderates, liberal Catholics, republicans and industrialists combined to defeat ministerial candidates. In spite of prefectorial and official pressure Villèle lost his majority and was forced to resign.

Charles X now called on Martignac to form a ministry in an attempt to pacify the centre. He made some concessions by restricting clerical control in education, restoring Guizot and Cousin to their posts, dismissing ultra prefects and relaxing controls on the press. His actions, however, only increased the fury of both sides. The left denounced Martignac for personal ambition, duplicity and 'Villèlist' policies. The press claimed for the Chamber an absolute sovereignty and demanded a ministry responsible to the will of the people. Lawyers and republicans led by Lafayette began to urge the need for further action and drew parallels with the English revolution of 1688. In 1830 Thiers founded a new paper, the *National*, with money lent by Talleyrand, which attacked the Bourbons and demanded a government entirely responsible to the Chamber. Ultras, meanwhile, countered by vindicating the rights of the Crown and justifying absolute sovereignty.

The intentions of Charles X at this moment remained somewhat obscure. Faced by a deliberate campaign of abuse from the left he was obviously entitled to rely on support from the right. The fall of Villèle had brought him a brief moment of popularity and he hoped to consolidate his position by a successful attack on Algiers. When Martignac failed to restore a centre party, Charles called in Polignac to form a new ministry. This was, however, an unfortunate choice as it seemed to identify the Crown, once and for all, with the ultra faction. Polignac was the son of a leading *émigré*[1] and chose a ministry of unpopular extremists. Moreover he was erratic, mystical and unrealistic. His policies only hastened the downfall of the monarchy.

In June 1830 new elections were held amid unparalleled excitement. By the winter of 1829 the industrial recession had created unemployment at Lyons and in the capital. Conditions had been worsened by a long and severe winter

[1] See p. 61.

and by rising bread prices which had been further inflated by
the tariff. The outcome was a decisive liberal majority and a
clear defeat for the government. The King, however, refused
to give way. On July 25th, determined to maintain the rights
of the Crown, Charles agreed to sign five Ordinances which
suspended press liberty, dissolved the new Chamber, restored
the Electoral Law of 1817, restricted the electorate to the top
25 per cent of the voters and listed more Ultras to hold high
office. His action was interpreted as an attempt to destroy the
Charter. It also threatened bourgeois interests. A revolution
broke out that night.

Agitation was led by journalists who deliberately ignored
the censorship. Thiers drew up a protest which justified disobedience and advocated revolt. Crowds soon assembled to
denounce the ministry and shout for the Charter. No action
was taken to disperse the mob. Charles, reassured by Polignac
and gratified by victory at Algiers, went hunting; the
Chamber, unwilling to take a lead, went home. By the following day, however, the revolution in the capital had got out of
control. Republican sympathizers, led by Cavaignac and
Favre, began to build barricades. They were supported by
students and by workmen who had been supplied with arms
by their employers. By July 28th left-wing insurgents had
captured the Hôtel de Ville, the Arsenal and Nôtre-Dame,
raised the Tricolour, and demanded an end to Bourbon rule.

The revolution took everyone by surprise. The ministry
was complacent and the military preparations inadequate.
The Algiers expedition had removed veteran regiments and
the army under Marmont was forced to withdraw from the
capital. Charles X cancelled the Ordinances and dismissed the
ministry. When this failed to stem the revolt he abdicated in
favour of his grandson, and appointed Louis-Philippe, duc
d'Orléans, Lieutenant-General of the Kingdom. Meanwhile,
however, the deputies had taken charge of the revolt. Lafayette was appointed Commander of the new National Guard
and undertook to restore order in the capital.

Bourgeois members now faced the problem of recon-
structing a constitution. Suspicious of the Bourbons and
exasperated by the Ultras, they were equally alarmed by a
possible revival of mob rule and republican activity on the
left. Thiers and Laffitte now launched a propaganda cam-

paign in favour of the House of Orléans and placarded Paris with bills praising the activities of the Duke. After some hesitation Louis-Philippe came to Paris on the 31st and with the support of the moderates and the cryptic encouragement of Talleyrand agreed to accept the Lieutenant-Generalcy offered by a delegation from the Chambers.

In the afternoon the Duke and a group of supporters marched in procession to the Hôtel de Ville where Lafayette now held sway surrounded by republican crowds and supporters from the lower bourgeoisie. Lafayette, who still retained great prestige from the first revolution, had lost none of his caution and hesitancy. Having failed to declare a republic, he joined Orléans on the balcony of the Hôtel wrapped in an outsize Tricolour. As they embraced, the crowds cheered the victory of the revolution and the end of the ultra régime.

The new constitution, however, had still to be determined. Louis-Philippe was only Lieutenant-General and had some doubts about accepting the crown. Charles X had abdicated in favour of his grandson and still appeared ready to impose a legitimate succession. He was only driven from Rambouillet by Lafayette leading a procession of the National Guard. His obstruction further weakened the Bourbon cause and when the abdication was proclaimed there was no reference to any successor.

Meanwhile the republicans led by Cavaignac were being equally obstructive in urging a crusade for liberty and universal suffrage. They showed nothing but contempt for Louis-Philippe's policies of peace, prosperity and reconciliation. For the deputies in the Chamber, however, these objectives appeared paramount. Determined to effect the least possible concessions to the left, they merely modified the Charter to eliminate divine right, press censorship and extraordinary tribunals. The Chambers were to share with the King the right of initiating legislation. Further amendments could safely be left to the future.

On August 9th Louis-Philippe accepted the crown and thus endorsed the new constitution. In essence, however, it was no more than a redefinition of the Charter – now neither legitimate, nor popular, but merely upper middle class. Both Bourbons and republicans felt cheated. The new citizen–monarchy was to have an uneasy passage faced by open hostility and frequent attack from both the left and the right.

4. The Belgian Revolt

Belgium achieved independence through a combination of revolutionary action and outside aid. The union with Holland had been the direct result of Britain's policy to create a barrier against French penetration.[1] It had been imposed in spite of a hostile majority and had failed to achieve 'the intimate and complete union' called for by the allied powers. The Belgians had gained certain advantages: trade had been encouraged by canal and harbour construction; Antwerp had been opened to shipping; manufacturers were able to expand into the markets of the Dutch Empire; new banking and credit facilities from Amsterdam stimulated the economy; coal output soared, mills and engineering works flourished. These benefits, however, were not enough to offset religious and political antagonism.

The Catholic Church remained a dominant factor in the old Austrian Netherlands. It had defied Josephinism, Bonapartism and liberalism. The Catholic revival after the war had led to the restoration of seminaries and schools. Jesuit influence revived and clerical authority was re-established in the rural parishes. The Church had been encouraged by developments in France and had demanded increasing independence to defend itself against rational criticism and state intervention. William I, King of the Netherlands, had, however, inherited both a severe Calvinist background and the mentality of an eighteenth-century despot. Dutch Protestants despised Belgian subservience; William's policies were designed to establish uniform control. Seminaries and schools were to be licensed, clerical activity controlled, and all priests trained at the philosophy schools at Louvain.

The King might have gained bourgeois support for his plans had he been prepared to compromise with a liberal constitution and an administration that took account of the differences between the Dutch and Belgian provinces. His methods, however, were absolute and his actions uncompromising. In the Lower House of the Estates General repre-

[1] See p. 168.

sentation was equal though the Belgian population was nearly twice as large. The administration was heavily weighted in favour of the Dutch: they held four-fifths of all government appointments and enforced the use of Dutch or Flemish to the exclusion of French, which had always been the language of the aristocracy and upper bourgeoisie in the southern, Walloon provinces.

William insisted on maintaining his sovereignty and refused to rely on ministers. His economic policies became increasingly unpopular, while demands for increased taxation roused protests from the peasantry and the bourgeoisie. In 1822 the protective tariff was reduced to encourage trade and stimulate the prosperity of the North. In the South, however, this exposed newly established industries to British competition and roused the opposition of both management and workers. When agriculture and industry were taxed the disparity between falling wages and rising prices led to bitter dissatisfaction.

It was not until 1828, however, that social, economic and political discontents combined to promote effective action. The aristocracy of the South, who were by tradition royalist, Catholic and favourable to France, had little sympathy for the mercantile and industrial bourgeoisie who appeared liberal, anti-clerical and socially inferior. Both regarded the peasantry and the growing proletariat with indifference or hostility. Neither were sympathetic to the advanced claims of the Church. In 1827, however, William concluded a concordat with the Papacy which allowed him to veto appointments. The Catholic hierarchy now became increasingly influenced by Lamennais'[1] appeal for an alliance between the Church and liberty and agreed in 1828 to join moderate liberals agitating for a free press, free schools, ministerial responsibility and a reduction in agricultural tariffs.

Opposition gradually increased. The press joined in a violent campaign and defied the censorship. Catholic, liberal and radical journals reflected every grievance and followed events in France with excited attention. Foreign exiles and agitators increased unrest and spread demands for a division of powers or for complete independence. The industrial recession of 1829 added to the discontent: the textile industry

[1] See p. 211.

Q

in Liége slumped and towns filled with growing numbers of unemployed. The majority, however, wanted reform and a separate administration under the House of Orange rather than a complete break, as this would retain the benefits of commercial association with the North. Events, however, were to leave no room for half measures.

In 1829 William began to make moderate concessions. The censorship was relaxed, educational restrictions were lifted, attendance at Louvain was made voluntary. As in France, however, this merely encouraged agitation. Press criticism now developed unchecked and repeatedly advocated the views of Lamennais or Benjamin Constant.[1] But the Paris revolution roused only limited enthusiasm and speculation. There was no immediate desire to follow the French lead; clergy and bourgeois were indeed far from reassured by events in France. Though a few radicals may have plotted revolt, and even publicized their intentions, the majority were prepared to wait and appeared more interested in the Brussels industrial exhibition on view at the time.

On August 24th, celebrations in the capital for the King's fifty-ninth birthday were not expected to cause much trouble. Nevertheless, the government cancelled some of the events as a precaution. When next day a riot broke out during the performance of a heroic opera commemorating a Neapolitan rising the authorities were taken by surprise. Crowds soon assembled, seized arms, sacked government offices and attacked the police headquarters. Within a few hours Brussels was in the hands of radical agitators backed up by artisans, foreign refugees and the unemployed. Aristocrats and bourgeois now combined to form a Committe of Public Safety and set up a National Guard to protect property. An assembly of notables sent a delegation to the King urging an immediate meeting of the Estates General to reform the constitution. William, after some delay, agreed and the Estates met and voted for the separate administration of the two nations, but for the preservation of a union under the House of Orange.

Meanwhile, however, the radicals in Brussels had seized control. The evacuation of Dutch troops appeared to confirm the victory of the rebels. Support poured in from the provinces where the clergy often helped to rally the towns.

[1] See p. 202.

Rogier led a march of supporters from Liége; Mons, Louvain and Aix followed the lead of the capital. Here the clubs and journals now demanded total separation, the Committee of Public Safety disintegrated and a new provisional government of the bourgeois left was established. William, relying on a split in the opposition, now determined to crush the revolt. Three days' bitter fighting failed, however, to break the barricades defended by fanatical workers, bourgeois and artisans. The use of force merely intensified the hatred and made partition inevitable. In October the Dutch were driven from Antwerp after a lengthy bombardment; by the end of the month, with the exception of Luxembourg and Maastricht, Belgium was free.

In November a national congress was summoned to draw up a new constitution. A majority of the electors were moderate bourgeois who were able to defeat right-wing Orange men and left-wing radicals. National sovereignty was proclaimed and vested in a monarch whose ministers were to be responsible to a Chamber of Representatives and a Senate. Freedom of worship, education and the press were guaranteed; censorship and police control were abolished. The franchise was extended to all above the age of twenty-five, with a low tax qualification which varied by region. In all some 46,000 became eligible out of a population of 3.5 millions, over double the French proportion. Provincial autonomy, however, was restricted and local government reorganized by communes on French lines. Democratic tendencies were thus limited and the revolution remained essentially a triumph for the middle class; nevertheless it was the most liberal constitution of its day, and was to become a model for many others throughout the century.

Meanwhile, immediate survival depended on the attitudes of the major powers. Austria, Russia and Prussia were violently hostile and demanded immediate intervention. Revolts in Poland and Italy, however, distracted their attention and settlement of the problem was left in the hands of Britain and France. Wellington was prepared to recognize Belgian independence if French influence could be excluded, a policy repeatedly emphasized by Lord Palmerston who became Foreign Secretary in November. Louis-Philippe, though anxious for peace, was under pressure from the left to restore

French initiative and in an effort to please all sides sometimes appeared to follow contradictory policies.

On December 20th a five-power protocol in London recognized Belgian independence. Next month her frontiers were drawn up, excluding Maastricht and Luxembourg, and her neutrality guaranteed. The election of a sovereign created some difficulty as the Belgians chose Louis-Philippe's second son, the Duc de Nemours, who was both a popular candidate and a guarantee of French support in the Luxembourg dispute. Louis-Philippe, however, was persuaded to turn down the offer when Palmerston threatened 'immediate war'. Leopold of Saxe-Coburg was eventually elected, and married Louise of Orléans in the following year. When Talleyrand, now ambassador in London, suggested some minor frontier adjustments in favour of France, Palmerston rejected them derisively.

In the summer of 1831, however, William refused to recognize Belgian independence and declared war. French troops were sent to drive out the Dutch, while the British fleet blockaded the Scheldt. Luxembourg was partitioned, Maastricht awarded to Holland and any French suggestions for territorial gains in Belgium or Luxembourg again rejected. In 1832 a combined Anglo-French operation finally cleared the citadel at Antwerp; but the blockade had to be continued until May 1833 before all danger of Dutch intervention was eliminated.

5. *East and West*

Anglo-French intervention in the Netherlands limited their freedom of action elsewhere. In Portugal and Spain some mediation was possible. In the rest of Europe disturbances were crushed by the efforts of the eastern powers who thereby consolidated their authority and strengthened the established order. Nicholas I had been outraged by events in Belgium and France and had threatened military intervention. Metternich and Wellington, however, had remained firmly opposed to any Russian advance, and in November the Tsar was suddenly tied down by the outbreak of a revolution in Poland.

Alexander I had granted the Poles a constitution in 1815 but the Tsar's autocratic liberalism had led to increasing conflicts with the Polish Diet. Absolutism hardened after the accession of Nicholas I who was determined to uphold a rigid control over all parts of the Russian Empire.[1] The Polish administration was closely watched by the police, press censorship enforced and the army maintained under the command of Grand-Duke Constantine, the Tsar's brother. This led to growing discontent in many sections of society: the nobility, who dominated the Diet, rejected the budget and criticized the royal prerogative; army officers with western experience joined in secret patriotic societies; university intellectuals, influenced by Herder and the German romantics, preached national liberation; students at Vilna and Warsaw formed *Burschenschaften* and agitated for greater freedom and a wider Polish union.

The revolutions in France and Belgium sparked off revolt. Led by the officer school in Warsaw the movement rapidly spread to include the aristocracy and other disaffected elements. Constantine withdrew and gave the Poles time to consolidate and set up a provisional government. Rival factions, however, soon split up the rebels. While moderates in the Diet urged negotiation, extremists demanded the deposition of the Tsar and staged a further rising in the capital. Neither party was prepared to grant concessions to the peasants who remained largely indifferent to the appeals of their feudal masters. In 1831 Nicholas was able to counter-attack. A *ukase* modified manorial dues and secured peasant neutrality. Conflicts between 'whites' and 'reds' paralysed resistance. Cholera weakened both armies and undermined the opposition. The Poles were defeated at Ostrolenka and Warsaw was reoccupied in September. Desperate appeals to London and Paris failed to produce more than medical supplies. Though Lafayette raised hope and urged action, both governments were fully occupied in Belgium. Morever, Poland was too remote and beyond the reach of the British fleet. Prussia and Austria were free to close their borders and give the Tsar full moral support. Poland was reoccupied, the constitution destroyed and the country erased from the map.

In Germany and Italy *Burschenschaften* and *Carbonari* agitation revived. Students and bourgeois liberals were

[1] See Ch. XII

stirred up by professors and press articles throughout the
German states. Göttingen, Heidelberg and Freiburg were the
scene of miniature revolutions; the rulers of Brunswick, Hanover and Saxony were forced to grant constitutions. But once
again enthusiasm was limited to an intellectual minority.
Though the peasants of Hesse-Cassel burnt their tax assess-
ments, the majority remained indifferent. The aristocracy
were hostile and the princes, led by Frederick William III of
Prussia, determined to counter-attack. Metternich's preoccupation in Italy, however, delayed action and for two years
liberalism was allowed to flourish. In May 1832 a festival at
Hambrach brought together students, professors, liberals,
journalists and exiled Poles. Dressed in romantic costume they
unfurled the national flag, sang patriotic songs and denounced
the Holy Alliance.

In June 1832 Metternich summoned the Diet at Frankfurt
and passed the Six Acts. Popular gatherings were banned,
tricolour flags suppressed, state diets were curbed, and the
press carefully censored. Constitutions once again lapsed and
agitation declined. A desperate attempt by students and
exiles to seize the Frankfurt Guard House in April 1833
failed. A commission meeting in Mainz expelled liberals and
curbed criticism. Opposition melted away; more than romantic
enthusiasts and disaffected intellectuals were needed to
threaten the combined power of reactionary governments.

In Italy opposition was equally unsuccessful. Anti-clerical
aristocrats, *Carbonari* officers, students and bourgeois groups
hoped to stir up revolt with the aid of France and the support
of Francis, the ambitious ruler of Modena. Secret negotiation
and conspiratorial rivalry, however, caused lengthy delay. By
1831 Louis-Philippe had secured his throne and was able to
reject republican plans for intervention. Francis, anticipating
action by Metternich, arrested the rebel leaders. Nevertheless
revolution broke out in the papal Legations and in Modena.
Francis fled to Mantua while the Pope appealed for aid.
Metternich, reassured by the news from France, was now free
to send in troops and crush the revolt. Police control was restored and agitation crushed. When *Carbonari* leaders retired
to Lyons to plan an invasion of Italy they were dispersed by

French troops. The secret societies disintegrated, filled with bitterness and a sense of betrayal.

In November 1831 Mehemet Ali of Egypt demanded payment for his intervention in the Greek revolt, launched an attack on the Sultan and rapidly swept through Syria. His victory at Konieh in 1832 opened the way to Constantinople and seemed to threaten the dissolution of the Ottoman Empire. As neither Palmerston nor Louis-Philippe were free to send assistance Mahmoud was forced to rely on Russia. In 1829 a secret commission had stated 'that the advantages offered by the preservation of the Ottoman Empire exceeded its inconveniences'. A fleet and 10,000 troops were therefore sent to the Bosphorus to repel any Egyptian assault. Palmerston, who believed quite wrongly that Russia wished to partition the Empire, now attempted to rally Austria and France. The Sultan was persuaded to surrender Syria by the convention of Kutahiya and Russian troops induced to withdraw in July. Before their departure, however, the Treaty of Unkiar-Skelessi (July 8th, 1833) bound the Sultan to close the Dardanelles to foreign warships and to rely on Russian aid for the next eight years in case of attack.

Reolution, unrest and the Mehemet Ali crisis persuaded the eastern powers to reaffirm their alliance at Münchengrätz in September. The Polish settlement was accepted and the preservation of the Ottoman Empire confirmed. A convention signed at Berlin in October called for a strengthening of the conservative system, the preservation of the 1815 treaties, and the need for mutual aid to destroy revolutionary movements. But, though Europe was divided into spheres of influence, effective action was limited to central and eastern areas. In the West, Palmerston was able with French support to give aid and encouragement to liberal agitation in order to counteract the influence of the eastern powers.

In 1826 the death of John VI had reopened the conflicts between the constitutionalists and absolutists in Portugal. The next in line, Dom Pedro, was also Emperor of Brazil and had abdicated the Portuguese crown in favour of his daughter, Maria, after issuing a new Charter and setting up a regency under his brother, Dom Miguel. Ultra-royalist forces had, however, been able to regroup in Spain and make a determined counter-attack which was only defeated when Canning sent 5,000 troops in 1827 to safeguard the government. The Wellington ministry, however, had withdrawn the troops in the following year and the Ultras had again been able to seize control. The army, aristocracy and clergy now welcomed the return of Dom Miguel from Vienna. In spite of an oath to the constitution he quickly dissolved the Chamber, recalled the old Estates and assumed the crown amid general enthusiasm.

Portuguese liberals were forced to retire to a life of exile in England until 1831 when Dom Pedro returned from Brazil to take up his daughter's cause. Using a small base in the Azores he made determined efforts to restore Maria's authority. At first Palmerston was unable and unwilling to give official aid, but Dom Pedro was able to raise a loan for £2 million on the London market. Louis-Philippe was more helpful, allowed Pedro to levy mercenaries in France and seized Dom Miguel's fleet on the pretext that the Portuguese government had failed to protect French citizens. In 1832 Pedro was thus free to land on the mainland and seize Oporto. There, however, he was besieged by the forces of Miguel who was able to rally the Church and the peasantry to his support. Pedro only survived with the unofficial assistance of French, English and Irish mercenaries. In 1833, Charles Napier became Admiral of Pedro's navy and with the aid of British seamen destroyed Miguel's fleet and seized Lisbon. Portugal degenerated into confusion with rival governments imposing varying degrees of terror and displaying equal measures of incompetence.

The end of the Belgian and Near East crises restored the possibility of French and British intervention. 'The principle of not interfering,' noted Grey, the Prime Minister, 'had to have its practical limits!' Action was hastened by events in Spain. The death of Ferdinand in 1833 revived the conflicts of the post-war years.[1] Liberals, army officers and anti-clerical aristocrats rallied to a regency for Ferdinand's daughter Isabella. A *Cortes* was summoned and a constitution based on the French Charter restored. In addition, Spanish aid to Dom Miguel was cut off and his position became increasingly precarious. Nevertheless, Don Carlos, Ferdinand's brother,

[1] See p. 436.

rallied the clergy, the peasantry and provincial interests in an attack on the new liberal government and threatened to reduce Spain to total anarchy.

In April 1834 a Quadruple Alliance was eventually negotiated between Britain, France and the constitutional governments in Spain and Portugal. Dom Miguel was expelled and Pedro and Maria persuaded to inaugurate a more moderate régime based on the Portuguese Charter, with a *Cortes* and a general amnesty. In Spain the liberals were assisted by the French and Don Carlos was defeated after five years of confused fighting.[1] Palmerston claimed that the alliance was a counter-weight to the secret Münchengrätz agreements. Its influence, however, was by no means equally effective. Constitutional governments in the peninsula remained unstable, exclusive and frequently corrupt, while in the East the Holy Alliance was able to maintain a rigid and purposeful authority.

Nevertheless, events in the West did illustrate a very gradual weakening of absolute control. The French and Belgian revolutions had achieved an obvious break from the established order of things and this had been at least partially reflected by events in Portugal and Spain. The development of France during the next two decades was to show that such hesitant moves were not enough to absorb the changes which were beginning to transform the social and economic structure of much of central and western Europe.

[1] See pp. 437–8.

X · THE JULY MONARCHY AND THE 1848 REVOLUTION

1. *Louis-Philippe and the July Monarchy*

IN France the July revolution had assured the supremacy of the upper bourgeoisie. The Charter was redefined to exclude the constitutional claims of both the ultra right and the republican left. Divine right, press censorship and special tribunals were swept away. The Catholic Church lost its monopoly as the religion of state. At the same time republican demands for decentralization and a wider franchise were carefully evaded. The new Electoral Law reduced the tax qualification of deputies to 500 francs and of electors to 200 francs. The franchise now totalled 168,000 and grew with the increasing prosperity of the next sixteen years to 241,000. The electors controlled local councils and jury service. The National Guard was reorganized and effective membership limited to those who paid direct taxation. Ultra prefects, sub-prefects and mayors were replaced by local bourgeois in a purge which swept away the officials of the old régime. The hereditary peerage was abolished and replaced by life peers who reflected the values and ambitions of a new middle-class plutocracy.

Louis-Philippe was himself in part a reflection and a personification of the new order. As 'King of the French' he was committed to share power with the nation's representatives and always governed with a ministry that was able to command a majority in the Chamber. He satisfied the bourgeoisie by a lavish distribution of suitable titles, offices and honours. He reflected their regular, cautious and complacent manner. He was affable and good humoured, ready to talk to anyone and to meet delegations from every quarter. He inspected the National Guard with regularity in the first ten years of his reign and talked with confident ease to almost all on any subject. His familiarity, however, became something of a liability: a combination of conceit and cultivated stooping roused increasing antipathy and brought the monarchy into ridicule and contempt.

From the beginning the July Monarchy was attacked by all those who felt themselves cheated or betrayed. The legitimist followers of Charles X were outraged at the usurpation of Orléans and tried to keep alive the memory of an ultra-clerical tradition. Republicans regarded the monarch with contempt and waited for further occasion to achieve their ambitions. The liberal Catholics led by Lamennais attacked a system that gave them neither God nor liberty. Secret societies, anarchists and idealists advocated violent action and attempted almost annually to assassinate the King. Louis-Philippe, however, maintained a surprising calm and slowly managed to stabilize the régime.

The King first tried to combine the moderates of both the left and the right in a centre coalition, and formed a government that included both doctrinaires from the '*partie de résistance*' and members of the moderate-left from a '*partie du mouvement*'. But its members were unable to co-operate and failed to cope with the Parisian mob, the trial of Charles' dispossessed ministers and the Belgian crisis. In November the King veered to the left in the hope that Laffitte and Lafayette would control the agitation of their republican supporters. This, however, they were unable or unwilling to do. The indicted ministers had to be rescued from a howling mob outside the court-house. Anti-clerical rioters broke up ultra services, burnt down the bishop's palace and threw the library into the Seine.

When Lafayette urged intervention in Italy, Poland and Belgium and threatened to plunge France into war,[1] the King swung back to the right. Lafayette resigned from the National Guard and a new ministry was formed under Casimir-Périer. The new Prime Minister was forceful and determined. With the aid of doctrinaires like Guizot, Molé and de Broglie he was able to exercise a measure of control. Cabinet responsibility was enforced and the administration reorganized. A Riot Act was passed to curb violence and a policy of 'order without loss of liberty at home, and peace without loss of honour abroad' proclaimed.

It was a year, however, before the '*partie de résistance*' could feel secure. Meanwhile the '*partie du mouvement*' opened a violent attack on the ministry in the press. The

[1] See pp. 235–6.

Tribune and the *National* ridiculed both the King and the government. Republicans incited unrest and extreme left-wing agitators led by Blanqui and Raspail stirred up revolutionary action. A revolt by the silk-workers of Lyons, who demanded new wage scales, was put down by the army; riots organized by *Les Amis du Peuple* were curbed by the National Guard. When Casimir-Périer died in the 1832 cholera epidemic, de Broglie became Prime Minister. He continued the work of reconstruction. The Local Government Act established bourgeois control in the provinces. Guizot's Education Act set up primary schools in every commune to build up the foundations of 'the new moral order'.

Extremist activity gradually discredited the opposition and brought increasing support to the régime. An attempt by the Duchess de Berry to rouse the Vendée ended in a miserable fiasco. Efforts by a new *Société des droits de l'homme* and isolated anarchists led to futile bloodshed A second rising in Lyons was crushed in 1834, and a revolt in the Paris sections was put down with some violence. A mass trial of conspirators brought out Blanqui, Buonarroti and Lamennais in their defence, but eventually disillusioned the public. When an 'infernal machine' of loaded gun barrels failed to kill the King and mowed down some three dozen spectators, the National Guard cheered and Louis-Philippe received an ovation. In September 1834 new laws strengthened action against libel, forbade attacks on the monarchy and allowed juries to give their verdicts in secret by a majority vote. All parties were to be free, but only within the framework of the constitutional monarchy. The *Tribune* and the left-wing *Réformateur* were heavily fined and forced to close down. The secret societies were rooted out by the police and began to disintegrate.

France appeared set on a course of increasing prosperity and stable government. The depression of the early 'thirties had been followed by a steady growth in agriculture and industry. A law of 1836 encouraged the upkeep of secondary roads; 1837 witnessed the construction of the first railways. Patriotism was roused by expeditions to conquer Algeria and by arches and obelisks designed to commemorate the triumphs of the past. It was therefore unfortunate that both the doctrinaires and the moderates should now split up into rival factions and undermine the solidarity of the centre. Louis-Philippe was encouraged to intervene personally in the political arena, and left-wing parties were given renewed opportunities for criticism and attack.

The main cause of the conflict was the personal rivalry between Thiers and Guizot. While Guizot elevated himself into the supreme apologist of the 'golden mean', *juste milieu*, with leanings to the right, Thiers was anxious to promote his own interests and ambition by an alliance with the moderate left. The split in the government led to its defeat in 1836 and the King now gave Thiers the chance to form a ministry. But his wild oscillations between left and right, between support for Metternich and for the Spanish liberals, threatened to lead to war with Spain.[1] Louis-Philippe therefore stepped in, dismissed Thiers and restored the doctrinaires under Molé and Guizot. The new ministry, however, soon collapsed. Guizot, who was put in second place, felt himself slighted and now joined up with Thiers to attack Molé and the growing influence of the King. To win support Thiers and Guizot then moved on to join up with Barrot and the moderate left and began to denounce the King's 'personal government'. When they won the 1839 elections, however, neither was prepared to serve under the other and no ministry could be formed.

Meanwhile France drifted into crises at home and abroad. An amnesty in 1837 had freed Blanqui who began rapidly to build up a new secret society, *Les Saisons,* with the assistance of Barbès and other Babouvists. The paralysis in government was considered a suitable moment to launch a revolution. On May 12th, 1839, the left-wing sections were roused, gun-shops looted and soldiers disarmed. But the masses refused to move, the leaders were arrested and rapidly returned to prison. In the Ottoman Empire the renewal of war between the Sultan and Mehemet Ali reopened the Eastern Question at a critical moment. France had poured increasing military, financial and economic aid into Egypt in order to build up her own presence in that area. The fortunes of Mehemet Ali were thus closely linked to both French prestige and France's commercial interests.

A caretaker ministry under Soult failed to satisfy Thiers or

[1] See p. 438.

the moderate left and appeared to sacrifice French interests in Egypt to the policies of the major powers. In 1840 Thiers began his second ministry with the support of moderate-centre and left-wing elements. Republican agitation revived and the *National* began to urge electoral reform and universal suffrage. Laffitte opened a campaign of 'reform banquets' in Lyons and Grenoble, and collected petitions advocating a moderate extension of the franchise. Simultaneously Thiers' activity threatened to plunge France into a war against the whole of Europe. The major powers, suspicious as ever of each other's motives, were united in their determination to preserve the Ottoman Empire and repel Mehemet Ali. On July 15th, 1840, they agreed to act in concert and put pressure on Egypt to abandon Syria. Thiers roused a war fever in France and prepared to defy all comers. The fleet was manned, defences prepared and invasion plans drafted.

Louis-Philippe, however, again stepped in to avoid a collision. Shares had dropped and a financial panic threatened the stability of the bourgeois régime. Moderates and doctrinaires were equally horrified by the revival of republican activity and the threat to their established order. A war against the whole of Europe was an obvious absurdity. Thiers was dismissed and a government formed under Soult with Guizot as its chief spokesman. Control swung to the right; the spectre of war and a republican revival were repelled. Guizot restored the King's policy of peace and prosperity, but with an intellectual rigidity that was in the end to provoke yet another revolution.

2. Guizot and the Golden Mean

Guizot, who dominated the ministry from 1840 to its fall in 1848, had decided views about both his own ability and the nature of government and society. He had been professor of history at the Sorbonne and a minister in the governments of Molé and de Broglie. He was determined to apply his academic principles to the politics of his day. He believed that the achievements of the upper bourgeoisie represented the highest limits of human progress; that the existing social order was a perfect combination of individual freedom and established authority; that the July Monarchy was thus the best system to harmonize society within a constitutional framework. The great conquests had been made and it remained only 'to assure the enjoyment of what had been conquered'. Property, the family and the foundations of society had to be defended, the Charter maintained, faction eliminated, and the electorate held down to its predetermined level.

Louis-Philippe found in Guizot his most accomplished minister. As the King approached his seventieth year in 1843 he became increasingly conservative. The accidental death of his eldest son, the popular Duc d'Orléans, was a tragic shock which undermined his interest, weakened his concentration and opened up acrimonious discussions about a regency. His main concern was now to preserve the dynasty. He believed, with Guizot, that the way to do so was by preventing change and by upholding a system which seemed to ensure a permanent equilibrium. Guizot had saved the King from the policies of Thiers and the demands of the left; he would now allow him to die in harness and preserve the achievements of the monarchy.

Guizot was indeed able to establish an illusion of permanence and stability that embraced the Chambers, the administration and most of France. With the aid of conservatives, doctrinaires, crown servants and persuasive bribes he maintained a majority in the Assembly. Prefects and mayors kept a tactful hold on the countryside and watched elections 'with impartiality but not with indifference'. In 1846 the government won a striking electoral victory, in spite of the combined efforts of the opposition, and Guizot was able, with increasing confidence, to predict the continuity of the régime.

Stability seemed assured by the expansion of the economy and the increasing prosperity of the bourgeoisie. Under the July Monarchy coal, iron and cotton production more than doubled. Coke furnaces began to overtake charcoal; mechanical looms and spindles displaced with increasing rapidity the hand-looms of cottage industries. Progress in transport was considerable and now included the maintenance and reconstruction of secondary roads. These enormously speeded the distribution of agricultural produce and opened up the countryside to new competitive pressures. Canal building was maintained and the first railways opened in the 1830s. These were planned by the State in keeping with economic and strategic interests, but financed and run by private companies who added rails and rolling stock to the national fairway. In the 1840s France was seized by a railway mania; between thirty and forty companies were formed and some two thousand miles of line constructed.

Expansion was only possible as a result of increased credit and a steady rise in note circulation. 'Now the bankers will rule,' Laffitte remarked after the July revolution. Their influence soon permeated the economy and the social framework. The Bank of France maintained a high cash reserve ratio and thus helped to stabilize the currency and keep a steady mean price level. Circulation rose by some 50 per cent, but as industrial output increased by over 200 per cent there was, if anything, a tendency for prices to fall. Provincial banks supplied loans to the cities and in the countryside. Funds were, however, inadequate to cover demand. Railways had to be financed by big bankers like Rothschild and Laffitte and by government subsidies and private companies. In addition nearly half the capital was drawn from the London money market.

Economic change came in slow stages rather than by any revolutionary development. Lack of credit, raw materials and communications were combined with an unwillingness among artisans and peasants to abandon traditional methods. Small workshops run by lower bourgeois craftsmen remained the basis of industrial activity. Peasant consolidation and land bargaining absorbed the attention of country life. Nevertheless, bankers and capitalists, joint-stock and insurance companies appeared to dominate the State and create a network of vested interests closely linked to the doctrinaires. Manufacturers were protected by high tariffs, investors by limited liability, the railways by state assistance, and employers by the free traditions of *laissez-faire*. For Guizot it was the 'conservative principle in everything'; unfortunately, it brought little benefit to any but those who so obviously proclaimed it.

Beneath the affluent surface of society there were signs of growing discontent. The rising population in the countryside created a land hunger and an accelerating drift to the towns. Competition from the new industrial areas undermined village manufacture and destroyed the alternatives to rural employment. This added yet another influx of labour into the cities where conditions became increasingly deplorable. In Lille one-third of the population lived in permanent poverty; at Rouen 60 per cent of the workers had not enough to live on; in Paris *les classes dangereuses* rose to number nearly 60,000. They often lived in holes or cellars, lacking light and air, and ate only bread or potatoes. Many found employment in the new factories and worked a twelve- to fifteen-hour day. By 1848 over a million Frenchmen were employed in 'large-scale' industrial plants employing over ten workers. Their condition was generally sickening. Their unions remained illegal, and any strike action was punishable by fines, dismissal and lengthy terms of imprisonment.

The effect on artisans and lower bourgeois enterprise was equally discouraging. While capitalist concentration squeezed them from above, cheap labour undermined their status and security from below. In 1850 1.5 million masters still employed 2.8 million men in small workshops in most of the cities. The large majority were concentrated in Paris which thus began to highlight the contradictions in the Guizot régime. Builders, printers and weavers formed secret associations and followed the socialist doctrines of Proudhon and Louis Blanc. In 1843 the *Réforme* under the editorship of Flocon, began a bitter attack on the government and demanded drastic social reforms.

But the ministry remained largely unaware of any need for action. Almost the only reform passed was the Factory Act of 1841 which prohibited the employment of children under the age of eight in factories using steam power or employing over twenty persons. Work for children between the ages of eight and sixteen was also restricted, but little was done to enforce these limits as no inspectors were appointed to put them into effect. Even less was done to protect women, who might earn only one franc a day, and conditions in factories and mines continued to deteriorate. Nevertheless, for Guizot such problems did not even exist. In 1847 he was confidently able to report 'that for the moment there was nothing, no grave questions, nothing!'

By then, however, dissatisfaction had spread to the middle ranks of the bourgeoisie. Rising prosperity had increased the electorate by some 50 per cent, but this was not enough to

R

satisfy the ambitions of the new bourgeois and the many respectable citizens who paid under 200 francs in tax. The *National* spread republican agitation and urged universal suffrage; in 1841 Ledru-Rollin became leader of the republican left and began to attack the social and political institutions of the country with increasing violence. Guizot may have been justified in claiming that such attacks were bound to destroy liberty and public order. But when the government rejected proposals for even a small extension of the franchise or any reduction in the number of state officials in the Chamber, Thiers, Barrot and the moderates were forced to join the republican camp to assure their own political survival. Guizot's complete inflexibility left them with no alternative but to unite with the moderate left. By 1848 even the National Guard had become affected. Though the higher officers remained loyal, the rank and file were increasingly disillusioned by the stagnation which permeated political life.

In 1843 Lamartine, poet, orator and romantic republican also joined in the attack and drew an increasing volume of support from students and intellectuals. 'France is bored,' he declared in 1839 and by 1846 he was predicting that nothing could galvanize it but a crisis: 'If man's genius was to remain immobile there was no need for statesmen, stake-posts would be enough.' Guizot, however, did not see it that way. For him factions were dead and the new order was universal.

Guizot remained preoccupied with education and foreign affairs where, however, his policies began to arouse widespread misgiving. Measures to strengthen state control over secondary schools and the University of France roused bitter opposition from the Catholic hierarchy and led to mounting attacks from the right. Attempts to solve the conflict had been shelved for nearly ten years before a bill was eventually introduced to allow recognized denominations the right to open schools under conditions laid down by the State. This compromise, however, pleased neither side and merely intensified the conflict.

Meanwhile Guizot's foreign policy had led to conflict with Britain and a closer alignment with Metternich. The fall of Thiers in 1840 had helped lessen Anglo-French hostility and in 1841 France rejoined the Great Powers to sign the Straits

Convention which stabilized the Eastern Question and placed the Dardanelles under five-power guarantee.[1] Relations continued to improve with the fall of Palmerston and the close *entente* established between Guizot and Lord Aberdeen. An exchange of royal visits appeared to cement Anglo–French understanding, though Guizot was accused of subservience to British policies and his peaceful intentions were attacked as unpatriotic. In 1846, however, agreement was shattered by the Spanish marriages crisis. The problem of finding a husband for the eleven-year-old Queen Isabella created a network of intrigue between governments and ambassadors. While Aberdeen advocated the claims of Saxe-Coburg, Guizot urged a Spanish Bourbon or the Duc d'Aumâle, younger son of Louis-Philippe. Discussions were left inconclusive and both sides agreed not to put pressure on Madrid, relying on a free choice in their own favour. Meanwhile rival ambassadors were urging their respective candidates. By 1846 a compromise was found in the Duc de Cadiz, and the problem shifted to Isabella's younger sister Maria Louisa. The French felt they now had a stronger claim and Montpensier, Louis-Philippe's youngest son was proposed. When Palmerston returned in 1846 and re-opened the Saxe-Coburg claims all the parties became exasperated and Guizot agreed to push ahead with the French proposals. Palmerston was furious, Queen Victoria shocked and the *entente* shattered beyond repair.

Queen Victoria liked to think that Louis-Philippe's troubles began with the Spanish marriages crisis. Its influence, however, was very indirect: uncertainty helped to hasten the financial crash in 1847; Guizot was forced to counter British hostility by opening negotiations with Metternich. As a result he was unable to support the liberal revival in Italy or protest with vigour at the Austrian annexation of Cracow.[2] In Switzerland he supported the Catholic cantons against the radical government without success. Palmerston rejected intervention and opened correspondence with Thiers and the opposition who attacked Guizot's policies as ineffective and reactionary. More significant, the government appeared preoccupied with foreign affairs and failed to take account of the worsening situation at home. Here an economic crisis increased the dissatisfaction of the

[1] See p. 309.   [2] See p. 306.

bourgeoisie, the artisans and the new proletariat, and further
undermined the confidence of the financial community. All
combined to demand varying degrees of parliamentary, electoral or social reform and, when faced by the total inflexibility of Guizot and the government, were swept forward by
extremist elements into a new round of revolutionary action.

3. *The Revolution of 1848*

The French Revolution of 1848 was the result of innumerable factors which, together, fused into violent, almost spontaneous erruption. Varied emphasis has been placed on the
economic, social and political elements involved. All are of
significance, as are the characters who failed or succeeded in
measuring up to the events.

The economic crisis, which marked the closing years of the
July Monarchy, is often taken as a basic cause of the revolt. In
1845 the harvest was disastrous. It was little better in 1846
when potato blight damaged much of the crop and added to
the food shortage. The price of bread doubled in some
regions; shops were looted and grain transports attacked.
Rioters were severely punished and the repressive measures
increased the bitterness felt by the hungry and the unemployed. But the 1847 harvest was excellent and, by the
autumn, prefects were confidently reporting an end to the
emergency.

The critical harvests were, however, partially responsible
for a financial crash and a general slump in 1847. Large sums
of cash were sent abroad to pay for grain imports and this cut
down the reserves available for domestic credit. The railway
mania had already led to the creation of companies whose
capital reserves were inadequate to carry out their commitments; when they were unable to obtain fresh loans, many
went into liquidation. A combination of falling demand and
declining output increased anxiety, promoted bankruptcy and
hastened a general recession. Unemployment rose, especially
in rural industries, vagrancy increased and Paris was filled
with the dispossessed and the demoralized. But the general
atmosphere was one of dejection and apathy rather than of
revolution. Many anticipated a revival of activity and a renewal of business confidence during the coming year.

The fragmentation of society was regarded by acute political observers like de Tocqueville as a far greater threat to the stability of the régime. Not only were the aristocracy divided between legitimists, Bonapartists and Orléanists, but the ruling bourgeois circle had become increasingly separated from the moderate core of the middle class and also from artisan and lower middle-class elements. They had become a *pays légal*, detached by their property and vested interests from the *pays reél*, in which the rest of the country lived and worked. In 1846 and 1847 a number of scandals appeared to suggest that their society was riddled with corruption. Doubtful government contracts, murders and suicides led to exaggerated accusations of vice which helped to discredit the ministry.

Guizot, however, remained unperturbed and continued to act as though in complete command of the situation. His doctrinaire attitudes had been conditioned by an isolated and academic atmosphere. His confidence had been confirmed by victory in the 1846 elections which could not be entirely explained as the outcome of bribery or forceful persuasion. Indeed Guizot's attitude to politics and economics reflected all too clearly the interests of the upper bourgeoisie: the exclusive detachment of the man of property, the indifference of the liberal economist to human misery and misfortune.

The opposition, meanwhile, was forming up into a formidable alliance. Thiers and the centre, who only wanted to limit the number of royal officials in the Chamber and to broaden the electorate, had already joined Barrot and the moderate left. Their paper, the *National*, agitated for a 100-franc franchise with special categories to include professional men and all members of the National Guard. The inclusion of the Guard was to be of special significance as many of the junior officers failed to reach the minimum tax qualification and became increasingly hostile to a government that refused to give them a vote.

Even more significant, however, was the further alliance between the moderate left and the republican opposition led by Ledru-Rollin. Many moderates who had originally supported the July Monarchy now appeared committed, even if unwillingly, to a policy advocating its overthrow. The republicans demanded universal suffrage which for Guizot appeared quite incompatible with the Charter. Their left-wing allies on the *Réforme* added demands for social reforms

and supported the policies of moderate socialists led by
Flocon and Louis Blanc. They represented the views of lower
bourgeois artisans and craftsmen anxious for their security
and social status.

On the extreme left were the advocates of violence –
Blanqui, Barbès and their followers – who were prepared to
exploit any division in the centre in order to revive revolutionary action. But their support was limited. Many workers
preferred the more constructive attitude of Louis Blanc while
others adhered to passive socialist or communist doctrines.[1]
Lines were blurred and interests obscured by the romantic
oratory of Lamartine who appealed to the idealism of young
and old, and believed that all could be satisfied within the
framework of a new republic.

The refusal of Guizot to make even a gesture in favour of
parliamentary or electoral reform finally split the supporters
of the dynasty and drove all the moderate opposition into the
republican camp. After the 1846 elections they realized the
hopelessness of constitutional action and began to rally support outside the Chamber by a series of reform banquets.
While Barrot spoke for moderate adjustment, Ledru-Rollin
and Louis Blanc urged more violent action. New histories of
the French Revolution by Louis Blanc, Michelet and
Lamartine glamorized violence and influenced student agitation. Jacobin traditions revived, new organizations and
secret societies were built up in the artisan quarters. Robespierre was openly praised and a network of revolutionary
cells revived in the capital. In 1847 Lamartine published his
Histoire des Girondins and told a large audience: 'My book
needs a sequel; you are making it.'

The crisis, which many had regarded as inevitable but few
seemed to expect, came to a head in February 1848. On
December 28th, 1847, the King had condemned 'agitation
fomented by hostile or blind passions' in his speech from the
throne. When a group of officers from the National Guard decided to hold a banquet in Paris authorization was refused.
The opposition parties denounced the government and a
hundred deputies led by Barrot decided to take the lead and
hold a Parisian banquet on February 22nd. A rising tide of
agitation, however, created alarm among the moderate

[1] See pp. 204-6.

deputies and on February 19th they reached agreement with the government to restrain their enthusiasm and modify the demonstration. This, however, encouraged the republican left to take independent action and on the 21st both the *National* and the *Réforme* gave marching orders to the National Guard and urged defiant demonstrations. The moderates, now thoroughly alarmed, cancelled the whole project and rallied to the régime. The republicans equally afraid of violence, also abandoned the demonstration, while Flocon and Louis Blanc realizing their isolation, urged caution and deprecated any real conflict.

It was now, however, too late to avoid some revolutionary action. On February 22nd angry students, left-wing agitators, artisans and unemployed seized arms, erected barricades and processed through Paris shouting 'Down with Guizot'. Their action, however, only hastened a renewal of moderate allegiance to the constitution. The demonstration failed to achieve its objectives and by nightfall Paris appeared under control. A series of accidents and miscalculations now precipitated the sudden and unexpected collapse of the monarchy. When the National Guard was called out next day many legions appeared apathetic or openly hostile. Louis-Philippe, who had clung to Guizot till the last moment, now lost his nerve, dismissed his minister and called on Molé to form a ministry. While negotiations proceeded the army was left without instructions and extreme left-wing groups were given time to organize renewed demonstrations. When a procession pressed against troops guarding the Foreign Office in the Boulevard des Capucines a shot led to panic and a volley which wounded or killed some fifty marchers. The bodies were immediately put in a cart and driven round the streets while the tocsin rang and barricades appeared in every quarter.

February 24th witnessed the final collapse of the régime. Thiers and Barrot were called in to form a government and General Bugeaud, an Algerian veteran, summoned to clear the streets. Louis-Philippe, however, was not prepared to authorize a general massacre and the army was allowed to disperse and fraternize with the revolutionaries. When the King went to inspect the National Guard outside the palace he was greeted by shouts denouncing the system and urging reform. Thoroughly demoralized, Louis-Philippe agreed to abdicate in favour of his grandson, the Comte de Paris. As angry crowds moved towards the palace between lines of indifferent troops, the royal family escaped to Dreux and to eventual exile in England.

4. Class and Conflict

The February revolution was won by the *petit bourgeois*, artisans and intellectuals who with the unemployed *classes dangereuses* had followed up the lead of a moderate bourgeois opposition and then seized the initiative. The moderates, however, only wanted to remove Guizot and if necessary force the King to abdicate without destroying the essential character of the régime. They now hastened to join with the conservatives in an attempt to restore the established order and proclaim a regency for the Comte de Paris. The Duchesse d'Orléans was brought to the Chamber to plead the cause of the dynasty together with her sons. But it was too late. The capital was in the hands of the mob: while some sacked the palace and occupied the Post Office, Police Headquarters and the Hôtel de Ville, others marched to the Chamber to prevent any repetition of the events of 1830. When the crowd poured in all thoughts of a regency were hastily abandoned; the Duchess and the moderates fled; the republican remnant was left in command.

The republicans in the Chamber thus had leadership suddenly thrust upon them and were forced to temporize with the crowd. Dupont de l'Eure, a veteran of over eighty, took the chair while members drew up lists of names for a provisional government. These had already been discussed in the offices of the *National* and were now acclaimed by the spectators. A final list of seven included Lamartine, Ledru-Rollin, Dupont and Arago, a distinguished astronomer; all were bourgeois of the moderate left, dedicated to order and the preservation of property. At the Hôtel de Ville they were faced by another crowd of some 200,000 artisans and unemployed demanding recognition of socialist and *petit bourgeois* interests; their policies had been formulated at the rival offices of the *Réforme,* where a second list of ministers had been drafted. Both parties now agreed to form an uneasy alliance. Louis Blanc, Flocon and Marrast were included in the government first as under-secretaries but finally as full members. Lastly, Albert, a workers' representative and a member of the *Nouvelles Saisons*, was added to the list as a result of popular pressure.

From the very start elements on the extreme left mistrusted the middle-class complexion of the provisional government. Both the original republicans and the additional socialist members believed in property and profit. Louis Blanc's 'right to work' might ensure survival in a competitive community but it failed to guarantee genuine security. Communists, left-wing socialists and secret societies were, however, divided and not yet prepared for action. Some were satisfied by the inclusion of Louis Blanc and Albert in the provisional government; many like Cabet, Fourier, Proudhon and their followers were idealists or theorists with a hatred of violence. Blanqui, the apostle of immediate action, only emerged from prison on the 25th of February and soon realized his isolation and the futility of an immediate revolt. Nevertheless the extreme left continued to agitate, demanded the red flag and shouted for a democratic republic and for social reform. The provisional government eventually agreed to declare a republic and guarantee work. But Lamartine in a rousing speech saved the Tricolour for France as the embodiment of past achievement and future hope. Red rosettes were to be worn as a compromise!

The Second Republic began on a wave of optimism and keen expectation. Universal suffrage was decreed and elections fixed for mid-April; slavery was abolished and the press freed from restraints; workers were promised the right to form combinations; prefects and nearly all sub-prefects were replaced by new *commissaires* with wide powers to carry the revolution into the provinces. In the towns a series of miniature revolts followed the lead of the capital. Artisans and unemployed seized arms, built barricades, attacked monastic and managerial property and smashed textile and printing machines. Trees of liberty were planted with the support of the bourgeoisie and the blessing of many of the lower clergy. Violence was in general confined to the older industrial towns like Lyons, Lille, Rouen, Rheims and Marseilles, where new capitalist methods had undermined the security of traditional industries and craft methods. Nevertheless it was enough to create anxiety in the minds of the moderate middle class anxious to preserve their property and their order.

Bourgeois interests soon began to influence the actions of the provisional government. The revolution had led to panic on the Stock Exchange; the value of government securities had fallen by over a half, railway shares had crashed and credit collapsed; business had declined by 54 per cent, creating alarm, despondency and mounting unemployment. Bankers and bourgeois demanded security and the government was forced to take immediate action. Notes were declared legal tender; foreign loans were drawn upon London and St. Petersburg; credit depositories were set up across the country and credit notes made interchangeable. When this failed a 45 per cent increase in the land tax finally re-established confidence, and stability was gradually restored during the summer. Meanwhile, however, the extreme left had been frustrated by a passive foreign policy designed to placate the bankers and the peasants had been enraged by increased taxation to keep up the value of government bonds, *rentes*.

Popular pressure and growing unemployment forced the government to implement its guarantees for work and a living wage. But its measures were both evasive and half-hearted; lacking money and opposed in principle to economic planning and social reform, the majority merely wanted to keep the workers pacified until the election of a National Assembly and the consolidation of bourgeois control. Louis Blanc's plans for a Ministry of Progress and for co-operative 'social workshops' were rejected. Instead a commission was set up at the Luxembourg Palace under Blanc and Albert to enquire into workers' grievances and find ways of improving working conditions. At the same time National Workshops were established under an engineer, Emile Thomas, to organize and discipline the rising mass of casual or unemployed labour. Men were grouped into squads under elected leaders and directed to work on roads, railways or in public parks. Members were kept out of politics, away from both the extreme left and from Louis Blanc at the Luxembourg Commission. They were paid two francs a day if employed and one franc if work were not available. As there was only enough for 10,000 men and the numbers of unemployed rose

in April to over 50,000 and in June to 100,000, it was soon
obvious that the workshops were failing to provide work and
merely becoming a form of dole which soon demoralized the
worker and drained the exchequer.

Meanwhile the government consolidated its authority over
the army, the police and the National Guard. When the Paris
police were taken over in February by Caussidière, an independent socialist, Lamartine and Marrast, now mayor of
Paris, set up a rival *Garde mobile* to absorb the unemployed
and use them to maintain order. In fact Caussidière, a
supporter of Louis Blanc, remained loyal, curbed crime and
helped to discredit Blanqui and the extreme left by leaking
information from secret police files. At the same time the
National Guard, which had been opened to all citizens, was
electing reliable bourgeois officers, and the army, hastily summoned by Lamartine, was affirming its loyalty to the new
régime.

The ambiguity of government action, however, soon
roused renewed agitation on the extreme left. In February
and March nearly 140 clubs representing every shade of left-
wing opinion had been founded in Paris where over 170
journals had also started publication. These, often carrying
lurid and passionate titles – the *Guillotine* was printed in red
ink, warned the workers of their imminent betrayal by the
bourgeoisie. Blanqui worked in desperate haste to co-ordinate
action, organize protest marches and effect a genuine inte-
gration of the National Guard. The left began to demand
postponement of the elections until the Guard had been amalgamated with working class contingents and until the country
had been educated in genuine republican principles. It was
becoming increasingly obvious that universal suffrage, far
from promoting the republic, would endanger its very existence by harnessing the peasantry and the provinces against
the revolution.

Popular agitation, however, only hardened moderate bourgeois resistance. The elections were postponed until April
23rd, but the selection of reliable Guard officers continued.
The position of the left-wing members of the government became increasingly precarious. Louis Blanc and Albert were
torn between loyalty to their colleagues and loyalty to their
principles. Too weak to dominate events they wavered from

side to side, supporting the socialists and left-wing clubs in their petitions, but joining the government when it came to any trial of strength. Thus they lost influence and were often branded as traitors by both sides.

On March 16th the bourgeois National Guard marched past the Hôtel de Ville, denounced Louis Blanc, and demanded the right to keep its exclusive uniform. Next day a rival demonstration organized by Blanqui revealed the rising power of the workers and terrified the government. It was Louis Blanc who finally persuaded the marchers to return home, but only at the expense of much of his popularity. April 16th was the occasion for another demonstration. By now Ledru-Rollin as well as Louis Blanc had become alarmed by the growing consolidation of moderate bourgeois control. For a brief moment it looked as if the left might unite; but when Blanqui led a march to the Hôtel de Ville, Ledru-Rollin rallied to Lamartine, and Louis Blanc again supported the government. The National Guard was called out and, assisted by the *Garde mobile,* surrounded the workers with bayonets and cannon. When the marchers went home they felt betrayed, bitter and disillusioned. A divided left could make little impact upon the combined power of the bourgeoisie.

The April elections confirmed bourgeois control and restored powerful right-wing Catholic and Orléanist elements. All were alarmed by the spread of agitation in the provinces and by the action of socialists and communists in the capital. The National Workshops were criticized for subsidising idleness; increases in taxation were attacked, and Parisian clubs and journals denounced for spreading anarchy and atheism. Catholics had been further alarmed by Carnot's[1] Education Bill which introduced free compulsory schooling for children up to fourteen. In a poll of 84 per cent the electors returned a Chamber of lawyers, officers, doctors, landowners and industrialists. Nearly 80 per cent came from the highest tax group and, though the majority declared themselves to be moderate republicans, over a half were Catholics and nearly a third legitimists or Orléanists. Even in Paris the moderates had led the socialists at the poll. Out of 900 deputies only some 82 left-wing supporters were elected.

[1] Son of Lazare Carnot, Minister of War during the Convention.

The result of the elections meant an inevitable if cautious move to the right. The situation in Paris was still too turbulent for a successful counter-revolution. Nevertheless the provisional government was replaced by a Commission of Five which excluded Louis Blanc and the left-wing representatives. A new labour committee which included the reactionary Vicomte de Falloux was established to examine the National Workshops which had become something of an obsession with the bourgeoisie. The workshops were now giving relief to over 100,000 unemployed, but this was not enough to satisfy the flood which poured into Paris from the provinces. Another 50,000 were estimated to be living without a fixed job in and around the capital, and this rising proletarian army filled bourgeois deputies with mounting anxiety.

In May and June the conflict moved to its tragic climax. On May 15th left wing socialists and extremists united for a demonstration of protest called officially in support of the Poles. Blanqui and a crowd which included some 14,000 from the National Workshops invaded the Assembly, abolished the government and seized the Hôtel de Ville. By now, however, it was too late. The National Guard and *Garde mobile* led by Lamartine and Ledru-Rollin crushed the revolt. Blanqui, Barbès, Albert and Raspail were arrested and imprisoned; Louis Blanc resigned from the Luxembourg Commission which was subsequently suspended.

The right now proceeded to strike back. Reliable generals were placed in command of the National Guard and *Garde mobile*. On May 21st the army was brought to Paris and reviewed at a so called *fête de la concorde*! Caussidière was dismissed and the police taken over by the government. In addition, new plans were devised to deal with the 'loafers in the workshops'. On May 24th Thomas was ordered to prepare to draft men into factories, into the army or back to the provinces. When he refused he was arrested and sent to Bordeaux. A decree to enforce these proposals was eventually issued on June 21st. Two days later the workers rose in revolt.

The June rising was a revolution of despair. The actions of the government provoked a last bitter gesture of defiance. Though the left-wing leadership had been imprisoned after the May uprising new men had emerged. The socialists of the

Luxembourg and the National Workshops had at last combined with extremists, communists and leaders from the clubs. In the by-elections of June 4th this had led to the election of Proudhon, Leroux, and Caussidière to the Assembly. Nevertheless, there is no evidence that official leaders had any hand in the June revolt. When a group of men from the workshops led by one of their lieutenants, Louis Pujol, swore vengeance and demanded 'bread or lead', artisans, mechanics, railwaymen, women and children built barricades and sparked off a spontaneous rising that was at once hopeless and heroic.

This time the Assembly was prepared for action. Emergency powers were voted to General Cavaignac who summoned the army, the *Garde mobile,* the National Guard and reinforcements from the provinces. In spite of the protests of Lamartine, he gave the workers time to dig in before launching an attack. The bombardment began on June 24th and in three days of bitter fighting the revolution was crushed. National Guardsmen were rushed to Paris by train – 3,000 from Amiens and others from up to 500 miles away. The dead numbered some 2,000 and included the Archbishop of Paris who had vainly attempted to mediate at the barricades. Defeat was followed by a wave of arrests, trials and deportations. The spectre of left-wing revolt was to be obliterated by mass repression.

The June days were followed by a summer of terror and reaction. Cavaignac was elected President of the Council and remained virtual dictator for the duration of the emergency. The National Workshops in Paris and the provinces were abolished, 2 million francs were voted to pay off the workers, and another 3 million made available in credit to help finance respectable industrial enterprise. A new Press Law restored caution money and a long list of libels. Left-wing journals were gradually suppressed throughout the country. The leading clubs had been closed during the June days. In July, secret societies were abolished and all clubs made subject to official approval and public inspection. Meanwhile the work of the Luxembourg Commission was largely ignored; plans for agriculture and industrial co-operatives, and for a system of social security during illness and old age were forgotten, though proposals to limit the working day to eleven hours were eventually put into effect. A commission of enquiry forced Louis Blanc and Caussidière to flee to England; all plans for social reform and guarantees of work lapsed. By the autumn of 1848 proletarian agitation had been crushed.

Paris continued under martial law until October 19th. The remainder of the country gradually returned to normal. A good harvest pacified unrest. Credit revived and government stock slowly recovered with the assistance of foreign loans. Beneath the surface, however, there remained a general and profound sense of shock and disillusion. Artisans and unemployed remembered the June days with bitterness and hate. Republicans felt betrayed, their ideals shattered. George Sand could no longer believe in a republic that began by killings its workers. Lamartine proclaimed that God would demand account for the bloodshed. The bourgeoisie were equally alarmed by the dangers of a dictatorship under Cavaignac and by the threats of a socialist or communist democracy. Legitimists and Orléanists, though active in opposition, were too discredited by past failure to provide any popular alternative. The way was thus open for a new and almost unknown claimant, Prince Louis Napoleon Bonaparte, nephew of the late Emperor, to step out of the shadows into the centre of the political arena.

5. Louis Napoleon and the Second Republic

Louis Napoleon, youngest son of Louis Bonaparte, King of Holland, and Hortense de Beauharnais, daughter of the Empress Josephine,[1] had been born on April 20th, 1808. After an early childhood spent amid the glories of the Empire he had lived in exile with his mother in Switzerland and was educated by French republican tutors and at the Augsburg gymnasium. From an early age he had been reminded of the significance of his name and the legacy of Napoleon. He soon began to identify himself with the many ideals which the Emperor had elevated into a powerful Napoleonic myth by his writings on St. Helena. Louis Napoleon made friends with Italian liberals and took part in the 1831 risings. In the following year he published his *Rêveries politiques* in which he advocated a combination of 'Napoleon II' and a republic. When 'Napoleon II', now officially Duc de Reichstadt, died,

[1] See Appendix 1.

Louis cast himself in the role of his successor and in *Des Idées Napoléoniennes*, first published in 1839, he outlined a programme that claimed to satisfy the need for order, equality, justice, liberty and peace.

His early efforts to make good his claims were, however, disastrous. In 1836 an attempt to rouse the garrison of Strasbourg in revolt failed and the Orléanist government had him ignominiously deported to the United States. In 1840 an attempted raid on Boulogne had been equally unsuccessful and he had been imprisoned for six years in the fortress of Ham. Here, however, he had met Louis Blanc and was able to write *L'Extinction du Paupérisme* which he rightly hoped would appeal to the workers and bring him fresh publicity. In 1846 he managed to escape to England where he waited patiently for events. When the revolution broke out in February he followed developments with a new caution and a shrewd sense of timing and political calculation.

On the outbreak of the revolt Louis Napoleon went to France, but when the provisional government declined his assistance he returned rapidly to England, professing full loyalty to the new Republic. He refused to stand in the April elections preferring to wait 'until people had lost their illusions'. By June a widespread publicity campaign organized by his supporters secured his election for Paris and in three departments. When, however, the government arrested his leading agent, Persigny, Louis Napoleon resigned his seat 'in the interests of good order'. After the June days his agents opened a press and propaganda campaign offering Napoleon as the only name able to reconcile the bitter divisions in the country. In September he headed the list for Paris and was also returned in four departments. He took his seat, shy and hesitant, on September 26th. His appearance seemed so out of keeping with his claims that the deputies withdrew a motion declaring him ineligible and abrogated the law excluding Bonaparte's heirs from France.

Meanwhile, however, the deputies were drafting a constitution which was greatly to assist Louis Napoleon in realizing his ambition. In an attempt to satisfy every requirement it failed in the end to guarantee any. A strong president was needed to keep order and head the executive. Lamartine swayed the house in favour of election by universal suffrage –

'the voice of the people' – rather than by members of the Assembly. In order to maintain a traditional separation of powers the legislature was to consist of a single chamber of 750 members elected by universal suffrage to which ministers were to be responsible. In order to prevent any subversion of the constitution a Council of State was given powers to check laws and their administration. A High Court was to pronounce immediately in case of any usurpation of power, and any amendment to the constitution required a three-quarter majority on three successive occasions. With such cast-iron guarantees the deputies felt free to leave the administrative machinery intact and to promise freedom of worship, education, association and the press within the framework of a new Republic.

Louis Napoleon was able to take advantage of the divisions in the country and the new principle of universal suffrage to project his image as saviour of France. 'Since 1815 the people have been waiting for Napoleon,' wrote Victor Hugo, and Louis rapidly formulated a programme which had something for everyone. To the socialists he promised employment, old age relief and popular reforms; to the rebels an amnesty; to Catholics he guaranteed order, freedom in education and the protection of the Pope; to the peasants he assured property and peace; to the bourgeoisie freedom, order and justice. He won the support of many Orléanists like Thiers, Molé and Barrot who hoped he would be a stepping stone to the restoration of their own fortunes. A press campaign secured increased coverage and won the support of royalist and Catholic journals. Above all, the name Napoleon conjured up the glories of the past and expectation for the future in contrast to the discredited politicians of the republic. Louis Napoleon was elected President by 5.5 million votes; Cavaignac polled 1.5 million, Ledru-Rollin nearly 400,000, Raspail 36,900 and Lamartine 17,910.

As President, Louis Napoleon faced a nation divided at every level by class and creed, and found a constitution where division of power threatened to create permanent deadlock. The aristocracy and upper bourgeoisie were divided between Orléanists and legitimists; the middle and lower bourgeois were split between republicans and socialists; workers and proletarians retained bitter memories of the June days and

S

were divided between socialist and extreme left-wing groups. Louis Napoleon exploited these divisions to secure his authority and manipulated the constitution to guarantee control. While ministers and deputies could carry the blame for unpopular measures, the President could always appeal over their heads to the people. A wide cross-section of the nation reinforced by the peasantry could be relied upon to give him massive support.

His first ministry was led by Barrot and contained reliable men of the right like Falloux and Faucher. It was designed to reassure the country and used to curb left-wing agitation. Barbès, Blanqui and Raspail were tried and convicted; left-wing agitators were deported from Paris and the provinces. The elections in May 1849 confirmed the supremacy of the right but brought a powerful challenge from the republican left: some five hundred monarchists and Catholics were returned to defend 'order, property, the family and religion'. A left-wing alliance of socialists and republicans led by Ledru-Rollin captured nearly 200 seats, mainly in the old industrial areas – Rhône, Alsace and the Massif central. The moderate republicans won barely 80 seats; both Lamartine and Marrast were defeated.

During the summer the policies of the Catholic right were maintained. Falloux drafted a law which freed education in primary and secondary schools from state control. The monopoly of the University of France was broken, church schools became officially established, and priests became the sole guardians of religious and moral instruction. In April an expedition was sent to Rome to mediate between the Pope and the New Republic.[1] A skirmish with Garibaldi's troops led to a breakdown of discussion and the capture of the city by storm. This was too much for the republican left: on June 13th left-wing regiments of the National Guard, socialist clubs and members of the old Luxembourg Commission rose in revolt. The rising was easily suppressed by the army and upper bourgeois guards under Changarnier. Disturbances at Strasbourg, Lyons and Toulouse were also crushed without difficulty; everywhere the proletarian workmen refused to follow the republican leadership. The Assembly passed laws to restrict the press and limit the right of association. Ledru-Rollin fled to England; republican organizations were driven underground.

Louis Napoleon now manoeuvred to gain independence from the right. When the Pope refused to accept the need for reform the President published a letter deploring his actions and advocating a general amnesty, a secular administration, the Code Napoléon and liberal government. When the ministry ignored the letter Louis Napoleon dismissed it, despite the fact that it had not lost its parliamentary support, and vindicated his right to select independent ministers in the interests of the whole nation. This miniature *coup d'état* was but the first step in the restoration of the Empire. Two years later, when the left had again been discredited by violence and the right by acts of repression, Louis Napoleon felt strong enough to seize ultimate control and establish a new imperial régime.[1]

1 See Ch. XV.

XI · THE REVOLUTIONS OF 1848

1. *Metternich's Europe*

THE failure of the 1830 revolutions in central and eastern Europe was followed by a decade of apparent calm. Kings, courts and aristocrats were entrenched behind a tight façade of military power, landed estate and clerical backing. The upper bourgeoisie remained dedicated to the accumulation of wealth; only a minority appeared interested in the problems of independence or the possibility of any future revolt. The Iberian peninsula continued to be a centre of disturbance and civil war, but its savage and uncontrollable politics defied solution within a European framework. The revolutions had generally failed as a result of mass indifference. Peasants and artisans were soon forced back to a routine of daily living; even the moderate bourgeois often refused to respond to Mazzini's heroic appeals or to the defiant gestures of students and intellectuals.

Herein lay the main justification for Metternich's diplomacy. Throughout Europe there was a general desire for stable government and peace. This was only disrupted by the agitation of a few disaffected artistocrats, idealists, romantics or bourgeois whose motives were essentially selfish. The interests of both Europe and the Habsburgs required that these subversive elements be held in check, and Metternich's policy was therefore dedicated to maintaining the existing order in Germany, Italy and throughout the Austrian Empire. The Carlsbad and Frankfurt[1] Decrees were vigorously enforced by armies of spies and by the action of the police. Publications were carefully censored and correspondence checked by agents in the Vienna post-office. In foreign affairs, Metternich hoped to contain crises by an extension of his alliance with Prussia and Russia. This was achieved in 1833 at München-grätz[2] and Berlin, and enabled him to mediate effectively in the Near East in 1840. Possible friction with Russia was skilfully avoided, and diplomacy was directed to maintaining the

---

[1] See pp. 174-5.   [2] See pp. 236-7.

interests of a conservative establishment throughout Europe.

Meanwhile, however, economic and social changes were subtly eroding the cornerstones of Metternich's world.[1] The major weakness in his much boasted claims to realism was his failure to appreciate the real and inevitable impact of these developments. The growth of agricultural and industrial activity, the expansion of trade and finance and the gradual redistribution of wealth led to renewed fragmentation and adjustment within the social structure. As new aristocracies came into conflict with the old, as bourgeois financiers, industrialists, nationalists and intellectuals struggled for leadership, and as artisans, skilled factory hands and peasants watched familiar landmarks slowly disappear, idealists, romantics, liberals and nationalist writers were once again able to attract wider audiences and plunge Europe into renewed periods of uncertainty and violence.

Isolated examples of unrest revealed a growing climate of dissatisfaction in the years before 1848. In Italy and Austria the landed aristocracy began to demand credit facilities and a relaxation of feudal restrictions. In Galicia and Hungary the lesser nobility added national rights and privileges to demands for mortgage banks and economic benefits. At court the death of Francis II in 1834 and the accession of the near imbecile Ferdinand introduced a new element of instability. Metternich found his policies increasingly undermined by rival factions led by Kolovrat and an assortment of archdukes.

Meanwhile the bourgeoisie became more and more impatient with the general paralysis in policy. In Germany the moderates demanded a constitution modelled on Louis-Philippe's July monarchy, while the radical liberals advocated more representative and popular plans. Similar views were spread throughout the Habsburg Empire where the German élite also urged moderate constitutional proposals, while Czechs, Croats and Slovenes began to agitate for a wider franchise. At the same time artisans, fearful of new competition, continued to demand security, while peasants were increasingly resentful of the *robot* and residual feudal obligations.

Dissatisfaction was reflected in the growth of newspapers

[1] See Ch. VIII.

and journals. The circulation of Paris dailies had risen from 70,000 to 200,000 in the decade after 1835, and the 1848 revolution had been in part the outcome of journalist initiative. In Germany, the Rhineland press was of almost equal significance. Among many was the *Neue Rheinische Zeitung* edited by the young Karl Marx in the interest of a group of lesser liberal industrialists. In the Habsburg Empire censorship restricted the distribution of news to official government publications. Criticism was spread, however, by the proliferation of scientific and economic journals which, by highlighting developments in England and France, were able to demonstrate the backward state of the Habsburg economy. Italy alone had over ninety such publications and their circulation, though limited, probably reached many more readers than Mazzini's clandestine *Giovine Italia*. In addition the poetry and drama of the romantics fostered the enthusiasm of the young who in mock debates between romantics and classicists disguised a more fundamental conflict between liberal and reactionary doctrines.

While agitation remained divided, however, Metternich was able to keep command without much difficulty. He could rely on the army with its aristocratic officer caste and obedient battalions, on the indifference of the majority and upon his control over the government, the princes, the police and the press. The Habsburg Empire itself was governed by bureaucrats who operated from Vienna. Rival nationalities were used to hold each other in check by being sent to administer or garrison each other's territories. Metternich even re-established national diets in Hungary, Bohemia, Austria and Croatia both to strengthen the direct ties between the Emperor and his estates and also, if necessary, to play off one against the other. Here, however, he over-estimated his own ability to manipulate the situation and the diets were to play an unexpectedly subversive role in the events leading up to 1848.

Metternich was more confident in his use of the censorship and the police. All letters passing through Vienna, including those of the royal family, were unsealed and copied for his perusal. He personally checked papers and journals, and with an almost infinite capacity for work kept a watch over liberal agitation throughout Europe. Dangerous captives were locked up in the Spielberg fortress; potential subversives were shadowed by ambassadors and spies. His attention was especially focused on neighbouring states and he felt it his duty to keep a general watch over the German princes, the Papacy and the many Habsburg dependants throughout the Italian states.[1] Though these activities roused considerable resentment from the rulers concerned this was of little immediate significance; while princes looked to Metternich for protection against the spread of subversive elements, his advice was always useful and his support an essential factor in their own survival.

The economic crisis of the mid 1840s, however, enormously increased the strength of each individual source of agitation and also encouraged all the elements to coalesce. The trade slump affected shipping and textile exports. Between 1844 and 1847 the export of unbleached linen yarn from the *Zollverein* fell by nearly 40 per cent. The collapse of credit hit bourgeois industrialists as well as railway shareholders and middlemen. Simultaneously the failure of both the grain and potato harvest in 1846 forced up the average price of food in Germany by almost 50 per cent. This led to a steep price rise in neighbouring areas and the outflow of funds soon brought a general fall in the demand for other goods on the home market. Aristocrats and bourgeois became more and more frustrated by government restrictions, while artisans were reduced to starvation and peasants found it impossible to pay mortgage and redemption dues.

As a result agitation and rioting broke out in several quarters. In 1844 the Silesian handloom weavers rose in revolt, driven desperate by the progressive decline of the mining, linen and cotton industries. Factories and managerial property were burnt until troops restored order, shooting eleven and wounding another twenty-four. These events were magnified into a general condemnation of working conditions. Regional distress was certainly evident elsewhere. At Aachen handicraftsmen rioted and smashed machinery, and similar disturbances were repeated in Saxony, Bavaria, Baden and in the industrial regions of Bohemia. In the spring of 1847, as food prices reached new heights, a wave of disorder spread throughout Prussia. For

[1] See Appendix 1.

four days 'potato riots' raged in Berlin before the army eventually regained control.

Meanwhile the bourgeoisie were rallying support for their constitutional demands. In Germany, Baden radicals met in September 1847 at Offenburg to demand the abolition of repressive legislation, a popular militia, freedom of speech, a free press and a national and representative parliament. Next month, the moderate liberals met at Heppenheim. These included a wide selection of Rhineland constitutionalists and urged freedom of speech and assembly, but within the established framework of social and political life. Anxious to maintain law and order, they were already alarmed by the danger of artisan revolts and by the radical riots in Baden. For them artisans, radicals and rioters had already become almost indistinguishable. In Italy and the Austrian Empire agitation also took on a more national flavour. In Piedmont the bourgeoisie demanded both economic and political reforms, and their attitude was echoed both in Rome and in the diets of the Habsburg Empire.

In both Italy and Habsburg territories agitation was taken up by members of the lesser aristocracy. In 1846 the nobility of Galicia revolted to assert their demands. The Government in Vienna retaliated by promising the peasants freedom from *robot* and encouraging them to massacre their landlords. In Hungary, Kossuth, the leader of the gentry, stirred up the Diet to demand the restoration of ancient Magyar rights and privileges. Revolts in Sicily and central Italy added to the general unrest. It was clear that Europe was going through a wave of disorder. Nevertheless the harvest in 1847 was good and by winter the economic crisis had passed its peak. Metternich might yet have survived the storm had not fissures appeared at the very apex of his political empire.

In 1846 Pius IX, the newly elected Pope, was persuaded to grant a general amnesty, a press, a civic guard and an advisory council to the Papal States. This move was greeted in Italy by an outburst of enthusiasm. Charles Albert of Piedmont, ambitious for leadership yet hesitant in action, was persuaded to offer constitutional concessions in the following year. Frederick William IV of Prussia also chose 1847 to summon a United Diet to ask for money for the construction of a new railway to his eastern provinces. In Austria itself court factions encouraged the demands of the national diets in order to undermine Metternich's authority. It appeared that the established order was crumbling around him. It only required the impetus of another French revolution to bring about its immediate collapse.

2. *The Revolution in Italy*

In Italy the revolution welled up from a variety of sources and proclaimed many and contradictory beliefs. In the North, the aristocracy led by men like d'Azeglio, Balbo and Cavour had joined with the upper bourgeoisie – bankers and industrialists – to advocate the need for economic reform and a moderate constitution. The Piedmontese Agricultural Association, founded in 1842, discussed problems of railway construction, tolls and tariffs that implied the possible unification of the North under a liberal régime. They attracted the support of Lombard proprietors equally frustrated by the lethargy of the Habsburg administration. Similar attitudes were adopted by aristocrats and influential bourgeois in Florence, Rome and Naples, where economic advantages were frequently associated with political and national gains. Meanwhile artisans and lower bourgeois in the big cities were increasingly disturbed by the harvest failure and slump of 1846 and began to agitate for some measure of reform. They hoped that liberal or national constitutions might also bring social and material advantages.

A number of alternative formulae had been widely publicized as the solution for Italy's complaints. In 1831 Mazzini had founded Young Italy to proclaim a free, united and democratic republic.[1] A decade of abortive risings had largely discredited his movement, though his ideas still lingered in the minds of many artisans and intellectuals. In 1843 the Abbe Gioberti's *Il Primato* had urged a federal union under the presidency of the Pope. This had been given unexpected support in 1846 when the election of Pius IX had led to a series of apparently liberal concessions in the Papal States. A general amnesty was followed up by plans for railways, gas lighting, education and prison reform, as well as the formation of a consultative committee and a National Guard. Italy was roused and Metternich horrified, especially by the

[1] See p. 208.

Guard. In 1847 Radetsky, the Austrian Commander-in-Chief, used the occasion of riotous celebrations to occupy the Papal city of Ferrara. Metternich, however, was forced to withdraw as a result of unanimous protests. The Papacy had won a moral victory for 'nationalism'. In fact, however, Pius IX had been driven further than he intended by a combination of calculated flattery and controlled popular acclaim. Metternich was right when he commented that the Pope did not understand the implications of his actions.

An alternative solution was urged in Balbo's pamphlet, *On the Hopes of Italy*, published in 1844 and by the writings of d'Azeglio and Piedmontese liberals who advocated the leadership of Charles Albert, King of Sardinia. The king had reformed the currency and encouraged agricultural and industrial development. He had purged the army of Mazzinian sympathizers and stationed a naval force in Genoa. At the same time, upholding principles of extreme absolutism, Charles Albert hated constitutions, crowds and liberal agitation. He was infected by that romantic and mystic vision which seemed to haunt princes. He hoped to lead Italy to eventual unification, but it was to be on his own terms and not as the result of outside pressure. He thus appeared at once idealistic, ambitious, deceptive, secretive and vague. He remained throughout his reign a lonely and isolated, almost ascetic figure. His determination to act alone, and his failure to harness support in either Italy or Europe were to have disastrous results. The lack of any co-ordination, the inability of leading revolutionaries to act in concert and the failure to find one formula acceptable to all parties were to be largely responsible for the ultimate defeat of the entire revolution.

Division and hesitation were apparent even at the start. When the Papacy suggested a customs union, Piedmont rejected such a rival initiative. Charles Albert had to be persuaded by processions and deputations to grant even minor concessions – a freer press law, the abolition of special tribunals and the broadening of membership of the Council of State. But doubts were soon brushed aside in the wave of revolts which swept up the peninsula in the early months of 1848. In January demonstrations against the tobacco tax led to riots in Milan. A more serious insurrection broke out in Sicily where the aristocracy declared their independence and

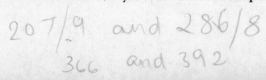

proclaimed the 1812 Constitution. Anxious to outbid them and harness bourgeois support Ferdinand II set up a constitution in Naples based on French lines. On February 8th, Charles Albert appointed a constitutional commission in Piedmont, while a new constitution was accepted in Tuscany three days later. The fall of Louis-Philippe hastened developments. On March 15th a constitution was proclaimed in Rome, and when news of Metternich's fall reached Milan, friction between citizens and the garrison led to a rising which after five days of street fighting forced the Austrian army to retreat to the fortresses of the Quadrilateral.

Events in Milan immediately raised the problem of the Austrian presence in the North. Charles Albert had already granted a constitution on March 4th which established an assembly based on a limited franchise (some 2.5 per cent of the population) and a ministry responsible to the King. He hesitated before taking the next step and declaring war on Austria. He was, however, now subject to increasing pressure from aristocratic liberals led by Balbo and Cavour who were anxious to extend their interests in Lombardy and unite the northern states into one economic unit. In addition, Charles Albert was worried by the rival claims of Tuscany and the Papacy. The former had already declared war, while, on March 24th, papal volunteers streamed north with the Pope's apparent approval. Charles Albert declared war on Austria the same day. Two days later his ill-prepared army crossed the frontier to drive the enemy out of Lombardy.

The advance of the Piedmontese, however, was laboriously slow. Supplies were lacking and there was a shortage of maps and medicines. The commissariat broke down and orders often failed to reach their destination. In addition the aristocratic and exclusive Piedmontese failed to absorb or train the many volunteers who flocked to join the cause. When Garibaldi landed in June from South America, Charles Albert, who mistrusted his republican views, passed him on to the provisional government in Milan. Tuscans, Lombards and Neapolitans were rapidly disillusioned by such treatment. In spite of Mazzini's support, the King failed to rouse the enthusiasm of the young or the loyalty of artisans and intellectuals, while the peasant majority remained, as usual, generally indifferent or even hostile to the sudden demands of war. As a result Radetsky was able to consolidate his position behind Mantua, repel the probing attacks of the Piedmontese army and wait for reinforcements from Vienna.

Delay hastened the fragmentation of the innumerable elements struggling for liberation. The governments of Naples and Tuscany already mistrusted the ambitions of Charles Albert. Neapolitan and papal troops were instructed not to cross the Po. On April 29th the Pope in an allocution declared himself opposed to any war against Austria and in favour of legitimacy and peace. His action destroyed papal claims to political leadership, undermined national enthusiasm and removed a possible rival to Piedmontese supremacy.

Political rivalry was cross-cut and complicated by social friction. In Milan the upper bourgeois municipal authorities relied upon Charles Albert for support. But there was already growing opposition from lower bourgeois republicans who, led by Cattaneo, demanded autonomy within a federal framework. They considered Mazzini a traitor for supporting Charles Albert, and were often more interested in increasing their own wages than in fighting the Austrians. Nevertheless, on May 29th, a plebiscite in favour of union with Piedmont was voted by a large majority. But by that time most of the Lombards had left the front line, thus further weakening Charles Albert's position.

Ferdinand II of Naples had by now withdrawn his troops. Preserved by the grant of a constitution in January, he used the occasion of subsequent disputes between aristocrats, peasants and bourgeois to destroy it. Rallying peasant *banditi* and *lazzaroni* against the liberals he bombarded Naples and restored a traditional Bourbon absolutism. He then ordered the recall of General Pepe and the Neapolitan army from the North in order to begin the reconquest of Sicily. Half the troops obeyed, and the remainder drifted to Venice where they helped organize the defences of a new republic set up by Daniel Manin.

As a result Charles Albert found his position dangerously isolated in the face of a growing Austrian build-up. In May the Piedmontese had captured Peschiera while the Tuscans staved off a fierce counter-attack from Mantua. By July, however, Radetsky had been reinforced by 35,000 men, while the Tuscans had been withdrawn. When the new Piedmontese Chamber met to confirm the plebiscite for the Union of Upper Italy the military backing needed to make it effective had largely evaporated. Papal and Lombard volunteers were brushed aside at Vicenza and the Piedmontese decisively defeated on July 24th at Custoza. Retreating in good order Charles Albert could only abandon Milan, amid the threats and curses of the population, and retire to Piedmont. On August 9th a truce brought the fighting to an end. The war of liberation appeared over.

Defeat, however, roused radical and republican elements to a new pitch of endeavour. The majority felt betrayed by the incompetence of princes, the exclusiveness of aristocrats and the complacency of the upper bourgeoisie. For Mazzini 'the war of kings was over and the war of the people had begun'. In Tuscany, the port of Leghorn, long a centre of Mazzinian propaganda, rose in revolt. The moderate liberals were swept aside and the Grand-Duke forced to accept a more popular, democratic ministry which demanded a Constituent Assembly and unification with Rome. Here the Pope's withdrawal from the war and his increasing opposition to liberal reform also aroused growing resentment. Artisans, officers, intellectuals and smallholders agitated for action. In an effort at compromise Pius appointed Count Rossi, a doctrinaire liberal of wide knowledge and considerable experience, to form a ministry. His moderation and opposition to war failed, however, to satisfy the radicals and he was assassinated when about to open the first sitting of the new Chamber. The Pope was forced to accept a new radical ministry and meet demands for a Constituent Assembly, a republican form of government and the renewal of war with Austria. In November he fled in disguise to Gaeta and from there denounced events in Rome as monstrous and treasonable. He was soon followed by the Grand-Duke of Tuscany who joined him in appealing to Austria for aid.

Meanwhile events in Piedmont had followed a very similar course. The abandonment of Lombardy and Venice had led to an outcry in the Turin press and the King was forced to accept a ministry under Gioberti to rally popular support. This, however, only helped to show up the permanent rivalry of the social and political groupings in the peninsula. When Gioberti opened negotiations to restore the Pope and a moderate constitution in Rome his proposals were rejected by both Pius and the republicans. When the Roman Constituent Assembly called for delegates from the whole of Italy, Gioberti refused to comply. His plans to restore a moderate constitution in Tuscany met a similar fate. Meanwhile he lost the support of the radicals and was forced to resign.

Charles Albert was now reduced to calling a left-wing ministry, dominated by Rattazzi, which urged the immediate renewal of war. A combination of despair, ministerial pressure, popular demand and the agitation of thousands of Lombard refugees eventually persuaded the King to take action. But Italy was again hopelessly divided. On March 26th the Piedmontese army was easily crushed at Novara by Radetsky's confident men. Charles Albert quickly abdicated to allow his son Victor Emmanuel to negotiate a favourable peace and died in exile four months later.

Novara shattered the hopes of the Italian republicans. In Tuscany the moderates now joined the aristocracy in suppressing the radical Assembly and restoring the Grand-Duke, while the Austrian army bombarded Leghorn into submission. In Rome the Constituent Assembly had meanwhile declared a Republic and, guided by Mazzini, embarked on an ambitious programme of social reform. Land was distributed among the peasants, apartments were provided for the poor and the unemployed were set to work excavating the forum. Lack of funds, however, soon created financial difficulties and excessive note issue led to rapid inflation. In any case the defeat of the Republic was only a matter of time in spite of the valiant efforts of Garibaldi to rally volunteers in its defence.

On March 30th representatives of the Catholic powers met at Gaeta to discuss the restoration of the Pope. Austria, France, Naples and Spain competed in offering assistance while keeping a careful watch on each other's actions. Louis Napoleon, anxious to please both Catholics and moderate bourgeois in France, rushed a French column to Rome under General Oudinot with instructions to restore the Pope with moderate liberal support. This, however, proved quite impracticable and the French were vigorously repulsed by Garibaldi. The arrival of reinforcements in May led to a renewal of the attack and, after a month's siege notable for the heroic conduct of the defence, Rome was reoccupied in July. Garibaldi led his battered volunteers towards Venice but after desperate escapes was forced to disband his force at San Marino. Meanwhile Austrian and Neapolitan troops mopped up in the rest of the peninsula. Sicily was reoccupied after bitter and savage fighting and Venice forced into submission. The revolution which had begun as an appeal for freedom, unity and the expulsion of Austria had foundered on the fragments of its own ideals and interests.

3. *The Revolution in Germany*

In Germany there was, if anything, an even greater variety of purpose and design. Regional differences were equally pronounced while the more rapid pace of industrialization had led to a greater degree of fragmentation within each class. As a result projects for reform and for German unification multiplied. Princes, aristocrats, bourgeois liberals and radicals, artisans and factory operatives all urged a variety of proposals designed to consolidate their position and satisfy their own immediate needs.

East of the Elbe the Junkers still retained an almost absolute authority over the peasants on their estates, upheld a traditional framework of feudal class barriers and provided the Prussian army with its dedicated officer corps. In the West these distinctions had been blurred as a result of French influence, but throughout the southern states, forest rights, feudal dues and servile obligations still remained.

Rhineland liberals and Prussian industrialists were the core of the upper bourgeoisie. Their general aim was a free economy and a moderate constitutional programme. But they only represented a small section of the middle classes. The remainder were often critical and even hostile to upper bourgeois plans. Radical liberals, though in favour of a freer economy, were anxious to relieve obvious distress and promote reform. Radical democrats were even more violent in their criticism, deplored the disruptive effects of liberalism and advocated greater social and industrial security. Their arguments were taken up by socialist and communist intellectuals in the Rhineland who denounced the spread of capitalism and urged direct working-class resistance to both aristocratic and bourgeois claims.

Workers, however, were by no means united in their desire

to resist. The prosperous artisans in Berlin and the larger cities preferred to develop middle-class affiliations. They hoped to rise to a higher status and deplored any proletarian labels. The skilled workers in the new mills and engineering workshops also hoped to improve their standard of living within a capitalist framework. They sought to increase wages and to regulate hours and working conditions rather than to attack the foundations of their own security.

It was the lower bourgeois artisans and craftsmen, often living at bare subsistence level, who formed the core of the radical and democratic opposition. Backed by sailors, coachmen, innkeepers and handloom weavers, all threatened by the progress of mechanization, they were struggling to maintain the shreds of their former security before falling into a limbo of vagrancy or unemployment. Even they, however, were not united. Though masters and journeymen urged the restoration of guilds, there was little co-operation between them. West of the Rhine, where French influence had been considerable, guilds had long since been abolished and all were forced to operate within a capitalist framework.

The political structure of Germany and the problem of German unification created almost as much difficulty as these social and economic differences. While princes and courts dreamt of gothic spires and medieval estates, East Prussian Junkers rejected anything likely to submerge their own identity into any such romantic reconstructions. While the bankers and industrialists of the *Zollverein* hoped for a union under Prussian leadership, the southern bourgeoisie preferred a more cultured Austrian supremacy. Artisans and proletarians hoped for greater benefits within a protectionist economy. All expected a new constitution to bring unity, security and guarantees for their particular interest. Though divided by region, religion and class all had vague hopes that a united Germany would cure their ills and solve all their difficulties.

The economic crisis of the mid-forties had led to a spate of congresses and manifestos advocating a variety of these solutions. In 1847 the moderate liberals had met at Heppenheim, the southern radicals at Offenburg, while guilds petitioned for special protection and hunger riots spread across the country.[1] Interest, however, soon concentrated upon a United Diet

[1] See p. 170.

called by Frederick William IV of Prussia in order to raise money to finance the new East Prussian railway. This monarch, intoxicated by the highest notions of divine right, Christian idealism and romantic fantasy, had, since ascending the throne in 1840, given a vaguely liberal impression. The censorship had been relaxed, disaffected professors like Arndt and Jahn had been restored, and biennial diets had been established in the provinces. The United Diet was hailed as a great step forward. For the King, however, it meant a return to the Middle Ages. No power on earth, he declared, would induce him to transform the natural relation between prince and people into a constitutional one. When the Diet asked for regular sessions Frederick William refused. When it rejected the railway loan it was soon dissolved.

The whole question was reopened dramatically by news of the February revolution in Paris. When students and crowds began to gather in Berlin, Frederick William promised a regular diet. News of the fall of Metternich brought hopes of a constitution, a free press, a German flag and a revised confederation. On March 18th, however, two shots, fired when the army moved in to disperse crowds, led to a sudden and furious uprising. Bourgeoisie, artisans, students and railwaymen constructed barricades and fought with every available weapon against the hated soldiery. The King, in an agony of indecision and remorse, prevented the army from reducing the capital, and agreed to summon a diet to draw up a constitution. Meanwhile the army had returned to Potsdam in fury and disgust, and Frederick William was forced to pay homage to the dead, and ride through the streets of Berlin wearing a new German Tricolour and guarded by the citizen militia. At the end of March he appointed a ministry of moderate bourgeois and liberal aristocrats, with Ludwig Camphausen as Prime Minister, and Hansemann as Minister of Finance. In April a royal patent promised a new constitution, a free press, a responsible ministry and an Assembly elected on universal suffrage through electoral colleges. But the King made it clear that ministers were to remain his servants and that no one was to tamper with his direct control over the army.

Meanwhile the revolutionary tide had been sweeping through the German states. Agitation broke out in Baden at

T

the beginning of March and spread rapidly through the South. Princes seldom put up more than token resistance, and appointed liberal ministers, granted constitutions and capitulated to moderate bourgeois interests. These, however, were but the crest of a massive wave of demands. Radicals advocated the abolition of standing armies and a republican constitution. Skilled craftsmen agitated for the return of corporations. Artisans exploded into violence and burnt down mills in Saxony and the Rhineland. Cutlers attacked iron works, hauliers tore up railway lines, while sailors threatened steamships on the Rhine and brought navigation to a halt. At the same time factory operatives struck for higher wages. In Berlin the printers won a quick pay rise and their victory led to similar concessions in Dresden and Leipzig. At Breslau a threatened general strike soon brought higher wages and a shorter working week.

The peasantry also joined in the general revolt. In the South castles were attacked, records burnt and manorial forests invaded. Destruction spread north into Saxony and Hesse as peasants demanded free land, the end of forest dues and the abolition of tithes. Rioting spread into Brandenburg, Pomerania and Silesia, in spite of Junker claims to the contrary. Everywhere the peasants demanded the realization of their hopes after half a century of manorial obstruction.

In the border states national interests often intruded into the pattern of the revolt. In Posen there was widespread agitation for a restoration of Polish autonomy. In the Austrian provinces of the German Confederation Czechs, Poles and Slovenes hoped to win a measure of independence.[1] In Schleswig-Holstein the German population revolted against the Danes, called the Duke of Augustenburg to the throne and appealed to the Confederation for assistance against a Danish counter-attack.

While Germany was in a state of general upheaval princes capitulated and authority collapsed. It was small wonder that liberals now assumed that their hour had come. With moderation and conventional propriety they took it upon themselves to restore order, set up a constitutional régime and constructed the framework of a new German Union. In Prussia the new liberal ministry appealed for order, rallied

[1] See p. 289.

the Civic Guard, protected factories and summoned troops to disperse artisan mobs and put down peasant risings. Fears of radical and republican agitation quickly replaced their earlier fears of royal or aristocratic action. Moderate liberals made little effort to rally support from democratic or working men's clubs in the capital and regarded any initiatives from that quarter with horror and alarm.

The policies of the new Prussian government soon turned out to be essentially liberal and bourgeois. It agreed to back loans in order to restore credit and end the post-revolutionary recession, and raised seventy-five million marks to support agriculture, industry and trade. Public works were organized in parks and on canals to pacify the unemployed, and cereal duties were cut to bring down food prices and promote freer trade. Meanwhile the Diet had drafted a constitution designed to give control to the bourgeoisie. But when the first Prussian Assembly met on May 22nd a large radical element appeared determined to advocate further social and democratic reforms. This, however, only added to the alarm of the moderates who soon began to turn back to the Crown for support.

Similar conflicts of interest were quickly apparent in the plans for German unification. To forestall any royalist proposals for a confederation based on medieval diets or estates, liberal leaders met at Heidelberg on March 5th and called for a meeting of state representatives at a preparatory parliament *Vorparlament*, to draw up a national constitution. This met at Frankfurt on March 31st and soon revealed the usual fragmentation between conservative, moderate and radical elements. The moderate majority, however, was able to draft proposals for a Federal Union, a liberal monarchy and a Constituent Assembly to be elected by all 'independent citizens'. Radical demands for the abolition of standing armies and aristocratic privileges, and for 'prosperity, education and freedom for all' were rejected. A popular revolution led by students and intellectuals in the South was easily defeated, and elections for the new Constituent Assembly hastily organized.

The interpretation of the qualification 'independent citizen' was, however, left to the different states. In Hanover and Würtemberg wage-earners were declared not to be independent. In Bavaria all who did not pay direct taxation were disenfranchised. Farm hands, servants and workers were generally denied a vote, while the provision of a secret ballot was frequently ignored. As a result the election took place in a mood of disillusion and barely half of the electorate even bothered to vote. On May 18th when the Frankfurt Parliament eventually assembled some two-hundred of its members were lawyers, one hundred were writers, teachers or professors, some fifty merchants or doctors, while only four were artisans and one a peasant.

It had already become clear that artisans, workers and peasants could expect little benefit from the revolution. By May the agrarian revolts had been crushed, while artisan demonstrators had been repeatedly dispersed by civic guards supported by regular troops. Lower bourgeois and workers, however, were quite unable to combine to press their own demands. Moderate artisans and factory operatives organized a congress in Berlin in August and urged a 'social democratic' programme of factory laws, improved social services and an end to internal dues. They set up a network of local branches in Berlin, Breslau, Leipzig and the larger cities, but emphasized their devotion to law and order and to the work of liberal parliaments.

At the same time radical artisans organized craft assemblies and petitions. Rhine boatmen continued to obstruct steamships while printers attacked machines and tailors demanded an end to the sale of ready-made clothing. These moves culminated in the formation of regional associations and in June 1848 a North German Artisans' Congress, meeting in Hamburg, condemned liberalism and urged that wages paid be related more closely to work done. In July an Artisan Congress met at Frankfurt and accepted an Industrial Code which listed the revival of guild controls, protective tariffs, sickness benefits and free education among its demands.

Even the radicals, however, remained divided. The Artisan Congress only represented the guild masters. Journeymen met in a rival German Labour Congress to demand minimum wages, shorter hours and freedom from guild regulations. Though the majority were in general agreement in their attacks on liberalism such moves were not supported by winegrowers and craftsmen from the west bank of the Rhine.

Radical intellectuals and socialists felt themselves at a loss when faced by so wide a variety of conflicting proletarian demands. Marx, who had no sympathy for medieval guild organization, deplored the revolutionary apathy of factory operatives and skilled artisans. A congress of workmen from the southern states did assemble at Frankfurt in August to set up a 'workers league', but efforts to stir them into revolt failed. A Socialist Congress organized by Cologne communists met in June; a Democratic Congress attempted to co-ordinate action in July. All failed before the general indifference or particular interests of the working classes.

Meanwhile the Frankfurt Parliament had been drafting a new German constitution. But cut off from lower bourgeois, artisan and working class support their deliberations threatened to become dangerously remote. Members had fatally undermined their own position when they denied the vote to peasants and artisans, and ignored popular petitions for security and social reform. They continued to operate in a vacuum, proclaiming liberal values to a society increasingly obsessed by its vested interests. For this they were for a long time severely and mercilessly criticized. Recently, however, some historians have begun to judge their actions in a more favourable light. They were at least honest to their own convictions and attempted to establish a constitutional framework which would incorporate a wide variety of civilized bourgeois virtues. If their horizons were limited, so also were those of every other class. If they failed to display the flexibility and subtlety needed for success, they nevertheless followed the precedents set by nearly every other constituent assembly of the nineteenth century. Like so many others they were to be defeated not only by the divisions within their own ranks, but also by the weight of the conservative opposition which rallied against them.

During the summer of 1848 the Parliament placed executive authority in the hands of an imperial Regent, Archduke Johann of Austria, who was to enforce the decisions of the nation's representatives and defend life and property against revolutionary attack. But the Archduke was a colourless aristocrat who lacked both the will and the power to be effective. While the several German armies remained in the hands of the separate states no so-called 'national' authority could really command respect. Schleswig-Holstein was assisted in its war against Denmark by Prussian, Hanoverian and Bavarian troops. When Frederick William agreed to a truce in August as a result of British pressure and internal unrest there was nothing the Frankfurt Parliament could do about it.

In spite of their apparent impotence, members continued to discuss a Declaration of Fundamental Rights which was to act as the basis for new constitutions in the German states. These rights included equality before the law, freedom of speech, religious toleration and guaranteed property rights. It was essential to have an agreed framework of values as the basis of a new German Union. France and the United States had both prefaced their revolutions by similar declarations of intent. At the same time the Parliament worked out detailed plans for German unity. The states were to be joined into a federal union with a monarch, a responsible ministry and a federal diet elected by universal male suffrage. Plans for common tolls, weights and measures and a uniform currency were also formulated. Some efforts were made to appease the peasants by abolishing aristocratic privileges and servile dues where these did not conflict with liberal economic principles.

Gradually, however, it became clear that all these proposals would remain entirely academic unless the Parliament acquired some power to put them into effect. Isolated from peasants, artisans and popular elements, suspected by princes and aristocrats and unable to satisfy nationalist aspirations in Schleswig-Holstein, it was soon apparent that liberal plans could only be realized with either Austrian or Prussian support. This led to a bitter dispute between the protagonists of Austria and Prussia which did little to enhance the Parliament's prestige. While most southerners and the many liberals who hoped to rely on Austria within the frontiers of a greater Germany formed a *Grossdeutsch* party, the northerners and members of the *Zollverein* who favoured a smaller state under Prussian leadership advocated a *Kleindeutsch* solution. When Frederick William wavered and abandoned Schleswig-Holstein to the Danes the majority swung in favour of Austria. But once the reaction had triumphed in Vienna[1] support gradually shifted in favour of Prussia.

[1] See p. 292.

The debates between the *Grossdeutsch* and *Kleindeutsch* parties, though founded upon a basic conflict of interest, showed up the total ineffectiveness of the Frankfurt Parliament. When radicals and democrats used the occasion of the truce with Denmark to stir up nationalist demonstrations, besiege the members and lynch two Prussian delegates, Austrian and Prussian troops had to be called in to quell the riots. The moderates became more and more alarmed at the rapid disintegration of authority and began to look back to the princes for security. Disillusion spread among intellectuals and bourgeois liberals, and gradually conditioned opinion for a restoration of the old order.

Meanwhile somewhat similar developments had occurred in Prussia. In the Assembly growing radical agitation had led to demands for the abolition of aristocratic privileges, hunting rights and tax exemptions, and for an oath of loyalty from the army to the new constitution. These were reinforced by riots in the streets and demonstrations organized by radical clubs which the Civic Guard seemed powerless to control. In June, crowds invaded the arsenal to seize arms. In October, a second Democratic Congress led to further mob violence in the streets. Moderates became increasingly alarmed at the growth of agitation and began to advocate the restoration of law and order.

These developments were watched with an appreciative eye by the aristocracy and the army. Anxious to make a comeback, determined to wipe out the memory of the March days, they only awaited a favourable moment to restore their power. In the early summer they merely caricatured the efforts of the Civic Guard to keep their fellow citizens in check. In July and August, however, the Junkers became increasingly active, opened a press campaign, set up associations for the protection of 'King and Fatherland', and in a 'Junker Parliament' held in Berlin attacked the liberals, the bourgeoisie, the Frankfurt Parliament and the whole concept of a unified German federation.

In Prussia everything depended upon the King. When Frederick William moved to Potsdam in April 1848 he gradually regained confidence and came to look back in horror at the March revolution. He was soon surrounded by officers, Junkers and a close circle of conservative advisors like the

Gerlach brothers and Manteufel all urging stronger measures against the anarchists in Berlin. He was incensed by demands that the army should take an oath to the constitution and considered it a gross violation of the royal prerogative. The end of the Danish war freed the army for use at home. General Wrangel was appointed Commander-in-Chief and with some victories against Denmark to his credit prepared to intervene at an opportune moment in the capital.

The October riots and the capitulation of Vienna[1] finally stirred Frederick William into action. At the beginning of November the liberal ministry was dismissed and replaced by another under Count Brandenburg, a strong conservative. The Assembly was prorogued and sent to the provinces, the Civic Guard disbanded, and Berlin occupied by General Wrangel's troops and placed under martial law. Wealthy citizens appeared to welcome the move and the Civic Guard returned their arms with scarcely a murmur. In December the Assembly was dissolved. In January 1849 the King granted a new constitution which retained many features of the old but assured royal control over the executive, the army and the ordinary revenue. When in April a delegation from the Frankfurt Parliament eventually came to offer Frederick William the German Crown he contemptuously rejected 'a crown from the gutter'.

Abandoned by all, the Frankfurt Parliament could only dissolve and vanish from the political scene. Even its national appeal had failed to rouse the Germans, and had merely alarmed Poles, Czechs and Slavs who found themselves in danger of absorption into a wider German union.[2] But more significantly it had failed to appeal to the vested interests of peasants, artisans, workers and lower bourgeois elements for whom nationalism was not merely an ideal, but an avenue to concrete economic and social advantages. In May 1849 radicals and republicans revolted in Baden and Saxony only to be relentlessly crushed by Prussian troops. No class was sufficient in isolation to curb the combined power of the army and the aristocracy. The failure of the Frankfurt Parliament brought failure for every other sector, and all were forced to make what terms they could with the triumphant forces of reaction. The latter were quick to exploit the situation to their

[1] See p. 292.   [2] See p. 290.

own advantage and to guarantee their own survival for
another seventy years.

4. *The Revolution in the Habsburg Empire*

The revolutions in the Habsburg Empire combined both
the social and the national conflicts apparent elsewhere. This
in itself gives them a decided historical interest. In addition,
Vienna was both the centre of Metternich's authority and the
source of political initiative throughout central Europe. Its
actions influenced events in Italy, Germany and the Austrian
provinces. Its failure encouraged reaction everywhere and
made the ultimate defeat of other revolutionary movements
practically certain.

Throughout the Empire social and national divisions were
hopelessly entangled. The higher aristocracy were closely tied
to the Court at Vienna and frequently absent from their
estates, though the Hungarians still exercised some political
leadership at home. The lesser nobles remained in the
provinces, loyal to the Crown, hostile to their superiors and
increasingly aware of their economic and regional differences.
In Hungary all free Magyars were noble and some 500,000
still lived in a state of traditional, near-feudal independence.
There was also a rising class of Croat, Czech and Rumanian
gentry all claiming vague traditional rights and jealous of
German and Magyar privileges. The upper bourgeoisie were
nearly all German and controlled commerce and city life.
Budapest, Prague and the larger towns had German majorities
and were the centres of cultural activity and bureaucratic
control. The lesser bourgeoisie, however, generally reflected
the separate nationalities struggling for recognition. Intellectuals, rising peasants and artisans competed by stressing
Czech, Croat or Magyar ties. They were largely responsible
for the growth of nationalism within each region and used
the literature of the past to stir up new hopes for the future.

The government controlled this varied assortment by a
policy of checks and balances. The economy was regulated,
publications carefully censored, political activity closely
watched in an attempt to frustrate agitation and maintain an
unruffled calm. In moments of crisis nationalists could be
used to keep each other in check, or peasants roused against
their lords as in Galicia. Nevertheless, the growth of dis-

content was obvious some time before the revolution. It was partially economic. In Austria, the aristocracy and bourgeoisie joined forces in an 'Estates Movement' to demand credit facilities and freer trade. Artisans, lacking employment and the benefits of new industrial development, were forced to live in deplorable conditions in the suburbs of Vienna. Discontent was also national. In Bohemia, Hungary and Croatia, authors and aristocrats continued, in spite of censorship, to proclaim their privileges in the new regional diets. There was also an element of liberal idealism among students and moderate bourgeois who hoped through a constitutional or national solution to bring a new vitality and a new meaning to the fossilized traditions of the Habsburg Empire.

In 1848 news of the Paris revolution precipitated events. In Hungary the Diet was in session at Bratislava. It had already proclaimed the unique authority of the Magyar tongue, and agitated for economic and political reforms. Spurred on by news of student agitation in Budapest, Kossuth, the fiery and passionate leader of the lesser nobility, now demanded radical reforms. Hungary was to have its own ministry and parliament elected on a restricted franchise. *Robot*[1] was to be abolished and landlords compensated. Viennese control was to be severed and the Habsburg link retained only as a personal union between Magyars and the monarchy. At the same time Hungary claimed all the lands of St. Stephen from Croatia to the Carpathians, and set out to liberate the Slavs within a rigid Magyar framework. Inspired by the Kossuth's rousing oratory the Diet passed these 'March Laws' with only limited opposition from the moderate court aristocracy.

In Prague, national and intellectual agitation also erupted in revolt. On March 11th moderate Czechs and Germans met to urge liberal reforms, linguistic equality and the abolition of *robot*. This, however, was not enough for radical Czech nationalists. By March 29th they had added demands for a responsible ministry, a parliament, and all the lands of St. Wenceslaus which included Bohemia, Moravia and Silesia.

Meanwhile the revolutionary tide had reached Vienna. The Lower Austrian Estates were due to meet on March 13th to discuss economic grievances and urge the resignation of Metternich. Intellectuals and university students used the

[1] See p. 267.

occasion to present a petition for reform and rouse the workers from the suburbs. As crowds pressed round the *Landhaus*, a copy of Kossuth's speech in the Hungarian Diet led to further agitation and to renewed demands for a constitution. A march to the palace created panic at court, Metternich resigned and left for London while troops cleared the squares and shot down a number of citizens. This provoked a general uprising. The bourgeoisie hastened to form a national guard, students seized arms and created an academic legion, while artisans burnt toll houses, destroyed gas lamps and wrecked machinery. On March 15th Ferdinand capitulated and promised a free press and a constitution. A new moderate ministry at the end of April published proposals for a liberal constitution with a restricted franchise. This, however, was not enough for the radical student and artisan opposition. On May 15th another rising in the suburbs forced through demands for universal suffrage. Two days later the Court fled to Innsbrück.

Ferdinand also gave way in Hungary, Prague and north Italy, where Radetsky was ordered to evacuate Lombardy. Paradoxically, this was the first step towards the eventual recovery of Habsburg fortunes. The apparent collapse of the Court allowed every sectional, national and class interest full scope. Once again general fragmentation occurred, only this time protagonists became engaged in bitter conflict and open warfare. As a result the Court, steadied by the army and the aristocracy, was able to make a spectacular come-back and crush all its rivals. Radetsky ignored instructions, held out in the Quadrilateral and sent Schwarzenberg to Innsbrück for reinforcements. With the aid of the loyal Minister of War, Count Latour, 25,000 were drafted to Italy by July. Windischgrätz, the Imperial Commander, when ordered to retire from Vienna, took the army on manoeuvres and remained ready to strike at the appropriate moment. He was soon given his first opportunity by events in Prague.

In Bohemia, Czech claims had led to conflict with the Germans, who made up most of the aristocracy and upper bourgeoisie. German plans aimed to promote a *Grossdeutsch*[1] union through the Frankfurt Parliament in order to enhance both their national and economic status. Such a policy, how-

[1] See p. 284.

ever, the Czechs refused to accept. Palacky, their leader, rejected an invitation to Frankfurt in a letter which began: 'I am a Czech of Slav descent.' He feared absorption into a greater Germany, and urged the preservation of the Habsburg Empire as a bulwark against the insidious advance of Russia. In June he called a Pan-Slav Congress in Prague with Bohemian, Slovak, Croat and Polish delegates. Their aim was to maintain a federal but unified Empire, free from Magyar and German domination, but at the same time safe from their differences. Such objectives appealed neither to the Germans nor to the radical Czechs. Windischgrätz, who had meanwhile been appointed Military Governor, played upon the situation to provoke a riot. This gave him an excuse to intervene and on June 12th Prague was crushed after five days of bitter fighting, the Congress expelled and the radicals eliminated. All hopes of a separate Czech movement were destroyed and the moderates moved to Vienna to join up with the new Constituent Assembly.

Meanwhile Magyar claims had created bitter opposition from the Slavs in the Hungarian provinces. A new government had been formed under a radical magnate, Batthyány, with Kossuth, Minister of Finance, as its driving force. On April 11th the 'March Laws' had been confirmed by Ferdinand, and Hungary had become a separate state. Kossuth now demanded ruthless Magyarization throughout, and the Diets of Croatia and Transylvania were summoned to vote their own dissolution. The outcome, however, was quite different. The Croatian Diet, meeting at Agram, demanded full autonomy, elected Jellačič, a local aristocrat, to be governor, and ignored instructions from Budapest. Batthyány persuaded Ferdinand to dismiss Jellačič in May. Once again, however, imperial instructions were ignored with the approval of the Court. When Jellačič rallied an army in June, Latour sent secret aid from Vienna for use in a future war to crush Magyar independence.

By the end of July, Charles Albert had been defeated at Custoza, Czech radicalism had been crushed and the Hungarians progressively insolated. The Court had also begun to placate moderate German sentiment in Vienna. Here the government was faced by a constant stream of radical demands. Student agitation, artisan riots and press abuse created a reign of terror that began to alarm moderate opinion. Efforts to introduce a limited censorship and curb the academic legion failed and merely led to renewed disturbances. Eventually on May 26th a Committee of Public Safety was set up in an attempt to regulate the government and curb disorder. The National Guard was reorganized and the unemployed set to work mending roads and clearing the Danube. In August, however, lack of funds led to a cut in pay and further violent artisan demonstrations. This time the National Guard restored order, firing into the crowd and killing eighteen. The moderate bourgeoisie greeted the news with enthusiasm. They were also gratified when Ferdinand returned to Vienna in response to a petition signed by 80,000 citizens. By the end of the month the Court was able to take the offensive. Anglo-French mediation in Italy was rejected, union under the Habsburg crown was declared indissoluble and Jellačič was restored to his post. Outside Hungary, imperial authority seemed assured. The Court now manoeuvred to defeat their last and most dangerous opponents.

In July the Constituent Assembly of the western provinces met in Vienna to draw up a constitution. Universal suffrage had given the vote to the peasantry, whose representatives generally remained loyal to the Crown and the aristocracy. Kudlich, the peasant leader, rallied enough support to abolish feudal obligations and *robot* with the usual provisions for compensation. After this the peasants rapidly lost interest in the revolution. The majority believed that their release was due entirely to the generosity of Ferdinand. Bourgeois members, anxious to restore credit, voted two million florins to back up loans and rally the exchange. Radical Germans, however, urged support for the Frankfurt Parliament and the recognition of Hungarian autonomy which would enable Austria to sever connections with her outer provinces and allow her to join a greater German union. These moves, however, met bitter opposition from the Czechs and Slovenes who were hostile to both Germans and Magyars, and from the aristocracy and the upper bourgeoisie whose economic and social interests still lay within a Habsburg Empire. These elements combined to reject Hungarian demands, and to undermine the *Grossdeutsch* party.

As in other revolutionary movements, the radicals were to rise in a last heroic act of defiance. On September 11th Jellačič had invaded Hungary only to be driven back before Budapest by a massed Magyar counter-attack. Kossuth became president of a new Committee of Defence and called for a fight to the finish. The imperial commissioner sent to dissolve the Hungarian Diet was murdered in the streets, while moderates and aristocrats fled from the capital or retired to their estates. As a result the government determined to send reinforcements to support Jellačič and crush the Hungarian extremists. They had, however, misjudged the temper of the radicals in Vienna. News of the draft led to an immediate revolt by students, artisans, unemployed and ardent German nationalists. Latour was torn to pieces while National Guards pulled up the railway track to prevent troop departures. The Court fled to Olmütz and was followed by the Czechs and the moderate Germans in the Assembly. The National Guard split, half of it deserting, while some 20,000 wealthy citizens left the capital. Vienna was left in the hands of radicals, students and artisans.

But the position of the capital was desperate. Abandoned by moderate bourgeois and Slav nationalists, and surrounded by an indifferent peasantry, it could only hope for aid from radicals in Hungary and Frankfurt. Kossuth, however, was pre-occupied, while the Germans were powerless. They could only send a delegation led by Robert Blum with a message of fraternal greetings! By mid-October Vienna was surrounded by the armies of Windischgrätz and Jellačič, who now claimed that his retreat from Hungary had been an advance into Austria. Even when Kossuth arrived on the frontier, suspicion of German plans made him hesitate to come to the city's relief. After fanatical resistance Vienna was bombarded into submission, radical leaders including Blum were shot, and the revolutionary movement finally expunged.

In November, a new ministry was appointed under Schwarzenberg which included able administrators like Stadion, Bruck and Bach. On December 2nd Ferdinand was persuaded to abdicate in favour of his nephew Francis Joseph, and Schwarzenberg now felt completely free to destroy the work of the revolution. He represented a new realistic approach in politics. He had nothing but contempt for the court aristocracy, and was prepared to tolerate the activities of moderates while building up his forces to destroy the Hungarians. Thus the Constituent Assembly was maintained at Kremsier where it was urged to draw up a liberal and united constitution. After four months it had drafted a new framework for the Empire which combined a central government with some measure of regional autonomy.[1]

Meanwhile, Hungary had been invaded by Jellačič and Windischgrätz from the West, and by Rumanians and frontier troops from the East. Budapest was occupied in January, and Kossuth and the Diet forced to retire to Debreczen. On March 4th Stadion[2] issued a new compromise constitution which united the Empire under one single authority but kept a number of liberal proposals. The historic units were retained and communal autonomy, linguistic and national rights were guaranteed. But there was to be one parliament, one citizenship, one law and one administrative machine operated from Vienna.

Though the constitution was accepted in German and Slav provinces, the Hungarian radicals were roused to new and desperate measures. In April, Kossuth declared the Habsburgs deposed and drove the Austrian army out of Budapest. But his actions alienated the moderates and a section of the army who had always maintained a tradition of loyalty to the Crown. Moreover, his passionate attacks on the Serbs and Croats also increased his isolation and alarmed intelligent Hungarians who realized they could never survive alone. Meanwhile Nicholas I offered unconditional Russian assistance to put down the revolt. Besides hating all revolutions in principle, he was especially alarmed by one on his own frontier and by its possible influence on Poland. Many Polish exiles were fighting in the Hungarian armies, and two of its best generals were Poles. Schwarzenberg accepted Russian help, and in May a Russian army entered Hungary. In August the bulk of the Hungarian army capitulated at Vilagos and Kossuth fled to Turkey. Hungary was reoccupied by imperial troops and subjected to a reign of terror directed by the Austrian Commander-in-Chief, General Haynau. Its defeat brought the revolutionary movements of the previous year to an end. Divided and disillusioned they rose to great-

[1] See p. 426.   [2] See p. 427.

ness in defeat. This was, however, poor consolation for the hopes and fears of half a century.

5. *The Policies of Reaction*

In 1849, kings, courts and aristocrats restored their authority throughout central Europe. Their armies were generally welcomed by the upper bourgeoisie, chastened by a year of social upheaval and economic collapse. Austrian troops imposed uniformity on the Empire, and restored Habsburg rule in Lombardy, Tuscany and Venice. The reoccupation of Rome was followed by the revival of the Inquisition and the gradual elimination of liberal critics. In Naples, Ferdinand filled the prisons with his political opponents. In Germany the Prussian army fulfilled a similar role. The Rhineland revolts were crushed in May, socialists expelled and censorship restored. A radical revolution in Saxony led by Born and Bakunin, in which the composer Richard Wagner played a prominent role, was defeated in June. While Prussian troops marched South to destroy the last democratic revolts in Baden, Würtemberg forces, their courage restored, expelled the radical rump of the Frankfurt Parliament from Stuttgart.

Nearly every class had been profoundly shocked by the tide of events and emerged disillusioned and cynical. The complacent assumptions of the aristocracy, the romantic vision of princes, the liberal convictions of the bourgeoisie and the trusting hopes of artisans and workers had been shattered. Constitutions had collapsed, national ideals had failed. The Poles had won no privileges in Posen,[1] Schleswig-Holstein had been restored to the Danes. German unification had proved an idle dream. Italy remained a geographical expression. Intellectual exiles in London indulged in bitter recrimination, blaming liberal leaders and bourgeois duplicity for their defeat. For Marx the middle classes had betrayed the revolution and united with the aristocracy to crush the proletariat. Failure, however, was in most cases due to a misunderstanding of the facts. The events of 1848 made this explicit.

Royal and aristocratic authority depended in the last resort on the deployment of force. In its armies, bureaucracy and police the old order had more effective weapons than liberals

[1] See p. 280.

had bargained for. The main asset of the bourgeoisie was money. In 1848 they were unable to transform it into power. They were governed by a natural desire to preserve their wealth, uphold an ordered community and assert liberal values. They assumed that others would accept their ideals without benefiting materially from the outcome. In this they relied upon a perfectionist but somewhat naïve view of human nature.

Other classes had little interest in liberal principles, and were largely concerned with their immediate social and economic benefits. When artisans found themselves unable to share bourgeois wealth they tried to destroy it. More advanced factory operatives, however, already realized the advantages of industrialization and merely hoped to even up their share of the profits. Hence the fragmentation among lower bourgeois and proletarian groups. The same applied to the peasantry. Once their interest in the land had been secured they lost all interest in the revolution. Even the upper bourgeoisie were, in fact, divided by similar considerations. The conflicts between *Grossdeutsch* and *Kleindeutsch* had also been in part the outcome of intense economic and political rivalry.

After 1848 politicians, political parties, authors and agitators paid increasing attention to the real as opposed to the ideal. Courts relied less on divine right and concentrated on consolidating and broadening the foundations of their power. Armies and administrators were carefully controlled, while the interests of others were skilfully exploited. This even allowed a certain degree of compromise with the social, economic and political demands of the community. Constitutions might preserve bourgeois loyalties and assure regular taxation. Reform would pacify social unrest and promote the accumulation of wealth.

The pattern was set by Schwarzenberg who, with a general contempt for others, exploited everyone in the Habsburg interest. Until the army was fully restored all parties were kept pacified. While nationalist rebels and radical threats remained, moderates were diverted to draft constitutions. But once the extremes had destroyed each other centralization was swiftly restored. Peasants were placated by the abolition of *robot*, the bourgeoisie by the restoration of order and Bruck's

U

plans for a wider German *Zollverein*. Slavs would be grateful for their newly won equality with Magyars, and Germans for their established status at the heart of the Empire.

Similar policies were adopted in the German states. In Prussia the constitution gave the King complete control over the army and pacified bourgeois anxiety. The Brandenburg ministry, observing events in France, insisted on universal suffrage in order to guarantee a conservative majority by harnessing the peasant vote. Meanwhile Manteufel[1] passed laws to commute manorial dues, establish loans banks and promote guild controls in order to rally support and undermine liberal claims. In May, however, the government felt sufficiently secure to limit the franchise and restore graded property qualifications. Other states soon followed the Prussian example. Peasant dues were abolished or commuted, feudal jurisdiction destroyed, and guild controls restored in many crafts. Liberal ministries were gradually replaced and constitutions slowly undermined by restricting the franchise and restoring an absolute royal authority.

Realism soon permeated political thinking. While the Habsburgs survived by juggling with the component parts of their Empire, Bismarck and Cavour were to unite Germany and Italy by a policy of opportunism that exploited every available factor to achieve their purpose. Socialists ceased trying to find utopian solutions, and began to organize effective weapons to force through their demands. The ideal anarchism of Proudhon slowly gave way before the disciplined determinism of Marx. Writers and artists were caught up in the same realistic analysis. Courbet, Daumier and Manet painted the harsh realities that Dickens, Hugo, Dostoyevsky and Turgenev were beginning to describe. Life was an infinite series of relationships, and success would come to those who could best harness and exploit them.

[1] See p. 352.

XII · RUSSIA AND THE CRIMEAN WAR

1. *Nicholas I and the Russian Empire*

RUSSIA was barely affected by the revolutionary upheavals of 1848. The extreme inflexibility of her society and of her institutions had a profoundly dampening effect. The community remained divided into traditional castes. The Crown and the aristocracy monopolised the land together with its forty-five million peasants. The bourgeoisie followed isolated careers in the widely scattered cities of the Empire. Doctors, lawyers and teachers could only rise through aristocratic patronage or by royal service. Twenty-five million private serfs lived a life entirely dependent upon the generosity or mania of their masters. Some landlords maintained a firm but benevolent paternalism. Others bullied, beat and even branded their serfs, while peasants in state communes still lived the simple and regular life of medieval villeins.

The State was co-ordinated by a government machinery dedicated to preserving distinction and designed to fulfil the wishes of an omnipotent Tsar. While nobles and towns were left to operate through their own assemblies, the country was supervised by an army of bureaucrats. These covered every department and frequently used blackmail and extortion to supplement their meagre pay. Instructions came from ministers personally appointed by the Tsar. The Council of State drafted laws, while the Senate acted as a supreme court and carried out occasional inspections of the bureaucratic administration. Order was maintained by regional governors assisted by the army and the police. The whole structure was vast, unwieldy and ineffective. The bureaucracy became paralysed with paperwork. In 1842 there were some 3,300,000 cases covering 33 million sheets of paper under consideration. All instructions remained secret; no one felt responsible for any decision; everyone lived by exploiting their inferiors.

Intelligent Russians generally felt helpless and depressed in face of the inefficiency, wastage and frustration of an autocratic semi-feudal state. Some had been influenced by eighteenth-century philosophers, others by romantic idealists. Both elements combined in the conspiracy of young officers and aristocrats that greeted the accession of Nicholas I. Many of them had been deeply affected by their experience in the West and felt outraged by the backwardness and brutality of Russian life. But their activities had to be kept secret and they remained divided among a variety of conspiratorial societies.

In December 1825, when Alexander died suddenly and in mysterious circumstances, revolutionaries in the Northern Society rose and proclaimed Constantine Tsar in opposition to Nicholas who had been designated to the title. But others in the South failed to combine and the rebels were easily crushed by loyal troops. The Decembrists were the forerunners of a tradition of revolt that lingered on and eventually grew into the revolutionary movements of the twentieth century. They had already given up hopes of any reforms from within. The reigns of the remaining Tsars would only have confirmed their doubts.

Nicholas I thus ascended the throne in the shadow of revolt. It probably left a lasting strain upon his nerves but it did not entirely cloud his judgement. The new Tsar was far more of a realist than his brother Alexander. He did not obscure issues in a mystical synthesis or imagine that he could absorb liberal and national ideals within the framework of an absolute state. He realised that Russia was an autocracy and was not entirely blind to its faults. He was not a man of half-measures and once set upon a policy carried it to its logical conclusions. He gave personal attention to the issues raised by the Decembrists, and set out to remedy some of their complaints. He hoped to consolidate control and maintain the traditions of a royal paternalism. He was aware of inefficiency and the evils of serfdom and tried to reform them. He realized the dangers of liberal criticism and revolutionary agitation and determined to eliminate both. His military background and commanding presence were well suited to such objectives. Unfortunately the task was too great, the area too enormous, and the obstructions too ingrained to allow for either reform or effective government.

From 1826 onwards Nicholas began to build up a private chancellery to supervise the nation and watch over state affairs. Various sections were set up to hear petitions, codify the law, supervise education, administer state peasants and provide a secret police. It was this latter Third Section, that gave the reign of Nicholas much of its notoriety. The secret police were to be the eyes and ears of the Tsar. With a network of informers they penetrated liberal societies and government departments, eliminated the unreliable and detected potential revolutionaries. They helped maintain censorship and destroy opposition. They were, in general, insidiously effective and completely overshadowed the limited achievements of the other sections.

The Second Section was designed to codify the laws. A complete list was eventually drawn up in the early 'thirties by Speranski, who had begun work under Alexander.[1] But its impact was negligible. Courts remained corrupt, their proceedings secret, their decisions delayed by infinite appeals. While serfs were tied to manorial rule half the population was, in any case, beyond the jurisdiction of the State. In government the private chancellery created yet more duplication in an already overloaded administrative system. In addition to bureaucratic, police and military supervision, each district was now liable to sudden inspection by the secret agents of the Tsar.

The official report on the Decembrist conspiracy had noted the inherent dangers of free thought and education. In 1826 a new censorship law curbed all criticism of the régime and restricted most speculative thought. It was, however, laxly applied in spite of the special supervision of the private chancellery, and a wide variety of disguised criticism was incorporated into the literature of the period. Education was also carefully controlled to exclude western ideas. Russia's seventy-four secondary schools were reserved for the privileged; her universities could only satisfy a small fraction of the population. Nevertheless, within the strict framework of a state institution, there was considerable room for development. Entry was based on intelligence. Promotion depended on merit. Valuable work was done in science and mathematics and discussion inevitably strayed into political and social fields.

Nicholas attempted to ensure conformity by rigid control over the Church and the elimination of independent Ortho-

[1] See p. 139.

dox or Catholic opinion. This led to a lengthy conflict with the Papacy. Not until the accession of Pius IX in 1847 was a concordat eventually signed. Elsewhere the Tsar was a firm supporter of conservative policies and dynastic control. He could only be secure if the sources of unrest beyond his borders were also eliminated. Hence his support for Metternich and his abhorrence of revolution and those who like Frederick William IV or Louis-Philippe appeared to compromise with liberal demands. In 1830 he was prepared to march into France to crush the July revolution and was only dissuaded by the violent protests of Metternich and Palmerston. The outbreak of the Polish revolt frustrated all plans for intervention and Nicholas vented a torrent of embittered rage upon the Poles.[1] Five thousand estates were confiscated. Thirty thousand families were deported to Siberia. Poland was eliminated and its affairs transferred to the Council of State.

In 1834 Nicholas joined Metternich and the King of Prussia in the Münchengrätz agreements to uphold the established order against revolutionary unrest. At home his attitude stiffened. Count Ouvarov, his Minister of Education, proclaimed the three corner-stones of Russian policy – 'Orthodoxy, Autocracy and Nationality.' Nationality meant observing the other two. The revolutions of 1848 led to further curbs. Talk of reform ceased. The censorship was strengthened. Even Biblical texts were purged. Study of philosophy and constitutional law was banned from the universities. The Tsar became 'Gendarme of Europe'. His troops crushed the Hungarian revolt; his attitude buttressed the Habsburgs and Danes and destroyed Prussian plans for Schleswig-Holstein and German unification. Queen Victoria considered him the 'greatest of all earthly potentates'. Even he, however, could not arrest the advance of Russian history. Though its progress might appear frozen, it moved with a glacial momentum and was to avalanche at the end.

2. *Social and Economic Change*

By the middle of the nineteenth century some changes had in fact begun to scratch the surface of the Russian economy. Though agriculture remained tied to the routine of the manor, industry, trade and transport were exposed to gradual

[1] See p. 235.

modification. The number of factories increased from 5,260 to 9,842 in twenty-four years, while the workers employed in them more than doubled. The output of pig-iron rose by twenty-five per cent to equal German production.[1] Most notable was the boom in textiles. After the relaxation of British export restrictions in 1842, new machinery was introduced into factories in Moscow and St. Petersburg. By the early 1850s some seventeen hundred mechanical looms were in operation and though their output was small in comparison to a vast mass of hand-loom weavers they did bring concentrations of industry into the suburbs of Russia's major cities.

Foreign trade also doubled during Nicholas's reign. Though almost entirely in alien hands, it did have a formative influence on the economy. Financial stability was essential and in 1844 a revaluation of the currency introduced a 'silver rouble' which had only depreciated 25 per cent by 1917. More significantly, attention was given for the first time to the problems of communication. As yet roads were barely tolerable, while railway construction had hardly begun. Railways were described by the Minister of Finance as a 'danger to public morals' as they encouraged purposeless travel and fostered the restless spirit of the age. Nevertheless in 1842 a line between Moscow and St. Petersburg was projected, financed by American capital, and completed in 1851. These changes, however, remained drops in an ocean of isolated communes and primitive cultivation. They could only anticipate further changes to come. Their impact upon the average Russian remained negligible or non-existent.

Prospects of change were blocked by the almost insuperable rigidities of Russian society. Life deferred to the vested interests and idle caprices of the aristocracy. Its court officials and army officers were the buttresses of the régime. The autocracy depended for survival upon the loyalty of the landed proprietor, who regulated peasant life and furnished quotas for the army from his estates. This restricted every effort at peasant reform. In state communes agricultural improvements, schools and social welfare services were introduced by the Fifth Section. Nothing much could be done to improve the conditions of the private serf. In 1833 their

[1] See Appendix 4.

public auction was prohibited. Subsequent edicts encouraged emancipation and allowed serfs to purchase freedom with their master's consent. No attempt, however, was made to interfere in the direct relationship between master and man. Many ignored every provision or principle of restraint. Labour dues were extracted regardless of statutory limits. Serfs were still sold, flogged or drafted into the army, generally as a punishment for disobedience. Nicholas accepted serfdom as a necessary evil. Freedom would undermine the security of the State; any reforms were left to his successor.

Serfdom appeared to enshrine the social and economic evils of Tsarist Russia. It brought out the worst characteristics of an aristocratic élite. It appeared to perpetuate an absolute state dedicated to repression and rigid class distinctions. It frustrated economic growth by tying capital and labour to the land, thus preventing capitalist accumulation and industrial growth. It led to repeated outbreaks of terror and violence, rising and repression. Peasant revolts increased by 50 per cent each decade throughout the reign. Altogether there were over seven hundred risings, some covering nearly twenty provinces. Landlords and bailiffs were murdered and estates destroyed. The reprisals were equally barbarous. Rebels were knouted, flogged to death and whole communities razed to the ground.

Intellectuals were well aware that Russia was weighed down by insuperable social and political burdens. Radishchev had described the tragic life of the peasantry in the eighteenth century.[1] The Decembrists had urged freedom for the serfs as well as constitutional reform. All the great authors of the nineteenth century described in moving terms the savage plight and resigned dignity of the Russian peasant. Nevertheless, it was practically impossible to do anything about it. Whenever critics met even to discuss a remedy they were quickly rounded up by the police. In the 1840s a group led by Petrashevsky, a clerk at the Ministry of Foreign Affairs, which included officials, students and artists, gathered to consider the need for action and the possibility of rallying the peasants in revolt. In 1849, however, they were arrested and sent to Siberia. Among them was Dostoyevsky, later to be-

[1] See p. 46.

come one of Russia's greatest writers. He wrote of his experiences in his novel, *The House of the Dead*, an epitaph upon the failure of Russian life.

Writers and reformers were further weakened by disagreements about ends and means. The impact of European thought upon the Russian mind created a variety of contradictory cross-currents. Some were influenced by the rational criticism of French philosophers, others by more romantic ideals. Some hoped to learn from the West, others from the collective traditions of Russian history. These eventually crystallized into two broad groups – Westerners and Slavophiles. In 1836 Chaadayev published *Letters on the Philosophy of History*, in which he described Russia as a desert, retarded and sterile, due to its lack of contact with the West. He urged a reunion with the Catholic tradition and a return to the mainstream of historical development. Khomyakov replied on the eve of the Crimean war that, on the contrary, Russia's condition was due to contact with the West. It was the alien policies of Peter and Catherine that had corrupted the aristocracy and diverted Russia from its true and natural path. He advocated a return to the ideal communes of the past and a restoration of Russia's traditional values.

Each group was further subdivided into active and passive elements. Chaadayev himself believed in gradual evolution and rejected the use of violence. Other Westerners such as Herzen and Bakunin were prepared to urge revolutionary methods and saw hope only in the complete destruction of the régime. Among the Slavophiles some dreamed of eternal truths smothered under an alien autocracy, others like Pogodin and Tyutchev hoped to organize a more militant Pan-Slavism and encourage agitation for a new Slav Order. After 1848 the failure of action and the futility of opposition created a growing climate of indifference and despair. While the greatest authors of the century like Chekhov, Tolstoy and Dostoyevsky were able to portray the conflicting ideals and frustrations of Russian life, the majority could only watch and wait. The hero of the time was 'the superfluous man', unable to succeed, empty, futile and bitter who could only end up by complete resignation or violent death.

Nevertheless, almost every Russian held in common a

passionate conviction of Russia's mission. For the Tsar it was
to uphold orthodoxy and autocracy. For the Westerner it was
to acquire new knowledge, reform the State and lead man-
kind to a nobler destiny. The Slavophiles hoped to convert
Europe to Russia's peculiar blend of free communal association. All were obsessed by the size of the Russian Empire, by
the power locked in her institutions, by visions of a bridge
between East and West. Liberation could bring fulfilment;
revolution would bring release. Though all looked in
different directions their national ambitions appeared clear.
Their propaganda filled Europe with alarm and created a
permanent fear of Russian intervention. Their effective influence, however, remained negligible. Nicholas I found the
agitation of both Westerners and Slavophiles equally dangerous. Though he exploited their feelings when it suited his
policy, he based his actions on the need to preserve power
and only expanded Russian claims as and when it appeared
practical to do so.

3. *The Expansion of Russia*

Russian expansion had continued intermittently since the
consolidation of European Muscovy. Explorers had reached
the Pacific in the seventeenth century and Peter and
Catherine had obtained footholds on the Baltic and the Black
Sea coasts during the next hundred years. Alexander had advanced westwards with the acquisition of Finland and Bessarabia and had brought Russia into the heart of Europe by
the absorption of Poland into the Russian Empire. This
appeared to end the possibility of immediate expansion to the
West. For the next hundred years Russian activities were to
turn in a more southerly direction.

Penetration followed four general lines of advance. In the
Far East Russian governor-generals occupied the Amur basin
with enough of the Pacific coast to establish a port free from
winter ice. In the centre, across the wide desert and steppe
lands between Lake Baikal and the Caspian Sea, expeditions
gradually absorbed the Khanates of Turkestan. Between the
Caspian and the Black Seas there were regular wars to subdue
Caucasian tribes. Finally in the South-West, Russian advance
appeared to threaten the mouth of the Danube and point a
sinister arm towards Constantinople.

Here Russian diplomacy became embroiled in the Eastern Question and the progressive disintegration of the Turkish Empire.[1] Russian policy was divided between a desire to gain control over the Straits leading to the freer waters of the Mediterranean and fear lest the intrusion of a foreign power should close this vital exit to Russian shipping. When Nicholas I ascended the throne he was immediately faced with this dilemma due to the recent outbreak of the Greek revolt. Alexander had become convinced in the last months of his reign that foreign intervention was imminent, and that Metternich was no longer reliable. As a result he was prepared to join with Britain and France to solve the Greek question. Nicholas continued this policy with notable success. Russian troops forced the Turks to grant Greek independence, and by the Treaty of Adrianople ensured the passage of unarmed shipping through the Straits in time of peace.[2]

In the same year (1829) an imperial committee reported that the advantages of preserving the Ottoman Empire outweighed the benefits of any possible dissolution. A weak Empire would inevitably fall under Russian influence. Partition could only bring other stronger powers into the area. In 1833 Russian troops landed on the Bosphorus to defend Constantinople against Egyptian attack. The Treaty of Unkiar-Skelessi which followed was purely defensive.[3] Russia agreed to defend Turkey if attacked, and in return the Turks agreed to keep the Straits closed to foreign warships. Palmerston, however, was convinced that Russia had imminent designs on the Ottoman Empire and had gained the right to send warships through the Straits in peacetime. He was not satisfied until he had torn up the Treaty of Unkiar-Skelessi by the Straits Convention of 1841.[4] This banned all foreign warships from the Dardanelles while Turkey was at peace. Nicholas thus had no qualms about signing it.

Between 1829 and 1848 Russia was fully engaged elsewhere. In 1829 the Caucasians launched a Holy War against Russian advance and her resources were fully stretched by a series of costly guerilla actions. In 1839 an expedition to occupy the Khanate of Khiva was a failure. The area, however, required constant attention, especially in view of the British

[1] See pp. 213-19.   [2] See p. 219.   [3] See p. 237.   [4] See p. 249.

expedition to Kabul in 1842. From St. Petersburg, British encirclement appeared as grave a threat as Russian expansion did to Palmerston. In 1842 the Treaty of Nanking, following Britain's opium war with China, forced the Chinese to open five treaty ports to international trade. In 1847 when Count Muraviev became Governor-General of Eastern Siberia he determined to re-open Russia's forward policy in the area by pushing down the Amur river and forcing a way into the warm waters of the Pacific.

Meanwhile Russian policy in the West had been essentially defensive. Nicholas was preoccupied with the problem of Poland. Even after the defeat of the Polish rebellion there was a continued danger of disturbance by exiles as well as incursions from neighbouring territory. The Tsar was therefore particularly sensitive to events in Austria, Galicia, Posen, Hungary and the Danubian Principalities. In 1846 Nicholas supported the Austrian annexation of Cracow which he described as 'the hotbed of a vast new conspiracy whose ramifications embraced all the former Polish provinces'. In 1848 he was enraged by liberal Prussian plans for Posen and kept a large army on the Polish frontier in case of disturbance. French demonstrations in favour of the Poles reinforced his determination to crush every symptom of revolutionary unrest. The use of Polish generals by the Viennese and Hungarian rebels only hastened his desire to assist the Habsburgs. The danger of agitation in the Principalities resulted in their occupation by Russian troops and the creation of a joint protectorate with Turkey until order had been restored.

Russian defensive action thus took on, as it so often did, a somewhat aggressive look. Pan-Slav propaganda, though not always favourable to Russia, appeared to suggest a growing threat from the East. The decisive influence of Russian arbitration in Europe in 1848 and 1850 seemed to confirm a dangerous accumulation of power.[1] When Nicholas demanded the extradition of two Polish generals who had fled to Turkey, and Austria followed by demanding some 4,000 Hungarians, the Turks appealed to Britain and France for support. As a result the British and French fleets were sent to the neighbourhood of the Dardanelles, though the Tsar

[1] See p. 351.

had already withdrawn his demands before the fleets moved. When they arrived and had to shelter in the Straits because of bad weather Palmerston quickly apologized for contravening the convention of 1841 in order not to give the Russian fleet any excuse for intervention, an action that must have caused the Tsar some secret amusement. Palmerston himself, however, did not really believe that Nicholas would intervene, while the British ambassador in Russia considered that no attempt would be made to subvert the Ottoman Empire during the Tsar's lifetime.

Nevertheless the Tsar's policies appeared dangerously enigmatic. Estranged from Prussia, he rejected a renewal of the Austrian alliance. He appeared to live in autocratic isolation, determined to maintain an absolutism at once impenetrable and overwhelming. Confusion and misunderstanding became inevitable. As a result the great powers allowed themselves to drift almost against their better judgement into the Crimean war.

4. *The Causes of the Crimean War*

Some wars may be classified as the outcome of obvious ambition, the grand design of monarchy, an expanding wave of revolution or the intoxicating dreams of military men. Others seem to emerge from an accumulation of events that grow almost inevitably out of a particular situation. Their causes create infinite room for speculation and debate. Emphasis may be placed on latent conflicts apparently embedded in the background out of which a pattern leading to war is almost certain to emerge. Alternatively, the events themselves may be analysed and stress laid on the decisions taken and the mistakes made. This again opens up further difficulties. At what point does a build-up of diplomatic manoeuvres and hostile demonstrations make war almost inevitable? Debates on the causes of the Crimean war have involved all these considerations.

The situation was the outcome of a number of factors known collectively as the Eastern Question.[1] The Ottoman Empire was in process of almost continuous disintegration. The Greek revolt, the autonomy of Serbia and the Principalities, and the activities of Mehemet Ali all appeared to indi-

[1] See p. 213.

cate its imminent dissolution.[1] The Constantinople régime, however, displayed sudden and repeated signs of revival. Mahmoud II, who had become Sultan in 1808 after a series of palace revolutions, had attempted to restore control by alternating policies of conciliation and repression. He had not been entirely unsuccessful and might have achieved more but for the intervention of the European powers. The latter were moved to act both as a result of genuine feelings of horror at the not infrequent slaughter of the Sultan's Christian subjects, and because of their own strategic and economic interests in the area. Lengthy debates have failed to disentangle these motives and any verdict remains as much a matter of opinion as of fact.

Russia, Austria, Britain and France were all involved in the area. The Tsar claimed vague but unsubstantiated rights of protection over the Orthodox Christians in the Ottoman Empire by the Treaty of Kutchuk-Kainardji (1774).[2] He was also influenced by the need to maintain free navigation in the Black Sea and an outlet for Russian merchant shipping into the Mediterranean. He was therefore determined that no foreign power was to be allowed to control the Ottoman Empire. Austria was anxious to ensure free navigation on the Danube and a free exit into the Black Sea. Her exclusion from the *Zollverein*[3] made her look to the South and East for new markets and in 1849 Bruck hoped to build up a large Danubian free trade area. Britain was anxious to exclude foreign powers from the eastern Mediterranean in order to protect her trade routes to India and safeguard her strategic and imperial interests. Palmerston was obsessed by recurring fears of Russian aggression and the dangers of partition. Though he may have been correct about the long-term dangers of Russian policy he was often wrong about the Tsar's immediate intentions. The object of Russian policy was to preserve the Ottoman Empire not to destroy it. The main threat to her security still appeared to come from France. In 1840 Thiers nearly precipitated partition by his support of Mehemet Ali. In 1849 a French forward policy was to be renewed under Louis Napoleon.

Sultans had come to realize that their survival depended on playing off one power against the other. In this they had be-

[1] See p. 243.　　[2] See p. 21.　　[3] See p. 351.

come increasingly adept. They were encouraged by a continuous state of rivalry between the embassies of the powers at Constantinople. Each attempted to bully or blackmail the Sultan into excluding the other, and tended to magnify the differences between them in an effort to acquire exclusive influence. In 1839 Mahmoud exploited this rivalry to win British support for a counter-attack against Mehemet Ali. After the Turkish defeat at Nesib the new Sultan, Abdul Medjid, was able to rely on Anglo-Russian support to defeat Mehemet and isolate the French. Ten years later he again appealed to the British ambassador, Stratford Canning, and to the French against Austrian and Russian demands. Ambassadorial appeals led to the immediate despatch of a combined naval force. Thus the Sultan felt he could rely on the jealousy of ambassadors and the rivalry of the great powers to allow him freedom of action, security against attack and liberty to ignore the demands for reform repeatedly presented to him by the major European powers.

In 1849 Russia again appeared to offer the greatest threat to Ottoman survival. In 1844 Nicholas had referred to 'the sick man of Europe' while on a visit to London and had suggested an 'honest and honourable understanding'. This had turned out to be a plan to partition the Ottoman Empire and had been officially noted by Aberdeen though more out of politeness than with any enthusiasm. The fortification of Sebastopol and the expansion of the Black Sea fleet seemed further cause for alarm. Russian intervention in Hungary and the Principalities roused the press and public opinion in the West and the Anglo-French naval action was greeted with enthusiasm. Anxiety, however, was largely misplaced. Russia withdrew from the Principalities in 1851. For the next two years she was fully engaged by Caucasian wars, and by a second expedition against Khiva. Her objectives in the Near East were essentially defensive and designed to preserve the established balance in the area.

In 1852 this appeared increasingly threatened by the intervention of Louis Napoleon. Anxious to win Catholic support in France and to enhance his personal prestige abroad, he took up the cause of the Latin monks in their quarrel with the Greek Orthodox Church over control of the holy places in Palestine. Louis-Philippe had begun the repair of the Holy

Sepulchre, and Louis Napoleon urged the Turks to recognize Catholic claims over some dozen sanctuaries in Bethlehem and Jerusalem. When the Sultan agreed there was an immediate outcry from Orthodox Greek Christians who appealed to the Tsar for assistance. Nicholas opposed any change and the Sultan was forced to make contradictory promises to both sides. In 1852, however, Louis Napoleon having re-established a French Empire[1] demanded satisfaction. A fleet off Tripoli and a gunboat in the Dardanelles finally persuaded the Ottoman government, and in December the Porte capitulated to French demands.

French intervention inevitably appeared to threaten Russia's security. The Ottoman Empire ceased to be a reliable buffer state once she had become subservient to another power. In 1852 it appeared to everyone in the Near East that she had fallen under French influence. Nesselrode, Russian Foreign Minister, warned the Tsar that Napoleon's actions had created 'an armed peace'. Nicholas refused to recognize the new Emperor's dynastic numeral, and tried to pacify Lord Aberdeen, who had just become Prime Minister, by again mentioning the question of partition with a view to guaranteeing British interests. In February he concentrated troops in Bessarabia and the Caucasus and reviewed the fleet at Sebastopol. Simultaneously Prince Menshikov was sent on an ostentatious mission to Constantinople to demand guarantees for Orthodox Christians and to offer the Turks a treaty of alliance against France.

In spite of Menshikov's pompous demands and abusive behaviour, the dispute over the holy places was settled in Russia's favour with the support of England and France. Though the French sent a fleet to Salamis and the British chargé d'affaires in Constantinople appealed for naval support, the Aberdeen government refused to be rushed. The cabinet blamed the French for all the trouble and sent Stratford Canning, now Baron de Redcliffe, to Constantinople with instructions to work for a settlement with Menshikov. The French were forced to follow suit and by April the rights of the Orthodox communities had been guaranteed.

Menshikov, however, determined to press additional de-

[1] See p. 386.

mands. Not only did the Tsar wish to redress the French initiative but he also wanted guarantees to ensure that in future the balance would remain in Russia's favour. He therefore required a defensive alliance and recognition of the Tsar's special protective rights over Orthodox Christians. This, however, the Sultan was determined to resist. He was supported by a surge of nationalist protest against Russian interference, and also by the British and French ambassadors. Aberdeen and Palmerston, now Home Secretary, were agreed that these demands were unreasonable and that a stronger line was needed. Menshikov, having uttered threats and warnings, left Constantinople in May, together with the embassy staff. In June the French and British fleets were ordered to Besika Bay. When the Russians occupied the Danubian Principalities in July a conflict appeared inevitable.

Nevertheless, serious efforts were made to avoid it. These failed, however, due mainly to misunderstandings and mutual fears. Austria was anxious to avoid a war which would be bound to expose her to pressure from East or West. She was equally alarmed at the prospect of Russian action on the Danube and by the possibility of French intervention in Italy. Schwarzenberg had died in 1852 and his successor, Buol, though equally opportunist was less decisive. When England and France sounded Austria for support, Buol persuaded them to join in a 'Vienna Note' which tried to pacify Russia by admitting her interest in the welfare of Christians in the Ottoman Empire. The Note, however, was rejected by Turkey as setting too dangerous a precedent, and was interpreted by Nesselrode as offering recognition of all Russia's demands. This merely confirmed British and French anxiety and the fleets were subsequently ordered to pass through the Dardanelles – though de Redcliffe delayed sending instructions in hopes of a last minute settlement.

In September 1853 Nicholas agreed to climb down, rejected Nesselrode's extreme interpretation and tried to win Francis Joseph on to his side at a meeting at Olmütz. Austria, however, refused to accept any Russian occupation of the Principalities and remained non-committal. Frederick William, anxious to stay neutral, declined to move without Austrian support. Meanwhile Russian activity roused the

X

press and Palmerston's fears of a revived Holy Alliance. Though Napoleon was at first prepared to accept the Tsar's pacific assurances the British government presumed the worst and ordered the fleet to Constantinople. The French, anxious to keep in step, followed suit.

Meanwhile the Sultan had already declared war on October 4th. Apparently assured of British support and encouraged by fanatical crowds and a belligerent war ministry, he had decided to set the pace. The arrival of the Anglo-French fleet created a new pitch of enthusiasm and persuaded the Turks to open hostilities, cross the Danube and attack Russian troops. The Tsar tried to exploit the Turkish attack and win support for mediation. But Austria and Prussia remained aloof and any British or French sympathy was destroyed when the Russian fleet sank a Turkish squadron at Sinope. The press made out that it was a 'massacre', the public were aroused and politicians clamoured for action. Palmerston threatened to resign from the government. In January the French and British fleets were ordered into the Black Sea to protect Turkish ships and confine the Russian navy to its base at Sebastopol.

This was, in effect, a declaration of war. In February 1854 the two western powers sent an ultimatum demanding Russian withdrawal from the Principalities. When she refused, war was officially declared. Britain fought to resist Russian aggression and preserve the Ottoman Empire. Russia fought to resist Western intervention and maintain her security and status in the Black Sea. These threats though apparent were, however, largely illusory. Neither wished to partition the Ottoman Empire and both assumed that their actions were entirely defensive. Louis Napoleon and the Sultan hoped to exploit the division, the one to gain prestige and the other to win independence. The Emperor was anxious to isolate Russia and win an established position at the centre of European diplomacy. The Turks hoped to rid themselves of the shadow of their powerful neighbour. Napoleon's ambitions had, however, been achieved before war began. Only the shadow of Russia remained to rouse the press, the public and the politicians into war.

5. *The Crimean War*

The conduct of the Crimean war illustrated much the same misunderstanding and confusion as the diplomacy which had preceded it. Britain and France failed to agree on a commander-in-chief and operations were repeatedly handicapped by divided counsel and mutual antipathy.

The Russian threat turned out to be far less substantial than anticipated. Instead of an expected 800,000 men the Tsar was only able to raise some 350,000 after immense exertions. Communications were primitive and, as in 1812, transport was still dependent on peasant carts. Medical supplies failed and military stores were generally delayed. Distances were immense – it was some thousand miles between St. Petersburg and the front – so that the Russians had little advantage from fighting on their own borders. In March they slowly crossed the Danube to besiege Silistria. They were soon fully engaged in warding off Turkish attacks.

Meanwhile the allies were assembling troops at Gallipoli and Scutari. It took three months for some 25,000 British and 30,000 French troops to arrive. Their original purpose had been to defend Constantinople from attack. When, however, an attack did not materialize they moved to Varna on the Bulgarian coast in order to relieve Silistria and expel the Russians from the Principalities. By the time they were ready to advance the Russians had already withdrawn as the result of a threat of direct Austrian intervention.

Austria was able to take advantage of the general delay to secure her own position on the Danube. In April, Buol persuaded Frederick William to join in an alliance designed to protect Austrian interests. In June he mobilized and demanded Russian evacuation of the Principalities. Threatened on their flank the Russians were forced to withdraw, and Austria occupied the Principalities herself with the agreement of the Turks. At the same time Buol negotiated with the western powers. In an attempt to persuade Austria to join the alliance, Britain and France agreed on four points: (1) no Russian protectorate in the Principalities, (2) free navigation on the Danube, (3) a revision of the Straits Convention in the interests of the 'Balance of power in Europe', and (4) no Russian protectorate over the Sultan's Christian subjects. Having assured her interests Austria, however, refused to join the alliance. With the Russian withdrawal three of the points had virtually been met. Indeed there seemed little reason for proceeding with the war. However, when Nicholas rejected the points, further action appeared justified.

The absurdity of the situation was emphasized by the fact that there was now nowhere to fight. Russia was peculiarly inaccessible and naval expeditions in the Baltic and Pacific made little impression. The Russian navy refused to challenge superior Anglo-French fleets and retired to safety behind powerful shore batteries. In the South the Russian armies retreated to Bessarabia, where the French failed to make effective contact. The allies thereupon returned to base where their troops soon began to suffer heavily from cholera and dysentery. In the circumstances the allies decided to proceed with plans first projected at the beginning of the year to land in the Crimea and capture Sebastopol. Troops would be moved from the unhealthy Danubian plain, a Russian naval base could be destroyed, control of the Black Sea would be assured and public opinion and national prestige would be satisfied.

In September 1854 some 60,000 allied troops were landed on the west coast of the Crimea after a brief and inadequate reconnaissance. The bulk of the Russian army was still in Bessarabia and Menshikov had difficulty in collecting some 40,000 men to resist the allied advance. At Alma he was defeated and forced to retreat before a fierce allied assault. Meanwhile, the Russians had hastily improvised defences at Sebastopol by using their naval guns on the landward side. But the allies now missed a vital opportunity when they failed to agree on a sudden attack and settled down to a methodical siege. Menshikov had moved north to link up with reinforcements from Bessarabia. These attacked the allies in the rear, but were driven back at Balaklava where the light brigade distinguished itself by a heroic but futile charge into the Russian positions. The battle of Inkerman (November 5th), though fierce and bloody, was also indecisive. The Russian army was unable to drive the allies into the sea, and they in turn were left too exhausted to capture Sebastopol by direct assault.

As a result a lengthy winter siege became inevitable. In November storms destroyed the allied transports. Unusually rigorous conditions exposed the armies to severe hardship and revealed the inadequacies of organization and supply. These could only be remedied slowly. Florence Nightingale and French nursing orders worked to improve the hospital services, while the War Office struggled to send reinforcements and new equipment. Meanwhile, however, a popular outcry led by articles in *The Times* was directed against the British government's conduct of the war. Aberdeen resigned and Palmerston became Prime Minister. His determination to bring the war to a victorious conclusion rallied the nation but probably protracted the fighting.

Nicholas died on March 2nd, disappointed and disillusioned. His successor, Alexander II, was anxious to restore peace if Russian interests could be secured, and negotiations were re-opened on the basis of the four points. In January, Nicholas had already agreed to a moderate Austrian interpretation of these proposals. Meanwhile, however, the British led by Palmerston had begun to demand stiffer terms. Point three was to include the demolition of Sebastopol and all Russian fortresses in the Black Sea, as well as a limitation of the Russian Black Sea fleet to four ships. While a conference in Vienna negotiated on the Austrian interpretation, Napoleon was invited to London and after an enthusiastic welcome was converted to the British proposals. These, however, Alexander refused to accept and the negotiations therefore broke down. In England the Peelites led by Gladstone attacked Palmerston's belligerent demands; Lord John Russell, the British delegate at Vienna, was forced to resign together with the French Foreign Minister; and Austria found yet another pretext for not joining the allies.

In the summer of 1855 Britain and France reopened the campaign in the Crimea. They had been joined by Piedmont who hoped to gain an advantage over Austria by committing herself to the allied side. Vast quantities of men and materials were shipped to the front. New siege guns and mortars made operations increasingly effective. Processed foods, improved equipment and regular medical attention eased the lot of the troops. A new cable and telegraph link between Balaklava and the West speeded up communications and commands. In

May the occupation of the Kertch peninsula cut off the supply of Russian reinforcements and the outer bastions of Sebastopol were slowly occupied during the summer. In August a Russian attempt to relieve the port was beaten back at the Tchernaya, and on September 9th, 1855, Sebastopol itself was abandoned after a lengthy bombardment.

The fall of Sebastopol satisfied Napoleon's military ambitions and turned his mind to the possible advantage of peace. Alexander, gratified by the capture of Kars in November, and alarmed by financial crises and peasant unrest, was also anxious to negotiate. Palmerston, however, still militant, seemed determined to continue the war and urged new campaigns in the Baltic and the Caucasus. Once again Buol stepped in to offer mediation. Alarmed by secret Franco-Russian talks he revised his four points to satisfy Britain and pacify the Tsar. Russia was to be excluded from the mouths of the Danube and the Black Sea was to be 'neutralized'. These proposals satisfied neither side. Palmerston demanded the right to add 'further conditions'. Alexander was determined to evade them and resented Austrian intervention. Nevertheless, a plea from Frederick William proved decisive. Russia accepted the Austrian terms and a peace congress was summoned to assemble in Paris on February 25th.

6. *The Peace of Paris*

The Peace of Paris was a decisive defeat for Russia. Isolated from her former allies and weakened by war, she was forced to accept the combined demands of Britain and France. Turkey acquired the mouths of the Danube. Russia was pushed back another twenty miles and the intervening strip was handed to Wallachia. Russia was forced to abandon her claims of protection over the Sultan's Christian subjects, and restored Kars to the Ottoman Empire. The Black Sea was neutralized and all warships and fortresses banned. Russia was saved from further humiliation by French support. Though forced to neutralize the Aaland Islands in the Baltic, Palmerston's demands for an independent trans-Caucasian state were rejected.

The Ottoman Empire was preserved and placed under European guarantee. All conflicts between Turkey and another party had to be submitted to the mediation of the powers. They also took note of a decree 'spontaneously issued' by the Sultan which gave Christians and Muslims equal rights to practise their religion and serve the State. The powers thereupon abandoned any right to interfere collectively or individually in the affairs of the Ottoman Empire, an action which enabled the Sultan to evade most of his promises. External pressure and internal disruption were to continue to dominate Ottoman affairs during the final years of the Empire.

This process was, if anything, hastened by the treatment of the Principalities. They received national institutions and administrative independence under Turkish suzerainty, and were also to be placed under European guarantees. Similar conditions were applied to Serbia. Both regions now existed in a state of autonomy which nevertheless denied them full independence. Both would hope to achieve this final objective and would try to embroil the major powers in their cause. Of these Russia would always be anxious to make a come-back, while the western powers would be equally prepared to mediate and defeat excessive Russian ambitions.

Austria found herself precariously balanced between these conflicting claims. The peace treaties established a commission to ensure free navigation on the Danube. Any further changes in the *status quo* were almost bound to be to her disadvantage. Fears of Russian penetration had dictated her policy during the Crimean war and continued to be of decisive importance up till 1914. French or British intervention was equally unwelcome, while the emergence of independent Slav states was an inevitable threat to the very existence of a multi-racial Empire. Habsburg policy, therefore, was almost fated to continue the conservative traditions of Metternich, buttress the Ottoman Empire and ward off the corrosive impact of national agitation. By 1856, however, she had lost the allies who were essential to make such a policy effective.

The disintegration of the Holy Alliance was one of the most significant consequences of the Crimean war. For forty years it had upheld the *status quo* in central and eastern Europe. In Poland, Germany, Italy and Hungary revolutions had been crushed by Russian, Prussian or Austrian action. Each had been free to act while the others held the ring. In

1830 French intervention in Italy and Poland had been prevented by combined Austrian and Russian protests. After 1856 the mutual understanding upon which a tradition of cooperation had been based was broken. Russia bitterly resented Austria's duplicity during the war, coming as it did so soon after her own unconditional assistance in Hungary. In future, agreements would only be based on immediate and practical advantages. Austria could no longer rely on Russian sympathy and support, while on the Danube their mutual hostility was to remain insoluble.

Russia was determined to retrieve her status in the Black Sea and restore her frontier on the Danube. An association with emerging Slav states was an obvious means to this end. Both actions, however, brought her into direct collision with Austrian interests. Future conflict thus appeared inevitable. Meanwhile, however, Russia was both isolated and ineffective. The war had revealed the deep social divisions, economic weaknesses and administrative inefficiency of the Empire. Alexander II set out to remedy these defects. At the same time he was anxious to find new allies. Austria had failed and Britain remained implacable. The alternatives were France or Prussia. In 1856 neither appeared to offer any immediate advantages and Russia remained isolated, preoccupied with reform and reconstruction.[1]

Prussia had also played an independent role during the Crimean war. In April 1854 Frederick William had agreed to sign a defensive alliance with Austria. This guaranteed her territories in Italy and on the Danube and was designed to protect her from revolutionary agitation. Frederick William only committed himself once he was assured that Austria would not fight. Torn between pride and a tradition of loyalty to the Habsburgs he agreed to support Austria at the beginning of the war. Thereafter, however, Prussian policy became increasingly hostile. In 1855 she led opposition in the Diet to Austrian demands that Germany be mobilized to enforce the four points. By 1856 Frederick William had taken up a position of strict neutrality and was thus able to urge Alexander II to accept allied terms without himself forfeiting Russian sympathy. In 1850[2] Prussia had been humiliated because of combined Austrian and Russian hostility. By 1856

[1] See Ch. XVI.   [2] See p. 351.

she was already aware of the possible advantages of their growing antagonism.

The disintegration of the Holy Alliance was greeted with obvious enthusiasm by Napoleon. Determined to end his personal isolation he had already committed himself to an understanding with Britain. Before the end of the Crimean war he was already preparing to exploit the situation in the interests of France. The Peace of Paris added renewed prestige to French diplomacy which could once again occupy the centre of the arena. Austro-Prussian rivalry might open up prospects of French expansion on the Rhine. Austro-Russian hostility could provide opportunities for intervention in Italy and Poland. At Paris he was able to act as host and probe possibilities for future action. The re-emergence of France was an obvious factor in European diplomacy. Napoleon, however, though determined to assert his prestige and fulfil his mission, remained cautious and hesitant. Anxious to follow his uncle's footsteps he never quite knew which ones to choose.

Piedmont had no such doubts.[1] Cavour had come to Paris hoping to rally support for the reconstruction of Italy and to denounce Austrian intervention. He was to be bitterly disappointed. Besides an inconclusive debate on Italian affairs and a British denunciation of foreign and papal misgovernment he gained nothing. Nevertheless the new fluidity in international relationships was to work to his advantage. Austrian isolation and Napoleonic ambition could be exploited in Piedmontese interests while Britain might provide valuable support in case of future action.

The Peace of Paris was thus of significance not so much as an end to the Crimean war — most of the conditions had been decided before the Congress met — but as a presage of developments to come. The old order had collapsed. The Holy Alliance was dead, at least for the time being. Ambitious powers were soon to exploit the situation — Piedmont to unite northern Italy, Prussia to acquire predominance in Germany, Serbia and the Principalities to win full independence. Napoleon, in turn, hoped to benefit from the general scramble in order to acquire territory, while Alexander waited

[1] See p. 329.

to restore Russian prestige and the Sultan schemed for survival. All approached diplomacy with a new ruthless detachment. 'We shall judge Austria by acts, by facts,' Alexander remarked in 1857 at a meeting with Francis Joseph. These were to depend upon essential economic and strategic considerations. Prestige and power created the incentives. New armaments and increasing prosperity provided the means. It was an extension of the new spirit of *realpolitik* into international diplomacy.

XIII · THE UNIFICATION OF ITALY

1. *The Risorgimento*

In 1849 most of Italy appeared to revert to the divisions and repressive traditions of a pre-revolutionary age. Radetsky retained control over Lombardy and Venetia until 1857. Austrian troops restored order in Tuscany and Modena, and crushed agitation in Bologna and the papal legations. In Rome the generosity of Pius IX was replaced by the more authoritarian policy of Cardinal Antonelli. Pope and Cardinal now realized the incompatibility of papal claims and liberal ambition. Advisory councils were modified and radical sympathizers expelled or imprisoned. Pius did, however, continue to encourage paternal reforms; poor houses, schools, gas and telegraph services were gradually constructed. Guilds were revived to regulate prices and preserve artisan interests. Nevertheless, the activities of the police, especially in the provinces, and the revival of the *Sanfedisti*[1] suggested to liberals the return of a blind reaction.

In Naples the activities of Ferdinand II roused widespread protest. His destruction of Messina earned him the title 'King Bomba'. Mercenaries were employed to guard the palace, while the Jesuits, the Sicilian mafia and Calabrian gangs were used to eliminate liberal and secret societies. Italian exiles once again flooded into France, Switzerland, England or the New World. Mazzini returned to London to organize a national Italian committee and begin yet another round of conspiracy and revolt. Only Piedmont, though defeated, appeared to survive with its *Statuo* as the sole achievement of two years of revolution and turmoil. Appearances, however, were deceptive. By 1849 the ingredients that were to lead to the ultimate unification of Italy had already been determined. Society had been stirred, ideas had spread, incentives had crystallized, foreign powers had been engaged. Only the instruments were lacking and these were to be forged during the coming decade.

[1] See p. 100.

The events of 1848 and 1849 left a legacy of disillusion and expectancy. Society had been agitated by war and revolution. The liberal aristocracy in the North had taken a lead in the struggle for independence. Piedmontese nobles like d'Azeglio, Balbo and Cavour, Lombard counts and Tuscan aristocrats had participated in stirring events that could never be entirely forgotten. Moderate bourgeois had also experienced brief tastes of leadership. In Milan, Turin, Venice, Florence and Rome, lawyers, doctors and intellectuals had struggled to set up constitutions and promote reform. In the larger towns artisans had provided the bulk of the fighting forces and had suffered the highest casualties. In Bologna, Leghorn and Genoa a genuine popular element had been roused by radicals and republicans to fight for liberty, equality and national unification. This had reached a climax in the brief achievements of the Roman Republic. The revolution left a legacy of martyrdom and sacrifice that brought new meaning to the ideals of poets and philosophers.

It also brought a new sense of realism. Liberal aristocrats became aware of their isolation in an essentially conservative society where landlord and peasant remained conditioned by the past. They were also aware of the dangers of excess and of the decisive influence of outside assistance. Reform would only come by careful preparation and the support of reliable foreign allies. The bourgeoisie were also increasingly conscious of their weaknesses. They too had failed when isolated from aristocratic support, or when divided between moderate and republican elements. They were too few, and were easily swept away by feudal reaction or the popular demands of republican agitators. As for the artisans, their efforts had been totally ineffectual when faced by the massive opposition of moderate and conservative elements. New alignments would be needed to break through the barriers of reaction, foreign occupation and mass peasant indifference.

The revolution thus led to a rapid distillation of political thought. The ideals of romantic authors such as Alfieri and Foscolo with their appeal to liberty had become embedded in the liberal mind. The work of Young Italy and the secret societies had kept agitation alive. Both had failed to achieve practical results. Though Mazzini was able to stir up further revolts in Milan and Venice in 1853 and in Naples in 1857, his activities were no longer of real significance. He had bequeathed an ideal that had captured the imagination of thousands. Others, however, would have to translate it into action. Of the possible leaders only Piedmont remained. The cause of the Papacy had been destroyed by the papal allocution of April 1848 [1] and by the Pope's withdrawal from the war against Austria. The federalist cause had foundered on inter-state rivalry at every level. Neither Naples nor Tuscany seemed likely to take the lead in any future moves towards reform. Everything appeared to point to the House of Savoy.

Victor Emmanuel II had ascended the throne after the defeat of Novara to save Piedmont from humiliation and dismemberment. Though Radetsky had demanded the abrogation of the Constitution, the King had refused, and Austria had moderated her terms to speed the pacification of Italy and conciliate British and French opinion. Piedmont thus retained her independence and the sympathy of other constitutional powers. She also kept her army. Victor Emmanuel was both a fighter and a realist. He intended to retrieve the reputation of his troops by future intervention against Austria. He also realized the value of a parliamentary Chamber to rally support and appeal to liberal opinion. He was aware of the need for patience and compromise and was determined to strengthen his own position and eliminate the threat of Austrian action by curbing both the extreme radicals on the left and the ultra-clericals on the right.

In 1849 Victor Emmanuel persuaded d'Azeglio to become Prime Minister and ratified the peace treaty in defiance of a hostile and radical Chamber. In November he appealed to the moderates for support in the Manifesto of Moncalieri which urged the nation to ratify his action and save the country and its *Statuo* from the dangers which surrounded them. The new Chamber accepted the treaty and confirmed policies designed to encourage reform, promote independence and pacify Austrian anxiety. A republican revolt in Genoa was easily defeated. In 1850 the Siccardi Laws abolished church courts, limited holidays and prohibited the growth of ecclesiastical property *in mortmain*. At the same time the d'Azeglio ministry embarked upon a careful programme of social, economic and military reforms designed to

[1] See p. 274.

strengthen Piedmont and ensure her future primacy in Italian politics.

Growing numbers of liberal Italians thus began to look to the North for leadership. Exiles from Naples and Sicily, like Crispi, congregated in Genoa, while Turin was filled with refugees from Lombardy. In 1853 the confiscation of their property gave them an added interest in the destruction of Austrian rule. Economic growth and the increasing prosperity of Piedmont brought renewed demands for the unification of northern Italy, and the creation of a liberal monarchy to consolidate the political and material interests of the bourgeoisie.

Nevertheless, powerful opponents remained. In Paris Daniel Manin led a group of republican exiles suspicious of Piedmontese expansion and anxious to promote a federalist union. Mazzini continued to advocate democratic ideals and appealed to artisan and lower bourgeois elements who had little to gain from the liberal policies of their masters. In every state the traditional aristocracy was anxious to maintain its exclusive interests centred on an independent court and a separate society. And over all brooded the conservative authority of the Church with its decisive hold over the peasant community and its determination to keep to its vision of the truth and uphold a timeless tradition in a changing world.

To disentangle this network of vested interests and conflicting idealism, and to construct a new and wider framework required exceptional understanding, clarity of mind and flexibility of action. The man who was able to realize many of these demands was Count Camillo Benso di Cavour (1810–61). Judgements upon him have, as usual, been varied and contradictory. For nineteenth-century liberals his achievements were of almost superhuman proportions. For idealist republicans they appeared limited and calculating. Recently historians have compared his political manoeuvres unfavourably with the forthright honesty of Garibaldi, and have criticized his activities for their devious and disingenuous opportunism. No doubt there is an element of truth in all these criticisms. Nevertheless, working through limited liberal institutions, Cavour was forced to fulfil his ideals by creating a consensus of individual interests which was bound to lead to a certain degree of ambiguity and misunderstanding. Negotiating from weakness he had to seize his opportunities and exploit them to the best advantage.

2. *The Rise of Cavour and the Recovery of Piedmont*

Cavour's early life brought him into contact with many of the formative influences of the Risorgimento. He was born in 1810 of a noble Piedmontese family. His father had been a member of the Napoleonic administration. At the age of ten Cavour was sent to the Sardinian Military Academy and was commissioned in the Engineers six years later. From an early age he studied liberal authors and read Adam Smith, Bentham, Ricardo, Benjamin Constant and Guizot with enthusiasm. He was soon attracted to the rationalism of the eighteenth-century philosophers and the free traditions of English political institutions. He came to believe in the value of free enquiry, free development and free trade, but always within the bounds of a balanced society. He thus appeared the incarnation of bourgeois virtues, equally opposed to clerical obscurantism and republican agitation.

There was also, however, a radical element in Cavour's earlier experiences. In 1830 he was stationed in Genoa where he met Anna Giustiniani, the one love of his life, who introduced him to friends on the left including members of the *Carbonari*. Implicated in the revolutionary activities of the time he was imprisoned for eight months and allowed to resign his commission. Cavour retained his more radical sympathies and was thus prepared to work with the moderate left against the extreme right. He was interested in social reform, poor laws and working conditions. He believed in the ultimate realisation of a democratic society, but considered that fulfilment should come by gradual stages and not by any sudden revolt.

Between 1831 and 1847 Cavour dedicated himself to estate management and practical economic reform. He introduced irrigation, crop rotation, fertilizers and new breeding methods, and became a founder member of the Piedmontese Agrarian Society. Soon he extended his activities to industry, banking and transport. He set up new sugar factories, steamship and railway companies, and helped to create the Banks of Genoa and Turin. Meanwhile, he wrote articles for scientific journals and travelled widely in western Europe and England where he was especially impressed by the policies and personal courage of Peel during the Corn Law crisis. He also noted the procedure of the House of Commons, and later used it as a model for the Piedmontese Chamber.

In 1847, with the relaxation of press censorship, Cavour became editor of a new paper, *Il Risorgimento*. For the next fifteen years it was to be a reflection of his ideals and aspirations. Freedom and progress were to be balanced by moderation and responsibility. A free press, free institutions and a free economy were to be tempered with caution, control and compromise. Society would advance neither by the action of democratic visionaries like Mazzini nor as a result of the authoritarian beliefs of the Church, but by a gradual extension of liberal Piedmontese principles. In 1848 he urged war to aid Milan and advocated the annexation of the northern states. In 1849, however, he opposed the radical campaign, and supported d'Azeglio in his efforts to promote peace and preserve the Constitution.

There was, therefore, a certain consistency in Cavour's basic attitudes to the problems of Piedmont and the ultimate unification of Italy. His use of parliament and liberal principles endeared him to nineteenth-century whig historians. Nevertheless, there were some notable gaps in his make-up. He was essentially northern, Piedmontese and aristocratic and found himself more easily at home in French or English political circles than among the majority of his compatriots. His knowledge of Italy was extremely limited. He knew little either about the south of the peninsula or of the traditional and parochial exclusiveness of peasant societies. He underestimated the influence of the Catholic Church and the strength of regional feelings within each province.

Cavour's approach was essentially intellectual and pragmatic. His memory was prodigious and his ability to master facts and outline arguments outstanding. He towered above his contemporaries in debate and could defeat critics in any argument. Yet he lacked warmth and failed to appreciate the loyalties of a simple mind. He outmanoeuvred Napoleon but misunderstood Garibaldi. His political calculations were sometimes masterly but he failed to evoke sympathy or affection. As a result he remained an isolated figure who dazzled his contemporaries but seldom moved them.

In 1848 Cavour was elected to the Piedmontese Chamber and supported the Siccardi Laws and the economic reforms of Santarosa. When Santarosa died in 1850 Cavour took his place in the d'Azeglio cabinet as Minister of Agriculture and Commerce. He dominated politics for the next decade. In 1851 he introduced freer trade, cut duties and abolished navigation acts. He also negotiated commercial treaties with Britain, France, Belgium and the *Zollverein*. From the start he attempted to involve the European powers in Italian affairs. As early as 1852 he remarked that it was above all on France that Piedmontese destiny was to depend. Every effort was therefore made to attract French capital. Joint-stock companies were founded to finance roads, railways and ports. Genoa was linked by rail to the Po valley and its port facilities reconstructed to rival those of Trieste and Marseilles. A new line was planned to link Turin and Grenoble with a tunnel under the Mont Cenis pass. Piedmontese exports of oil, silk and wine boomed. Prosperity brought both the approval of foreign investors and liberal ministers, and the support of growing numbers of bourgeois and intellectuals throughout northern Italy.

In 1851 Cavour also became Minister of Finance to deal with the deficit created by his free trade policies and to liquidate the Austrian indemnity. He soon reorganized the treasury, restored efficiency and accurate accounting, and made up for cuts in customs and excise revenue by increasing direct taxation. He was aware of the vital role of credit in stimulating an under-developed economy. He raised an internal loan to repay the Bank and restore liquidity. He played off rival firms abroad to get loans at lower interest rates and used them to pay off the indemnity, cover state debts and finance port and railway construction. In three years, revenue was increased by thirty-two million lire and expenditure cut by twenty million. The deficit was thus reduced from seventy-seven to twenty-five millions but was never eliminated. Deficit finance and the rapid expansion of credit led to mounting inflation. Though this brought profits to the commercial community, it did nothing to relieve the hardship of artisans and smaller craftsmen. For them, free trade, increas-

Y

ing taxation and rising costs meant growing hardship and ultimate ruin. Hence Cavour's economic policies only appealed
to limited class interests and did little to benefit the peasant
or urban majority.

Cavour's parliamentary pre-eminence soon led him to dominate the cabinet. In order to reinforce his position he reached
an agreement with the moderate left led by Rattazzi behind
the back of d'Azeglio and his conservative colleagues. This
famous *connubio* (marriage) was for a number of years the
basis of Cavour's majority in the Chamber. In 1852 right-
wing demands for a new press law to curb criticism of foreign
developments – notably adverse comments on Napoleon's
coup d'état in Paris[1] – brought the alliance into the open.
D'Azeglio resigned and Cavour, after a show of reluctance, became Prime Minister. He was entirely convinced of his own
qualifications. Having gained supreme office he now felt fully
entitled to manipulate the Chamber, the press and foreign
politicians to his advantage.

In Piedmont, Cavour maintained a tradition of liberal reform. The modification of the penal code brought bitter
attacks from the Catholic right and led to an intensification of
the conflict between Church and State. Determined to destroy
clerical privilege and also ease his financial deficit, Cavour
introduced a bill to suppress three hundred and thirty-four
lesser monasteries and transfer their assets to the Exchequer.
This measure caused bitter dissension for a number of years
and was only passed in 1855. By then Piedmont had become
involved in the Crimean war and Cavour was increasingly
preoccupied with foreign affairs.

Abroad, Cavour was from the start anxious to gravitate to
the front of the stage in the hope of advancing Piedmontese
interests. He had the active support of Victor Emmanuel and
the army, anxious to recover after the disastrous campaigns of
1848–9. The King and the Minister of War, La Marmora,
had reorganized the army, restored discipline, opened prospects of promotion to all and modernized equipment, while
the navy had also been reformed and moved to a new base at
Spezia in 1854. The outbreak of the Crimean war appeared to
offer Piedmont an occasion for more positive intervention in
European diplomacy.

[1] See p. 386.

Britain, France, Cavour and Victor Emmanuel all wanted Piedmont to participate in the war, but at different times and for different reasons. In the winter of 1853–4 Cavour and Victor Emmanuel may have made tentative offers of support. Cavour, however, met almost unanimous opposition from the cabinet, who could see no advantages in a war against Russia. In 1854 France appeared more anxious to negotiate an alliance with Austria and merely hoped to keep Italy pacified.[1] Only Britain wanted to engage Piedmont from the start and opened negotiations behind the back of her ally. But while France remained indifferent the advantages of intervention were negligible and neither Cavour nor the King were prepared to over-rule the opposition. In December 1854, however, the situation changed. Both the great powers now urge an alliance. When the Foreign Minister continued to insist on conditions, such as the restoration of Lombard property, Victor Emmanuel threatened to dismiss the liberal cabinet and call in the conservatives. Faced by a threat to his position, Cavour now over-rode the cabinet, took over the Foreign Ministry and signed a treaty of alliance himself.

In August a Piedmontese expeditionary force under General La Marmora distinguished itself at the battle of the Tchernaya. Victory wiped out the stigma of earlier defeat and revived hopes for the future. Piedmont had staked another claim to Italian leadership. Nevertheless, the immediate benefits appeared negligible. Even Cavour had grave doubts about his position when he left for the Congress of Paris at the end of the war. Though treated as an equal by the allies, he was unable to get any French backing for territorial adjustments in north Italy. Though Lord Clarendon was persuaded to launch a bitter attack on Austrian maladministration, Cavour received little encouragement when he visited London later in the year and was treated with growing suspicion by the British government. Piedmont had thus emerged as a recognized power, but her strength remained small and her policies tentative and lacking in foreign support.

[1] See p. 313.

3. The War of 1859

The war of 1859 was a turning point on the road to Italian unification. By involving France in war against Austria, Cavour precipitated a chain reaction the results of which were as much of a surprise to himself as to Napoleon. Though the possibilities of unification were often in his mind, Cavour doubted if Italy was as yet adequately prepared for it, especially the under-developed South. He even went so far as to describe the whole idea as nonsense. Nevertheless, by bringing almost every element into play he certainly prepared the ground. He also promoted a variety of apparently conflicting movements which he was later able to exploit in the general interests of Piedmontese policy. Thus while he cannot be given all the credit for the final outcome, his preparatory work and adroit diplomatic manoeuvres should not be denied.

The causes of the war and the opening moves of Cavour and Napoleon remain somewhat obscure on account of the secretive and ambiguous methods of both parties. The first probes almost certainly came from the Emperor. Napoleon had always displayed a keen interest in Italian affairs, was anxious to extend French influence and hoped to restore France's Alpine frontier by the acquisition of Nice and Savoy. Cavour was only too anxious to feed the Emperor's appetite and to encourage intervention in the Piedmontese interest. In December 1855, when Cavour and Victor Emmanuel were visiting France, Napoleon asked for a confidential note suggesting what he might do for Piedmont and Italy. Cavour forwarded a number of proposals drawn up by d'Azeglio and himself for reforms in the Italian states, the withdrawal of Austrian troops from central Italy and the acquisition of Modena and Parma by Piedmont.

By January 1856 Napoleon was already speaking to La Marmora of a confederation of Italian states with a diet, based on the Frankfurt pattern, to be held in Rome. But at the Congress of Paris nothing came of any of these suggestions due to Austrian opposition and to Walewski, the French Foreign Minister, who retained a rooted antipathy to Napoleon's plans. Nevertheless, Italian affairs were openly debated, and Napoleon appeared genuinely interested and made encouraging remarks about the actual peace not lasting long.

As a result Cavour felt free to launch a violent diplomatic offensive against Austria, and began to harness support for an eventual war to drive her from the peninsula. Alessandria was refortified and a national subscription organized to provide a hundred cannon. In February 1857 Cavour broke off diplomatic relations with Vienna over the expulsion of a Sardinian senator from Lombardy and spoke of 'Italy marching towards independence and liberty'. Meanwhile he opened secret negotiations with a new Italian National Society founded by Manin, Pallavicino and La Farina, and met its vice-president, Garibaldi.

The National Society united many of the leading elements of the early Risorgimento and brought them into line behind Piedmont and Cavour. Manin and Pallavicino had been northern federalists, La Farina had been a Sicilian republican and Garibaldi remained the hero of the democratic left. All had come to realize the futility of isolated insurrection and saw in Cavour a possible ally to co-ordinate action. Cavour met La Farina, secretary of the Society, almost daily in secret to discuss future plans and plant cells of loyal agitators throughout the peninsula.

While Cavour made unofficial agreements with the left, he appeared to move officially to the right in order to reassure Napoleon that he had no national or revolutionary intentions. In June a Mazzinian revolt in Genoa caused some anxiety, but it was easily suppressed and its significance minimized. Cavour, however, thought it wiser to drop Rattazzi and the left, especially after conservative gains in the 1857 election. By now he was indispensable and could juggle with parties as with politicians.

Everything, however, depended on the initiative of Napoleon. Throughout 1857 he appeared to be weighing up the alternatives. Economic unrest at home and the need to maintain a Napoleonic image gradually focused attention on Italy and by the end of the year he was urging a marriage between his disreputable cousin, Prince Jerome, and the daughter of Victor Emmanuel. Opinion, however, is almost unanimous that the Emperor was eventually stirred into action by the Orsini incident in January 1858. Orsini, sometime a

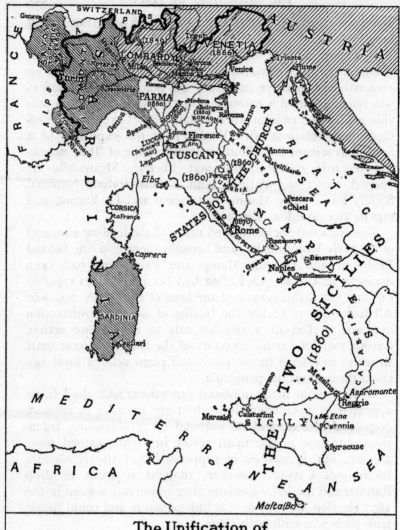

The Unification of
ITALY

English Miles

0   50   100   200

Austrian territory in 1859 ///   Kingdom of Sardinia 1815–1859 ▨
Boundary after 1870 ～～～

*The dates (1860) are those of the union of the various States with
the Kingdom of Sardinia, forming together the Kingdom of Italy.*

member of Young Italy and deputy to the Roman Republic, hoped to promote the Italian cause by assassinating Napoleon in front of the Paris Opera House. His bombs killed eight and wounded one hundred and fifty but missed their essential target. Napoleon emerged from the general carnage alive but shaken, and sent violent notes of protest to Piedmont and Great Britain where the bombs had been manufactured. A firm reply from Victor Emmanuel and Cavour's ruthless elimination of the Mazzinian press mollified his rage and made him decide on immediate intervention. Napoleon published Orsini's last appeal to the Emperor urging him to set Italy free, renewed his marriage proposals and offered Piedmont a treaty of alliance.

After some secret preliminaries Napoleon invited Cavour to a meeting at Plombières in July. Here the Emperor outlined his future plans for Italy: an upper Kingdom from the Alps to the Adriatic, a central State, Naples and the Papacy were all to be formed into a confederation under the presidency of the Pope. In return Piedmont would surrender Nice and Savoy and agree to the marriage. Napoleon would isolate Austria while Cavour was to provoke a war that satisfied public opinion and was not in support of any 'revolutionary cause'. Cavour remained cautious and reserved when presented with these proposals. He must have realized that they were impracticable and was himself secretly working towards a very different goal. Nevertheless he needed an 'event' which could subsequently be exploited, and made no effort to destroy the Emperor's illusions.

For the next six months Cavour hastened preparations for war. In January 1859 a treaty of alliance between France and Piedmont was eventually signed. It was limited to defend Piedmont against Austrian attack, create an upper Kingdom, and maintain papal sovereignty, but made no mention of a federation or of any specific state boundaries, though Napoleon certainly assumed that these were to be based on his Plombières proposals. Cavour instructed La Marmora to prepare the army for war in the spring of 1859, and warned Lanza, the Minister of Finance, to raise the necessary loans. In October 1858 Cavour also informed La Farina of his intentions and began to plan for progressive risings in the northern and central states. The National Society, through its committees, prepared arms depôts and circulated manifestos supporting the leadership of Victor Emmanuel. In December, Garibaldi was instructed to form groups of volunteers to harness national support and reinforce the Piedmontese army.

This move was part of a deliberate plan to provoke Austria. Many of the volunteers were Lombards and the Austrian government could not remain indifferent to the build-up of hostile forces on her frontier. In January, Victor Emmanuel spoke of the 'cries of grief' that were reaching Piedmont from many parts of Italy, a provocative comment added on the advice of Napoleon. As a result the Austrians brought in more troops and Cavour was able to use this as an excuse to raise a war loan, reorganize the National Guard and maintain a stream of agitated propaganda. War appeared imminent.

Nevertheless, at the last moment, Napoleon seemed to falter. His diplomatic manoeuvres had not worked out as favourably as he had hoped. The Tsar had agreed to observe a benevolent neutrality and treat Austria as she had treated Russia during the Crimean war. Prince William, now Regent of Prussia, however, remained noncommittal and appeared to favour Austria, while the defeat of Palmerston, over a 'Conspiracy to Murder Bill' to deter future Orsinis, led to the return of Derby and the conservatives who tended to favour Austria. In January, Napoleon made a deliberate remark to the Austrian ambassador about the unsatisfactory state of relations between Austria and France and this was immediately taken as an omen of war. Shares fell on the stock exchange, the German states became increasingly agitated and Walewski openly hostile. In February the British sent a mission to Vienna to mediate and urge demobilization. Cavour merely ordered total mobilization in an effort to force the issue. Eventually the Russians suggested another congress in Paris and Britain, France and Prussia agreed. Austria, however, delayed and demanded Piedmontese disarmament first. On April 19th Napoleon, anxious to appear pacific, forced Cavour into line.

The apparent failure of all his plans almost drove Cavour to suicide. Paradoxically he need not have worried. His strategy had been successful. On April 19th Buol persuaded the Austrian government to deliver a direct ultimatum to

Piedmont. They were determined to humiliate their opponent and destroy a mounting threat to the Habsburg Empire at what seemed a favourable moment. Cavour rejected the ultimatum and on April 27th, convinced of their superiority, the Austrians attacked. Buol, however, had gravely miscalculated. France fulfilled her treaty obligations, England and Prussia remained neutral while the Tsar held the ring on Napoleon's behalf and warned the German states to keep the war localized and not to intervene on the Rhine. Napoleon was thus given a free hand. In three weeks 100,000 men were rushed to Italy through Genoa and the new Mont Cenis tunnel. They soon threatened the lumbering Austrian advance by an attack from the South. An Austrian probe was defeated at Montebello and forced to withdraw to defend the crossings of the Po. Napoleon, however, did not follow his uncle's line of attack along the southern bank of the river, but decided to take advantage of the railways and turn the Austrian flank from the North. On June 3rd he outmanoeuvred the Austrians at Magenta and forced them to withdraw from Lombardy. Three weeks later the French came into headlong collision with the advancing Austrian army at Solferino. In a bloody engagement which cost in all some 40,000 casualties Napoleon drove the enemy back to their bases in the Quadrilateral.

On July 11th, after only a brief warning, Napoleon signed an armistice with Francis Joseph at Villafranca. Though this sudden move has never been fully explained a number of factors seemed to have weighed on Napoleon's mind. His victories had been both indecisive and costly. Austrian resistance had not been broken and the Quadrilateral remained a formidable obstacle. Napoleon lacked siege guns and his supply system had broken down. The sight of the dead on the battlefield undermined his will to fight. Moreover, events in Italy had been disquieting. Few had come forward to enlist, though Garibaldi had played a valuable role in the North with his volunteers. Cavour and the National Society had appeared more concerned to stir up revolts in Tuscany, Parma, Modena and Bologna. This had upset Napoleon's calculations and contravened what he had understood to be the conditions of the Plombières agreement. In addition, it had seriously alarmed Catholics at home, and had begun to

worry Alexander II who was always on the look-out for a possible spread of revolutionary activity through Austria or
Hungary into Poland. As a result he relaxed his policy of
friendly neutrality and allowed Prussia to mobilize her
armies and rally German support in case of a French attack.

The armistice, however, also failed to fulfil the terms of the
Franco-Piedmontese alliance. As a result Napoleon forfeited
his claims to Savoy and Nice. He was able to acquire Lombardy as a gift for Victor Emmanuel, but Austria retained
Venetia and the dominating fortresses of the Quadrilateral.
The princes were to be restored to their states and Italy
united in a confederation under the Pope. Three days later
Napoleon hurried home to prepare a victory parade leaving
liberals in Italy stunned and bitter. Cavour after a furious
scene with Victor Emmanuel resigned and left for Switzerland. The King with calculating and calm statesmanship refused to be rushed and appointed Rattazzi Prime Minister to
carry out the terms of the Villafranca agreement.

4. *The Unification of Italy*

The war, however, had set in train events that made any
implementation of the armistice impossible, and seemed to
lead almost inevitably to the unification of the peninsula.
Even before its declaration, the Piedmontese minister in
Florence had begun a round of intrigue and agitation. When
the Grand-Duke rejected an alliance, the National Society
organized demonstrations in the streets. On April 27th
Leopold fled and a new government was formed under Baron
Ricasoli which offered Victor Emmanuel the 'dictatorship'
and urged union with Piedmont. Though the King only
accepted the 'protectorship', Cavour sent secret instructions
in May urging preparations for annexation. A visit from
Prince Jerome had aroused speculation but, once reassured
about the restoration of order, he had moved on to the front
disgusted by the lack of volunteers for his army. Tuscany was
left in the firm hands of Ricasoli who remained determined
to effect a union with Piedmont and frustrate the return of
the Grand-Duke or the creation of any middle Kingdom.

After Magenta, agitation broke out in Parma and Modena,
resulting in the flight of the dukes and appeals for union with
Piedmont. As these areas were within the Plombières agree-

ment Palieri and Farini were sent as royal commissioners to take over and hasten annexation. When, however, revolts flared up in Bologna and the papal Legations the situation became increasingly confused. Napoleon had agreed to a Piedmontese occupation, but had also undertaken to respect the integrity of the Papal States. When a provisional government offered Victor Emmanuel the dictatorship and d'Azeglio was sent to maintain order this was explained in the French press as a 'temporary measure'. Nevertheless, Pius IX had the gravest doubts about its temporary nature and sent his own Swiss troops to crush revolts in Perugia and the Marches.

The armistice of Villafranca appeared at first sight to shatter Cavour's plans. In fact it removed the restraining hand of Napoleon and allowed the northern states to demonstrate their determination to unite with Piedmont. Though d'Azeglio left Bologna, instructions were sent to Tuscany and the Duchies to hold firm. When Farini retired as Royal Commissioner he was immediately elected 'dictator' by Parma and Modena and subsequently by Bologna and the Legations. He at once began to reorganize the customs and post office on a Piedmontese pattern and to arrange demonstrations in favour of Victor Emmanuel. Similar policies were followed by Ricasoli in Tuscany who ignored all protests, began to 'Piedmontise' the administration and called an assembly to vote for union in a constitutional state under the House of Savoy. It thus became clear that the terms of Villafranca could only be put into effect by force.

The mutual jealousy of the great powers, however, prevented any such intervention. When Austrian, French and Piedmontese delegates met at Zürich to convert the armistice into a permanent peace the French, though opposed to an enlarged Piedmontese union, rejected the use of force and thus, in effect, prevented Austrian intervention as well and made the union inevitable. Meanwhile Britain had become increasingly opposed to any French action. Palmerston had returned as Prime Minister in June with Lord John Russell as Foreign Secretary. Both were anxious to promote Italian independence and hasten the withdrawal of French and Austrian troops. In January 1860 Lord John presented 'four points' which urged France and Austria not to interfere in Italian affairs. The situation appeared to have reached deadlock. But while Austria retired in sullen discontent, Napoleon was already involved in schemes to retrieve his prestige and make what he could out of his Italian adventure.

In December 1859 Napoleon launched an anonymous pamphlet under the title *Le Pape et le Congrès,* which urged the advantages of ending the temporal power and establishing an Italian confederation. This roused a storm of protest in France: Walewski resigned and the Emperor appeared committed to a new initiative. Cavour, who had returned to Piedmont in September, quickly formulated new plans to exploit Napoleon's ambition. In January he was again Prime Minister, and prepared to bargain Savoy and Nice in return for Tuscany, the Duchies and the Romagna. The deal was settled by treaty on March 24th; Napoleon's troops quickly marched in to organize a plebiscite while Cavour prepared for elections to the first North Italian Parliament.

Cavour's calculations were, however, suddenly interrupted by events in Sicily. A combination of feudal aristocrats, peasants, *banditi,* radical citizens and liberal lawyers made the island a permanent centre of unrest. In April the Mazzinians, despairing of any genuine unification of the peninsula and deeply suspicious of Cavour and his diplomacy, stirred up another revolution in Palermo. Though the revolt was deplored by moderate opinion it roused the enthusiastic support of Sicilian exiles led by Crispi who urged Garibaldi to lead an expedition to assist the rebels. Garibaldi, outraged by the surrender of his native Nice to Napoleon, was soon persuaded and began to gather arms and volunteers with the obvious intention of launching a direct attack on southern territory.

Garibaldi's activities placed Cavour in something of a dilemma. While keeping the possibility of ultimate unification in mind he would have preferred time to consolidate the North before moving on to absorb Venice and any additional southern territory. Gradual growth was essential to integrate the new provinces and to keep control over developments. The revolution had so far been carefully directed from above and had avoided any Mazzinian or social disturbances. Garibaldi now threatened to disrupt the entire programme. His independent action introduced another incalculable factor and might stir up republican agitation and social unrest, undermine Piedmontese leadership and even threaten the authority of Cavour himself. In addition his action could disturb the great powers, and especially Napoleon, whose plans had already been somewhat disrupted. Any attack on the South was bound to raise the question of Rome and this again might precipitate intervention, especially by France where the Emperor was always sensitive to Catholic opinion.

On the other hand Garibaldi was enormously popular and had long since abandoned any republican views. He was completely loyal to Victor Emmanuel, who was known to hold him in high regard. Cavour, who had just abandoned Nice and Savoy was in a weak position, and could not take effective action to stop Garibaldi's expedition until the surrender of the territories had been ratified in the Piedmontese Parliament. Meanwhile Austria appeared paralysed while Britain could be relied on to counter any French activity. The whole affair might in any case prove a complete fiasco. Cavour, therefore, embarked on a tortuous and ambivalent policy designed to take account of almost every eventuality and pacify all the interested parties. This resulted in a chronicle of contradictions that confused contemporaries and has continued to confuse historians ever since.

Though Cavour sent instructions to stop Garibaldi at all costs, a ramshackle expedition of two steamers and some 1,150 fighting men was allowed to sail. Their impact on Sicily was immediate. The revolt which had been on the verge of collapse suddenly revived. Garibaldi roused enthusiasm in the countryside and in the towns. Peasants hoped to secure their tenures, artisans to find new employment, while bourgeois liberals and even aristocrats expected new opportunities with the collapse of the Neapolitan government. Within a month Garibaldi had virtually cleared Bourbon troops from the island, seized Palermo, declared himself 'dictator' and established a new government under Crispi to restore order and win the confidence of moderate Sicilians.

Garibaldi's unexpected success, however, only increased Cavour's difficulties. Italians everywhere were now thoroughly roused, while the Catholic powers began to protest forcefully at so blatant a violation of international law.

Cavour could only play off one party against another, make desperate efforts to keep up with events and try to maintain an element of control. Though Garibaldi had proclaimed Victor Emmanuel King and set up a moderate ministry, Cavour was obsessed by fears that the dictator would stir up a social revolution and ally himself to Mazzinian and republican elements. He therefore sent La Farina to Sicily to arrange for the immediate annexation of the island to Piedmont by plebiscite – a course which would inevitably appeal to Napoleon III. La Farina's activities, however, roused the opposition of Crispi and Garibaldi who were determined to unite the whole of Italy into one unit and not allow each province to be absorbed piecemeal. They favoured the election of an assembly to bargain with Cavour and assure the full and free unification of the peninsula. When La Farina attempted to undermine their position by rallying moderate and federalist support he was arrested and deported. This only confirmed Cavour's suspicions of Garibaldi's plans and accelerated the widening rift between the two men.

Cavour's anxieties were redoubled when Garibaldi crossed the Straits and attacked Naples. A threat to Rome and a social revolution in the South appeared imminent. French intervention and the collapse of Piedmontese policy seemed highly probable. While previously Cavour had tried to negotiate an alliance with the Neapolitan government, he now hoped to stir up a liberal revolution to forestall Garibaldi's radical allies. When this failed he was forced to take decisive action. While on the one hand he was ready to temporize in Sicily and rely on the British fleet to cover Garibaldi's advance, he simultaneously persuaded Napoleon of the dangers of the General's republican ambitions and the imminence of a threat to Rome. Napoleon was induced to agree to a Piedmontese attack on the Papal States to cover the Holy See and prevent the advance of the Neapolitan *sans-culottes* and Mazzinian agitators.

On September 8th 1860, the day after Garibaldi's triumphant entry into Naples, Piedmontese troops attacked the Papal States on the flimsiest of pretexts and reasserted the leadership of the North. Many who had doubted the genuine patriotism of Cavour's policy now rallied to Victor Emmanuel. The victory of the royal army at Castelfidaro and the occupation of Ancona further enhanced Piedmontese prestige. Though Garibaldi continued to reject demands for an immediate plebiscite, the stiffening of Neapolitan resistance on the river Volturno and the defences of Capua forced him to abandon his plans to occupy Rome. Meanwhile the Piedmontese army was able to interpose an effective barrier to any further advance on Rome. In October, Victor Emmanuel entered Naples and Garibaldi, loyal to the end, surrendered his authority to the royal government and retired unrewarded and almost unrecognized to his island of Caprera.

Cavour rapidly gathered all the threads into his own hands. On October 2nd Parliament met in Turin and gave the Prime Minister an overwhelming vote of confidence. Sicilian aristocrats and moderates rallied to the North to avert further confusion and rural unrest. In October, Sicily voted almost unanimously for annexation. Naples voted at the same time; promises of order and liberty persuaded the nobility and bourgeoisie to join Piedmont as the only alternative to a Bourbon reaction. Already the revolution had lead to widespread violence in the countryside and the growing unrest of the *lazzaroni* and peasant population ultimately persuaded the moderates to vote for unification.

The apparently overwhelming verdict of the plebiscites did much to forestall foreign intervention. Napoleon withdrew his minister from Turin as a formal gesture. Though the three eastern powers met in conference at Warsaw, any threats of a revived Holy Alliance were frustrated by Lord John Russell's note of October 27th which declared that 'the people in question are the best judges of their own affairs', and deplored the severe censure administered by Austria, France, Prussia and Russia. As a result annexation was able to proceed without interruption. When Gaeta fell in February 1861 Bourbon rule in the South finally collapsed. Naples and Sicily joined the northern Kingdom and all Italy with the exception of the Patrimony of St. Peter round Rome and the Venetian territories was united under the House of Savoy.

The unity of Italy, however, was deceptive and barely skin-deep. Sicilian and Neapolitan moderates had voted for unification merely to escape the threat of revolution or reaction. Vague assurances of regional autonomy led them to anticipate some federal independence. When Cavour sent La Farina back to advise on the government of Sicily they were rapidly disillusioned. In Naples the situation was even worse. Few moderates existed outside the larger towns. The country-side was dominated by the aristocracy, the Church and the peasantry. All were hostile to Piedmontese controls and customs. Once free from Bourbon rule the landowners were anxious only to retain their feudal independence, while the Church incited the villages to oppose the encroachment of the anti-clerical laws of an alien North. The peasants, disappointed in their earlier hopes, were soon roused and by the spring of 1861 a full-scale revolt had broken out in the Abruzzi. Farini, who had been sent to reorganize the government of Naples, found himself increasingly unpopular and isolated. It was soon clear that the South would remain united only if held down by force.

In January 1861 Cavour nevertheless won a triumph in the elections. As these were based on a general application of the very narrow Piedmontese franchise[1] this was not altogether surprising. Peasants and artisans were excluded; the aristocracy remained generally indifferent. The liberal and radical representatives of the middle classes became the voice of the nation and constructed a framework to suit their own attitudes and interests. Unity could only be assured by the extension of a centralized Piedmontese system. Though Minghetti, a moderate southerner, proposed some autonomy for the South in his constitutional amendments these were rejected by the North as too dangerous and by Sicilians as inadequate. Cavour, who persistently refused to visit the South, accepted the verdict of Parliament as final. He had little sympathy for the Neapolitans whom he considered to be 'rotten to the core' and was determined to unite Italy under the more progressive and liberal institutions prevailing in the North. For this he has been alternatively praised or blamed, depending largely on the political bias of his critics.

Cavour's attitude, nevertheless, left a legacy of bitterness and disillusion. The moderate left attacked the whole process of unification as unreal, while federalists resented the dominant position of Piedmont in the peninsula. Garibaldi, angered by the indifferent treatment of his volunteers and

[1] See p. 273.

convinced of Cavour's duplicity, came to denounce him publicly in the Chamber. Radicals and republicans felt betrayed by the failure to capture Rome and build a new society and a new state around Italy's historic capital. More significantly, Cavour's determination to impose Piedmontese laws on the South, dissolve the monasteries and introduce civil marriage led to the permanent and bitter hostility of the Church. Though he foreshadowed the future by his ideal of a 'free Church in a free State', outlined in one of his last and most memorable speeches, his actions did little to soothe papal feelings and delayed the implementation of his principle for some eighty years. Clerical hostility, which fostered the opposition of the aristocracy and the peasantry, was to be a dangerous weakness in the structure of the new Italian State.

In June 1861 Cavour died, exhausted by his exertions, embittered by the attack of Garibaldi and alarmed by the unrest in the South. His death was acknowledged by most liberals and moderates as an unmitigated disaster. He alone had grasped the many threads of foreign diplomacy and domestic change. He had manipulated them to build a shell which was as yet hollow and incomplete. It was left to his successors to finish the job. Cavour, himself, had been forced to improvise and work within a confused cross-current of conflicting events. Nevertheless he had generally managed to keep his balance and remain sufficiently detached to steer a course calculated to achieve the maximum advantage and move towards a dimly projected goal. As such he was undoubtedly the prime architect of Italian unification, even though his efforts depended upon the support of Victor Emmanuel and the heroic initiatives of Garibaldi. Amid the tumult Cavour retained a grasp of the factors involved and was thus able to harness the many elements needed to build the framework of a united Italy.

5. *Venice and Rome*

The framework, however, remained unfinished. Cavour had made it clear that only Rome would unite the historical, intellectual and moral conditions needed to form the capital of a great state. His successors were equally determined to complete unification by the acquisition of Rome and Venetia.

z

While both remained under the control of foreign powers
Italy could only wait for a suitable diplomatic moment to
assert her claims. Meanwhile internal division and economic
weakness sapped enthusiasm and frustrated growth. Unification had been the work of small groups of liberals, idealists,
townsmen and northern rationalists. Garibaldi and Mazzini
had between them roused momentary excitement among the
peasantry and town proletariat, but this had been smothered by the use of the Piedmontese constitution and the
application of northern custom and law. The *Statuo* restricted the franchise to some 250,000 literate taxpayers in
a population of nearly twenty-two millions. The majority
thus became increasingly indifferent; a minority actively
hostile.

The old aristocracy of the South, denied autonomy and
resentful of northern control, retired from active political life
to the feudal isolation of their estates. Many remained loyal
to the Pope, the Bourbons and to their provincial privileges.
Traditional loyalties assured them of influence among
peasants and artisans. The latter, denied the expected benefits of the revolution, were easily incited by radical and reactionary extremists. In the cities Mazzinian and republican
agitators were soon at work. Throughout the countryside the
Church encouraged resistance to Piedmontese laws and
northern secularization, and assisted groups of *banditi* in
their struggle with the new national government.

The hostility of Pius IX and the Catholic Church encouraged fragmentation and undermined the authority of
government. Napoleon, Cavour and a strong section of liberal
opinion hoped that the Papacy would reach a compromise
with the new order. But Piedmontese actions appeared to
contradict their more moderate arguments, and the Pope
determined to stand fast on the traditional and territorial
claims of the past. Pius regarded Napoleon as little less than a
traitor who, while promising to support the Church, had
allowed her territory to be seized and violated. When the
Emperor decided to withdraw his troops and signed a convention with the Italian government in September 1864, Pius
replied with a Syllabus of Errors which denounced liberalism, rationalism, atheism, communism, state education,
toleration and the whole spectrum of progressive thought.

This was interpreted as a declaration of war upon the State of Italy, and indeed upon the whole non-Catholic world.

The Italian economy remained quite insufficient to support the superstructure of the new State. The inherited debt of the several states stood at nearly two thousand million lire while the annual deficit was some four hundred million. Railways, roads and port facilities were inadequate, industry was restricted to the North, vital raw materials such as coal and iron barely existed, while agriculture remained essentially feudal and primitive. In the South 90 per cent of the population were illiterate and a vast educational programme was required to make people aware of the significance of unification. Poverty inevitably forced Italy to rely on loans and the assistance of foreign powers. This again dampened the ardour of patriots who found their future mortgaged to the financial demands of French or British banking houses.

Progress was further undermined by the instability of political life. The death of Cavour left a vacuum impossible to fill. After ten years of stable government, ministries now began to change almost annually as the King manoeuvred to find suitable men among the several parties in Parliament. The extreme left, the 'party of action', of some eighty members followed Garibaldi or Mazzini in demanding the immediate occupation of Rome or the creation of a federal republic, and were regarded as too irresponsible to hold office. The moderate left, led by Rattazzi, was to prove dangerously unreliable when dealing with Garibaldi, while the liberal right, Cavour's old supporters, was soon weakened by the influx of a 'consorteria' of Tuscan and northern members hostile to Piedmontese leadership. The fragmentation of the right and the growth of sectional rivalry soon led to the proliferation of parties and factions. This became a characteristic of Italian politics and soon made government continuity increasingly elusive.

Baron Ricasoli, sometime dictator of Tuscany, followed Cavour in 1861. His unbending autocracy failed, however, to persuade Parliament, irritated the King and alarmed Napoleon. His attempts to control internal unrest by increased centralization and his dissolution of southern monasteries led to bitter opposition from the Church and the regions. Attempts to reorganize a national army and elevate Italy to great power status brought mounting costs and increased taxation. Banditry continued to ravage the South and received open assistance from the Papal States. Italy's problems appeared to multiply and defy solution. Soon all were to be dwarfed by the revival of the Roman Question.

In March 1862 Ricasoli resigned and the King chose Rattazzi as Prime Minister, even though he lacked a majority in the Chamber. As a result he was forced to rely on the left and appeal for popular support to retain office. Garibaldi considered it an opportune moment to attack Rome and landed in Sicily where he soon collected two thousand volunteers. In spite of government opposition and a royal reprimand he was allowed to land on the mainland. The widespread belief that the ministry was following an ambivalent 'Cavourian' policy encouraged officials to ignore instructions. Garibaldi and his men had to be pursued into the mountains by Italian troops. At Aspromonte the volunteers were dispersed and the hero shot in the leg. The ensuing outcry forced Rattazzi to resign.

The Minghetti ministry, which relied upon the anti-Piedmontese 'consorteria', was able to take the Roman Question a step further in 1864 by negotiating the September Convention with Napoleon. France agreed to withdraw her troops in two years if Italy guaranteed papal territory, agreed to a papal army and moved her capital to Florence within six months. This, Napoleon hoped, would satisfy the Italians and divert attention from Rome. The majority, however, regarded it as a half-way stage to their final objective and as a way of limiting the power of Piedmont. Bitter rioting in Turin was only put down with the loss of fifty lives. Minghetti resigned and Piedmontese influence was restored by the appointment of La Marmora as Prime Minister.

While developments in Rome now waited upon the withdrawal of French troops, an opportunity arose to occupy Venice. Austro-Prussian rivalry in Germany had reached a new climax over the partition of Schleswig-Holstein.[1] In 1865 Prussia made tentative offers for an Italian alliance – probably to frighten Vienna – but La Marmora was evasive and anxious to sound Napoleon's views first. Meanwhile the Convention of Gastein patched up the quarrel and the negotiations lapsed. They were resumed in the following

[1] See p. 371.

year. Bismarck had meanwhile pacified Napoleon at Biarritz and the Emperor, anxious to fulfil the Plombières agreement, encouraged the alliance which was eventually signed in March 1866. Indeed, he assured the eventual transfer of Venice to Italy by signing a treaty with Austria which ceded the province to France to ensure French neutrality in the coming war.

The war of 1866 brought nothing but humiliation to Italy. Her army, though superior in numbers, was defeated at Custoza due to defective staff work. Her new navy was shattered by an inferior Austrian force at Lissa. Prussia, after a short but decisive campaign, made peace with Austria without consulting her ally. Italy received Venice from the hands of Napoleon to whom she appeared increasingly indebted. After a plebiscite the new province was handed over to the new Kingdom, but without the Tyrol or the Trentino which were retained to pacify German and Austrian opinion within the Confederation.

The withdrawal of French troops from Rome at the end of the year encouraged yet another Garibaldean invasion of the Papal States. In 1867 Rattazzi was again Prime Minister and the pattern of his previous ministry was repeated. While volunteers flocked to the frontiers the government pursued an ambivalent policy. Though intervention was officially to be stopped at all costs volunteers were often provided with free transport and free arms. The invasion, however, was a complete fiasco. Rome failed to rise. The irregulars were easily defeated at Mentana by an army of papal volunteers. Napoleon, alarmed by the outcry of French Catholics, was forced to restore his garrison; his ministers declared that Rome would never become the capital of the Italian State. With increasing bitterness Italians were forced to watch and wait.

Meanwhile the problems of the peninsula continued to fester. Brigandage flourished in the South and was inflamed by new demands for conscription and taxation. In Sicily prolonged agitation led to a general revolt in 1866 when elements of the extreme left and right combined to defy the central government. The debt continued to mount while ministers of finance struggled in vain to curb the deficit. Though trade gradually increased and though industry was encouraged by exhibitions and the construction of a national railway network, this was not enough to cater for the massed poverty of the majority. The closure of southern monasteries and the sale of monastic property to cover state debts further embittered relations with the Papacy. Pius IX used the temporary security of French troops to call an Oecumenical Council in Rome in 1869. This upheld the supremacy of faith, denounced rationalism and proclaimed the infallibility of the Pope. It was to be a beacon of light amid the confusion and misery of a liberal world. To many, however, it merely signified a final refusal to compromise, an eternal barrier to any genuine unification of the peninsula.

The occupation of Rome came in the following year. The Franco-Prussian war led to the withdrawal of French troops and the Italian government took cautious steps to occupy the capital. The great powers were notified and after token resistance Rome was taken, though without the enthusiastic support of the population. Papal independence was guaranteed and a free Church within a free State established by a Law of Guarantees. But the Pope refused to agree and retired, a 'prisoner in the Vatican', to reaffirm his claims and deny the validity of any unilateral solution.

When Victor Emmanuel and the government entered Rome the unification of Italy was complete. But the problems remained. As d'Azeglio put it: 'We have made Italy, now we have to make Italians.' The poetry had already been lost; the process had soured. Ten years of disappointment and defeat, of civil war and religious bitterness had left a permanent scar upon the peninsula. Though the economy developed and political institutions survived, the framework remained hollow. It was a legacy that dogged Italy into the twentieth century and was only eradicated after decades of violence, warfare and democratic reconstruction.

XIV · THE UNIFICATION OF GERMANY

1. *Germany after 1848*

THE failure of the 1848 revolutions left the German middle classes disillusioned and divided. Their reform plans had failed; their ideals had lacked substance and support. Liberal proposals had been rejected by both Austria and Prussia. Radical agitation in the South had been vigorously suppressed. Artisans had failed to find security in either liberal legislation or in their own divided associations. Workers and left-wing intellectuals had been isolated and ineffective. The mass of the peasantry remained equally powerless. In the East, occasional riots had been easily crushed, while west of the Elbe security of tenure only encouraged the sub-division of property and the proliferation of a 'dwarf' economy. Peasants had received little or no help from the middle-class lawyers who dominated state assemblies. The ideals of philosophers and poets had been reserved for an enlightened few and had failed to provide any concrete social benefits. The majority turned back to the more reliable protection of kings and aristocrats. They at least appeared to have learnt from their experiences. The Junkers now advocated guild restoration and land reform in order to ally with artisans and peasants against the bourgeoisie. A new Brandenburg ministry[1] soon put these proposals into effect and within a year had prepared laws to protect guilds, commute peasant dues and set up loan banks to help pay for their redemption.

All the policies of the new Prussian government were not, however, equally practicable. Frederick William and Radowitz hoped to take advantage of Austria's preoccupation with the Hungarian revolt to unite Germany into a confederation of princes under Prussian leadership. Both hankered after a romantic fusion of medieval estates and middle-class interests. In 1849 a new constitution, granted by royal favour, proclaimed equality before the law and set up a *Landtag* with a nominated upper house and a lower house of representa-

[1] See p. 286.

tives elected by universal suffrage through electoral colleges. While the chambers retained a measure of control over taxation, ministers were entirely responsible to the King, and the army remained firmly under royal command. Though little more than a gesture to liberal sentiment, the constitution did mollify the upper middle classes who eagerly voted for new property grades in order to exclude artisan or radical representatives.

Meanwhile, as Prussian troops crossed Germany to destroy any lingering revolts in the South, Frederick William and Radowitz negotiated a *Dreikaiserbund* between Prussia, Hanover and Saxony as the nucleus of a new German Union designed to appeal both to princes and to moderate liberal opinion. In June 1849, 148 members of the Frankfurt Parliament meeting at Gotha urged acceptance of the Radowitz proposals. By the end of August twenty-eight states had joined the new *Bund*, set up an administrative council and agreed to hold elections for a diet at Erfurt in the following year.

By now, however, the Habsburgs had reasserted their authority in Hungary,[1] and Schwarzenberg set out deliberately and skilfully to undermine and ultimately destroy the Prussian initiative. Bavarian loyalty to Austria had never been in doubt, and Schwarzenberg exploited fears of Prussian domination to detach Hanover, Saxony and Würtemberg from the alliance. While Frederick William delayed, confident of the outcome of his romantic vision, Schwarzenberg launched a bitter attack on the Prussian plans. While the *Bund* busied itself preparing for the elections, he put forward rival proposals to restore Austrian leadership. In May 1850 he summoned the Diet of the old Confederation to discuss reform and began to concentrate troops on the Prussian frontier.

In October, Prussian and Austrian plans came into direct conflict in Hesse-Cassel. Here the Elector's drift towards reaction was suddenly interrupted by a liberal revolt. The Elector fled and appealed to the Diet for support. Hesse-Cassel, however, was in the Prussian Union, at the heart of the *Zollverein* and in a key military position. Prussia, therefore, intervened instead. The Diet declared this move illegal

[1] See p. 293.

and threatened war, while Austria deployed a quarter of a million men ready for action. Though Berlin cheered belligerently, Frederick William completely collapsed. Schwarzenberg had already secured the agreement of the Tsar, who had been hostile to Frederick William's liberal ideals from the start. In November Nicholas recognized the Diet, denounced Prussian intervention and advised the restoration of the old Confederation. Radowitz resigned and Manteufel was appointed Prime Minister. In December he travelled to Olmütz and abandoned Prussia's claims. The new Union was dissolved, the troops in Hesse–Cassel withdrawn and the Confederation restored under Austrian leadership.

Prussia's humiliation was completed when Anglo-Russian pressure forced her to withdraw from Schleswig-Holstein and make peace with the Danes. In 1852 the Treaty of London left the Duchies united and settled the succession in favour of the Danish Crown. Thus Frederick William had failed to satisfy any of his aristocratic, liberal, or national dreams and hopes of a revived medieval empire faded,[1] together with the ideals of Herder, Heine and the romantics of an earlier age. Nevertheless, within a year Prussia had already begun to turn the tide. The Manteufel ministry, conservative, bureaucratic and Junker had no use for speculative ideals and embarked on a policy designed to maintain Prussian solidarity and preserve her essential interests.

Though the old Confederation was restored, Prussia was able to exclude the Austrian Empire from the Union. Manteufel rallied support from both Russia and the south German states to defeat the Austrian proposals and thereby retained a balance between the two powers. Prussia also succeeded in excluding Austria from the Zollverein, and destroyed Bruck's plans for drawing off the German states into a wider Danubian free trade area.[1] By 1853 the Zollverein treaties had been renewed, and in the following year the addition of Hanover helped to consolidate Prussia's influence in the North. In 1851 Prussia had agreed to sign a defensive alliance with Austria in order to guarantee her territory from revolutionary attack. But this had only been designed to last for three years and by the end of the Crimean war she had

[1] See p. 428.

already embarked on an independent policy destined to challenge Austria for leadership in Germany.

Meanwhile, the Manteufel ministry worked to consolidate its authority at home. Frederick William was dominated by a *Camarilla* of Junkers and conservative aristocrats led by the von Gerlach brothers who urged the need for paternal reconstruction to improve the public welfare and secure popular support. The King was quick to agree, and the government introduced a broad programme of artisan and peasant reforms. In 1853 and 1855 legislation carefully regulated the working conditions of children. Child labour under twelve was prohibited, while those between twelve and fourteen were to work no more than six hours a day. Children were to be exempt from nightwork, were to receive daily rest periods and were to attend public or factory schools. These terms, which were vigorously enforced by government inspectors and the regular courts, were well in advance of any comparable legislation in Britain or France.

In 1854 laws were passed to promote guilds, regulate wages and hours of work, encourage trade schools and facilitate state loans. Over 4,600 new crafts corporations were founded to protect the artisan classes, though these could in the long run do little to stem the tide of capitalist enterprise. Legislation did, however, attempt to introduce the social benefits denied by middle-class revolutionaries. Agitation declined and radical intervention in the 1855 elections was a complete failure. In subsequent years the lowest property grades were to provide the highest proportion of government supporters, revealing yet again the relative isolation of the middle classes and the widespread appeal of authoritarian rule.

The Manteufel ministry also promoted a vigorous programme of peasant reform. The 1850s and 1860s witnessed the end of manorialism on the east German estates. Nearly 640,000 peasants were freed (some three times as many as between 1811 and 1848). Their labour services were commuted and redemption backed by land credit schemes. Nevertheless, the majority were too small and too poor to maintain an independent livelihood and were forced to sell out to their landlord and become labourers or factory hands. Between 1850 and 1860 nearly a million emigrated to the New World. But 90 per cent came from the small, overcrowded freeholds

The GERMAN QUESTION 1815–1871

a = Part of Luxemburg excluded from the Confederation in 1839

Prussian Territory in 1866 ....

Prussian Acquisitions in 1866 ....

Boundary of German Confederation, 1815–1866 ..

Southern boundary of North German Confederation, 1866–1871 ....

Boundary of German Empire, 1871 ....

English Miles
0   50   100   150   200

west of the Elbe. Once again, it appeared that it was the spread of freedom rather than the weight of authority that was to inflict the greatest hardship upon the majority.

The aristocracy exploited the post-revolutionary years to consolidate their power. Junker apologists praised the benefits of paternal government and denounced the destructive liberties of the bourgeoisie. Throughout Germany, constitutions were curtailed and artisan and peasant reform encouraged. In Prussia, aristocratic entails were restored and the Upper Chamber elevated into a House of Peers. In 1856 landowners regained their earlier police powers and thereby restored an almost absolute authority on their estates. Meanwhile, the middle classes could only protest ineffectively at the follies of restrictive regulation and the arbitrary powers of the police. Wedged between fear of revolution from the left and fear of reaction from the right they were left to exploit the years of relative peace to their own best advantage. Though the 'reaction' inevitably received a bad liberal press it gave the majority a greater sense of security than the upheavals of 1848. Even the old Confederation allowed Germans of different interests and ideals a period of peaceful co-existence. Prosperity became once more a practical consolation for loss of political power and the transience of popular acclaim.

2. The 'New Era'

The post-revolutionary decade was one of unprecedented economic development. The reorganization of the Bank of Prussia in 1846 had established a stable financial base, encouraged the development of joint-stock banks and accelerated the distribution of credit. Some twenty note-issue banks were founded in the boom conditions which prevailed between 1850 and 1857. This promoted the growth of limited liability companies covering every branch of industrial enterprise. During the peak years of the middle fifties over one hundred and sixty were registered and though a recession in 1857 brought a sharp decline, the economy was sufficiently buoyant to make a rapid recovery in the early 1860s.

The period also witnessed the completion of the German railway system. General planning was directed by August von der Heydt, Prussian Minister of Commerce, who drew up an overall national plan, thus by-passing innumerable particular state interests. Eastern Prussia was linked by three strategic routes to the industrial Rhineland, while the southern states were joined to the Baltic and the North Sea ports, diverting traffic from the Austrian Empire. In 1851 branch line construction was opened to private enterprise and by 1860 Germany led the continent of Europe in its rail coverage.[1] Shipping boomed and the tonnage handled at Hamburg rose by some 300 per cent in ten years. Industry was stimulated and the economy launched on a new age of 'self-sustained growth'.

As elsewhere it was textiles, especially cotton, that led the way. By 1860, 310 cotton mills were employing 23,000 power looms and absorbing four times the quantity of raw cotton purchased in 1836. The Rhineland, Saxony and the South became centres of a growing textile industry which, including the more traditional woollen, linen and silk manufacturers, employed some 750,000. Coal and iron were quick to follow. In 1851 new laws cut the coal tax by half and encouraged free enterprise and investment. Steam engines, pumps, rails and new safety devices were introduced. By 1864 some 670 mines were employing 99,000 men and six years later German coal output had become second in the world. The iron industry, which had lagged behind Belgium and France in the first half of the century, rapidly overtook its neighbours. Though the Silesian mines continued to decline, development in the Ruhr and Saar basins made spectacular progress. The rapid spread of coke furnaces more than doubled output in each decade. The introduction of Bessemer's and Siemens' steel processes led to a rapid growth in production in Berlin and the Ruhr.

German engineering also made rapid strides. By 1861 some 715 firms of all sizes were employing 37,000 men. Besides engines, locomotives, machine tools and other mechanical appliances, important improvements were made in the manufacture of field guns and smaller armaments. A striking example was the Krupp works at Essen. By 1864 it was employing six thousand men – as against only seven in 1826 – and manufacturing a wide variety of engines and steel can-

[1] See Appendix 5.

non. The Borsig works in Berlin followed a similar pattern and gave a lead to a growing number of smaller industrialists throughout the country.

Such economic expansion enormously increased the combined interests of the upper middle classes. They were able to enforce demands for the renewal of the *Zollverein* treaties and for the gradual liberalization of the economy in spite of opposition from conservative governments. Handloom-weavers and craft industries thus continued to decline with growing rapidity, while the erosion of guild controls in mining and metallurgy allowed increasing numbers to move from the overcrowded countryside into the new industrial towns. The inter-dependence of economic activity created a new awareness of national problems. Monetary conferences urged standardization of the German currency. In 1858 a congress of German economists demanded free trade and a closer union to combine the commercial, financial and political interests of the nation.

Any reform tended to increase the solidarity of the *Zollverein* and to undermine the influence of Austria. Her exclusion became a fundamental principle of Prussian policy, and the addition of Hanover to the customs union in 1854 was an obvious victory for her diplomacy. Three years later Austrian efforts to negotiate a currency agreement were also defeated. Prussia systematically excluded the circulation of south German notes from her territory thus achieving a measure of standardization entirely on her own terms. At the same time, investment was encouraged in German enterprise to build up industry and counteract the dominant position of British, French and Belgian capital in the Rhineland.

Increasing independence was also shown in Prussia's foreign policy. During the Crimean war her neutrality had gradually swung away from Austria towards Russia.[1] Though a defensive alliance had been renewed in 1854, on the clear understanding that Austria was not going to fight anyway, Prussia led the opposition to German mobilization in 1855 and thus won Russian approval for holding Austria in check. At the Congress of Paris the Prussians had been almost entirely ignored. Yet by remaining detached they obtained a freedom

[1] See p. 318.

to manoeuvre which was to be fully exploited in the years ahead.

In 1857 Frederick William suffered a stroke, and his brother William became regent the following year. His accession brought to a head all the conflicting elements within the Confederation and these were further agitated by the example of Italian unification and the defeat of Austria in her war against Piedmont and France. William I had no use for the *Camarilla* and the vague paternalism of the Gerlachs. He was essentially practical and level headed, aware of the realities of power and suspicious of ambivalent and contradictory policies. His first ministry brought back the moderate aristocracy and the Rhinelanders led by Prince Karl Anton von Hohenzollern and Rudolph von Auerswald. This was immediately hailed as the dawn of a 'new era'. But enthusiasm was premature. William was essentially a conservative and a military man. His aim was to find an alternative government, not to modify his exercise of power or alter the structure of the State. Nevertheless, small gestures are easily misconstrued and the response illustrated the keen sense of anticipation that existed throughout the Confederation.

The elections of 1858 reflected the complexion of the new government. The extreme conservatives were defeated and the moderates led by Vincke, a Westphalian landowner, won 210 seats in the Diet. They represented the cautious and restrained liberalism of the new aristocracy and upper middle classes anxious to promote a liberal economy yet retain established political safeguards. The formation of a new progressive party in 1861 introduced a growing challenge from the rising industrialists and intellectuals of the middle bourgeoisie. Rhineland businessmen and liberal manufacturers from Saxony and Silesia combined to demand free trade, lower taxes and the elimination of guild restrictions. In addition they urged the need for economic union and began to look to Prussia to achieve the unification of Germany within a constitutional framework.

Their demands were strengthened by the example of Italy. In 1859 a German National Association, *Nationalverein*, was founded to urge the need for action under the leadership of Prussia. Treitschke predicted the imminent realization of union, while Bennigsen raised the total membership to some

25,000 by 1862. The Association appealed to both the middle and upper bourgeoisie. Small businessmen, intellectuals, professionals, officials, financiers and industrialists expected to achieve greater political influence and higher material returns from a combination of liberal and national institutions. Both the moderate and progressive parties hoped to find in Prussia an agent ready and willing to shape Germany to their own design.

Others, however, suspected that Prussia would be a dangerous and deceptive ally. Klopp was already warning Germans of the dangers of enslavement, and many of the southern states preferred a wider federal union which would retain Austria as a counterweight to Prussia's growing preponderance. In 1862 they founded a Reform Association to urge German unification with the inclusion of Austria. In February, Vienna had already taken the initiative and urged a conference to strengthen the executive of the Confederation. Throughout Germany agitation for union appeared to be rising to a vociferous climax. In 1861 a National Chamber of Commerce was set up to co-ordinate liberal economic demands. In 1862 a German Union of Handicraftsmen at Weimar appeared to unite artisans in a final struggle against mechanization. In 1863 factory operatives were united by Lassalle into a German Workers Union that combined agitation for higher wages and shorter hours with demands for national unity under Prussian leadership. Almost every articulate class appeared infected with an urge to unite and to add national colours to their individual demands.

William I, however, remained quite unmoved by all the clamour. He was more concerned with retaining control over the chief instruments of power, the army and the administration, than with any national considerations. Indeed, he regarded all popular representation with obvious distaste and was anxious to remove any sign of it from the armed forces as rapidly as possible. In 1859[1] attempts to mobilize the Prussian army to counter any French pressure had revealed glaring weaknesses in organization. As a result Albrecht von Roon had been appointed Minister of War. In February 1860 he submitted plans to extend compulsory military service to all eligible recruits and also to reduce the role of the *Land-*

---

[1] See p. 336.

wehr[1] and bring it under the control of regular officers. These proposals were bitterly attacked by the moderates in the Prussian *Landtag* both on account of their cost and because of the reduced influence of the popular *Landwehr*. When the proposals were withdrawn, however, the *Landtag* nevertheless voted the additional funds. This allowed the government to carry out its plans without parliamentary consent.

In 1861 the rift between the King and the *Landtag* widened. In January, William assumed personal responsibility for the army and in October assumed all the attributes of divine right at his coronation in Königsberg. In December, however, the elections brought in a majority of liberals and progressives who refused to pass either the government's proposed army reforms or the increased budget, and demanded detailed inspection of all financial expenditure. As a result the liberal Auerswald ministry resigned and William turned for support to Heydt, von Roon and the Junkers. When the May elections further increased the representation of the progressives the deadlock between the government and the Lower House appeared complete. William I considered abdication, but when the liberal Crown-Prince refused to replace his father the King was persuaded to call Count Otto von Bismarck-Schönhausen to resolve the crisis. Bismarck soon dealt with the *Landtag* and left the King with complete control over the army. He subsequently went on to deal with the problem of unity as well. He was to save the King and Prussia from any Austrian, liberal or progressive alternatives by completing the process of unification himself. To save Prussia from Germany he was to absorb Germany into Prussia and in the process exploit and undermine German ideals in the interests of a Prussian empire.

3. *Bismarck and his Background*

Otto von Bismarck was born on April 1st, 1815, two and a half months before the battle of Waterloo. His father came from a long line of Junker landowners, who had farmed their Schönhausen estates east of the Elbe for several centuries. Poor, proud and aristocratic they were consciously Prussian, determined to preserve their status against the advance of

[1] See p. 149.

revolutionary ideals from France, Poland or the new Rhine-land provinces. Bismarck's mother, on the other hand, was the daughter of a middle-class civil servant from Leipzig. She brought intellect and distinction into the crude outlines of junker life, and her restless perception was inherited by her son. Bismarck, however, bitterly resented his mother's in-fluence and attempted to erase it from his life. His own his-tory and that of Germany was to become a reflection of this struggle in which the finer attributes of German civilization were to be crushed by the brazen fetters of a junker domina-tion.

Bismarck at first tried quite deliberately to follow a junker line. He resented the liberal grammar school to which he was sent in order to train for the civil service. He resented the university of Göttingen where he became a reactionary rebel, proud of his own lack of culture and contemptuous of middle-class values. In 1836 he joined the civil service, but was unable to put up with his superiors. Two years later he re-signed, determined 'to play only the music I like, or none at all'. When, however, he tried to find independence on his estates he became miserable, frustrated and bored. Assuming complete control after the death of his father, he found no gratification in the routine of agrarian life and the minor offices of a provincial landlord.

For a while Bismarck tried to find satisfaction in a series of desperate attachments. Having pursued innumerable women he fell violently in love with Maria von Thadden, who came from a devout pietist family and was already engaged. She attempted to convert him to a personal faith and her sudden death came as a violent shock. He subsequently married Joanna von Putkammer, one of Maria's friends, who pro-vided the basis of a quiet and stable home life for forty-seven years. She was the opposite of his mother, homely, retiring and entirely devoted to her husband. Bismarck was thus freed to direct his explosive energy at the disturbed currents of German political life.

In 1847, some six months before his marriage, the first United Prussian Diet had met in Berlin.[1] The sudden illness of a sitting member gave Bismarck an opportunity to repre-sent his district. He immediately launched a violent attack on

[1] See p. 278.

every liberal proposal, denounced the emancipation of the Jews and defended the game laws. In a few weeks he built up a reputation for extreme and uncompromising reaction. The 1848 revolution filled him with fury. Resentment of middle class liberals, civil servants, Poles and Rhinelanders drove him to Berlin where he immediately tried to organize a counter-revolution. He had no sympathy for Frederick William whose moderation only appeared to encourage popular demands. When informed of the King's sleepless nights he declared 'a King must be able to sleep', and urged Crown-Princess Augusta to assume the regency for her son. Her refusal only outraged Bismarck still further and opened a lasting feud between them.

In the summer of 1848 Bismarck joined Manteufel, the Gerlachs and the *Camarilla* to plan for a reaction. He rapidly appreciated the weakness of the liberal opposition and urged an alliance with artisan and peasant groups to frustrate the middle classes. He helped rally the 'Junker Parliament'[1] in the autumn to protect aristocratic privileges, and tried to persuade the King to re-occupy Berlin and dissolve the new Prussian Assembly. In the spring of 1849 he directed his attacks against the Frankfurt Parliament. He denounced its 'organized anarchy' and demanded 'no dishonourable connections with democracy'. Frederick William's rejection of the imperial crown filled him with delight. Bismarck's reputation for diehard conservatism appeared confirmed. His views were too extreme to justify an appointment in any Prussian government, and the King's opinions of him were well expressed in the comment: 'red reactionary, smells of blood, only to be used when the bayonet rules'.

Bismarck thus remained free to attack any proposals that appeared to threaten junker independence. He attacked the new Prussian constitution as smacking of liberalism, though he could not deny the King his right to grant it. Bismarck was even more bitter about Radowitz's national proposals. 'We are Prussians and want to remain Prussian,' he stormed and denounced the 'German Swindle' in which Prussia might lose her junker identity. He toasted the fall of Radowitz in champagne and praised the Olmütz settlement. Once again liberal proposals had been defeated and the dangers of utopian

[1] See p. 285.

vision destroyed. Bismarck even went on to praise Austria as the protector of German interests against the Slavs, and denounced the Rhineland liberals for provoking civil war! Bismarck liked to compare politics to a game of chess. In it he played the black pieces, using every stratagem to defeat the initiatives of any rivals until he had cleared his opponents off the board!

His support of Austria brought him the position of Prussian representative at the new Diet of the Confederation in Frankfurt. On arrival, however, he immediately set out to challenge Austria's presiding claims. A characteristic action was to light a cigar in order to break the custom whereby the Austrian plenipotentiary was the only one allowed to smoke. He criticized Austrian demands on every occasion and tried to destroy her leadership over the German states. In 1852 he went to Vienna and played a leading part in excluding Austria from the *Zollverein*. During the Crimean war he advocated strict neutrality and the Austro-Prussian treaty of 1854 filled him with disgust. In 1855 he was able to renew his attack when he rallied the German states against Austrian demands to mobilize the Confederation in her defence.[1] In 1856 Bismarck was confidently predicting: 'Germany is too small for both of us ... only a war will put right the clock of Germany's development.'

During his years at Frankfurt Bismarck also came to realize that victory could not be won by a policy of static conservatism. Social, economic and national developments were creating new sources of power and opening up alternative solutions to the German problem. If these were not harnessed and diverted the Prussian element would be overwhelmed. Thus Bismarck abandoned his earlier support for the powerless artisans and urged a closer alliance with the bourgeoisie who could be outmanoeuvred and deflected by promises of economic reform. 'The side that seizes the initiative in this matter whether it be the Diet ... the *Zollverein* or Prussia alone, will enjoy a great advantage with respect to the sympathy of the participants.' It was Bismarck's avowed objective to play everything up in the name of Prussia rather than in the name of the Confederation or any other rival authority.

By 1858 Bismarck had extended his horizons to incorpor-

[1] See p. 318.

ate national and foreign elements. During the Crimean war he had already anticipated the need for an alliance with Russia. After the Peace of Paris he even urged an understanding with Napoleon III, much to the disgust of the *Camarilla* in Berlin. He was prepared to exploit anyone in Prussia's interests and advised the government to 'beware of sentimental alliances where the consciousness of good deeds is the only compensation for noble sacrifices'. His views were far too unprincipled for the conservative and right minded William. With the 'new era' Bismarck lost his position in the Diet and was sent as ambassador to St. Petersburg. Passing through Berlin he remarked that 'the only reliable ally for Prussia is the German people'.

Once again Bismarck had sensed a rising current that was at once a threat and a challenge to Prussian domination. From St. Petersburg he watched the growth of national institutions that followed the unification of Italy and welcomed the weakening of Austrian power. He bitterly attacked proposals to support Austria and urged that her war with France be allowed to eat deeply into her substance. Meanwhile he learnt Russian and tested the reactions of Gorchakov, the Russian Chancellor. An understanding would guarantee junker interest in Poland and also provide possible support in case of any future Prussian challenge to Austria.

Bismarck's final leap to power was due entirely to internal circumstances. The deadlock between William I and the Prussian Diet appeared to present a decisive challenge to the Crown. Eventually the King was prepared to go to any lengths to retain control and complete his army reforms, and summoned Bismarck for consultation in May 1860 and again in July 1861. On each occasion Bismarck's demands for a free hand in foreign affairs and his talk about German parliaments and universal suffrage were too much. Moreover, he was suspected by the Junkers for his wildly opportunist views, by liberals for his reactionary statements, by Queen Augusta and by William himself who could never be brought to understand the apparent contradictions in Bismarck's brilliant mind. In May 1862 he was sent as ambassador to Paris, where his soundings of Napoleon III were to prove advantageous, though his advocacy of a Franco-Prussian alliance continued to outrage the King. Nevertheless, by

September, William was desperate. On September 18th Roon
summoned Bismarck by telegram. When the Crown-Prince
refused the throne and the King felt ready to surrender, Roon
was able to produce Bismarck as the only alternative. On
September 22nd, 1862, William eventually agreed and two
weeks later Bismarck came to power as Prime Minister and
Minister of Foreign Affairs.

4. Bismarck and Prussia

Bismarck's advent to power was greeted by a chorus of protest. Junkers, liberals, nationalists, parliamentarians and civil
servants were almost all hostile. The King himself only gave
grudging support and was repeatedly reproached by his wife
and the Crown-Prince Frederick who, married to a daughter
of Queen Victoria, was known to be sympathetic to English
ideas. Bismarck lacked experience in both government and
parliamentary procedure. He had few friends and appeared
aloof and isolated. His early moves were by no means uni-
formly successful. But gradually as he learnt to handle the
King and to manipulate his opponents he gained confidence.
Eventually his actions could appear to follow an almost predetermined course. This, however, was certainly not so
apparent at the start.

Bismarck's immediate problem was to resolve the constitutional question and gratify the King's demands. The day
after his appointment the Lower House had defiantly cut the
army estimates and sent an amended budget to the Peers.
Bismarck characteristically first tried to get his way by peaceful means. In the Chamber he took out an olive branch as a
gesture of reconciliation. He visited Vincke and other opposition leaders, blamed the King for his excessive demands and
offered to withdraw the budget and separate the reform proposals from the financial estimates if the liberals would be
prepared to accept a new budget for the following year.
When they refused, he withdrew the budget altogether and
prepared to spend the money without parliamentary consent.
In a notable speech he declared that Germany did not look to
Prussia for her liberalism but for her power. 'It is not by
speeches and majority resolutions that the great questions of
our time are decided. That was the great mistake of 1848 and
1849. It is by iron and blood.'

The speech caused an immediate sensation and was received unfavourably in every quarter. Treitschke ridiculed the vulgarity of a shallow Junker, Roon considered his words excessive, while the liberal press exploded in denunciations. Even William found the speech too provocative and returned to Berlin with the apparent intention of dismissing his Prime Minister. But Bismarck, who admitted the speech had been a mistake, intercepted him in his railway carriage and after lengthy discussion persuaded him that death was preferable to any surrender to a liberal chamber. As a result Bismarck was given a free hand. The Upper House rejected the amended budget, accepted the government's proposals and left the Prime Minister with some pretext for ruling without a budget at all. Bismarck thereupon adjourned parliament and continued to spend the money needed for the army reforms quite arbitrarily. The liberal opposition have often been criticized for not taking more effective action at this point. But there was little they could do. Members had no powers either to impeach ministers or to impede the collection of taxes, while speeches and press agitation left Bismarck totally unmoved.

The conflict between Bismarck and the Lower House became increasingly violent during the next few years. In 1863 members condemned a government that placed 'might before right', and voted by 274 to 45 to make Bismarck personally accountable for any unauthorized expenditure. The elections in the middle of the year returned an even larger liberal majority and the government could only rely upon some 37 firm supporters. Bismarck, however, only became increasingly provocative. In June he passed a Press Law designed to curb opposition journals during the elections. This brought protest from the Crown-Prince which created a widespread sensation and encouraged further agitation until the Law was withdrawn five months later.

Elsewhere, however, Bismarck stood his ground. He rejected compromise and even strengthened his hold over the King by heightening the crisis atmosphere. While the Lower House remained hostile he was indispensable. At the same time he became increasingly adept at playing off his opponents. He exploited William's anger towards the critical attitude of the Crown-Prince. He used the Upper House to pass estimates rejected by the Lower. In 1863 he began discussions with the socialist leader Lassalle for a possible alliance between the government and working classes against the bourgeoisie. At the same time he was already angling for national support to bring the Germans into line behind Prussia. 'In the long run we have certainly one thing on which we can always rely. It is the national strength of the German people, so long as it sees its champion and the hope of its future in the Prussian army.'

While Bismarck was holding moderates, liberals and progressives at bay, his attention was also riveted on threats from abroad. Once again his opening moves appeared conciliatory and disarmingly frank. Though he was later to claim that he had planned war against Austria from the day he took office, his contemporary view that 'events are stronger than the plans of men', ring truer, and he certainly began by suggesting a direct and somewhat ruthless bargain with the Austrian government. Prussia was to be given a free hand north of the Main where 'she needed enough air to keep alive'. Austria should shift her centre of gravity to Hungary where Prussia would be fully prepared to guarantee her interests. Francis Joseph, however, was not yet ready to surrender influence in Germany, especially after the loss of Lombardy, and Bismarck was quick to exploit possible alternatives.

In 1862 Bismarck ratified the free trade treaty between France and the *Zollverein,* and probed French reactions to Prussian control in north Germany. Napoleon III remained conciliatory but evasive. Bismarck may have mentioned possible adjustments on the Rhine. He considered the Emperor's intelligence over-rated and Napoleon was to find himself repeatedly out-manoeuvred while Bismarck exploited his indecision to Prussia's advantage. In the same year he began to attack every Austrian initiative in Germany. Rechberg's plans to reform the legal procedure of the Confederation by an assembly of delegates from the several state parliaments were bitterly denounced, even though Bismarck had himself advocated a similar form of representation a few years earlier. 'Now', he declared, 'to give the German people due influence in their common affairs it must have a representation directly elected by the whole people'; a complete contradiction of all his earlier views.

In 1863, however, these considerations were suddenly interrupted by the outbreak of another revolt in Poland. Bismarck, who had a bitter and lasting hatred of the Poles, was seized by a moment of panic and without reflecting on the implications sent General von Alvensleben to St. Petersberg to conclude a 'secret' convention against the common enemy. This, however, led to a chorus of protest from France, Britain and the Prussian liberals, all outraged by Russia's savage repression of the Poles. Bismarck was forced to ask for a suspension of the convention, and refused Alexander's request for a firm alliance against France. As a result he offended both the Russians and the French, increased his isolation in Germany and roused renewed protests in the *Landtag*. When he subsequently claimed that the convention had been a triumph of diplomacy and had won Russia to the Prussian side, he was twisting the facts in an attempt to magnify his foresight and justify his behaviour.

In fact the Polish crisis placed Bismarck increasingly on the defensive. Assailed on all fronts he became nervous and suffered from violent headaches which forced him for days on end to work lying on a sofa. In the summer of 1863 Austria decided to take the initiative in Germany and invited all the princes to a congress in Frankfurt to discuss a possible reform of the Confederation. Francis Joseph handed the invitation to William personally and for a brief moment the King appeared favourable. But Bismarck made every effort to dissuade him and William eventually declined. When the Emperor sent the aged King of Saxony with a final plea Bismarck was forced to bring all his energy and argument to bear. The debate ended with the exhausted monarch weeping on a sofa and Bismarck smashing the crockery in his room. But he had won his point. William refused to go to Frankfurt and without his agreement the Austrian reform plans could not be put into effect. Once again Bismarck had defeated his rivals. Once again his victory had been entirely destructive. Suddenly in November 1863 the death of King Frederick VII of Denmark and the reopening of the Schleswig-Holstein question gave Bismarck an opportunity to break the deadlock, and opened the way towards the reconstruction of Germany under Prussian leadership.

5. *The Defeat of Austria*

The Treaty of London[1] had put the Schleswig-Holstein question into cold storage but had failed to satisfy any of the parties in the dispute. The historic union of the Duchies was reaffirmed, and their rights to separate representation under the Danish Crown assured. The Duke of Augustenburg, who had claimed the Duchies by virtue of the Salic law, agreed to withdraw and refrain from disturbing the peace. But these terms entirely failed to satisfy the Germans in the Duchies. As they numbered almost the entire population of Holstein and a majority in south Schleswig, they resented Danish rule and refused to accept the withdrawal of the Augustenburgs. They were supported by a majority in the Diet of the Confederation, which had never ratified the Treaty of London anyway, and by a growing mass of German liberal opinion. As Holstein was a member of the Confederation the Diet felt entitled to intervene and exert pressure to guarantee the liberties of the Duchies.

Meanwhile the Danish crown had found it impossible to work out a constitution which satisfied both German and Danish national opinion. As a last resort Frederick VII had planned to incorporate Schleswig by itself, and a decree to this effect had been awaiting the royal signature at the time of his death. Christian IX, who succeeded to the throne by an indirect female line, quickly signed the necessary patent that precipitated the crisis. The Germans in the Duchies and the Diet joined in furious protest. Frederick, son of the Duke of Augustenburg, suddenly stepped in to take over his father's claims. Denmark looked towards Britain for support as Palmerston had made a rash speech in favour of the Danish position in the summer of 1863. On December 7th the Diet voted to send Hanoverian and Saxon troops into Holstein to support Augustenburg and the German population. Some ten years earlier Bismarck had noted that, 'great crises are the very weather which stimulates Prussian growth, if we turn them to our account fearlessly and maybe, very recklessly'. He was now to put his views into spectacular effect.

Nearly all of Bismarck's biographers admit that his handling of the Schleswig-Holstein question was one of the most

[1] See p. 351.

brilliant feats of his career. From the start he was determined to get both the Duchies for Prussia. In order to do so he had to browbeat Britain and the European powers, defeat the Danes, eliminate Augustenburg claims and bluff the King who at first opposed annexation and supported the Augustenburg candidature. Bismarck had to defy the Lower House of the Prussian *Landtag,* the Diet of the Confederation and German liberal opinion. He had to harness the support of Austria to suit his own plans, deceive his friends, compromise with his enemies and employ every argument and counter-argument to fit his purpose. Throughout, he was almost completely isolated, playing off each element against the other in a series of carefully calculated and daring moves.

Bismarck was fortunate that the foreign situation allowed him room to manoeuvre. The Crimean war had destroyed the Holy Alliance; the unification of Italy and the Polish revolt had broken the Anglo-French and Franco-Russian *ententes.* All the great powers eyed each other with suspicion. Bismarck was able to pacify Napoleon with vague hints about the Rhineland and promises of a plebiscite in Schleswig. He could rely on Russia to remain aloof, and could even taunt the British government about the feebleness of its protests. His real problems lay at home where it was essential to by-pass the Diet and harness national feeling in the Prussian cause. By the end of December the troops of the Confederation had occupied Holstein and installed Frederick at Kiel. In order to dislodge them Bismarck needed the King's approval and Austrian support. He persuaded William that Augustenburg was too favourable to Austria and thus a threat to Prussia, and simultaneously pressed the need for an Austrian alliance. It is hardly surprising that the King's mind was often in a state of confusion!

In January 1864 Bismarck persuaded Austria to join in action to uphold the 1852 treaty, invade Schleswig and 'settle the Duchies by mutual agreement'. Rechberg, the Austrian Foreign Minister, saw in Bismarck a conservative statesman anxious to uphold treaties and crush revolutions. Afraid of allowing Prussia to take the lead, he agreed to join in an action that was to damage Austrian prestige and undermine her influence among German liberals and throughout the southern states. The Austro-Prussian action led to bitter protests from liberals and progressives. When the Prussian Lower House refused to vote funds for the war, Bismark prorogued the *Landtag* for a year and continued his policy undisturbed. In the Diet, however, the attacks continued, and here it was the Austrians who inevitably bore the brunt of the criticism for having attached themselves to Bismarck's reactionary plans.

By April the Austrian and Prussian armies had brushed aside confederate troops in Holstein and occupied Schleswig. But it was soon clear that Bismarck had no intention of implementing the 1852 treaty at all. When a conference of the signatory powers was held in London in May he sent a petition signed by 20,000 demanding the separation of the Duchies from Denmark and in a joint Austro-Prussian declaration suddenly upheld the Augustenburg claims. As a result German opinion swung to Bismarck's support. William, already gratified by the performance of his troops, felt renewed confidence, and Prussian liberals began for the first time to detect the advantages of Bismarck's tortuous diplomacy. Needless to say the Danes refused to accept the Prussian demands and, relying on British support, rejected Anglo-French proposals for plebiscites or possible partition. As a result the war was renewed. France and Russia remained aloof. The British government, divided on the issues, lacking a continental ally and unprepared for war, refused to intervene. By August the Danes had been defeated and had handed over the Duchies to Austria and Prussia.

Bismarck had now to consolidate Prussian claims and expel Austria, Augustenburg and confederate forces from the Duchies. He first tried to get his way by peaceful means. At a meeting at Schönbrunn, Francis Joseph offered the Duchies to William in return for guarantees in Venetia and for aid to recover Lombardy. But William replied somewhat naïvely that he had 'no right to them', while Bismarck refused to be tied down to any commitments. Both, however, agreed to reject Augustenburg as too liberal and to undertake a joint administration of the area. Bismarck evaded Austrian requests to enter the *Zollverein*, showing quite clearly that he was not prepared to accept the presence of any rival power in north Germany. He subsequently expelled confederate forces from the Duchies without consulting his ally, and proceeded to harass the Austrian administration with a spate of abusive and bad tempered demands.

During the winter of 1864–5 Bismarck worked on the King and with the aid of crown lawyers persuaded him that since the Duchies had been surrendered by Denmark he was entitled to them after all. At the same time he frightened Augustenburg by threatening to demand money to pay for the war and by producing an alternative claimant distantly related to the Tsar. As a result Frederick was persuaded to hand over all effective power to Prussia. Any protests were used to discredit him in the eyes of the King. Meanwhile Bismarck had occupied Kiel and turned it into a naval base. Austrian and popular protests were treated with contempt and exploited as signs of deliberate provocation.

As Rechberg had clearly lost the initiative he was replaced by Mensdorff and Biegeleben who were determined to support Augustenburg and restore Habsburg leadership.[1] This, however, played into Bismarck's hands. He could now demonstrate to the King the obvious danger of Austrian hostility and predict war to be only a 'matter of time'. He opened secret negotiations with Italy; to frighten the Austrian government he sent the despatches through the Vienna post-office. Outwitted and outmanoeuvred Mensdorff was forced to play for time. In August 1865 he proposed discussions and at Gastein Austria and Prussia agreed to partition the Duchies 'provisionally'. Prussia acquired Schleswig and Kiel, while Austria took Holstein – where she found herself almost entirely surrounded by Prussian territory. The Gastein convention roused another storm of protest among the German liberals and led to bitter comment in much of Europe. Bismarck had progressively destroyed every treaty and inverted every argument in pursuit of his objective. Now that he had one of the Duchies it would clearly only be a matter of time before he took the other. By now, indeed, he had already fixed his eyes on a 'higher goal'.

At what moment Bismarck decided to extend the scope of his plans into a full-scale attack on the Austrian position it is difficult to decide. Certainly by 1865 he had thought of the possibilities of such a development and his deliberate provocation of Austria after the end of the Danish war would

[1] See p. 433.

suggest a policy designed to humiliate the Habsburgs and to hasten their withdrawal. But Bismarck was always ready to achieve his ends by peaceful means, and the Gastein convention, which gave him half his objective, was of obvious advantage to Prussia. It was his readiness to go to the very brink and even to use war that distinguished him from many other statesmen. Though he often got his way by calculated risks, he was prepared to accept war as the inevitable climax of a long diplomatic campaign and even welcomed it once he knew that it could not be avoided.

After Gastein, Bismarck deliberately set out to isolate Austria, harness support and provoke retaliation. As he remarked, 'it was vital to assume the role of an injured party'. He met Louis Napoleon at Biarritz and reassured himself that the Emperor's evasive neutrality would be maintained in case of any Austro-Prussian conflict. Napoleon was clearly preoccupied with Italy and Mexico and could only keep half an eye on the Rhine.[1] Bismarck simultaneously continued a violent attack on Austrian policy and the Holstein administration. In 1866 he persuaded a crown council that war was inevitable and reopened negotiations with Italy. After some time the Italians agreed to an alliance. Italy would open a second front against Austria if Prussia declared war within three months. William signed the alliance with reluctance as it broke the constitution of the Confederation. By now Bismarck was clearly out to destroy it anyway. North Germany, he wrote, was to be reorganized on lines similar to the 'National Constitution of 1849'!

In April, Bismarck published plans for a German parliament based on universal suffrage. This move, designed to rally support and divide the opposition, failed completely as by now no one believed his proposals to be genuine. Treitschke denounced his 'adventurous policy' while liberals deplored his lack of any moral sense. As rumours of war spread so opposition to the conflict mounted. Even here Bismarck exploited the situation agreeing to a peace mission while simultaneously anticipating its failure. This time events came to his rescue. The Italians continued to arm, the Austrians refused to demobilize and Bismarck could brand them as the aggressor. When Napoleon advocated a con-

[1] See pp. 396–7.

ference the Austrians laid down conditions that assured their rejection elsewhere. As in 1859 they had been driven by a ruthless assailant to breaking point. On June 1st they submitted the Schleswig-Holstein question to the Diet. This was a breach of earlier Austro-Prussian agreements and Bismarck ordered Prussian troops to occupy Holstein. When a tactful commander allowed the Austrian troops to withdraw peacefully Bismarck was furious. But on June 11th Austria demanded the mobilization of the German Confederation against Prussia. This persuaded William of Austria's hostility and after an ultimatum to the German states Prussian troops invaded Saxony, Hanover and Hesse on June 16th.

The Austro-Prussian war was over with startling rapidity. The reforms of Roon and Moltke had developed the Prussian army to a new peak of efficiency. With Krupp's steel cannon, new needle guns, an efficient general staff and a well trained officer corps the army had a greater speed of mobilization and manoeuvre and a greater striking power. Resistance in the German states soon crumbled. The Austrians were decisively defeated on July 3rd at Sadowa, or Königgrätz, when the Crown-Prince brought up his reserves just in time to roll up the Austrian flank.

For Bismarck a rapid peace now appeared vital. Prussia was supreme in the North and could only benefit by placating Austria and offering a generous settlement. Russia was already protesting at the disruption of the Confederation and the deposition of legitimate dynasties in the North. Napoleon, taken aback by the suddenness of the Prussian victory, was offering to mediate, a move which Bismarck hastened to accept. William and his generals, however, now expected to gain the fruits of victory and punish Austria for her aggression. Once again Bismarck had to use threats, tears and broken crockery to win his point. He was even forced to rely on the assistance of the Crown-Prince. By July 26th the peace preliminaries had been signed at Nickolsburg. Austria was excluded from Germany, and Schleswig-Holstein and the states north of the Main were annexed by Prussia to form a North German Confederation. The southern states, however, retained an independent and separate existence. This satisfied both Napoleon and Bismarck who considered them alien to the true Prussian tradition. Elsewhere, however, Napoleon was disappointed. While negotiations had proceeded, his demands for compensation had been evaded. Once peace had been signed Bismarck could reject French requests with equanimity.

The battle of Sadowa determined the course of German history for almost a century. Austria was excluded; the influence of the Rhineland and of the South declined. Prussia became the model state and imposed herself upon the imagination and the mind. Her bureaucracy, army and economy were to captivate the German people and gradually undermine their liberal and individual traditions. Blood and iron was to harden the spirit and subjugate the soul.

6. *The Unification of Germany*

The defeat of Austria enormously increased Bismarck's prestige. The ambition of liberals, nationalists and millions of Germans had been realized, and few were prepared to scrutinize the reasons. As a result parties and social groups split up and reformed in opposition or in support of the new Prussian framework. The aristocracy divided between the old Junkers like the Gerlachs, who bitterly attacked Bismarck's apparent betrayal of their exclusive interests, and the 'free conservatives', who represented those in the North and West anxious to consolidate political and economic power within a unified state. Meanwhile, moderates and national liberals abandoned their opposition, hailed the triumph of Prussian diplomacy and agreed to work with Bismarck in formulating a new constitutional settlement. Only a minority of progressives remained outraged by the calculated duplicity and ruthlessness of his policy and refused to compromise with what they felt would be a disastrous development in German history. The mass of workers and artisans were also divided. While the northern socialists hailed the strengthening of the state as a guarantee of future security, a new Social Democratic party, founded in the South in 1869, deplored the triumph of Prussian militarism and warned against the dangers of future enslavement.

Assured of widespread support Bismarck proceeded to consolidate his gains and strengthen his position. While previously he had been forced to rely entirely upon the King he was now in a position to bring the national liberals, together with his conservative and popular supporters, into play. Elections held on July 3rd had cut the liberal majority in the *Landtag* and greatly increased right-wing representation. Before the outbreak of war Bismarck had already made his peace with the moderates and added von der Heydt to the ministry in order to assure the necessary estimates. In return he had agreed to introduce an indemnity bill in the Lower House after the war to gain retrospective approval for his unconstitutional expenditure since 1862. This was now passed by 230 votes to 75. It has been variously interpreted as a triumph for Bismarck and for the national liberals. They reasserted the principle of budgetary control; he was exonerated for his previous defiance. The liberals won in principle, but Bismarck triumphed in practice. He held the whip hand, and William was quite prepared to follow the same unconstitutional procedure again if necessary. While the national liberals appeared ready to condone Bismarck's violent actions, he merely added another dimension to his diplomacy and soon began to exploit them for his own ends.

Similar considerations determined the constitution of the North German Confederation. Schleswig-Holstein, Hanover and northern Hesse were annexed and opposition dismissed as a 'legitimacy swindle'! The remaining states north of the Main were to be united into a federal union with a *Reichstag* elected by universal suffrage to pass laws, and a *Bundesrat* of state representatives to act as an executive council. Here Prussia was to have a controlling voice and apply the directives of her government to the whole union. But the national liberals protested and demanded constitutional guarantees, a responsible ministry, a budget, secret ballots and regular sessions. Bismarck agreed to compromise. He accepted one responsible minister, a *Bundeskanzler*, who was to place government proposals before the Lower House. Budgets could be voted regularly on condition that the army estimates were accepted for four years. Secret ballot, universal suffrage and regular sessions were also agreed.

Thus the liberals appeared to have triumphed. But here again their victory was incomplete. In practice the initiative continued to lie with the King and his ministers. Bismarck became *Bundeskanzler* and continued to direct policy. The King as Commander-in-Chief had even greater control over the army. While Bismarck could play on parliament, it had no effective power to restrain him. He only gave way in order to outwit them at their own game. His ability to be almost all things to all men and say anything to anyone with apparent conviction was one of the outstanding features of his disarming genius.

Bismarck rapidly set about co-ordinating the North. Here again he found the national liberals useful and employed them to undermine regional loyalties. Bennigsen, a Hanoverian, became a leading supporter, while earlier critics such as Twesten, Forckenbeck and Lasker came over to his side. Delbrück was appointed to regulate the economy and rapidly introduced common factory laws, currencies, weights and measures. New civil and criminal codes were drafted to harmonize legal procedure. Moltke reorganized the army to absorb the new drafts from the northern provinces. The Prussian civil service, in spite of Bismarck's scorn, worked with patience and skill to achieve his purpose. It was one of the less attractive features of his character that he seldom showed any gratitude.

It was almost inevitable that the ultimate unification of Germany should have become a dominant theme after 1866. The national liberals had demanded a genuine constitution in the hope of attracting their supporters in the South and Bismarck may also have had this in mind as a useful weapon with which to undermine reluctant princes. As usual his comments were ambiguous and reflected his listeners' views rather than his own opinions. In practice, however, Bismarck did assure his leadership in two vital fields. In August 1866, while the French were pressing for a return to the 1814 frontier, he forced the southern states to sign secret defensive alliances which placed their troops at Prussia's disposal in case of war. When the *Zollverein* treaties were renewed in the same year he established a *Zollverein* parliament, elected by universal suffrage, which included all the German states. Though it only dealt with customs matters, it was an important gesture possibly designed to anticipate future developments.

Nevertheless, Bismarck's plans during the next few years appear to reveal a considerable degree of doubt and uncertainty. The southern states remained divided and partially hostile. Baden and Hesse favoured union but Bavaria and Würtemberg opposed Prussianization and Bismarck refused merely 'to skim the milk'. As Bavarian opposition increased, however, it obviously became desirable to hasten on a final solution. Here Bismarck had to take France into account. He had evaded all Louis Napoleon's requests for German compensation and refused to comment on a draft treaty presented at the end of August 1866 which proposed French gains in Belgium and Luxembourg in return for union with the South.[1] To Bismarck, however, it was clear that French opinion regarded Sadowa as a bitter blow and that the Emperor could not allow the unification of Germany without acquiring some visible benefits for France. But of course he could never be certain and therefore embarked on a policy designed both to harness national support and probe French reactions.

In 1867, Luxembourg provided the first test. Like Schleswig-Holstein it was in an ambiguous position, a member of the old German Confederation with a Prussian garrison and a Dutch king. Napoleon was anxious to purchase it from the King of Holland, who found it something of an embarassment, and Bismarck appeared at first sight vaguely sympathetic to the French proposals. He was, as usual, prepared to work for either a compromise or a conflict and urged Benedetti, the French ambassador, to act swiftly and present Europe and the King of Prussia with a *fait accompli*. Napoleon, however, delayed and the King of Holland refused to act without Prussian agreement. Bismarck, who had refused to commit himself, was thus forced into the open, especially as rumours of the deal began to circulate and inflame public opinion. In March he published the military alliances with the southern states, and on April 1st arranged for Bennigsen to question him in the *Reichstag* about the negotiations. Though he gave a cautious reply the general outcry in Germany brought an end to further discussion. Luxembourg was neutralized at a conference in London and its Prussian garrison withdrawn. But this did not pacify Louis Napoleon or French opinion; both felt disappointed and somewhat insulted by the entire episode.

After the Luxembourg crisis, conflict with France was generally reckoned to be inevitable. Bismarck seized the occa-

[1] See p. 404.

sion to renew the south German treaties and rouse national
opinion. But this did not necessarily mean that he deliberately worked for war. No doubt he hoped to follow a number
of alternative policies and his statements reveal a similar pattern of ambivalent and contradictory views. Nevertheless, he
was clearly prepared to test French reactions once more and
to provoke another trial of strength. Though he might have
hoped to further Prussian prestige and consolidate her hold
in Germany by peaceful means he was quite ready to go to
war in the end. In the circumstances it is hard to deny that
his actions were deliberately provocative.

In 1868 the Queen of Spain, Isabella II, was expelled by a
military revolt. The search for a suitable monarch led the
Spanish government to Prince Leopold, the son of Prince
Karl Anton[1] von Hohenzollern-Sigmaringen, a junior branch
of the Prussian royal house. In 1869 Napoleon made it clear
that the choice of Leopold would be an affront to France herself. William was also opposed to the candidature. But Bismarck, while playing down the whole affair and maintaining
that acceptance was anyway unlikely, sent secret agents to
Spain with the apparent object of encouraging the Spanish
to repeat their offer. In March 1870 he pressed the King and
the Prince to agree. The 'liberal Empire'[2] in France
appeared less belligerent, and a Hohenzollern on the Spanish
throne would enhance Prussian prestige and strengthen her
position in case of a future war. There is nothing to prove
that Bismarck regarded the candidature as a likely occasion
for the war itself.

In June 1870 Prince Leopold was at last persuaded to
accept and William reluctantly agreed. Bismarck planned to
present France with a *fait accompli,* but the news leaked out
in Spain due to an error in the decoding of an official telegram. France immediately exploded in rage and Napoleon
was forced to take action to save his throne. Benedetti was
sent to William, now at Ems, to urge him to withdraw the
candidature. The King, alarmed by the uproar, refused any
public renunciation, but persuaded Leopold's father to withdraw in the name of his son, who had meanwhile vanished
into the Alps. The crisis appeared over. Bismarck who returned to Berlin too late to affect the situation was deep in

[1] See p. 357.   [2] See p. 403.

gloom and almost ready to resign. But the French overplayed their hand. Urged on by the Empress and by Gramont,[1] Louis Napoleon agreed to send Benedetti to Ems to ask for guarantees that the candidature would never be renewed. These William refused to give and, having firmly but politely rejected the ambassador's request, sent Bismarck a telegram with details of the discussion. Bismarck, who was dining with Moltke and Roon, re-edited the telegram to emphasize French demands and the King's refusal. Once assured that the army was ready, he published the telegram in all the foreign papers. Swept away by the public outcry Napoleon was driven to war amid the cheers of the French Chamber and the applause of the press.

Bismarck was quick to underline French aggression and used it to consolidate his hold on the southern states. He published Napoleon's 1866 draft treaty in the London *Times* thereby assuring British neutrality, and could feel confident that none of the other great powers would intervene. Mobilization plans were already complete and by the end of July three armies had been transported over the new railway network to the Rhine. In August they swept in a broad arc across eastern France, isolated a French army at Metz and forced a second with Napoleon himself to capitulate at Sedan. By September the Prussians were able to begin the siege of Paris. When Strasbourg and Metz capitulated, Moltke brought up reinforcements to contain any French counter-attacks. In a war of frequent confusion and general incompetence, Prussian discipline, her superior artillery and Moltke's planning turned the scales.

Meanwhile Bismarck exploited the occasion of war to complete the unification of Germany. The conflict had roused widespread enthusiasm in the North and the South; national liberals, parliamentarians and popular opinion united in favour of a new Reich. But Bismarck remained determined to frustrate any alternative initiative and to decide the issue himself. The princes were now to make the Empire; the people would follow their example. Government delegations were called to Versailles and after some months of bargaining the southern states were persuaded to join the North. Ludwig of Bavaria was bribed to offer the imperial crown to the King

[1] See p. 407.

of Prussia. On January 18th, 1871, in the great hall of mirrors at Versailles, William was proclaimed German Emperor among the princes and generals who had created the new Empire.

The Reichstag accepted Bismarck's negotiations and sent a delegation to add its own plea to the national cause. It was led by the man who had headed the delegation from Frankfurt that offered the crown to Frederick William in 1849. This time, in spite of deep misgiving, the King was forced to accept. Bismarck had so contrived to manipulate events that there could be no escape. He had tied down kings, princes, parliaments and peoples almost in spite of themselves. In the end Germany had surrendered to Prussia though not without some signs of protest. When Prussian policies led to destruction much of Germany was to be destroyed with it.

A peace treaty was eventually signed at Frankfurt in May 1871. France lost Alsace and Lorraine and paid an indemnity of five milliard francs. Though Bismarck had his doubts about taking French territory the generals insisted and, convinced that a war of revenge was inevitable, he agreed that Germany would need the provinces as a buffer for her future defence. Believing in war he could not calculate without it and thus made its eventual outbreak all the more probable. The means that Bismarck had used to forge his Empire were in the end to lead to its destruction.

XV · LOUIS NAPOLEON AND THE SECOND EMPIRE

1. *The Second Empire*

LOUIS NAPOLEON remains one of the most enigmatic characters of the nineteenth century. His background, beliefs, political programme and private life reveal a series of contradictions that appear to defy rational analysis. He has been described at various times as a sleep-walker, an adventurer, a benevolent autocrat and a sphinx. In 1848 his election manifestoes promised the protection of property and religion, freedom of worship, free enterprise and a free press, as well as social reform, old-age relief and industrial progress. Every interest was to be fused under one Napoleonic image. Church and state, freedom and order, liberalism and nationalism were to be combined in a name that stood for all that was great and glorious in the history of France.

Louis Napoleon deliberately modelled himself upon the legends propagated by his uncle on St. Helena. For twenty years he had absorbed a Napoleonic myth, incorporated it into his writings and extended its implications to cover the social and economic problems of the age. Nevertheless, doubts remained. In the first place the ideals outlined by Napoleon I differed widely from the Emperor's actual behaviour. Secondly, Louis Napoleon, though able to express himself clearly on paper, had up till 1848 displayed none of his uncle's genius in practice and had merely engineered a series of desperate fiascos.[1] He adopted a role which, though acted with conviction and courage, often appeared to retain an element of artificiality. Finally, the objectives outlined in his Napoleonic elixir were in practice contradictory and sometimes even incompatible. Theories of revolutionary empires and authoritarian republics could only be realized in a romantic mind. In an era of practical politicians, Louis Napoleon was a visionary, a lover, a political outsider. While he pondered how to resolve the contradictions created by his

[1] See Ch. X. 5.

381

conflicting ideals others, often more ruthless than himself, were able to step in and exploit him to their own advantage.

Nevertheless, while Louis Napoleon was working for defined and limited objectives, such as the restoration of a Napoleonic Empire,[1] his policies were consistent and his manoeuvres skilful and generally realistic. He could display the same ruthlessness and duplicity in exploiting a political situation as Bismarck or Cavour. He appeared detached, watching events and waiting for opportune moments to strike. Political parties were left to devour each other while Napoleon gradually consolidated his position. In the Chamber the right-wing majority was encouraged to curb the left by making trade unions and strikes illegal, restricting the press and accepting the *Loi Falloux,* which set up free Catholic schools. By October 1849 the right-wing ministry had become so unpopular that Napoleon felt strong enough to dismiss it and replace its members by some of his own supporters.

In 1850 the pattern was repeated. When the extreme left won a few seats in the supplementary elections, the conservative majority panicked and passed a Franchise Law that deprived some three million vagrants of the vote. This was followed by a Press Law designed to extend stamp duties and enforce the registration of all publications. The increasing unpopularity of the Chamber gave Louis Napoleon an opportunity to appeal above parties. On provincial tours he claimed to speak for the nation and proclaimed himself a champion of order, prosperity and popular sovereignty. He criticized the actions of the politicians, and rallied the army by revues, inspections and increases in pay. The rivalry between Bourbon and the Orléanist factions was not healed by the death of Louis-Philippe, and the President was able to exploit the divisions on the right while using them to smother his opponents on the left. In January 1851 he dismissed Changarnier, the unreliable commander of the Paris garrison and National Guard, and replaced him by his own men.

By now it was clear to most observers that Louis Napoleon was moving towards a restoration of the Empire. The only question was the method by which it was to be achieved. As

[1] See Ch. X. 5.

the alloted four years of his presidency drew to an end the problem took on a new urgency. The constitution could only be revised by a three-quarter majority in the Chamber. In spite of extensive tours, speeches and a flood of carefully engineered petitions, a proposal to allow the President a second term did not gain the necessary votes. Confident of support from the army, the police and the rural areas, Louis Napoleon carefully and deliberately prepared for a *coup d'état*. As a gesture to the left he proposed the repeal of the 1850 Franchise Law. When this was rejected by the Chamber its unpopularity was only increased. In October, cabinet changes brought a further influx of reliable supporters to prepare for action. Saint-Arnaud, a veteran from Algeria, was placed in command of the Paris regiments and promoted Minister of War. Maupas was put in charge of the Police and Louis Napoleon's half-brother, the Comte de Morny, was appointed Minister of the Interior.

The *coup d'état* was planned for December 2nd, the anniversary of Austerlitz. In a well organized police operation leading opponents – Thiers, Changarnier and Cavaignac – were arrested and troops placed at key points in the capital. The Chamber of Deputies was occupied, all press offices seized and Paris covered with proclamations appealing to all Frenchmen to rally to the new order – 'a France regenerated by the Revolution, a France reorganized by the Emperor'. The response in Paris, however, was generally lukewarm, while in republican districts it was openly hostile. Though the divided and demoralized deputies were unable to put up any effective resistance, barricades were constructed on December 4th by radical elements. Since the defeat of the 1849 revolt, left-wing republicans had prepared to resist a coup by building a network of workers' clubs and democratic cells in Paris, the Rhône and the older industrial areas. In the capital, however, they remained a small minority and were soon eliminated by Saint-Arnaud's Algerian methods. Sporadic risings in the South were also defeated. Once again workers and socialists on the extreme left refused to follow a moderate lead, while the bourgeoisie remained generally indifferent and only became alarmed when some indiscriminate shooting killed fifty spectators in the middle-class districts.

Louis Napoleon's coup, far from creating any spontaneous

enthusiasm, had been baptized in blood. It was followed by an extensive and ruthless purge of 'republicans and socialists' all over the country. Of some 27,000 arrested, over 9,000 were transported to Algeria; the majority were smallholders, craftsmen and artisans – all leaders of the moderate, lower bourgeois opposition. Nevertheless, in the plebiscite held on December 21st to sound popular reaction to the new régime, 7.5 millions voted in favour and only 600,000 against. But in Paris less than half registered support; the majority were hostile or failed to vote altogether. The bloodshed and the widespread repression that ensued were never forgotten or forgiven, especially in the capital. Louis Napoleon had not begun by reconciling the conflicting elements in French society, but by reopening past sores and creating renewed bitterness.

The new régime was thus bound to take on an authoritarian character. The popular myth had been undermined, and Louis Napoleon had first to restore order and consolidate his power. For three months, before a new constitution could become effective, he ruled by decree. The French estates of the Orléans family were confiscated and the proceeds spent on social relief and welfare. The National Guard was abolished. A new Press Law combined all the restrictions of previous legislation and allowed the suspension of any journal after three warnings. Louis Napoleon was not to tolerate possible rivalry or criticism. This was made clear by a constitution that gave the Prince-President supreme executive power for ten years. Besides command of the armed forces, war and peace and the usual ministerial appointments, he alone could initiate laws, summon the Legislature, nominate the Senate and command an oath from all officers and magistrates. He could even recommend a successor, though ratification would still depend upon the French people. Once again France was to be dependant upon the will of one man. The powers and prerogatives of empire had already been restored.

Government and administration depended upon the effectiveness of the bureaucracy. Some 250,000 civil servants became the executive agents of the State. Their role was rapidly clarified and their status assured. Prefects were given extensive powers, higher salaries and direct control over the police. Their functions were to implement instructions from the

Ministry of the Interior covering crime, press control, election propaganda and economic regulation. Below them mayors controlled the communes; the *gendarmerie* was trebled to maintain order and control crime.

Louis Napoleon, like his uncle, recognized the social significance of the Church. The electoral influence of *curés* remained of considerable importance in ensuring an overwhelming Bonapartist majority in plebiscites and elections. Louis had already accepted the *Loi Falloux* and sent assistance to the Pope. Closer co-operation, however, foundered over the Organic Articles. Pius demanded abrogation, but Louis could not afford to relax his hold. As a result he had to meet constant and powerful opposition from liberal Catholics led by Montalembert, and could only maintain an uneasy alliance with the Papacy. The ambiguity of his religious policy was to become a centre of friction and a dangerous weakness to the régime. It was the inevitable outcome of his contradictory principles, and characteristic of the ambivalent policies created by his rule.

Popular representation was to be assured by two legislative chambers. But their powers were severely restricted and ultimate authority was vested in the President. He nominated members of the Senate, whose role was to watch the constitution and amend it on request. The Chamber of Deputies was to be elected by universal suffrage, but could meet for only three months in the year, discuss bills set before it, and was not to be reported in the press. In addition, elections were to be 'guided' by prefects, who were to publish official lists of candidates and restrict the activities of the opposition. It came as no surprise that in the 1852 elections all but nine of the two-hundred and sixty-one seats were won by government supporters.

Yet the régime did have a powerful basis of popular backing. Universal suffrage was retained. The Code Napoléon assured civil rights and equality before the law. The peasant majority, even though guided, gave Louis Napoleon massive support. The bourgeoisie was assured of their property and prosperity, and relieved of any fears of 'red' revolutions or left-wing coups. While monarchists on the right and republicans and socialists on the left remained divided, there was little likelihood of any effective alternative government.

In the summer of 1852 Louis Napoleon set out to test opinion on a long provincial tour. Carefully arranged demonstrations and cries of 'Vive l'Empereur' soon persuaded him to take the final step and restore the Empire. At Bordeaux he proclaimed that the Empire would mean peace, and would bring consolidation at home, renewed prosperity, and economic reconstruction. In November, the Senate passed the necessary decree. In the plebiscite a month later nearly 8 millions voted 'Yes' as against 25,000 'No' with 2 million abstentions. On December 1st the Empire was proclaimed and Louis assumed the title Napoleon III to underline the continuity of the Bonaparte dynasty.

Nevertheless, a degree of uncertainty remained. How was Napoleon to unite the myth and the reality? How were conflicting interests and contradictory factors to be resolved? The creation of an Empire helped to obscure rather than clarify these dilemmas. Fundamental social and political problems could be gilded by a veneer of pomp and pageantry. Any decisions became dependant upon the wishes of one man. While the Empire brought years of stability and increasing wealth France was prepared to sacrifice her political freedom for the sake of material benefits. But these in turn soon created new problems which only magnified the basic contradictions in the régime. The policies of the Empire seemed all too often to defeat the very purposes for which they were intended; Napoleon's eventual failure was in part due to his inability to measure up to the implications of his own ideals.

2. Economic and Social Development

The first decade of the Second Empire were years of increasing expansion and economic growth. It was Louis Napoleon's deliberate intention to promote prosperity by government intervention and guidance. He thereby deviated from the more general laissez-faire approach of nineteenth-century constitutional governments and returned to policies of a benevolent paternalism. In his speech to the Bordeaux Chamber of Commerce in October 1852 he had declared that the Empire meant peace and had elaborated the many benefits this could bring: 'We have immense uncultivated regions to improve, roads to construct, harbours to dredge, rivers to render navigable, a railway and canal network to complete.'

By 1852 Louis Napoleon had already taken steps to create the machinery to realize his plans.

Easier credit was assured by low interest rates. In 1852 the Bank of France was persuaded to cut the bank rate to 3 per cent, thus encouraging investment and stimulating demand. More important, two credit companies were founded to channel funds into new development and make France increasingly prosperous through public works. The Crédit Mobilier, backed by the Péreire brothers and the Minister of Finance, Fould, was to raise credit for railways, gas works, shipping lines and industrial developments. Though its shares were high and limited to the wealthy, it became the model for less ambitious investment companies throughout France and western Europe. It played a vital role in economic expansion until the disastrous slump at the end of the reign. The Crédit Foncier was set up in the same year to encourage investment in land and offer easy mortgages. It was to stimulate agricultural development and assist in the reconstruction of many French cities, notably Paris.

Communications were essential instruments of expansion. Secondary roads were built to open up outlying villages. The canal system was rationalized and a Saar canal dug to help link up the industrial regions of eastern France. One of the most significant developments of the Empire was the completion of a railway network which connected Paris to all the outlying provinces. A multitude of small companies were amalgamated into six regional networks radiating from the capital to Lille and the northern industrial belt, Brest and Cherbourg, the Loire valley, Bordeaux, Marseilles and Strasbourg. Once again the government stimulated action by granting ninety-nine-year concessions, and encouraging reorganization. When a recession threatened construction in 1857 a new Railway Law, passed the following year, stabilized interest rates under state guarantee and laid down plans for new cross-country lines. Recovery was swift and railway shares soon became a favourite security for the small investor. By 1870 over 17,000 kilometres of line had been built, all but 3,000 during the Second Empire.

The railways were only part of a general plan to expand trade and open up new economic horizons. Dockyards and harbours were developed to launch French mercantile interests into neighbouring continents. Marseilles became the outlet for Mediterranean, eastern and north African enterprise. Cherbourg, Brest, Bordeaux and Le Havre were the terminals for new Atlantic and Far Eastern shipping companies. Passengers and freight moved with greater speed and in greater numbers. Goods and raw materials could be transported in bulk from Strasbourg to Brest, Lille to Marseilles and out into the wider world. In 1857 plans were even prepared for a Channel tunnel. Though these came to nothing, the construction of the Suez Canal was to be a notable monument to the enterprise of the Empire. Discussed by Napoleon I, debated by St. Simonians and Mehemet Ali, it was eventually constructed under the direction of Ferdinand de Lesseps between 1859 and 1869, in spite of opposition from Great Britain, the merchants of Alexandria and the Sultan of the Ottoman Empire. Its opening, in the presence of the Empress Eugénie, in 1869, was perhaps the last notable occasion of the régime.

Communications and easy credit, rising prices and growing demand created a boom in industry and a gradual expansion in agriculture.[1] Coal output doubled in a decade after 1850. New mines were opened in the North. Iron and steel production rose, notably in Lorraine. Coke smelting eventually overtook charcoal in 1853, and accounted for 90 per cent of pig iron output by 1870. Puddling techniques spread rapidly in the 1850s, while the Bessemer and Siemens processes for steel were introduced in the 1860s. By 1860 the French cotton industry had become the largest in Europe with five to six million spindles and nearly 400,000 operatives. The use of steam engines increased threefold between 1850 and 1860, and new machinery was introduced to develop the printing and finishing processes. Similar developments stimulated growth in the woollen and linen industry, though silk output was slow to expand due to disease among French silk worms and a shortage of alternative sources of raw materials.

The government also tried to stimulate agriculture by setting up institutes and model farms, and by initiating schemes for drainage and land reclamation. Courses in chemistry encouraged the spread of fertilization, while roads, canals and branch lines opened up prospects of wider markets

[1] See Appendix 4.

for agricultural produce. In ten years output and wealth increased by some 25 per cent. In 1871 over half the population
were still employed in agriculture. Throughout the Second
Empire it remained basic to the economy and an essential
prop to the imperial order.

This may explain why, in spite of official stimulus, the
economy expanded less rapidly than in Britain or Germany.
French agriculture remained essentially conservative, dominated by small proprietors. The birth rate was still the lowest
in Europe, limiting demand and hampering the mobility of
labour. In addition, resources of coal and iron were restricted.
In 1870 French coal imports reached five million tons – over
25 per cent of total consumption. This had an adverse effect
on shipping, which had reached a tonnage of only a million by
1869 – a sixth of the British displacement. French industry
still remained the preserve of the small man. Old established
iron firms continued to use charcoal, especially in the central
highlands. Linen and woollen manufacture was dominated
by workshops and domestic organization. Not until the end of
the period had specialization and the principles of combination begun to spread into these industries.

It was to overcome some of these deficiencies that Louis
Napoleon abandoned a traditional policy of protection, and
attempted to introduce the more competitive conditions of
free trade. He was influenced both by his experiences in England and by the example of the *Zollverein*. Wider markets
promoted growth, encouraged efficiency and helped to stir up
the complacent or the incompetent. Such a policy, though
welcomed by bankers, merchants and a few large industrialists, roused the bitter opposition of small manufacturers and
bourgeois artisans. The Emperor therefore decided to impose
his policies surreptitiously or in secret. Railway requirements led to a cut in the duty on imported rails in 1853. Cuts
were gradually introduced elsewhere, protests were ignored,
and opposition softened by a generous distribution of state
loans to encourage productive investment. In January 1860 a
secret treaty was signed by Cobden and Chevalier representing Britain and France. While the former agreed to cut
duties on silk and wine the latter undertook a progressive
tariff reduction to 25 per cent after five years. In spite of an
outcry from manufacturers and small industrialists, similar

treaties were signed with Italy and the *Zollverein* during the next few years, thereby exposing the French economy to the full rigours of foreign competition.

Trade and capital nevertheless continued to expand. Exports and imports more than doubled under the Empire, and France maintained throughout a favourable trade balance. French financial interests percolated through western Europe. Spanish gas works and railways, Austrian mines and steamship companies,[1] Piedmontese docks, and Swiss and Russian[2] railway lines were largely financed by French capital and promoted by French companies. The Paris Bourse rivalled the London Stock Exchange as the centre of European finance. In 1852 the opening of the new telegraph network enabled prices to be quoted in both capitals on the same day.

The Emperor set out to make Paris a fitting monument to his economic and imperial designs. Reconstruction was in the hands of Haussmann, prefect of the Seine department between 1853–69, but Louis Napoleon took a personal interest in the replanning of the city. Slum clearance involving some 20,000 dwellings improved health and curbed cholera. Wide avenues and geometric designs relieved congestion and hindered the building of barricades. The whole operation provided work, relieved unemployment and made Paris the cultural and economic capital of Europe. New parks, public buildings, museums, theatres and an opera house were spread out among fashionable shopping centres, markets and residential apartments. All were lit by new gas lighting and washed by new water-works. International exhibitions held in 1855 and 1867 illustrated the triumphs of the Empire and revealed France as second only to Britain in the industrial development of Europe.

But Paris also reflected the growing rifts in the social composition of the Second Empire. Its very size was bound to magnify any distinctions: eight new districts were absorbed outside the walls, and a population of a million in 1851 had nearly doubled by 1870. The wealthy lived in the spacious boulevards on the western side, enjoying the profits of the commercial boom and the culture of a sophisticated society. While the rising bourgeoisie struggled in the wake of the affluent, increasing numbers found themselves depressed by

[1] Also see p. 440.   [2] See p. 418.

economic change and imperial planning. Paris was still essentially the preserve of the lower bourgeois and artisan classes. In 1860 some 100,000 manufacturers employing 416,811 workers in small *ateliers* found their livelihood undermined by foreign competition, new combines and government contractors. Tradesmen and shop keepers were hit by big stores in the centre of the city. Slum clearance led to the transplanting of increasing numbers of artisans to the eastern districts and northern suburbs, which soon became areas of proletarian discontent. The Cité meanwhile became the administrative and official centre of the capital – increasingly isolated between rival areas of western affluence, eastern poverty and an intellectual left bank.

Parisian distinctions were reflected in other parts of France. By 1860 some 3 million manual workers were variously distributed among 1,450,000 workshops, the vast majority in small units. In the 1850s their wages, which rose some 18 per cent, failed to keep up with a general price rise of 44 per cent. Standards deteriorated. Living conditions were often depressed. Small textile manufacturers suffered. Traditional iron works and charcoal foundries collapsed. But though Lyons, Marseilles and the North had concentrations of labour, workers were too widely dispersed and regionally segregated to become politically effective. Moreover, many areas benefited from the new textile and mechanical boom. The iron and steel works at Le Creusot employed 10,000 men. The mechanization of the Alsace cotton industry brought new opportunities for skill and working class enterprise. Employees were more concerned with shorter working hours, higher wages and the elimination of piece work than with remote political arguments. The interests of a declining artisan class and of the new factory hand continued to conflict. While the former looked back to a *petit bourgeois* security, the latter struggled to make the most out of existing conditions.

Similar divisions continued to operate in the countryside. While middle-size holdings increased, small holders and *métayers* declined. Unable to support themselves they moved to the towns to find employment in new industries and public works. Rural society, however, remained stable and essentially traditional. In 1876, 67·6 per cent of the popula-

CC

tion could still be classed as rural, and this provided the un-changing element in French society. As before, the tempo of change was to be set by the towns, especially Paris with its concentrations of class and contrasts of wealth. The redistri-bution of the lower bourgeoisie between a rising level of affluence and a falling standard of living was to create re-newed unrest, undermine the Empire and threaten the very framework of France itself.

3. Foreign and Colonial Policies

During his first ten years as President and Emperor, Louis Napoleon was able to promote affluence at home and win prestige abroad. It was almost inevitable that the heir to a Napoleonic tradition should feel a need to take the initiative in foreign affairs. Memories of the First Empire, of his uncle, as well as the needs of the army and the demands of popular opinion required some expansive gestures. The problem was to determine the direction these were to take and the means that were to be used to implement them. Once again Louis Napoleon was a victim of his own background, his dreams, myths, fears and dominant ambition. From St. Helena, Napo-leon had proclaimed himself the champion of nationalism, liberty and peace, guardian of the Catholic Church and advocate of a European confederation. His nephew had somehow to reconcile these contradictions. In addition, his early adventures had given him a real sympathy for Italian nationalists, a repugnance for Austria and a genuine admira-tion for Great Britain. Any attempt to amend the 1815 treaties was bound, however, to bring him into conflict with British policy. Thus Louis Napoleon was faced by a number of conflicting interests and elusive aims. It is hardly sur-prising that he was to rely more on 'the force of circum-stances' than on any 'premeditated plans'. He was in general more successful when exploiting the openings of others and following events than in his own initiatives.

Louis Napoleon's opening probes revealed a restless desire for prestige, allies, territorial acquisition and peaceful change. He urged a congress to consider threats to European peace, joined Britain in backing the Ottoman Empire against Austrian and Russian demands,[1] and tried to mediate be-

[1] See p. 309.

tween Austria and Prussia with a view to possible gains on the Rhine.[1] Subsequently he joined Britain and Russia in recognizing Danish sovereignty over Schleswig-Holstein[2] and supported Prussia in opposing the inclusion of the whole Austrian Empire within the German Confederation.[3] While trying to win good will on every side, these actions nevertheless failed to bring any material advantages. Moreover, his one decisive initiative in sending troops to Rome in 1849 to forestall the Austrians should have been a clear warning of the dangers ahead. Vague notions of reconciling the Pope and the Republic proved quite impracticable and Louis Napoleon found himself shouldered with a Roman Question that was to weigh upon him for the rest of his life.[4]

The proclamation of the Empire did little to ease Napoleon's difficulties. His declaration that 'The Empire meant peace' only confused the issue. His power depended largely upon the army and his promise to observe the treaties of 1815 was something of an anomaly since the very existence of a Napoleonic Empire obviously contravened their whole purpose. Nevertheless, his assurances mollified Britain and her readiness to recognize the dynastic numeral 'III' meant that Austria and Prussia soon followed, in spite of Russian hostility. This, however, did not amount to fraternal acceptance by the established dynasties of Europe. The new Emperor's attempts to find a bride from among the older royal families failed. In 1853 he married a twenty-seven-year-old Spaniard, the Countess Eugénie de Montijo, with whom he had recently become infatuated. The birth of a Prince Imperial three years later secured the dynasty; but the marriage failed to reconcile the aristocracy at home, while the Empress's headstrong papal and imperial policies were to become an added liability in foreign affairs.

The Emperor's first excursions in diplomacy were, however, reasonably successful. The outbreak of the Crimean war afforded considerable scope for manoeuvre.[5] By urging the rights of the Latin monks he won Catholic approval. He worked with Britain to resist excessive Russian claims and paced the British fleet into the Black Sea, thus appearing both to hold an initiative and yet to follow a united front. At the same time he worked with Austria to outline peace

[1] See p. 350.   [2] See p. 351.   [3] See p. 351.   [4] See p. 364.   [5] See Ch. XII. 4.

proposals and deplored the military preparations of the Ottoman Empire. When ambivalence and misunderstanding
eventually led to war Napoleon signed a formal alliance with
Britain and agreed to an expeditionary force in the Black
Sea and subsequently in the Crimea. He was also able to conclude an alliance to neutralize Austria in December 1854 and
a few months later appear to encourage Sardinian participation in the war. The multiplicity of Napoleon's schemes was
never fully fathomed by his ministers. In 1855 Drouyn de
Lhuys, French Foreign Minister, resigned rather than an-
tagonize Austria and was replaced by Walewski, son of
Napoleon I by his Polish mistress. Policy, however, remained
entirely in the hands of the Emperor who continued to steer
with apparent confidence between the reefs.

The outcome of the war was a notable triumph for French
diplomacy. British demands were successfully modified,
Russia partially pacified and the great powers lavishly entertained at a congress held in Paris.[1] The Holy Alliance had
been effectively crippled while France had emerged as a
formidable power. Yet, though prestige had been enhanced,
the practical advantages gained had been negligible. For the
next ten years Napoleon was to attempt to remedy this de-
ficiency by independent initiatives. His actions, however,
generally rebounded with disastrous repercussions elsewhere
so that the more he tried to do the more his difficulties
appeared to multiply.

Napoleon's next moves were largely guided by his cloudy
belief in the significance of nationalities. In the Balkans he
followed up the Congress of Paris by demanding regional
autonomy for the Danubian provinces. A further conference
held in Paris in 1858 paved the way for new elections and the
ultimate unification of Rumania in 1861. At the same time
the intervention of the French fleet helped to achieve
Montenegrin independence. Such action, however, roused
the inevitable opposition of Austria and was viewed with increasing alarm in Britain, always anxious to preserve the
integrity of the Ottoman Empire. But while Russia, anxious
to detach France from Austria and Britain, remained indifferent, Napoleon was able to get his way and dabble in
foreign enterprise with little thought for the consequences.

[1] See Ch. XII. 6.

When Napoleon turned to Italy, however, the situation was far more complex.[1] Here national, papal and international interests were dangerously intertwined and support for any one party was likely to rouse bitter hostility from the others. It was therefore unfortunate that the commitment to Cavour should have been so ill-defined. Napoleon's vision of a northern Kingdom from the Alps to the Adriatic, a central state and a confederation under the Pope were outlined at Plombières, but the details were not incorporated into the final treaty of alliance and Cavour, having committed the Emperor to action, was left to exploit the results.

From the start Napoleon had reservations about his Italian policy. Walewski was hostile and the reaction of the great powers ambiguous. Once again he was able to rely on Russia to restrain Austria, but Prussia remained watchful on the Rhine and Britain, under a conservative administration, was opposed to any violent changes in the status quo. In the early months of 1859 Napoleon therefore adopted the role of peacemaker, encouraged negotiations and eventually forced Cavour to agree to disarmament proposals. Nevertheless when Austrian intransigence led to war he stood by his commitments, poured troops into northern Italy and defeated the Austrians at Magenta and Solferino. War, however, revealed that he was neither a tactician nor that he had any stomach for the fight. The revolutions in Italy, especially in the Papal States, the clamour of Catholics at home and the ambivalent attitude of Prussia and Russia all persuaded him to propose a rapid armistice at Villafranca. This enabled Napoleon to extricate himself from Italy and revue a victory parade in Paris, but left Italians bitterly disillusioned and the European powers increasingly hostile.

Subsequent developments only increased Napoleon's dilemmas. Left to themselves the north Italian states conspired their own unification and the Emperor, unwilling to intervene again, was prepared to accept the situation in return for Nice and Savoy. His readiness to sacrifice papal territory and his suggestion, first indicated in La Guéronnèire's famous pamphlet, Le Pape et le Congrès, that the temporal power was not necessarily advantageous to the Catholic Church, caused an outcry in France. This was only

[1] See Ch. XIII.

increased when the activities of Garibaldi in Sicily and Naples forced Napoleon to tolerate or even encourage a Piedmontese invasion of the Papal States and witness the creation of a united Italy on his doorstep. As a result Napoleon felt bound to maintain French troops in Rome, thereby incurring renewed Italian hostility. Meanwhile the acquisition of Nice and Savoy roused indignation in Britain and destroyed all the good will built up by the free trade treaty signed earlier in the year.[1] Palmerston and Russell refused to countenance any intervention in Italian affairs, left Garibaldi a free hand, and frustrated any French plans for mediation. The cordiality of the mid-fifties was never to be restored and Britain watched the flounderings of Napoleon with growing hostility or indifference.

By the mid 1860s Napoleon had contrived to alienate Russia, while his efforts to settle the Roman Question merely increased opposition from both French clericals and Italian nationalists. As before it was the conflicting impact of his actions that led to disaster. The outbreak of the Polish revolt in January 1863[2] created serious difficulties. Napoleon, anxious to retain the Russian *entente*, hoped to avoid action, but popular pressure and the demands of radical nationalists and Catholics at court forced him to make ineffective gestures. A combined French, Austrian and British note demanding an armistice and an autonomous Polish state was angrily rejected by the Tsar. When Palmerston refused to go to war and Austria remained firmly neutral Napoleon was reduced to advocating yet another congress. This, however, was denounced by all the great powers. France was again isolated and Russia turned towards Prussia as a country more likely to provide a reliable buffer between Poland and the West.

Attempts to resolve the Roman Question were to prove equally unsuccessful. First approaches to negotiate the withdrawal of French troops in 1862 were thwarted by opposition from the Empress and the Catholics. The Convention of September 1864, which eventually agreed to a settlement in 1866, provoked general misgiving and was to prove an irritating failure. Italian nationalists had long since lost any feelings of gratitude for France, while Pius IX regarded Napoleon as little short of a double-dyed traitor.

[1] See p. 389. [2] See p. 415.

Growing isolation and loss of face were all the more serious when combined with disastrous colonial ventures. As in other fields, the first decade of the Empire was a period of successful expansion. Freer trade encouraged economic development. Anglo-French co-operation led to the capture of Canton, an expedition to Pekin and the opening up of China to European commerce and Catholic missionaries. An ambitious forward policy in Senegal laid the foundations of a West African empire, while the construction of the Suez Canal and intervention in Montenegro and Syria seemed to assure French influence in the Middle East. In the 1860s, however, the pace of development declined. Though advance was hastened in Indo-China, Napoleon was faced with mounting difficulties in Algeria and met complete disaster in Mexico. As both crises were in part due to his personal intervention, this was bound to reflect unfavourably on the régime.

In Algeria the conflict between growing numbers of settlers and the Arab population created a permanent source of unrest. With the final conquest of warlike Berber tribesmen in the 1850s the colonists expected to consolidate their authority and their military rule, and assimilate or exclude the native inhabitants. In 1860, however, Napoleon visited Algeria, confirmed military control and began to plan measures to assist the Arabs. In 1863 he outlined proposals to end European land purchase and give the natives equal rights. These well-intentioned plans, however, infuriated the settlers and failed to satisfy the tribes. In 1864 a general revolt broke out and had to be crushed at considerable military cost. Napoleon's second visit in 1865 to urge toleration and mutual respect did nothing to heal the wounds. Algeria remained 'a bullet in our leg', and a permanent drain on France's resources and reserves.

Dreams of intervention in Central America had lingered in Napoleon's mind since the days of his captivity at Ham. In 1861 civil war in Mexico and the victory of a 'liberal', anti-Catholic régime, which cancelled all foreign debts, appeared to offer a favourable opportunity. With the United States paralysed by civil war, Britain, France and Spain signed a convention to send an expeditionary force to Mexico to enforce the repayment of European loans. Napoleon, however, influenced by the Empress and unreliable Mexican exiles, was already committed to the creation of a Catholic empire and had approached the Archduke Maximilian of Austria as a suitable candidate for an imperial crown. After a preliminary landing, however, Britain and Spain alarmed by French plans withdrew and Napoleon was left to continue on his own. Mexican support failed to materialize and some 30,000 troops had to be committed to the expedition before Mexico City could be occupied and Maximilian elected Emperor by a selected body of notables. When the Archduke arrived, reassured by promises of permanent French support, he was unable to rally reinforcements against republican and native guerillas. The civil war continued into 1865 when an ultimatum from the United States and mounting difficulties in Europe forced Napoleon to withdraw. Maximilian refused to abdicate; in 1867 he was captured by the republicans and shot. In the words of the Austrian ambassador, 'it was the Moscow of the Second Empire'.

The Mexican entanglement and the Algerian revolt distracted Napoleon from European developments. Between 1863 and 1866 he lost the initiative in foreign policy. Attempts to mediate between Austria and Prussia in 1865[1] were ignored. In 1866, with his troops still in transit, he was unable to take advantage of the Austro-Prussian war or influence the settlement in Germany. Though he assured the surrender of Venice to the Italians, this failed to make up for the continued occupation of Rome. Sadowa was soon accepted as yet another French defeat. Humiliation abroad weakened Napoleon's position at home and persuaded him to experiment in renewed political reconstruction and a 'liberal Empire.' This, however, was taken as yet another sign of weakness and failed to halt the progressive break-up of the régime.

4. *The Liberal Empire*

A 'liberal Empire' had always been one of the theoretical axioms of the Napoleonic creed. Napoleon I writing from St. Helena, had claimed that had he won in 1812 his 'constitutional reign would have begun'; that the Additional Act[2] drafted during the hundred days was a proof of his real intentions! Louis Napoleon advised Maximilian on his ill-fated voyage to Mexico to summon a nominated congress, acquire

[1] See Ch. XV.   [2] See p. 153.

absolute power, yet agree to work towards a constitution. His own amendments, however, appeared neither as the outcome of victory nor as the benefits of an enlightened absolutism. However much Louis Napoleon may have believed that he was working from a position of strength, his actions could all too often be interpreted as signs of weakness and generally encouraged further agitation and a revival of political demands.

The first eight years of the Empire had seen power entirely concentrated in the hands of the Emperor. Ministers were merely executives; prefects curbed the press and guided the elections. The 1857 results had echoed the victories of 1852, though there were signs of renewed opposition in the towns. France basked in an economic boom, enjoying a period of affluence that appeared to make up for any loss of political liberty or social dissatisfaction. Republicans were divided or in exile. Legitimists retired from politics while many Orléanists even began to give tacit support to the new régime. Abroad, prestige had been enhanced by the Crimean war and by French expansion in Africa. Yet it was only after initial setbacks and disappointments that Napoleon began to make tentative moves to liberalize the constitution.

Louis Napoleon's Italian policy aroused bitter Catholic opposition. The publication of *Le Pape et le Congrès* was furiously attacked in the ultramontane press and the government was forced to suppress the *Universe*, a leading Catholic paper, in January 1860. In the same month the publication of the Cobden Treaty[1] led to an outcry from industrialists and manufacturers. Thus two important interests, previously sympathetic to the Empire, had been alienated simultaneously. By the end of the year Napoleon had begun to make concessions. He believed it was time to show generosity from a position of strength. Many, however, considered that he was merely trying to retrieve his position.

The constitutional modifications of 1860-1 made a number of minor concessions to the left. The Chambers could vote a reply to the speech from the throne, as in 1815. There was to be a greater freedom of debate, minutes were to be published and ministers appointed to defend government measures in the Legislature. In 1861 the Chambers were given control over expenditure, with powers to vote each section of the budget

[1] See p. 389.

separately and approve all supplementary estimates. Ministers, however, remained responsible only to the Emperor. With government majorities assured, Louis Napoleon ruled supreme. Meanwhile he continued to urge a 'new era of peace', to encourage industrial development and to promote a speculative boom. Plans were prepared to gratify the workers with provident societies, old age pensions, and schemes for state insurance. In 1861 the Press Laws were modified and efforts made 'to weaken the importance of leading opposition journals by allowing the creation of a large number of rivals' – a proposal that turned out to be yet another example of wishful thinking.

During the next six years the opposition continued to grow. In 1861 the Catholics were able to rally almost half the Senate and ninety-one members of the Legislature in defence of the Papacy's position in Italy. The debates in the Chamber added new wind to republican sails and encouraged renewed speculation. Thiers could point out the irony of France bestowing liberty on others while deprived of it herself. Meanwhile workers had not been won over by Louis Napoleon's ineffective paternalism. Though prices rose less rapidly in the 1860s, wages continued to lag. The American civil war cut supplies of raw cotton and the numbers unemployed soon rose to 100,000. Industry was further undermined by foreign competition and the organization of illegal strikes. When a workers delegation was sent to the London exhibition in 1862 they made contact with British trade-unionists and helped lay the foundations of the first Socialist International three years later.

The 1863 elections were fought in an atmosphere of increasing excitement. The opposition parties joined in a 'liberal union', including Catholics, moderate republicans and old Orléanists such as Thiers. Though the government still polled over five million, two million voted for its opponents. The Catholic right won fifteen seats while the republicans won seventeen including eight in Paris and others in Lyons and Marseilles. Thiers, who won the ninth Parisian seat, now urged a return to individual and electoral freedom, liberty of the press and a ministry responsible to parliament.

Louis Napoleon and his ministers, however, showed little sign of pleasure at the election results and no intention of meeting Thiers' demands. Persigny was retired from the Ministry of the Interior for his failure to 'manage' the elections. The press was curbed with renewed stringency and inspectors sent to tour the provinces. Evidently the policy of encouraging more papers 'had not weakened the opposition but multiplied the government's adversaries'. Efforts were made to restrict the efforts of the Legislature. The right to control supplementary estimates was evaded and a Minister of State, Rouher, appointed to guide the Chamber. At the same time Louis Napoleon tried to rally support by gratifying the left. Amendments to the legal code gave employers and workers equal rights. A ban on Pius IX's Syllabus of Errors was followed by efforts to encourage state schools at the expense of religious institutions.

These reforming gestures were, however, not enough to restore the popularity of the régime or to secure it against the crises of the mid 1860s. The Algerian revolt was followed by the Mexican fiasco, an ineffective German policy and the diplomatic defeats following Sadowa. By 1866 the liberal opposition in the Legislature was able to muster sixty-three votes. Once again Louis Napoleon hoped to retain the initiative by making concessions. In January 1867 he allowed deputies to question ministers and promised a major reform of the Press Laws. Meanwhile he hurried on preparations for a great exhibition – the last and most successful of the reign. But elsewhere his policies appeared dangerously indecisive. Ministers remained entirely dependant, while Rouher vigorously defended the record of the Empire. Press reforms were delayed by lengthy debates between conservative and liberal advisers. The effect of the great exhibition was somewhat spoilt by the news of the execution of Maximilian in Mexico, and the efforts of a Polish patriot to assassinate the Tsar.

The last years of the Empire are often described as exuding an atmosphere of impending doom. Louis Napoleon was certainly dogged by growing misfortune and bad luck. A painful stone in the gall bladder undermined his health. Many of his associates including Walewski, his half brother de Morny and Fould had died. Abroad he was faced by the ruthless and subtle opposition of Bismarck. At home, the economic and financial framework of the Empire itself appeared to founder. A temporary collapse of the credit market in 1866 and a mild recession during the next two years were enough to topple the Crédit Mobilier and the Péreires, banking empire. Over-ambitious investment and lack of reserves forced the company into liquidation. Conservative financiers, the Bank of France and the Rothschilds welcomed the collapse, refused support and blamed the government for encouraging unsound speculation and faulty finance.

Lack of confidence affected industry where manufacturers continued to blame the Emperor's free trade policies for unemployment and unrest. In 1867 rioting broke out at Roubaix and in the older industrial regions. In Paris the rents for Haussmann's new apartments took up to a third of the workers' wages. Increasing numbers were forced to move to tenements and slums in the east end – an area ironically named Belleville. In 1868 Louis Napoleon hoped to pacify the workers by allowing trade unions and combinations. This, however, only led to a dramatic growth of union activity among employees in the new industries. The next two years witnessed a wave of strikes at St. Etienne, Le Creusot and Sotteville with demands for shorter hours, increased wages and the abolition of piece work. Though these demands were not political the fact that strikers had to be dispersed by troops, sometimes with violence, rebounded unfavourably on the government and did little to support the picture of a benevolent 'socialist' Empire.

When the Press Laws were eventually liberalized in January 1868, a wave of criticism and abuse was poured over the government. While moderates demanded further concessions and reforms, extreme republicans like Rochefort and Delescluze attacked every institution in the Empire, lampooned the royal family and compared the Emperor to Nero or Caligula. Though outrageous criticism was suppressed, attempts to prosecute Delescluze for raising a subscription to commemorate an almost forgotten revolutionary, Baudin, misfired. At the trial Gambetta, a young republican advocate, was given an opportunity to pillory the régime, denounce the creation of the Empire and reveal the history of bloodshed and repression that followed the December *coup d'état*. The press went on to attack the Péreires' and Haussmann's extravagant schemes. When these were debated in the Chamber, revelations of financial irregularities and unauthorized loans led to renewed scandals which eventually forced Haussmann to resign.

The 1869 elections, though not disastrous, revealed a decisive swing away from the government. Its supporters only polled 4.5 million votes while the opposition rose to 3.3 million. The republicans won 30 seats mainly in the big towns, while the moderate liberals were able to rally 116 supporters in the new Legislature. Louis Napoleon therefore decided, in spite of opposition from the Empress and the Court, to introduce further constitutional reforms. In July he gave the Chamber powers to amend and initiate legislation, elect its own officers and modify the tariff. In addition Rouher was eventually forced to resign and in 1870 a new 'liberal' ministry was formed under Emile Ollivier after months of negotiation and clandestine manoeuvres.

The Ollivier ministry appeared to introduce the first responsible parliamentary cabinet of the Second Empire. Nevertheless, Napoleon still retained considerable power. He appointed the Ministers of War and Marine, and expected to dominate the framing of government policy. The constitution of May 1870 which was 'short and obscure', conforming to the maxims outlined by his uncle, left ministers dependent on the Emperor and gave the Senate the right to initiate and alter legislation. Under the leadership of Rouher it could be relied on to safeguard the imperial interest. The new régime was therefore a mixture of monarchy and parliamentary government. As such it was immediately attacked by republican and left-wing groups. A general amnesty in 1869 brought back leading exiles including Victor Hugo, Blanqui, Barbès and Louis Blanc. But their policies were divided and their supporters disorganized and isolated. The Socialist International was split between militant Marxists and passive Proudhonists. Moreover, Napoleon had retained his right to appeal to the nation by plebiscite. On May 8th, 7.3 million voted for the new constitution, while the opposition could only muster 1.5 million and some 2 million abstained.

Thus the Empire appeared to have weathered its most serious crisis. The Emperor seemed calm, trade revived, the stock exchange rallied. The plebiscite had given massive support; the opposition was weak and divided. Yet the outcome was still in the melting-pot. Would the final result turn out to be liberal or authoritarian? How could such a structure divided within itself survive? It was tragic that this was the moment when its survival had to be put to the test. Obsessed by a need for prestige to wipe out the defeats and disappointments of the past, imperial fanatics drove the Empire into a war that brought the entire edifice crashing into ruin.

5. *Collapse and Commune*

For half a decade Louis Napoleon had failed to gain any tangible benefits from his foreign policy. Victim of his own conflicting ideals and confused initiatives, he continued to alienate his allies and aggravate his friends. Protests about Poland angered the Tsar. Action in Italy failed to satisfy the nationalists and outraged the Catholics. In Germany he wavered between supporting Prussia or the Danes, preserving Austria and maintaining the independence of the southern states as a third force. Yet he had not been entirely unsuccessful. Italy had acquired Venice at last. Prussia had been held at the river Main. The south German states had retained their independence. But these achievements had been qualified by unsuccessful attempts to win territorial compensation and by the interminable Roman entanglement.

The rapidity of the Prussian victory in 1866 had taken France by surprise. News of Sadowa was followed by an offer of French mediation. Drouyn demanded immediate mobilization and a token force to threaten Prussia on the Rhine. But the Emperor, ill, undecided, committed to Italy and with an army in Mexico, preferred diplomatic negotiations. Bismarck's moderate peace proposals helped decide the issue. Mobilization was deferred and Benedetti was sent to Nickolsburg to gain compensation for French neutrality. This may have been anticipated at a meeting between Louis Napoleon and Bismarck at Biarritz in the previous year. But, once again, nothing had been defined and Bismarck now affected to evade French demands for Luxembourg and the 1814 frontier while he hastened peace negotiations with Austria. Once these had been signed he refused to surrender 'a single German village', leaked the French demands to the press and used them to frighten the south German states into signing secret defensive alliances with Prussia. Benedetti had to depart empty handed and Drouyn was forced to resign. It was the first of many humiliations that France and Louis Napoleon were to suffer at Bismarck's hands.

In August 1866 Rouher proposed a Franco-Prussian alliance which would assure the unification of Germany in exchange for future French control over Belgium and Luxembourg. But Bismarck again evaded these embarassing proposals, though he kept the draft treaty for future use. Meanwhile a note, circulated by La Valette, the Foreign Minister, justified French policy by asserting the principle that big national units were destined to absorb smaller states. When, however, Louis attempted to put this doctrine into practice by purchasing Luxembourg he provoked violent protests in Germany and aroused growing suspicions in Britain. It was Bismarck again who appeared to offer the greatest provocation. While French opinion raged, Bismark published his secret treaties with the German states, thereby adding insult to injury. Amid the subsequent outcry war against Prussia was seriously considered for the first time.

Louis Napoleon was aware of his growing isolation and the need for allies in case of future conflict. Once again, however, conflicting interests led to inconclusive policies and prevented firm commitments. Attempts to reach agreement with Austria were never completed. Francis Joseph refused to align himself against Prussia unless France agreed to defend Austrian interests in the Near East. As this would conflict both with the nationalists in that area and with Russian diplomacy Louis Napoleon became equally evasive. Plans for a triple alliance with Austria and Italy were also unsuccessful. In 1867 French troops had once again been forced to occupy Rome after Garibaldi's renewed attempts to capture the city.[1] In 1869 the Italian government refused to sign any alliance until the French troops had been withdrawn – a demand Louis Napoleon found quite impossible to fulfil. Meanwhile a French plan to take over the Belgian railways had roused fresh antagonism in Britain, while efforts to patch up an *entente* with Russia merely led to vague reassurances. The Tsar had in fact become increasingly aloof and hoped to exploit a war in the West to denounce the Black Sea clauses of the Peace of Paris.

Besides being diplomatically isolated France was also

[1] See p. 347.

dangerously unprepared. Sadowa had demonstrated the power and progress of Prussian arms and Louis Napoleon had formulated plans to raise an army of a million men from a combination of an active army, a full time reserve and a Garde Nationale Mobile. This would submit all those who had previously evaded service, or purchased 'substitutes', to regular military training. These proposals, however, met a barrage of opposition from every quarter. Professionals had no use for part-timers, peasants and proletarians resented call up, the Chamber denounced the cost, and the bourgeoisie attacked compulsory conscription. Marshal Niel was only able to present compromise reforms in 1867. These allowed for a regular and reserve force of 800,000 by 1875 but cut training for the Garde Mobile to a fortnight and retained the system of allowing 'substitutes' for those who could afford to pay them. Niel died in 1869, his reforms incomplete. Though the French army had been issued with *chassepots*, new breach loading rifles, little had been done about the artillery. Mobilization plans were to remain rudimentary in spite of the evidence of chaos that had been noted during the 1859 war. The army, nevertheless, appeared confident, reassured by success in Africa, a reputation for courage and a tradition of victory from the Crimea and the Italian campaigns.

Meanwhile, however, the 'liberal Empire' far from unifying the State was accentuating its divisions. In the struggle for survival every faction hoped to win prestige and glamour by some victory or sensational success. While the Ollivier ministry urged disarmament and the Chamber cut the army estimates, Louis Napoleon continued his efforts to reach agreement with Russia and opened unofficial military discussions with Austria. While the army planned for war the republican opposition cried for peace. It was in an atmosphere of growing excitement and frustrated anticipation that France suddenly heard of the Hohenzollern candidature for the Spanish throne.[1]

Louis Napoleon had already proclaimed that the choice of Leopold of Hohenzollern as king of Spain would be an affront to France herself.[2] Ollivier had warned that *'un échec ... c'est la guerre'*. There was little doubt that Bismarck was out to provoke a trial of strength. Gramont, re-

---

[1] See p. 378.   [2] See p. 378.

cently appointed Foreign Minister, roused the Chamber with belligerent statements, while the Empress urged action and the press cried for revenge. Louis Napoleon, however, preferred diplomatic methods: appeals were despatched to the great powers, and Benedetti was sent to demand an official withdrawal of Leopold's candidature. Though William refused any formal declaration he urged Leopold to withdraw. On July 12th Leopold's father renounced the candidature and the crisis appeared over. Louis Napoleon was satisfied, Ollivier thought the grounds of quarrel over and Thiers declared that Sadowa had been almost avenged.

The Prussian withdrawal, however, was not enough to satisfy the extremists. Gramont was determined to humiliate Prussia, the Empress anxious to safeguard the dynasty, while the popular press agitated for further satisfaction. The Minister of War, General Leboeuf, had already begun discreet preparations and on July 11th 1870 Louis Napoleon himself issued new mobilization plans to concentrate the army at Metz. At a private meeting on July 12th the Empress and Gramont persuaded Louis to agree to a further demand for Prussian guarantees. William I was to be asked to declare that the candidature would never be renewed. On July 13th William firmly but politely refused. When Bismarck edited and published the official telegram, however, both France and Prussia felt equally outraged.

While the crowds in Berlin and Paris shouted for war the Council of Ministers appeared to waver. Louis Napoleon was again hesitant and a majority even considered Gramont's demands excessive. The growing national outcry, however, could no longer be ignored. Gramont and the Empress felt that only action could save the Empire. Leboeuf threatened to resign. Publication of the Ems telegram was clearly a deliberate affront. Louis was persuaded to act and the Council agreed to mobilize. The news was greeted with frenzied cheers. The Chamber, assured that France had Austria's support and that the army was ready for war, voted the necessary fifty millions. The protests of Thiers and republicans like Favre and Gambetta were drowned amid shouts for war. Louis Napoleon had been overwhelmed by the pressure of events. Incapacitated by illness and quite unable to control the mounting cross-currents of passion and

DD

propaganda he was now at the mercy of the tide. Within two months it had swept him and the Empire to destruction.

For the French speedy mobilization was essential to out-manoeuvre the Prussians and encourage Austrian inter-vention. But Louis Napoleon's sudden change of plans and the lack of advanced preparation created massive confusion. The railways were choked by reservists crossing the country in every direction while equipment piled up haphazard and unrecorded at regimental depôts. When Louis Napoleon reached Metz on July 28th it was impossible to take the offensive. The army merely trundled forward to occupy the heights above Saarbrücken – a manoeuvre that was acclaimed in Paris as a notable success. A week later, however, illusions were shattered by defeats at Spicheren and Froeschwiller, where the superior Prussian artillery played a decisive role in scattering French resistance.

The news of defeat spread confusion in Paris. When Ollivier demanded an advance the French army was bundled into Metz, where it was quickly surrounded by the Prussians. Meanwhile the Legislature had met in emergency session, forced Ollivier to resign and accepted a new right-wing ministry under Palikao. Determined to save the Empire, he hastened the formation of a new army at Châlons. Louis Napoleon was persuaded to hand over command to Mac-Mahon. Urged on by appeals from Paris he moved forward across the front of the advancing Prussians in an attempt to relieve Metz. The move was disastrous. Defeated at Beau-mont, the French army was pushed against the Belgian frontier and surrounded at Sedan. After a heroic but futile defence Louis Napoleon surrendered on September 2nd. Next day he left, a prisoner, for Germany from where after six months he was to retire to England for the last two years of his life.

The defeat of Sedan led to an immediate revolution in Paris. Once again the moderate republicans led by Favre and Gambetta struggled for power with socialist republicans under Delescluze, Pyat and the now venerable and aged Blanqui. As before the moderates won and with Trochu as President prepared to defend the capital. But when the siege began on September 18th the failure of the moderate govern-ment to achieve any notable success and the growing hard-

ship inflicted on the population led to renewed agitation
from the left. In October a series of isolated demonstrations
built up to a full-scale revolt. National Guard battalions
from Belleville stormed the Hôtel de Ville and installed
Delescluze, Pyat and Blanqui as a rival government before being cleared out by bourgeois guardsmen and Breton
reservists.

Left-wing leaders were imprisoned and the moderates restored. But the government was unable to effect any recovery
in the war. Strasbourg capitulated at the end of September
and Metz fell a month later. Though Gambetta escaped from
Paris by balloon to rouse the provinces he failed to co-ordinate plans with Trochu. Attempts to break out of Paris failed
and a brief advance at Orléans was soon pushed back by Prussian reinforcements. Hunger, cold and the fear of 'red'
revolution finally persuaded the government to surrender.
France was to give up Alsace and much of Lorraine, pay an
indemnity of five milliard francs and suffer the final humiliation of a Prussian march through Paris. In February 1871,
new elections brought a decisive swing to the right and a
massive victory for the peace party. Led by Thiers the
Assembly agreed to the terms, though the surrender of Alsace-
Lorraine was denounced as 'war in perpetuity', and Victor
Hugo already felt the smouldering fires of revenge.

In Paris hatred burst out into the Commune – a climax to
the social conflicts of the century. Embittered by surrender,
the Prussian march and the reactionary policies of the Assembly, which abolished pay for the National Guard and
demanded immediate payments of arrears in rent, the republican and socialist left blazed into revolt. A *comité central* of the
National Guard organized elections to a Commune which
contained a wide cross-section of lower bourgeois and artisan
opinion from Blanquistes, now on the moderate left, to
terrorists such as Rigault, and isolated members of the
Socialist International. The majority were Jacobins led by
Delescluze, anxious to achieve the ideals of 1793 and the
hopes of 1848. All, however, had been taken by surprise and
none were prepared to control events. While Thiers organized massive forces at Versailles to crush the capital, the
Commune leaders quarrelled. Blanquistes, Jacobins and
Internationalists urged rival plans to the end. After a second

siege and a week of bloody street fighting the revolt was ruth-lessly suppressed.

Over 20,000 were killed in the Commune. Of some 40,000 prisoners at least 9,000 were deported to the colonies. Radicals and socialists had once again been crushed and Thiers was free to set up a conservative republic. But it was born out of bitterness and defeat, and failed to satisfy either the idealism of the left or the ambition of the right. It had been Louis Napoleon's aim to reconcile these extremes which, with the passions and prejudices of his age, were to tear Europe apart during the next hundred years. But, in the words of a recent biographer, 'he was a man too small for the great things he set out to do'. His failure was to prove a disaster and leave a lasting scar upon the history of France. For a brief moment Frenchmen had found a solution for their conflicts in the personality of one man. It may appear ironical that a majority were to accept a similar solution a century later.

XVI · REFORM AND REACTION IN EASTERN EUROPE

1. *The 'Tsar Liberator'*

ALEXANDER II succeeded his father, Nicholas I, in 1855, the year of Russia's defeat in the Crimean war. Military failure was to provide a powerful incentive to reform and hasten changes that had been held up for decades by the iron will of an absolute Tsar. Incompetence, demoralization, and lack of supply had been revealed in every department; but these had only been the symptoms of a deeper malaise. The rigidity of a serf-owning society, the inflexibility of an overworked bureaucracy, the slow rate of economic development and the isolation of Russia from the scientific and industrial developments of the West were all now equally apparent. Even Nicholas had become aware that his methods had failed. He left his son with a clear realization of the need to promote reform and further reconstruction.

The new Tsar combined his father's military interests with a wayward sensitivity possibly inherited from his mother, the daughter of Frederick William III and Queen Louise of Prussia. He preferred the parade ground to any liberal or scientific studies and believed in dutifully following his father's lead. He was also well meaning and vague, anxious to win popularity and averse to studying details or dealing with difficulties. Thus he was not entirely suited to effect any radical transformation in Russian government or society. But his father had carefully trained him for his imperial role. Alexander had sat on secret committees appointed to study the serf question and had become aware of the savage corruption in the administration. He had been sent on a tour of the provinces and had noted the misery and degradation of peasants and exiles. A visit to western Europe confirmed his impression of the backwardness and isolation of Russian life. Convinced that he was fulfilling his father's will and satisfying the needs of the Russian people, he set out on the road to reform without at first either grasping the implications or defining his goal.

In 1856 Alexander's peace manifesto appeared to suggest a coming 'thaw': 'May Russia's internal welfare be strengthened and perfected; may justice and mercy reign in her courts; may the urge towards enlightenment and every form of useful activity grow with new strength; and may everyone under the protection of laws equally just for all and equally protecting all enjoy in peace the fruits of their labour.' At his coronation the Tsar eased the persecution of religious sects, freed the remaining Decembrists[1] and revolutionary exiles, relaxed controls on foreign travel, the press and the universities, and cancelled the tax arrears from devastated areas. Polish nobles were allowed to return to their country and Catholics were granted wider toleration. Enquiries were opened into bureaucratic corruption and a new consortium set up to hasten railway construction with the aid of foreign capital and western technical assistance. But these gestures were not enough to satisfy radical elements, and landowners soon become alarmed by the implied abolition of serf labour.

Alexander's well-intentioned clemency released a flood of agitation and debate. The aristocracy split between the 'planters' anxious to retain their serfs and 'liberals' ready for reform. A spate of specialist journals on medicine, agriculture and economics soon added a familiar pattern of disguised criticism. The army and the administration feared change and government investigation; radicals demanded far more decisive measures. Alexander Herzen, now in London, advocated a free press, freedom and land for the serfs, and the end of corporal punishment. His journal, *The Bell*, was smuggled into Russia to stir up the growing student population. Chernyshevsky demanded better education, railways and a 'redistribution of economic forces', in the more cautious language needed to allow free publication inside Russia. These conflicts underlined the basic dilemmas facing Alexander in any efforts to move the sluggish mass of the Russian Empire out of its established rut. Though described as a weak and ineffective man he nevertheless persevered. His first achievement, the liberation of the serfs, was probably the most spectacular. It conditioned many of his other reforms and left a lasting tribute to his memory.

Addressing a delegation of nobles, Alexander made his own

1 See Ch. XII. 1.

attitude to serfdom quite clear. 'It is better to abolish serfdom from above than to await the time when it will begin to abolish itself from below.' He hoped to achieve abolition by stages with the support of the nobles, and set up a secret committee in 1857 to examine the problem. His hopes, however, were soon disappointed. The nobility refused to take any initiative, while the 'planters' on the secret committee and in the provinces obstructed every move. Alexander, nevertheless, pushed ahead determined to complete the measure himself. In the end he was criticized for leaving the landowners too much, but it is difficult to see how he could have done anything else within the existing framework of society. In the last resort the Empire still depended on an aristocratic hierarchy and the maintenance of a governing élite. Any reform was bound to provoke opposition from this sector and present the Tsar with a number of conflicting arguments and dangerous dilemmas.

The basic difficulty was the land question. When the Lithuanian nobility, supported by the secret committee, petitioned to free their serfs without any obligation regarding land, Alexander signed an official decree setting out his own policy. This had been drafted by Lanskoi, his reforming Minister of the Interior, assisted by Miliutin and Soloviev, and required liberation with land. Serfs were to gain personal freedom, and acquire their huts and allotments in return for compensation; they were also to retain their existing rights to any land then in use for a fixed rent or by labour dues. In 1858 the nobles of every province were instructed to elect committees to work out the details. At the same time two central committees were set up under Rostovtsev in St. Petersburg to co-ordinate their proposals.

The sudden publication of the Tsar's plans provoked a national debate that split Russian society. While Alexander had the support of liberals and westerners at court, a radical intelligentsia and a few enlightened landowners in the provinces, the majority on the provincial committees and on the secret, now Central Committee, in St. Petersburg remained hostile. The Tsar had repeatedly to reaffirm his determination to carry the matter to a conclusion. In 1858 he toured the less hostile provinces to appeal for support and divide the opposition. He also took over the presidency of the Central

Committee himself to hasten proceedings and deflect criticism.

In 1859 the provincial committees finished their work. The reports were co-ordinated in St. Petersburg where the two committees had been joined into one editing commission. Here Rostovtsev selected the liberal proposals and rejected 'planter' protests. When provincial representatives were summoned to Moscow, Alexander reprimanded the critics and urged more effective measures. Nevertheless, he was forced to agree to some concessions. The hereditary and legal rights of the nobility were confirmed, the size of the ordinary peasant allotments reduced and a 'beggar's plot' accepted as well. In addition the State finally agreed to pay immediate compensation and collect the necessary redemption dues from the peasants. By 1860 codification was complete. Alexander, assisted by his brother, the liberal Grand-Duke Constantine, and Lanskoi steered the final draft through the Central Committee and the Imperial Council against considerable opposition. In February 1861 the Emancipation Decree was eventually signed and read in all the churches of the Empire.

Alexander had hoped that 'this great work be accomplished in a manner not hurtful to anyone and satisfactory to all', a remark that might suggest that he was not fully aware of all the issues involved. In the event, most felt dissatisfied. The nobles lost a third of their land, suffered in status and sank deeper into debt. Seven-tenths of their serfs were already mortgaged and nearly half the compensation therefore went to repay their creditors. Most landowners failed to reinvest the remainder or to reorganize their estates. By 1870 renewed borrowing had made their debts higher than ever. The serfs on the other hand felt cheated. Though allotments were impartially distributed they appeared small, while redemption dues at 6 per cent over forty-nine years seemed high. Peasants now had to pay more for less land, continue to pay customary dues for the remainder and lost their rights to woodland and waste. In 1861 over six hundred riots broke out. At Bezdna fifty peasants were killed and over three hundred wounded. By 1878 only half the serfs had been adequately endowed; the remainder lived below subsistence level. Thus the hopes of the Tsar could not be fulfilled. The vested interests of the landlords and the claims of the serfs were indeed quite incompatible. Rostovtsev was more realistic in his comment: 'they are right from their points of view – we from ours.' In the last resort there could be no satisfactory compromise.

Similar conflicts bedevilled Alexander's relations with the Poles. The 'thaw' had brought considerable benefits and a new measure of tolerance to Polish affairs. Exiles returned, Catholics were granted greater freedom, a new medical school was opened in Warsaw, and an Agricultural Society was allowed to set up branches throughout the country to promote economic reforms. But such measures still denied full independence and could never satisfy the militant Poles. Exiles, officers, student societies and Catholics combined to agitate for more. The Agricultural Society became a network of intrigue linking up the nobility with other disaffected bodies. In 1860 they began to organize memorial services, anniversary marches and protest meetings. By 1861 there were widespread riots and clashes with the police leading to violence and bloodshed.

At first Alexander tried to maintain a policy of pacification. Russian police were withdrawn and citizen committees allowed to assume responsibility for law and order. A national commission was set up under a moderate Pole, Wielopolski, to draw up reform plans for Polish schools, provincial councils and a council of state. These measures, however, only served to whet Polish appetites. Agitation increased and Wielopolski was forced to close the Agricultural Society and curb the nobles' clubs. When Constantine was sent as viceroy in 1862 it was already too late. Extremist agitation led to assassination and riot, violence and counter-violence. Finally efforts to draft agitators into the army provoked a full-scale revolution. Nobles, clergy, officers and students fought with bitter fury for over a year. But, as before, the peasantry remained apathetic and foreign powers failed to provide any effective support.[1]

By 1865 the Poles had again been crushed. The nobility were executed, deported and fined. Estates were confiscated and Catholic monasteries dissolved. The peasants were freed and given land on more favourable terms than their Russian counterparts. Redemption dues were lower, plots larger and the use of waste assured. In Poland the government did not have to compromise with an aristocratic opposition! Russian became the official language of the administration. Poland was designated the Vistula region and all political or regional autonomy destroyed. For fifty years the Poles were officially erased from the map.

Alexander's relationship with the Finns provided an unexpected contrast. He had, as Tsarevitch, been Rector of Helsinki University and had remained surprisingly popular in the province. Russia encouraged the economic development of the area, building docks and railways, and stimulating agriculture, timber and fishing. After considerable misgiving Alexander allowed a Finnish Diet to meet in 1863 to vote funds for these new developments. The moderates were able to win a majority and worked with the Russians to set up a National Bank, new schools and encourage currency reform. The Finns were allowed to use their own language and develop separate institutions in partnership with the Russian authorities. Though relationships were not always easy and extremists continued to make threatening demands, the majority appeared ready to work out a practical compromise with their more powerful neighbour.

2. *Reform and Reaction in Russia*

The liberation of the serfs led inevitably to further reform. The destruction of manorial courts required the creation of a new administrative and legal framework. The end of 'peasant quotas' meant a reorganization of the army and new recruiting methods. Moreover, liberation had only been a step to encourage a more general development that required economic reform, a greater degree of social mobility and new opportunities for education. These changes, however, had to be carried through within the existing political and social order. Alexander had learnt that it was difficult to allow any class to participate in public affairs as it was never possible to stop such a development at any appropriate point. Yet without such participation many were bound to remain dissatisfied and continue to undermine and ultimately to destroy Alexander's well-intentioned plans.

After emancipation the peasants were reorganized into village communes, *mirs*. Elected elders allocated the land, assessed local rates and were held responsible for law and order. In 1864 a *Zemstvo* Statute added a superstructure of local councils, *zemstvos*, at district and provincial level. The district *zemstvos* were elected on a three grade property franchise by landowners, townsmen and peasants who were only allowed an indirect vote. They met each year to approve a budget, formulate plans and elect an executive bureau. This had powers covering rates, health, hospitals and education. It remained, however, subordinate to the central authority which controlled both taxation and the police. Thus efforts were made to reach a compromise between central and local government and between several class interests. But the centre retained effective control and the nobility their dominant position. They invariably made up a majority on the district council and up to 75 per cent of the membership of the provincial *zemstvo*. This was part of a deliberate policy advocated by Alexander to placate the aristocracy. In fact it soon brought them into headlong collision. By 1866 *zemstvos* were demanding a central *zemstvo* in which to air their grievances. When the St. Petersburg members became too insistent, Alexander was forced to exile their leaders to Siberia.

Nevertheless, the *zemstvos* were able to perform several useful functions and gradually spread a number of reforms over the vast expanses of the Russian countryside. Rates and taxes were more equitably assessed. Medical aid was promoted, together with veterinary services and improved agricultural techniques. Rural industries were encouraged, as were the first fire services and insurance schemes. Above all, Russia obtained its earliest sprinkling of elementary schools. In 1856 there had only been some 8,000, but by 1880 the number had risen to 23,000. In 1870 a Municipal Statute extended similar institutions to the towns. Here a *Duma* was to be elected on a similar three-tier suffrage with equivalent powers over health, education, water, light and local life. Once again, however, its limited powers were to encourage further demands and create new obstacles. The Tsars were to find the greatest difficulty in encouraging reform with one hand and restraining it with the other.

Judicial reform was the outcome of a deliberate study of western procedure. Manorial and police courts were replaced by a series of criminal courts with trained lawyers and juries to deal with serious offences. Petty crime was dealt with directly in courts held by justices of the peace. Their role was to act as arbitrators and to settle disputes along lines suggested by common sense rather than complicated legal procedure. This provided cheap and speedy justice and soon made them very popular. Their approach remains the basis of petty indictments in Russia today. The courts of first instance were followed by courts of appeal. All were open to the public. At the summit of the judiciary the Senate acted as a supreme court. A new and independent spirit was clearly revealed when juries began to acquit notorious terrorists at the end of Alexander's reign.

Reforms in the army and navy did away with brutal punishment, branding, excessive flogging and semi-penal service conditions. Radical reorganization, however, was bitterly opposed by both the aristocracy and the middle classes and it was not until 1871 that Alexander felt strong enough to set up another reform commission. This instituted compulsory military service for all with six years in the colours and nine in the reserve. Final selection was to be by ballot and special categories were allowed exemption. But evasion by purchase was banned; all had to be ready to defend the fatherland. Simultaneously officer training was improved by new staff colleges, and medical and engineering services were brought up to date. Military courts were regulated and an education corps set up to combat illiteracy. Many soldiers first learnt to read in army schools, though this was hardly to help the dynasty in the long run. It has often been noted that the army reforms were among the earliest attempts to introduce the idea of equality into Russian life. This, however, could only contrast unfavourably with the obvious inequalities elsewhere.

The second half of the nineteenth century witnessed the gradual acceleration of industrial development. All the essential ingredients were now at hand. Emancipation released a flood of cheap, surplus labour. Foreign credit was available from the booming stock markets in London, Paris and Amsterdam. Raw materials in the Urals and the Ukraine could be linked by new railway networks. Western entrepreneurs could be encouraged to harness Russia's vast, almost untapped resources. Progress, though slow and erratic, was nevertheless of significance especially in minerals, textiles and engineering.

Financial reform encouraged foreign investment and the growth of joint-stock companies. The Treasury was reorganized and the Minister of Finance given more effective control. In 1862 the first publication of a budget aroused public interest and helped create confidence. Meanwhile the foundation of the Bank of Russia in 1860 promoted further activity and some 278 municipal banks and 727 savings associations had been set up by the end of Alexander's reign. After the Crimean war the silver rouble had been made inconvertible, and though paper money fluctuated with changes in the European trade cycle, the basic standard remained surprisingly stable. This helped promote a boom in joint-stock companies: whereas only 72·1 million roubles had been invested between 1799 and 1853, the figure from 1855 to 1860 was 317 millions. By 1881 some 556 companies had been registered covering railways, cotton, mining, heavy industries and oil.

As so frequently elsewhere it was cotton and the railways that provided the spearheads for industrial growth. Both relied heavily on foreign capital and expert advice. Cotton mills had already been established at Ivanovo, Moscow and St. Petersburg in the early nineteenth century, but it was only in the second half that steam engines, power looms and spinning machines were imported from Britain and installed by English engineers. By 1860 some 57 mills were employing over 42,000 operatives. Thirty years later the numbers had more than doubled. In 1855 Russia had only some 650 miles of railway track in use. Soon a new consortium and Russian joint-stock companies were linking Moscow and St. Petersburg to Warsaw, the Black Sea ports and the western provinces. Some 150 million roubles were spent on imported rails during the 1870s and by 1881 over 14,000 miles were in operation.

Railway development helped to promote the coal, iron and engineering industries. Coal production increased more slowly due to the vast reserves of timber available throughout the country, but iron output rose with the introduction of British blast furnaces and rolling techniques. In 1869 the New Russia Company, founded by two Hughes brothers from

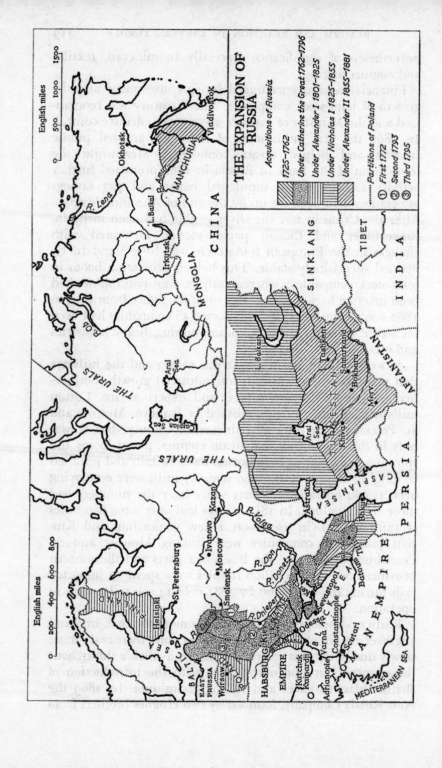

THE EXPANSION OF RUSSIA

Acquisitions of Russia

1725–1762
Under Catherine the Great 1762–1796
Under Alexander I 1801–1825
Under Nicholas I 1825–1855
Under Alexander II 1855–1881

Partitions of Poland
① First 1772
② Second 1793
③ Third 1795

Wales, began to exploit coal and iron in the Donetz basin, an area that was to become one of the centres of Russia's industrial development. Meanwhile new engineering works at St. Petersburg were constructing mining machinery and railway equipment. An essential feature of Russian industry was its concentration into large units of production. Both private companies and state enterprises operated on a larger scale than their counterparts in the West, a factor that was eventually to have considerable social and political significance.

Economic expansion led to a new surge in material progress. Trade boomed, exports and imports doubled in a decade. In the 1860s oil was discovered at Baku in the Caucasus, and, after some years of primitive distribution in leather bottles, a new company was founded in 1873 by Nobel of Sweden in order to exploit it. Fairs flourished and capital investment soared. But these developments also hastened the disintegration and fragmentation of Russian society. The landed aristocracy generally failed to exploit these new opportunities and fell deeper into debt and into a morose contemplation of their own grievances. The peasants, unable to subsist upon their meagre plots, overwhelmed by poverty and a rising population, drifted to the towns where they were drawn into the new factories and suffered the worst horrors of early industrialization. The new bourgeoisie was able to acquire wealth but neither power nor status within the framework of a Tsarist régime.

Russian writers and intellectuals continued to be intensely critical of the political, social and economic developments in their country. Chernyshevsky soon denounced the liberation of the serfs as totally inadequate, and students were provoked to riot by news of the massacre at Bezdna. Agitation reached new proportions in 1861. While the nobles demanded an assembly, Mikhailov in an 'appeal to the younger generation' urged the need for a constitution and a radical transformation of society. Attempts by the government to arrest students and agitators led to renewed violence. Once again Alexander tried to temper the wind and introduce educational reform. A University Statute allowed increased autonomy, rectorial elections and separate disciplinary control. Foreign exchanges were encouraged, new subjects such as science and modern languages introduced and scholarships endowed for poorer students. Secondary schools were opened to all according to merit, new subjects were introduced and better teachers promoted. But these changes were also accompanied by efforts to control the excessive agitation of students and intellectuals. In 1862 Chernyshevsky and Mikhailov were banished to Siberia and the activities of the Third Section revived to root out revolutionary authors and intimidate defiant critics.

Here again the basic contradictions implicit in Alexander's policy were revealed. Educational reforms only encouraged further criticism. A Young Russia movement demanded elected assemblies, nationalized factories and the destruction of monasteries. Anarchists influenced by Bakunin urged the dissolution of society and the abolition of marriage. Pisarev incited students to action by proclaiming that 'what can be smashed must be smashed', and spread the ideals of a new 'nihilism'.[1] But the Polish rebellion and the growth of violence frightened many of the moderates and by 1865 much of the agitation appeared to have been subdued. This, however, only drove extremists to further acts of desperation. In 1866 these culminated in an attempt to assassinate Alexander himself.

The Tsar was by this time exhausted, disillusioned and profoundly disturbed by the turn of events. Repeatedly on edge and increasingly excitable he found consolation in a new mistress, which split him from a majority of the Court and further increased his isolation. After 1866 a drift towards reaction slowly gathered momentum. Liberal ministers were dismissed, education brought under increasing control and the Third Section given further powers under Shuvalov. Science teaching was curtailed for promoting material values, and schools and universities carefully watched for disaffected elements. Students were soon expelled and officers purged for any revolutionary affiliations. By 1870 Alexander had become a prisoner of the police, bitter, restless and remote. 'All I have to do to make an enemy,' he remarked, 'is to do someone a favour.'

By 1870 there were also signs of renewed revolutionary activity. The Populists attempted to stir up the peasants and propagate the idealism of a communal society, but were quite

[1] See p. 425.

unsuccessful and soon eliminated. They were followed by
'Land and Liberty', the first carefully organized revolutionary
body. By the mid-1870s it had created a network of secret
agents and begun to indulge in violent terrorist activities. Its
militant wing 'the Peoples' Will' condemned Alexander to
death. In 1881 he was assassinated. Few grieved at his death.
His reforms had long since been forgotten. The aristocracy
resented their lack of influence, the middle classes remained
bitter at their inferior status, the peasants complained of redemption dues and their growing poverty; workers attacked
the long hours and low wages of factory life; students and intellectuals joined to condemn the failure of reform and the
revival of police regulations. Alexander's reforms had indeed
been incomplete and his failure had brought violent retribution. But he died the victim of his own ideals, a prisoner in
the framework of an absolute state and an obsolete society.

3. Russia and the Wider World

The contradictions and paradoxes within Russia had their
counterpart in foreign policy and in the literature and political thought of the period. Both were to have a disturbing
impact upon world affairs. In 1856 Alexander and Gorchakov
proclaimed the need for peace; yet Russia continued to expand. In 1861 the Tsar protested at Garibaldi's intervention
in Naples and at the unification of Italy; sixteen years later
he was to intervene himself on behalf of the Slav nationalists
in the Balkans. Such ambivalence aroused inevitable mistrust
among foreign powers and Russia found herself increasingly
isolated. This was clearly apparent during the Polish revolt
when European protests led to growing alienation from
France, Britain and Austria. Bismarck's impulsive intervention[1] was also received with suspicion, especially as it was
soon apparent that he was only anxious to exploit the situation to his own advantage. Nevertheless, Prussia's friendly
neutrality was appreciated and reinforced by a personal relationship and mutual understanding between Alexander
and his uncle William I.

In the East, Russia had maintained a policy of ruthless imperial expansion. As Gorchakov explained in a note to the
great powers in 1864: 'The United States in America, France

[1] See p. 367.

EE

in Africa, Holland in her colonies and England in India were all forced to take a road on which the chief difficulty is to know where to stop.' In addition, Russia's size made it almost impossible to control the activities of proconsuls on her distant borders, and the militant actions of regional governors often appeared in flat contradiction to the peaceful claims of Gorchakov's official declarations. On the Pacific coast Muraviev[1] continued to advance down the Amur and acquired the whole of its northern bank and a strip of coastline down to Korea by the treaty of Pekin. In 1860 Vladivostok was founded at its southern tip to give Russia an ice-free port in the Pacific.

At the same time Russian armies were completing the conquest of central Asian and the Caucasian tribes. Tashkent was occupied in 1865 and Khiva ten years later bringing Russia to the Afghan frontier. In the South, the Caspian region was opened up to new economic development. Cotton growing was extended to Turkestan to replace American sources, and fishing, oil, salt and sulphur exploited with increasing vigour. The construction of a trans-Caspian railway was to link this area to the growing industrial regions in the West and help accelerate the growth of the Russian economy. Expansion inevitably aroused increasing alarm, especially in Britain which viewed Russia's creeping advance towards India with growing apprehension. This, however, did not lead to open conflict until the last quarter of the century.

After 1856 Alexander was determined to denounce the Black Sea clauses of the Peace of Paris at the earliest favourable moment. In 1864 Count Ignatiev was sent as Minister Plenipotentiary to Constantinople. He represented a forward Pan-Slav tradition, first formulated by Pogodin and Tyutchev in the 1840s,[2] but was also a shrewd and able propagator of Russian interests. In 1870 the Franco-Prussian war provided Gorchakov with the occasion to denounce the Black Sea clauses. Though Gladstone protested at this unilateral violation of an international engagement, Britain was isolated and incapable of intervention. Bismarck was nevertheless sufficiently alarmed at possible complications during the siege of Paris to agree to a conference in London. Here in 1871 the Black Sea clauses were officially abrogated. Though the

[1] See p. 306.   [2] See p. 303.

Straits remained closed to warships in time of peace, Russia regained her freedom of manoeuvre and reasserted her military control over the area.

This achievement did not, however, mean full approval for other Pan-Slav proposals. Though the Empress and a limited court circle spoke in their favour, Alexander was cautious and fully aware of the dangers involved. The Polish revolt had revealed the weakness of any Pan-Slav association. At a congress in Moscow in 1867 the Minister of Education urged the visiting Slav delegations to study languages and master their grammar. Alexander had no desire to provoke renewed revolutionary unrest. Slav idealism, whether directed at the development of Russian communes or Czech and Serb liberation, was not necessarily to the advantage of a Tsarist government.

The literature of the time reflected the tensions and paradoxes created by so wide a variety of interests. Danilevsky urged the ideals of a Slav commune that united nations and peoples into a free but ordered whole. Herzen advocated a peaceful transition to a liberal state by educating the people to freedom. Chernyshevsky urged action; Bakunin advocated anarchy. Turgenev, noting the critical and apparently destructive attitude of the younger generation, coined the title 'nihilism' to describe a probing scientific attitude that rejected everything in the present in order to construct a more rational future. Dostoyevsky and Tolstoy explored the conflict of ideals in everyday life and emphasized the wisdom of the peasant and the understanding embedded in centuries of experience and development. But they could not resolve the conflicts of history or reshape the structure of the State. They could only echo the paradoxes in Russian society and the clash of interests contained within its vast horizons.

The year 1870 also saw the birth of Lenin. Using western ideas and methods he was to destroy the old social and Tsarist framework and reconstruct it on Russian communist lines. Slavophil ideals were extended to absorb the requirements of an industrial and scientific society. But many of the political and economic problems remained and contemporary ideological disputes often retain a vaguely familiar ring. Perhaps the very size of Russia, situated between East and West, imposed its own conditions. Herzen noted as early as 1851 that 'Com-

munism is the Russian autocracy turned upside down!'
Whoever ruled would experience the same difficulty in
equating the old and the new, in maintaining freedom and
authority, peace and power, and in establishing a tolerable
compromise between the conflicting elements within the
Russian State.

4. *The Habsburg Empire*

The Habsburg Empire suffered from even more conflicts
than the Russian. There were the same class rivalries between aristocrats, bourgeois, peasants and artisans. There
were similar constitutional difficulties between a centralized
autocracy and varied political and regional interests. In addition some dozen different nationalities added to the confusion, while interests in Italy, Germany and the Balkans
created a web of foreign entanglements. In 1848 all these elements had fallen apart and the Empire had appeared on the
point of disintegration. But Schwarzenberg had, by a ruthless
policy of expediency and exploitation, begun to gather up
the fragments.[1] Moderate Germans and Czechs had been
harnessed against popular and passionate extremists. Croats
and Rumanians had been brought into alliance against Kossuth's Magyar demands. By 1849 the Empire seemed ready
for reconstruction.

Four alternative solutions were to dominate the events of
the next twenty years. The first was advocated by the 'old
conservatives' at court and by the feudal aristocracy. They
hoped to return to the pre-March days and to the diets[2] in
which they had always played a dominant role. The second
was urged by German and Czech liberals and combined a
limited regional autonomy within a constitutional but united
Empire. The old historic units were to be retained and all
national groups were to have equal rights. At the same time
there was to be a central *Reichstag* of two chambers, a single
citizenship and a unified administration. Like so many liberal
proposals it attempted to get the best of both worlds. The
third solution was advanced by the bureaucracy and powerful
monarchists like Schwarzenberg and Alexander Bach who
advocated complete centralization under direct imperial control. All were to be treated as equal and subjected to the same

[1] See p. 292. [2] See p. 288.

laws and to the same administrative procedure. The last was a federal solution that proposed the separation of the nationalities under the personal authority of the Habsburg Crown with common institutions to cover questions of general concern such as foreign policy, finance and defence.

The Habsburg monarchy, unfortunately, was never prepared to come down in favour of any one of these proposals. Federalism, whether aristocratic or national, led to loss of imperial control. Constitutionalism created friction and undermined the authority of the Court. Centralization, though ideal in theory, proved unworkable in practice. Thus the Crown tried to reach a compromise which embraced the advantages of all these solutions without committing itself to any. It is thus hardly surprising that the history of the last eighty years of the Habsburg Empire is often confusing and sometimes obscure.

In March 1849 Stadion, Minister of the Interior, issued a constitution to pacify German and Czech liberals. It accepted many of their proposals such as an imperial parliament and equal linguistic rights, but also emphasized the need to maintain a strong centralized state. It was, however, only designed to appeal to Germany and to rally support until the defeat of the Hungarian revolt. Bach, who quickly replaced Stadion, ruled under emergency decrees all ready to impose a rigid and centralized uniformity upon the Empire. As soon as the Hungarians had been defeated this policy was clearly exposed. Hungary itself was divided into five districts and administered by state officials known as 'Bach hussars'. The tariff barrier between Austria and Hungary was abolished and German language and law imposed as the basis of all official transactions. Poles, Czechs, Croats and Germans were subjected to similar treatment. As one Croat leader remarked somewhat bitterly to a Hungarian friend: 'What you have got as a punishment, we have been given as a reward.'

By 1851 it was unnecessary to maintain any constitutional pretence. The aristocracy at court had been urging their claims and hoped to regain power by elevating the authority of the Emperor and creating an imperial council to restrain the Bach bureaucracy. Francis Joseph seized the opportunity to establish a new compromise. By a patent of December 1851 he assumed absolute power and accepted an imperial council to offer advice. But he retained the same ministers. Bach continued to rule the Empire on a rigid and uniform basis. Schwarzenberg tried to consolidate Austria's position in Germany.[1] The Emperor was now supreme and the Empire policed and regulated from Vienna. Local councillors were little more than civil servants and the old aristocracy merely a decorative appendage of the Court.

The Bach system, which eminently suited Francis Joseph's detached and unimaginative mind, was bitterly criticized by aristocratic Magyars, Slav nationalists and German liberals. But opposition was divided. Déak, who had taken over the leadership of the Hungarian moderates, advocated passive resistance, while the old aristocracy hoped to regain their influence through contacts at court. Many Slavs found opportunities for promotion within the bureaucracy, and the Czechs even came to predominate among the nationalities represented in the 'Bach hussars'. The Germans were gratified by their official position as administrators of the Empire, while the lesser subject races were too small and too divided to offer any resistance. Once again, however, the factors of change and the impact of reform were to undermine the best intentions of government. When these became combined with dissatisfaction at home and defeat abroad the new system was once again to collapse.

Economic development, though slow, was nevertheless significant. The peasantry had emerged from the revolution as the one satisfied class. Some three million had acquired their lands at low rates of redemption and now helped promote an agricultural boom. Bruck, the Minister of Commerce, planned to open a commercial empire of 'seventy million' by combining all German and Habsburg territory into one free trade area. Chambers of trade were opened to encourage development and a new Südbahn built to link Vienna and Trieste. Subsequently lines were built to Bucharest and the Black Sea and to Lombardy-Venetia. Bruck also founded the Austrian-Lloyd steamship company to encourage commerce, and opened a new network of postal and telegraph services to ease communications throughout the Empire.

But progress was constantly frustrated by lack of finance.

[1] See p. 350.

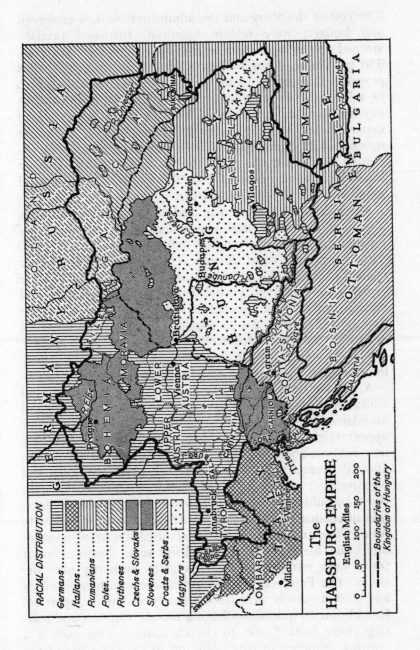

The cost of the army and the administration was enormous and budgets were seldom balanced. Increased taxation aroused protest from the peasants and the commercial classes. The government was forced to raise loans and sell crown property. During the Crimean war the state railways had to be sold to the banking houses of Péreire and Rothschild to pay for Austrian mobilization. Though Bruck set up a loan department to play the role of the Crédit Foncier,[1] there was never enough capital to launch an industrial boom. The exclusion of the Empire from the *Zollverein* added another limitation. Austria remained on the whole a land of rural enterprise and peasant agriculture.

Meanwhile some effort was made to modernize the State. The abolition of manorial jurisdiction led to a series of legal reforms. Courts were created at communal and district level, with a supreme court of appeal in Vienna. Trials were opened to the public and juries used in some cases. But the police still exercised a vital role checking agitators and officials, and keeping a watchful eye on both the press and the population. In 1852 the government introduced measures of censorship largely copied from the French Second Empire. Under the more effective control of the police these were enforced with an even greater severity than before the revolution.

A similar blend of reform and reaction was evident in education. Elementary schools taught in native languages and maintained a tradition of regional loyalty and popular appeal. High schools and gymnasia were reformed to include new subjects and more technical training. Universities were allowed greater freedom in choosing their curricula and electing their staff. Yet official communication had to be in German, publications were exposed to censorship and education increasingly handed over to the direction of the Church. A new Concordat in 1855 completed the retreat from Josephinism:[2] the hierarchy was freed from state control, church funds were restored and bishops given authority over the clergy. The Pope was allowed direct access to the episcopacy and church schools were freed from government inspection. In addition all questions affecting morals, manners and marriage were handed over to church control. This gave it a growing influence in education and in the daily life of the

[1] See p. 387.　　[2] See p. 42.

community. It became once again a basic prop of the social order, an essential corner-stone of the monarchy.

These contradictions in the régime inevitably exposed it to growing criticism. The old aristocracy deplored their ineffectiveness; others criticized the lack of capital. Middle class Germans attacked increased taxation and administrative waste, the mounting deficit and their failure to penetrate the German market. The nationalities bitterly resented German administrative controls and linguistic barriers. Failure abroad and financial disaster at home hastened collapse. The 1857 recession created widespread panic. While wealthier nations were able to ride the storm, the precarious credit structure of the Empire led to a general slump. Even Bruck was unable to restore confidence, and financiers demanded further guarantees. These implied a responsible financial policy, a return to constitutional rule and an increase in taxation that could only be effected by agreement with Hungary and the subject races of the Empire.

Austrian foreign policy proved equally calamitous. The death of Schwarzenberg in 1852 had removed the chief protagonist of a forward strategy. Buol, his successor, was probably more calculating but also more cautious. During the Crimean war he played an ambivalent but not unreasonable role.[1] Afraid to join Russia for fear of provoking French intervention in Italy, he was unable to join the West in case of a Russian attack through Poland or the Principalities. Attempts to compromise, however, brought criticism from both sides; mobilization led to bankruptcy, and the occupation of the Principalities was followed by a humiliating withdrawal. In the end Austria was isolated, having failed to rally even the Germans on to her side. As a result she was forced to meet the combined attack of France and Piedmont alone. Lack of finance and hope of a quick victory helped to hasten the ultimatum that provoked the war. Defeat discredited the army, one of the main pillars of the régime. Bach and Buol resigned. A new period of constitutional compromise began.

5. The Making of Dualism

Francis Joseph first tried to make a compromise with the old conservatives. He hoped they could create stability at

[1] See p. 313.

home and renew the Holy Alliance abroad. Loyal Bohemian
and Hungarian magnates led by Szecsen had assured the
Emperor that the loyalty of the nationalities would be reaffirmed once the Imperial Council and the old provincial
diets had been restored. A diploma in October 1860 revived
both institutions, but retained the bureaucratic machine
which was essential for running the Empire. The result
pleased no one. The aristocracy felt defrauded and attacked
the bureaucracy and the remaining vestiges of Bach's
policies, while the Germans and the bureaucrats attacked the
revival of archaic aristocratic institutions. Financiers deplored the lack of ministerial responsibility, and national
leaders resented a revival of feudalism that left them without
any effective voice in government. The bitterest opposition
came from Hungary where the court aristocracy had totally
misjudged the temper of the Magyar gentry. Led by Déak
they were determined to hold out for the March Laws of 1848
and regarded the diploma as totally inadequate. Meanwhile a
relaxation of the press censorship led to a dangerous revival
of criticism. By February 1861 Francis Joseph had suspended
the diploma and issued a new patent.

The February patent reverted to a compromise between
the bureaucracy and constitutionalism. The Imperial Council was transformed into an elected parliament, *Reichsrat*, of
343 deputies. The provincial diets became electoral colleges
with some administrative powers. German ascendancy was
assured by four grades of electors – landowners, trading corporations, townsmen and peasants – which gave greater
weight to the towns and thus guaranteed a German majority.
The *Reichsrat* was given legislative powers over all subjects
not reserved for the diets. But Francis Joseph retained control over the army, the executive and the financial departments. The bureaucracy remained the effective agent of
government. Anton von Schmerling, who was appointed to
manipulate this sham constitution, was in fact a convinced
supporter of Bach. It was thus hardly surprising that he failed
to rally much support.

The patent was attacked as violently as the diploma. The
old conservatives resented their loss of influence, while Slavs,
Poles, Czechs and Croats attacked the restoration of German
control. The main centre of resistance again came from

Hungary. At elections for the Hungarian Diet the old conservatives were swept away and membership divided in
roughly equal proportions between Déak and a radical wing
of 'Kossuthites' led by Koloman Tisza. Déak, who was
anxious to restore the 1848 laws within the framework of a
Habsburg Empire, appealed to the Crown to accept their validity, and refused to send delegates to the central *Reichsrat*
until they had been restored. At the same time he skilfully broadened the base of his appeal by appointing a
committee to work out a new nationalities law which would
offer equality to the Croats and to Hungary's Slav neighbours.

In 1861, however, Francis Joseph was not prepared to compromise with Hungarian demands. The Diet was dissolved
and the country restored to bureaucratic rule. Foreign developments, however, soon forced the Emperor to change his
mind. Abroad, both his conservative and his German policies
failed. In 1860 he had met Alexander but had been unable to
reach any agreement. The Tsar demanded support in the
Black Sea and on the Danube, which might have exposed
Austria to an attack from the West. In Germany, Rechberg
failed to reform the Confederation, while Bismarck destroyed
Francis Joseph's attempt to rally the princes.[1] In 1864 Rechberg had followed Bismarck into Schleswig-Holstein in the
belief that it was part of a conservative crusade. After the
Schönbrunn discussions,[2] however, he realized that Bismarck
was in fact a dangerous rival. By October, Rechberg had been
replaced by Mensdorff who began to challenge Prussia for
German leadership.

The German challenge forced Francis Joseph to agree to a
Hungarian compromise. In 1865 he opened direct negotiations with Déak and visited Pesth where he declared his intention of doing everything to satisfy his Hungarian peoples.
Diploma and patent were suspended, Schmerling dismissed
and discussions opened on the possibilities of a federal solution. These were interrupted by the Austro-Prussian war during which Déak remained loyal to the dynasty and refused to
exploit the situation to Hungary's advantage. As a result
Francis Joseph achieved what was to be his last, federal, compromise. In 1867 Hungary was officially reinstated, the March

[1] See p. 367.   [2] See p. 370.

Laws accepted and Francis Joseph crowned king. A common council was created to deal with defence, finance and foreign affairs. Hungary was left a free hand to deal with her own Slav subjects. In 1868 the Croats were given a limited measure of autonomy. Otherwise, in spite of earlier promises, the Slavs in the Hungarian provinces were kept subordinate to Magyar authority. They were to demonstrate their resentment in 1919 when the Habsburg Empire finally disintegrated.

In the western provinces Francis Joseph reverted to a compromise with constitutionalism. Beust, who had become Foreign Minister in 1866, hoped to restore Austrian leadership in Germany and attract German support in the Empire. The liberal rights of the Kremsier[1] constitution were confirmed, languages and nationalities were declared equal, the *Reichsrat* was retained as a parliamentary forum. But executive control remained in the hands of the Emperor who chose ministers at will. Bureaucracy and police, though more civilized than their counterparts in Russia, were still the essential agents of the régime. Furthermore, Schmerling's 'electoral geometry' continued to give the Germans a decisive majority. Czechs and Slovenes, though offered linguistic equality, could never compete in political power.

Thus the Dual Monarchy was a bargain between Germans and Hungarians at the expense of the remaining nationalities of the Empire. It was a compromise between a federal solution, a centralized state and a liberal constitution. As such it could not reconcile the Slav peoples who were denied any political powers and the benefits of a full federal system. It failed to satisfy the demands of the Germans who lost their over-riding authority yet could not gain full control over their own affairs. They looked increasingly to the new Germany for leadership and support, and their exclusion only made the bait appear the more appetizing. Meanwhile the Magyars held to their pride and their privileges; they remained determined to exclude Slavs from participation in politics and continued to advance their own economic and strategic interests.

As a result the Habsburg Empire could not pretend to reconcile its many subject races or bridge the differences be-

[1] See p. 293.

tween German, Magyar and Slav. Francis Joseph could find no mission except to maintain the *status quo*. Further constitutional development was frustrated by the very conditions of the 1867 compromise. Economic growth was handicapped by isolation and social change by the apparent dominance of the master races. The Empire was to remain frozen but fragile until the end of the First World War. The war was itself partially the outcome of the desperation created by the imposition of the Dual-Monarchy upon the Empire. To achieve independence the Slavs had to destroy it. To retain their interests Germans and Magyars had to preserve it. To maintain any identity Francis Joseph was forced to defend it. Defeat shattered the framework and hastened dissolution. But the subsequent partition of the Empire only led to further periods of instability and unrest. Though the Habsburg Empire failed, its failure brought little comfort; conflicting classes and national interests survived to compete for power in a struggle to impose centralized or federal solutions.

XVII · THE WESTERN SEABOARD

1. *The Iberian Peninsula*

In Portugal and Spain regional differences and social divisions appeared to defy the demands of rational government. By 1834 limited assistance from Britain, France and Spain, under the terms of the Quadruple Alliance,[1] had helped to confirm the authority of Queen Maria in Portugal and assure the preservation of the 1826 Charter. But this document, modelled on the French Charter of 1814[2], soon failed to satisfy 'progressive' elements. While a 'moderate' party of clericals, conservatives and courtiers advocated an increase of royal control, liberal bourgeois and discontented officers demanded a more democratic constitution. Portugal embarked on a round of political confusion, court intrigue and popular revolt punctuated by military coups which provided the few moments of stability in a generally fluctuating situation. It was not until 1846 that General Saldanha was able to establish a measure of control. After a series of revolutions and counter-revolutions, he eventually secured some degree of order, encouraged investment and trade, and laid the foundations of a new colonial empire in Angola and Mozambique.

In Spain the opening years of Isabella's reign were a scene of almost unrelieved anarchy, atrocity and civil war.[3] Ferdinand VII had restored an absolute régime by methods of brutality and terror. But in his last years he had married Maria Cristina, his fourth wife, and repealed the Spanish Salic law to assure the succession of his daughter. This had led to a conflict with his brother Don Carlos, who had secured conservative and clerical backing and thereby forced the Court to draw upon moderate and progressive elements for support. These were ranged between a liberal aristocracy, a widely scattered middle class, and the army which was to play a leading part in Spanish affairs. But due to their widespread dispersal and particular distinctions no single group was as

[1] See p. 239.   [2] See p. 220.   [3] See p. 238.

yet able to retain control for long, and Spain soon became a hotbed of conspiracy, violence and regional discontent.

The geographical divisions of Spain were exceptionally pronounced. In the North, independent peasant smallholdings supported a conservative population anxious to retain its privileges and uphold regional rights. To the East, a fertile Mediterranean coastline was the basis of Catalan prosperity, the centre of a culture and a tradition that had retained its own language and literature for centuries. The highlands of Castile provided the essential backbone of the country, an area of large estates, struggling peasants and isolated villages. In the South arid wastes, prosperous ports and mineral workings created enormous contrasts of poverty and wealth. Almost every area suffered from lack of capital, poor communications and industrial failure. Barcelona had developed a thriving textile industry; Cadiz and Seville had retained their trading connections; iron and coal had been developed in the North, copper, lead and mercury in the South. But years of unrest had undermined the economy, handicapped investment and retarded industrial progress. Most Spaniards found security in land and in official employment, rather than in the promotion of new resources and the encouragement of economic growth.

The aristocracy and the Church were united in their determination to defend their privileges and their property from the ambition of middle-class financiers or court politicians. Together with the independent peasants of the North, they formed the basis of a conservative party which supported Don Carlos in his claims to the Spanish throne. They were opposed by a variety of interests, which were seldom allied for more than a few moments of revolutionary action. Anti-clerical aristocrats, generals, rentiers and upper bourgeois merchants formed the basis of a 'moderate' party that took as its model the French Charter of 1814. 'Progressive' lawyers, officers and intellectuals looked to the English Reform Bill of 1832. In the 1840s ambitious regional interests and radical thinkers became increasingly influenced by French republican and socialist ideals. In the South and in the isolated peasant communities of the centre, a vague and primitive anarchism roused hopes of a nobler purpose and a better standard of life.

The army was to remain the essential arbiter between these conflicting interests. It provided opportunities for promotion at every level and was the chief avenue for ambition and enterprise. As the aristocracy had long since retired from military leadership, the way was clear for the sons of peasants and the professional classes. Many were to play a key role in Spanish history during the next hundred years. The army was to act as kingmaker, establish dictatorships and subsequently destroy them. Competition for promotion acted as a further incentive. High ranking officers would manoeuvre for advantage to assert their authority and increase their security and status. During the minority of Isabella (1833–43) Spain was devastated by the Carlist revolt. Maria Cristina, who acted as regent, was quite unable to control either the army or the politicians. A round of ministries gravitated between moderate and progressive, court and military interests. Attempts by any one party to consolidate its authority invariably provoked a revolt from the remainder. Constitutions were made and modified according to the party in power. The state was in a permanent condition of bankruptcy and only paid its way by the regular confiscation and sale of monastic property. The main towns were centres of constant unrest, while the countryside was ravaged by a violent and barbarous warfare which continued up to 1839.

In 1840 Maria Christina abdicated and was replaced by General Espartero, the first of a line of *caudillos* who were to dominate Spanish affairs. The son of a peasant, he had won fame in the civil wars and played a significant part in the defeat of the Carlist cause. He introduced a number of 'progressive' reforms, liberalized the constitution, regulated the treasury and advocated freer trade. But these measures, together with his efforts to curb municipal independence and regional privileges, only stirred up further unrest. Barcelona, Seville and the northern provinces broke into open revolt. Rival generals mutinied, declared Isabella of age and forced Espartero to flee to England.

For the next decade political life was dominated by General Narvaez who preferred a 'moderate' constitution and established a far greater degree of control. The Upper Chamber of the *Cortes* was reappointed and the franchise for the Lower House reduced. The press and the universities were effectively curbed. Liberals were prosecuted, brigands pursued into the mountains and wide areas of the country placed under martial law. These measures aroused bitter opposition and Isabella used the occasion of the Spanish marriage crisis[1] to get rid of her over-mighty minister. But her own rule was irresponsible and confused, caused mounting protest and threatened total collapse. In 1847 Narvaez was recalled and his strong arm effectively contained the isolated revolutionary outbreaks in Madrid and Seville during the following year. He even expelled the British ambassador for encouraging the rebels, and sent troops to Italy in 1849 to assist the Pope.[2]

The gradual stabilization of the peninsula during the next fifteen years was assured by the continued rule of generals who stepped in to expel aspiring court politicians and crushed continuing Carlist and urban agitation. Between 1854 and 1863 General O'Donnell rallied moderate and progressive elements into a 'liberal union', modified the constitution and stabilized the national finances. Budgets were published and efforts made to consolidate the floating debt and cover expenditure by the sale of ecclesiastical property. A Concordat with the Papacy regulated Church affairs, settled the land question in favour of the State, but accepted Catholicism as the only recognized religion. This move initiated a century of censorship and persecution directed against all Protestant and non-conformist doctrines that has only recently shown any signs of being relaxed.

In 1860 Spain once again began to launch out into a series of new colonial ventures. A war in Morocco provided an outlet for military enterprise denied by the loss of the American Empire during the first decades of the century.[3] Though fought with fury and incompetence it brought new popularity to the army and the government, and made the reputation of General Prim who was to play a major role during the last years of Isabella's reign. Spanish intervention in Mexico was less successful. Prim withdrew, together with the British, leaving the field open to Napoleon III.[4] This created bitter resentment in Spain, which still hankered after the prestige of her old imperial possessions.

Spain's loss of Empire helps to explain the lack of dynamism in the economy and the lack of purpose in political life.

[1] See p. 249.   [2] See p. 276.   [3] See p. 181.   [4] See p. 398.

FF

Thrown back on her own resources, she lacked the capital and the enterprise to embark on the agricultural and industrial developments that were beginning to change the face of western Europe. Nevertheless, the growing stability of the 'fifties and the 'sixties did encourage foreign investment and lead to isolated examples of economic progress. A Credito Mobiliaro, modelled on the French Crédit Mobilier and supported by French capital, promoted the construction of gas works, railways and other public utilities. A rudimentary railway network linked Madrid to Barcelona, Cadiz and the major cities. New telegraph services accelerated the distribution of information. New canals and roads gradually brought outlying areas into closer contact with provincial capitals.

Industrial and agricultural development, though slow, showed some signs of growth. The textile industry of Barcelona expanded in spite of the competition of foreign imports. These were encouraged by the gradual reduction of tariff barriers, which undoubtedly eased the import of manufactured goods but created considerable unrest in Spanish industries. In the North mining was promoted by close ties with the British market. High grade iron ore was exported in growing quantity for the steel industry, while the Rio Tinto mines remained the chief source of copper until the discovery of central African deposits. Agriculture was encouraged by the gradual destruction of entails, the abolition of feudal dues and the redistribution of ecclesiastical property. A central school was set up to urge new methods and promote development. But the growth rate remained slow; while adequate to modify the several regions of the peninsula it did not promote the unification of its overall structure.

As a result sectional interests evolved in parallel to any central authority. Exiles and foreign contacts spread republican and socialist ideals in the cities. Cells of artisans, printers and intellectuals met to discuss the works of Fourier and Proudhon. The trade recession of 1867 hit the industrial towns and created renewed agitation. In 1868 an emissary of Bakunin introduced his anarchist philosophies into Spain and further encouraged the fragmentary tendencies in the peninsula. Anarchism, with its rejection of authority and its regional appeal, was to exert a greater influence in Spain than the more disciplined doctrines of Karl Marx. Any failure in government led to the rapid disintegration of the State which in turn generally promoted a quick return to military rule.

After 1863 the reign of Isabella hastened to its chaotic end. O'Donnell resigned and a series of court ministries soon reverted to a familiar pattern of confused constitutional conflicts and increasing clerical control. From 1866 Prim consistently plotted to overthrow the monarchy. After a number of abortive coups he eventually succeeded in 1868, when Cadiz led another revolutionary movement which culminated in the deposition of Isabella from the Spanish throne. This promoted a series of Carlist, clerical and republican outbursts. But the moderate majority still favoured a monarchy and Prim was left with the task of finding a suitable monarch. At first no one was prepared to take on so unenviable a position. The Hohenzollern candidature precipitated the Franco-Prussian war,[1] and Prim was finally left with Amadeo of Savoy, the son of Victor Emmanuel. But on arrival in Spain the new monarch was greeted by news of Prim's assassination and two years later he abdicated from a hopeless task. After a year of republican rule and the almost total disintegration of the State, an equilibrium was eventually restored by another military rising. Spain was then able to enjoy almost half a century of comparative tranquillity before plunging into renewed cycles of revolution and civil war.

2. Holland and Belgium

The development of Belgium and Holland proceeded within a more balanced constitutional framework. The revolution of 1830 had created an independent Belgian state out of the assorted provinces of the old Austrian Netherlands.[2] In the North, Flanders and Brabant, which had been reconquered by the Habsburgs in the sixteenth century, spoke Flemish and still worked a long established cloth and linen industry. The countryside followed a tradition of peasant smallholdings and Catholic worship. The towns traded on their earlier prosperity, though Antwerp, once the unrivalled entrepôt of the area, had been strangled by foreign intervention and Dutch control over the mouth of the Scheldt. In the South the Walloon provinces spoke French

[1] See p. 378.   [2] See p. 234.

and were more closely linked to the liberal and radical traditions of their Gallic neighbour. The region was rich in coal and iron deposits and had already begun to benefit from the new techniques of the industrial revolution.[1] It was the centre of a growing commercial and financial bourgeoisie who were to dominate Brussels and Belgium for the next hundred years.

Though Belgians of every class and creed had combined to win independence the constitution limited the electorate to some 46,000 upper- and middle-class citizens. Nevertheless, it was considered a model of its kind, was to prove easily adaptable and excited liberal admiration throughout Europe for several generations. Liberal freedoms, popular sovereignty and ministerial responsibility were proclaimed. A parliament of two elected chambers controlled government and finance. The King was a genuine constitutional monarch, dependant upon parliamentary ministers and popular support. Leopold of Saxe-Coburg, though autocratic by nature, had had previous experience of the workings of the British constitution and was anxious to promote political consolidation. His marriage to Louise of Orléans, daughter of Louis-Philippe, appeared to symbolize a balance between French and British influence. His beliefs in a moderate and united ministry were to counter regional divisions and attempt to associate varied and conflicting interests into a new Belgian state.

For the first ten years rivalries were restrained to fortify the country against the Dutch. Moderate Catholics and liberals combined in a series of 'unionist' ministries to consolidate the administrative framework and encourage economic expansion. Local government was remodelled with communes and provinces on a French pattern, but with elected councils from whom the government chose a burgomaster or mayor. In 1834 Belgium was the first country to plan a national railway network. This covered the main commercial routes, linked up separate regions and provided a useful connection with the Prussian Zollverein. In 1835 a new Banque de Belgique guaranteed the stability of the currency, which had been adapted to the franc system three years earlier, and promoted the spread of credit which had already been stimulated by the Société Générale during the previous decade. Provincial

[1] See p. 191.

banks in Flanders and Liége also encouraged the distribution of capital, and this was soon supplemented by French and British sources.

The result was a cumulative acceleration of industrial growth. Belgium was to lead Europe in economic development. In 1830 75 per cent of the population was still employed in agriculture. By 1850 the proportion had dropped to about a half. 350 iron works employed some 7,500 men; 300 collieries produced over 6 million tons of coal, and this figure was to double in the next twenty years. The greatest concentration was, as elsewhere, in cotton which employed over 20,000, the majority in larger units. But joint-stock companies mushroomed in every sector; between 1834 and 1838 an average of twenty-five a year were registered to cover metallurgy, shipping and the lighter industries.

These developments accelerated the social changes that generally accompanied the spread of new industrial techniques. While the upper bourgeoisie profited and a new commercial and intellectual class emerged, the established handloom weavers in the linen industry were gradually ruined. Exports fell by 50 per cent, unemployment spread, and rioting broke out in the northern cities. Meanwhile the countryside remained Catholic and conservative, tied to a more primitive agrarian routine. By 1840 liberals and Catholics had begun to demand new policies to satisfy the requirements of a changing social and economic framework. But Leopold continued to favour 'unionist' coalitions and these were to survive until 1845. An Education Bill in 1842 set up primary schools which provided religious instruction and also received a subsidy from the State – a rare compromise between Catholic and liberal principles. The economic and political crises of the forties were soon, however, to destroy the 'unionist' centre and establish a pattern of rival parties and alternative governments.

Belgium had weathered its first crisis in 1838 when conflicting financial interests, agitation for the incorporation of Luxembourg, and uncertainties in the American market had led to a wave of unrest. In 1839 the Dutch had eventually recognized Belgian independence, while the great powers had guaranteed the independent status of Luxembourg. This, however, had only helped to spread disaffection. The end of the Dutch threat and the failure of foreign claims focused attention on Belgium's domestic difficulties and hastened the disintegration of a 'unionist' government. In 1844 and 1845 the failure of the potato and the wheat crops sent prices soaring and brought famine and unemployment to the countryside. The financial panic of 1846 added to the trail of disaster. Artisans suffered severely, particularly in the Flemish areas where some 30,000 were forced to abandon the textile industry. Rioting spread in the cities where gangs destroyed machines, tore up railway lines and looted the shops.

The crisis assisted the formation of a new liberal party under Rogier, who was largely responsible for setting up one of the first electoral organizations in Europe. Liberal associations were created in every province with cantonal committees to push party candidates and spread a party programme. They advocated freer trade, greater provincial freedom, a broader franchise and the end of compulsory religious instruction in schools. In 1847 the liberals won the election with a decisive majority and formed the first all-liberal ministry. This was to become a factor of major significance in the following year, when Belgium was able to escape the revolutionary wave which swept across Europe. Rogier extended the electorate to 79,360, which included the newer middle classes, instituted a programme of public works, cut tariffs and promoted a gradual upswing in the economy. Civic Guards were created to stop violence. A Belgian legion which tried to invade the country from France was easily disarmed on the frontier. The Church and the aristocracy co-operated to curb any agitation in the rural areas. By June 1848 Rogier felt sufficiently secure to hold another election and won a spectacular vote of confidence. Like Britain, Belgium was able to forestall revolutionary agitation by constitutional action.

The next twenty years were, with a momentary lapse, dominated by the liberal party. Their reforms reflected the commercial and financial needs of the bourgeoisie and the ideals of a moderately liberal society. Tariffs were progressively cut, the corn laws repealed, and a free trade treaty negotiated with Napoleon III. A new national bank was established together with new savings banks and additional credit companies. The unemployed were absorbed by a major programme of canal construction, road building and public works. The development of branch lines was opened to private enterprise and created a new spate of limited liability companies. As a result the economy boomed. Between 1850 and 1860 exports and iron production both doubled. Belgium appeared set on a course of unrivalled prosperity and industrial development.

The stability of the nation, however, was soon threatened by a revival of the religious question and the growth of regional and social divisions. In 1850 an Education Bill, which set up secondary schools without compulsory religious teaching, roused the bitter opposition of Catholics and led to the temporary defeat of the liberal government. Antwerp decided that the 'religion of the majority' was to be taught. This regulation was generally accepted, but led to a renewed attack from liberals and eventually brought about a split in the liberal party between 'moderates' and a body of young uncompromising 'progressives'. Meanwhile the introduction of taxes on beer and tobacco, and the creation of new estate duties and restrictions on religious bequests also provoked violent protests in every quarter. Each sector attacked the demands of the other and bitterly resented a levy apparently designed to benefit another region.

By the 1860s it was clear that peasants, artisans and factory hands were deriving little gain from the economic boom. Child labour was only restricted in 1858. Little was done to improve factory conditions or to introduce reform legislation. Opposition became especially militant in the Flemish provinces where Catholics, peasants and artisans combined to attack the linguistic and financial superiority of the Walloon South. The Catholic Church was inspired by the French Ultramontaines to lead a bitter attack on liberal values. The Flemings were roused by a revival of national traditions and regional interests to press their demands for separate institutions. In 1869 Catholics and Flemings combined with the 'progressive' minority to defeat Rogier and form a new Catholic ministry in the following year.

But the constitutional framework survived. Leopold died in 1865, widely mourned as 'father of the nation'. He was succeeded by his son, Leopold II, whose acquisitions in the Congo were to open up new prospects of African development. In 1877 the liberals returned to power, introduced the secret ballot and again widened the franchise. Catholic and Flemish interests, however, continued to compete for pride of place with liberal Walloon and subsequently socialist parties. Their conflicts still threaten to disrupt the development of Belgium today.

During the first half of the nineteenth century Holland also began to develop on more constitutional and liberal lines. In 1830 William I still ruled as an enlightened despot with an aristocratic court and a States-General which was really only employed for consultative purposes. Agricultural prosperity and the steady expansion of inland and overseas trade assured the well-being of merchants and smallholders, and weakened the supporters of a moderate middle class reforming movement. But the Belgian war of independence and the mounting costs of a 'confrontation' policy which refused to admit the loss of the severed provinces led to growing criticism. Taxes rose, the national debt soared, and a liberal opposition began to formulate demands for constitutional guarantees and closer financial controls. In 1840 William abdicated and was succeeded by his son William II. A 'voluntary loan' liquidated state debts, and reforms gave the States-General powers to vote a budget and cut the civil list.

Further action was avoided until the revolutions of 1848. The economic crisis of the previous years, potato disease and a trade recession had already led to riots and provided an obvious warning of possible revolt. William II was not a man to fight the storm, and rapidly appointed a reform commission to draft a new fundamental law. This established the framework of a liberal state with a royal but ministerial executive, two elected houses and a liberal pattern of local government. Though elections to the Upper House were based on a restricted franchise, the electorate for the Lower House and for provincial assemblies was on a more popular basis. Opportunities were opened to smallholders and a wide section of the middle classes. Holland had become transformed into a constitutional monarchy like her southern neighbour.

Liberal ministries assured a period of constitutional and economic reform. The franchise was widened still further and the powers of local authorities increased. The introduction of free trade policies encouraged exports and doubled the carrying trade. Rotterdam boomed and became a leading port connecting Britain to the European market. Amsterdam flourished as the centre of a prosperous East Indies trade and the heart of an international financial network. New companies were set up to develop canals and provide basic light industries. Land reclamation extended the area under cultivation and broadened the base of a thriving agrarian economy.

As in Belgium, religion and education were to provide the main sources of conflict. In Holland the established Calvinist Church attacked liberal measures with considerable ferocity and demanded the introduction of strictly denominational schools. When the Pope took advantage of liberal toleration to restore Catholic bishops, the Calvinists incited riots in the streets and forced the resignation of the government. But the progress of reform continued unchecked. In 1857 mixed schools were secured after all. Railway construction and the development of waterways were maintained. In 1860 slavery was abolished in the Dutch Empire. When the liberals returned in 1862 it was to carry on the work of constitutional consolidation and assure a future of growing prosperity and toleration.

3. Scandinavia

Norway, Sweden and Denmark, countries often pointed out today as models of their kind, were slow to respond to the changing developments of nineteenth-century Europe. For the first quarter of the century the society of Denmark and Sweden was dominated by the older aristocracy. Though feudal dues had generally been abolished, a wide variety of tenant obligations and rents remained. Only in Norway had a population of free peasant proprietors succeeded in consolidating their position. The middle classes appeared isolated and ineffective unless supported by the wealth and ambitions of a new aristocracy. In Denmark prosperity had been undermined by war and the destruction of Copenhagen by the British fleet.[1] In Norway and Sweden activity was still concentrated in regional industries and Baltic trade. Coasting and fishing were important items, though both were ham-

[1] See p. 132.

pered by quarrels over tolls payable on sailing through the Sound.

Government was still dominated by the Crown and run on the enlightened but despotic principles of the eighteenth century. Marshal Bernadotte, who had been adopted by Charles XIII of Sweden and had succeeded to the throne in 1818 as Charles XIV, acquired Norway in return for aid to the allied cause during the last years of the Napoleonic war.[1] He ruled both his kingdoms as independent units, Sweden with a nominated council and a traditional diet of four Estates, and Norway with separate councils and an elected parliament. In Denmark, Frederick VI governed with the aid of a privy council which debated but had neither executive nor legislative authority. Both monarchs, however, carried out policies of a generally benevolent and paternal nature designed to increase the wealth and well-being of the State.

The stabilization of finance was an essential first step towards the renewal of prosperity. In 1815 the Danish deficit amounted to ten years revenue, while Sweden lacked any financial reserves. The foundation of a new National Bank and the creation of a network of savings banks soon helped to stimulate the Danish economy. Currency reform, joint-stock banks and the adoption of a new decimal system laid the foundation for Swedish recovery. Seventy-five per cent of the population was still engaged on the land, and the introduction of new farming methods and British techniques soon led to a boom in agriculture. In Norway the number of small proprietors doubled in twenty years. In Sweden and Denmark new agricultural colleges and rising demand hastened enclosure and the spread of new crops and improved methods of cattle breeding. The influx of American wheat in the second half of the nineteenth century was to change the pattern of production and make Denmark a leading exponent of an intensive dairy farming that catered especially for the growing English market.

Industrial development was more uneven. Denmark and Norway built roads, constructed railways and developed a few industries but remained essentially agrarian. In both, the accumulation of surplus capital was to depend upon agriculture and fishing. In Sweden, however, industrial progress

[1] See p. 148.

was of greater significance. The introduction of British steam engines and puddling and rolling techniques doubled the output of iron which in 1860 reached a total of five million tons. Between 1840 and 1860 exports and manufactures trebled in value and Sweden began to develop a growing connection with the Russian market.[1] During the next decade Nobel invented dynamite and made the fortune with which he was later to endow his prizes for literature, science and peace. The Swedish industrial revolution was closely associated with timber development and railway construction. Timber, pulp and paper played a role similar to cotton and textiles in Britain and France. Financial investment, canal and rail construction and commercial and tariff negotiations were frequently connected with forestry, or with the growing iron and steel industries.

Economic progress fostered social adjustment and promoted the changes visible in other western states. New aristocrats, freeholders and middle-class interests soon began to agitate for influence and increased power. The example of Britain and France led to demands for easier credit, freer trade and electoral reforms. In 1834 Frederick VI set up provincial diets to advise on finance and law, and pacify the growing agitation in Schleswig and Holstein, which was already being inflamed by rival German and Danish claims. In Sweden the Estates urged financial reform, rejected the budget and imposed a new ministry upon the Crown. But liberalization remained slow. Press censorship was relaxed, compulsory church attendance abolished and elementary schools set up in every parish. New monarchs, Oscar I in Sweden (1844-59) and Christian VIII in Denmark (1839-48), though apparently liberal in outlook, quickly reverted to authoritarian methods after ascending the throne.

The 1848 revolutions found few echoes in the North. In Sweden the moderates held reform banquets while radicals rioted in the streets. In Stockholm a number were shot down by troops, but further agitation quickly subsided. Oscar was congratulated for his action by Nicholas I and followed a conservative line for the next ten years. In Denmark change was hastened by the crisis in Schleswig-Holstein. Frederick VII (1848-63), and his Prime Minister, Karl Moltke, had be-

[1] See p. 421.

gun to support the Danes there openly and planned a United
Diet to include representatives from the Duchies. This,
however, had led to a German revolt and had brought the
intervention of the armies of Prussia and the German Confederation.[1] In 1849 Frederick agreed to a constitution for
Denmark in order to rally support. A ministry was to be
responsible to a diet of two chambers. Liberal freedoms were
guaranteed. The way was cleared for the emergence of a new
national-liberal party.

These developments, however, only created increasing
difficulties in the Duchies where neither the Germans nor the
supporters of Augustenburg desired incorporation into a
Danish constitution. After the Treaty of London the government tried a variety of experiments. A period of direct rule
was followed by efforts to set up a Common Council including representatives from Schleswig and Holstein. This was
opposed by the Germans and rejected by the great powers. In
1863 Frederick eventually determined to incorporate Schleswig, which had a militant Danish party, and grant the Germans in Holstein separate institutions. This, however, led to
Bismarck's unexpected intervention[2] and the subsequent loss
of both duchies. As a result the national-liberals were discredited and the conservative landowners consolidated their
influence and gained increased control over the Upper
Chamber.

In Sweden, the accession of Charles XV (1859–72) gradually
hastened the progress of reform. A new ministry led by Baron
Louis de Geer encouraged economic growth and recognized
its close association with constitutional development. Legal
reforms, the spread of secondary schools and the introduction
of free trade policies were incompatible with autocratic
government. In 1865 the Estates were reformed into a diet of
two elected chambers, an Upper House controlled by the
wealthy and a Lower House elected on a wider franchise.
Ministers could address the chambers which had the power to
vote and check finance and legislation. Sweden thus became a
semi-constitutional state. This, however, soon led to growing
difficulties in Norway. Here parliament had supported the
liberals and welcomed the accession of Charles XV. The
country benefited from the commercial prosperity and peace-

[1] See p. 284.   [2] See p. 368.

ful policies of their more powerful neighbour. But the gradual extension of freedom and wealth, the discoveries of Norse legends and ancient sagas soon encouraged the rise of a Young Norse party, anxious to break the connection with an alien crown. Once again, a process of fragmentation had begun. In 1905 it was eventually to lead to the creation of an independent Norwegian state.

4. *The European Experience.*

Developments on the western seaboard illustrated a wide variety of social, political and economic change. The entrenched positions of the aristocracy were slowly undermined leaving them increasingly exposed to the ordinary pressures of daily life. Upper and middle bourgeois elements acquired greater influence in trade and politics and planted new industries and new commercial links across the Continent. Capitalization had begun a gradual redistribution of artisan and craft labour; some workers swelled the ranks of a new bourgeoisie; others were reduced to the status of landless or vagrant proletarians whose only future lay in the factories or in fulfilling the services required by a new industrial society. On the land, wealthy peasants also consolidated their holdings at the expense of the smallholder and share-cropper. These had been unable to compete and had moved on to swell the growing numbers concentrated in the towns.

Europe was becoming increasingly urban. A society conditioned by the ordered regularity of the countryside was being replaced by one dominated by the varied activity of city life. Kings had been forced to reach a compromise with these new developments. Their personal predilections and family ties were beginning to appear increasingly irrelevant to the needs of the State and the welfare of society. Constitutions made governments more and more dependant upon a franchise representing new class interests and varied levels of popular consent. Some were still restricted to an upper bourgeois electorate. The majority, however, were slowly moving towards a more democratic form of representation. But the process was halting and irregular. It took Britain nearly a hundred years to introduce universal suffrage after the 1832 Reform Bill had made the first inroads into the vested interests of an established order.

Change was the outcome of a variety of inter-related interests. It was also influenced by a wide range of ideals. This is not the place to debate how far beliefs are the outcome of social or economic factors or how far these factors could themselves be the result of various beliefs. No one would deny the importance of ideas and their profound impact upon social and political development. They catered for every contingency, satisfied every class and spread conviction and confusion throughout society and the State.

The major creeds of the century had been clarified and defined. Paternal and authoritarian governments found new justification in attacking social disruption and revolutionary unrest. The Church had reasserted its claims to guard principles and guarantee security. Liberalism and constitutional ideas had been applied to government, industry and trade, and had revealed the frustrations of liberty and the limitations of free enterprise. Socialists, communists and anarchists had formulated ideal solutions and absolute claims. Over all had emerged the attitude and techniques of scientific investigation. It imparted a new clarity and a new realization to philosophers, politicians, scientists, sociologists and many more. Doubts appeared clearer, solutions nearer, convictions sincerer. But all were to be equally elusive in practice. If there were many who made claims, there were now as many to contradict them. The clash of ideas and ideologies was to add to the European experience and subsequently to spread similar debates and doubts throughout the world.

European expansion and settlement scattered a combination of traditional attitudes and revolutionary ideas on a wide front. Areas of white colonization moved through varying stages of liberal and democratic development. Economic and industrial changes created familiar social and political problems. In homogeneous areas these could be solved within a united framework. Where races clashed, Boers and British in South Africa, British and French in Canada, patterns of conflict and compromise emerged. These often echoed the national rivalries of Europe and worked through a similar range of bitter and hopeful experiences.

Where colonization came into contact with native populations it rapidly opened up a variety of new and complex processes. Industrial and commercial developments, conflicting

ideals and contradictory attitudes were projected indiscriminately in the interests of traders and missionaries. All
assumed that their particular faith and their collective experiences were uniquely suited to the development of Indian,
African or South-East Asian communities. The majority
appeared to expect their solutions to be accepted ready made
as the gift of a superior intelligence and the order of a
wealthier civilization. Such assumptions were soon to be
proved equally unrealistic. It was to be difficult if not impossible to short-cut centuries of European development.
Settlers soon suffered the same fate as the exclusive élites of
the eighteenth century. They were replaced by native aristocracies or middle-class rulers. New industries, trades, scientific developments and academic achievements brought about
a complex pattern of change that reflected, even if it did not
parallel, many of the changes in nineteenth-century Europe.
New generations, rising classes, military leaders competed for
control. Agrarian communities and established crafts were
dislocated and destroyed by the impact of the industrial
revolution and the adoption of scientific techniques.

These, however, were not the only contributions of European society. Great achievements in mechanization, medicine, law and literature created new opportunities for progress
and survival, for reconciliation and understanding. Industrialization and agrarian reforms raised living standards;
medical services created new hope and brought a renewal of
compassion and relief. International law created a new
machinery for solving the disputes caused by rivalry and warfare. In 1864 the first Geneva Convention regulated conditions for the sick and the wounded. In 1871 the example of
Great Britain and the United States in submitting their
Alabama claims for arbitration, anticipated the creation of a
permanent court at the Hague. International societies and
unions worked to standardize communications and distribute
information. European legal codes were to provide the framework for a multitude of states and the growth of a wide
variety of new societies and novel institutions.

Experiences and developments were distilled and recorded
in the great artistic, literary and musical achievements of the
century. Ideals, attitudes and interests were blended in a record of human conflict, endeavour, and hope. A complex

interplay of factors had created the scenes and associations from which men could extract the essence of things and record them for posterity. They touched upon the passions and the problems that still afflict the world today, and often provided valuable clues to the problems that historians and sociologists were beginning to analyse. It was such analysis that was to contribute the essential first steps towards a wider understanding. Here again the nineteenth century opened up new horizons and laid the foundations for twentieth-century discovery and debate. Historians and scientists, philosophers and political thinkers had began to redefine the nature of man, the role of the State and the meaning of the universe with a new sense of precision and a new purpose.

Thus most of the elements that were to reshape modern Europe had come into play in the years between the mid-eighteenth and mid-nineteenth centuries. Social changes, industrial developments and the evolution of politics had begun to create the foundations of a modern world. Classes had become more articulate, machines more dominating and governments increasingly complex and effective. New roads, railways and means of locomotion had started to draw together the scattered precincts of the State. New newspapers, schools and technical colleges had prepared the way for the education of a mass age. New men had shown how to manipulate these developments in the interests of the nation or for the benefit of a selection of the people in it.

The outward appearance of Europe was to undergo many changes during the next hundred years. Further developments in science, technology, government and war continued to quicken the tempo of change. Increases in population, swifter communications and growing economic resources created new dimensions of prosperity and power. Yet the outlines of a modern society could be discerned and the lines of economic and political progress clearly recognized. Statesmen and philosophers had begun to argue in terms with which we are still familiar and tried to prescribe remedies which still appear relevant if not entirely up to date. The foundations of modern Europe had been effectively laid. The factors that emerged in the nineteenth century are still among those that dominate many of the changes in the world today.

(*a*) THE HOUSE OF BONAPARTE

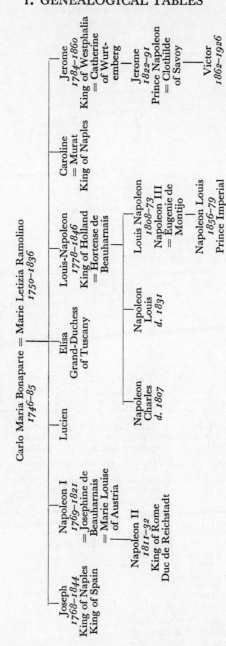

Carlo Maria Bonaparte = Marie Letizia Ramolino
1746–85   *1750–1836*

Joseph
1768–1844
King of Naples
King of Spain

Napoleon I
1769–1821
= Josephine de
Beauharnais
= Marie Louise
of Austria

Napoleon II
1811–32
King of Rome
Duc de Reichstadt

Lucien

Elisa
Grand-Duchess
of Tuscany

Louis-Napoleon
1778–1846
King of Holland
= Hortense de
Beauharnais

Napoleon
Charles
d. *1807*

Napoleon
Louis
d. *1831*

Louis Napoleon
1808–73
Napoleon III
= Eugenie de
Montijo

Napoleon Louis
1856–79
Prince Imperial

Caroline
= Murat
King of Naples

Jerome
1784–1860
King of Westphalia
= Catherine
of Wurt-
emberg

Jerome
1822–91
Prince Napoleon
= Clothilde
of Savoy

Victor
1862–1926

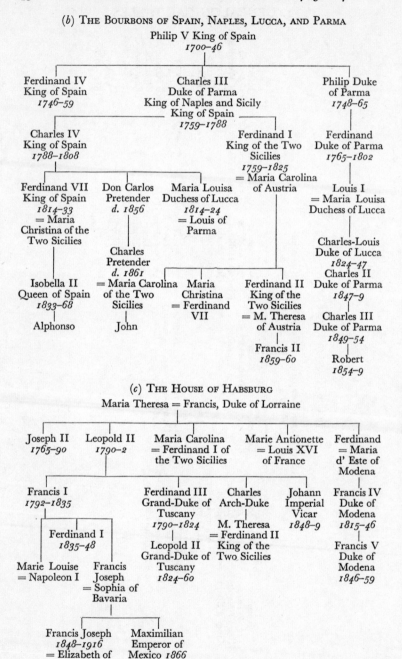

(b) THE BOURBONS OF SPAIN, NAPLES, LUCCA, AND PARMA

Philip V King of Spain
1700–46

Ferdinand IV
King of Spain
1746–59

Charles III
Duke of Parma
King of Naples and Sicily
King of Spain
1759–1788

Philip Duke
of Parma
1748–65

Charles IV
King of Spain
1788–1808

Ferdinand I
King of the Two
Sicilies
1759–1825
= Maria Carolina
of Austria

Ferdinand
Duke of Parma
1765–1802

Ferdinand VII
King of Spain
1814–33
= Maria
Christina of the
Two Sicilies

Don Carlos
Pretender
d. 1856

Maria Louisa
Duchess of Lucca
1814–24
= Louis of
Parma

Louis I
= Maria Louisa
Duchess of Lucca

Charles
Pretender
d. 1861
= Maria Carolina
of the Two
Sicilies

Charles-Louis
Duke of Lucca
1824–47
Charles II
Duke of Parma
1847–9

Isobella II
Queen of Spain
1833–68

Maria
Christina
= Ferdinand
VII

Ferdinand II
King of the
Two Sicilies
= M. Theresa
of Austria

Alphonso

John

Charles III
Duke of Parma
1849–54

Francis II
1859–60

Robert
1854–9

(c) THE HOUSE OF HABSBURG

Maria Theresa = Francis, Duke of Lorraine

Joseph II
1765–90

Leopold II
1790–2

Maria Carolina
= Ferdinand I of
the Two Sicilies

Marie Antionette
= Louis XVI
of France

Ferdinand
= Maria
d' Este of
Modena

Francis I
1792–1835

Ferdinand III
Grand-Duke of
Tuscany
1790–1824

Charles
Arch-Duke

M. Theresa
= Ferdinand II
King of the
Two Sicilies

Johann
Imperial
Vicar
1848–9

Francis IV
Duke of
Modena
1815–46

Ferdinand I
1835–48

Leopold II
Grand-Duke of
Tuscany
1824–60

Francis V
Duke of
Modena
1846–59

Marie Louise
= Napoleon I

Francis
Joseph
= Sophia of
Bavaria

Francis Joseph
1848–1916
= Elizabeth of
Bavaria

Maximilian
Emperor of
Mexico 1866

(d) THE HOUSE OF HOHENZOLLERN

Frederick William I
1713–40

Frederick II, the Great
1740–86

Augustus William
d. *1758*

Frederick William II
1786–97

Frederica
= William V
of Holland

Frederick William III
1797–1840

Frederick
William IV
1840–61
= Elizabeth
of Bavaria

William I
1861–88
= Augusta
of Weimar

Charlotte
b. *1798*
= Nicholas
Tsar of
Russia

Louisa
b. *1808*
= Frederick
of the
Netherlands

Albert
b. *1809*
= Wilhelmina
of the
Netherlands

Frederick III
1888
= Victoria,
daughter of
Queen Victoria
of
Great Britain

William II
1888–1918

(e) THE HOUSES OF OLDENBURG, AUGUSTENBURG AND GLUCKSBURG

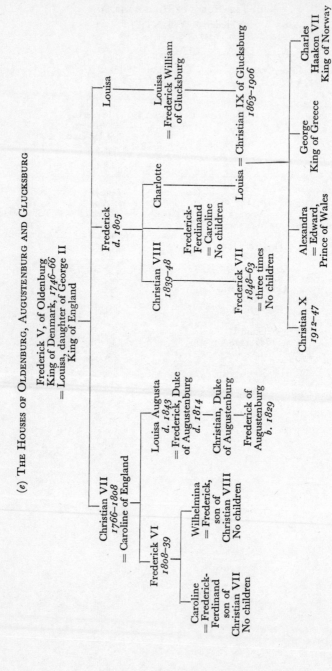

(ƒ) THE HOUSE OF ROMANOV

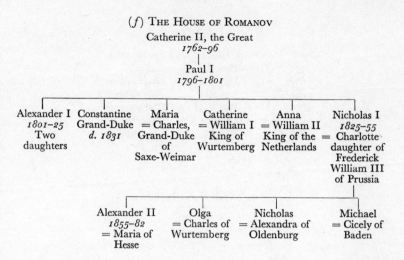

Catherine II, the Great
1762–96

Paul I
1796–1801

Alexander I	Constantine	Maria	Catherine	Anna	Nicholas I
1801–25	Grand-Duke	= Charles,	= William I	= William II	*1825–55*
Two	*d. 1831*	Grand-Duke	King of	King of the	= Charlotte
daughters		of	Wurtemberg	Netherlands	daughter of
		Saxe-Weimar			Frederick
					William III
					of Prussia

Alexander II	Olga	Nicholas	Michael
1855–82	= Charles of	= Alexandra of	= Cicely of
= Maria of	Wurtemberg	Oldenburg	Baden
Hesse			

(g) THE HOUSE OF SAVOY

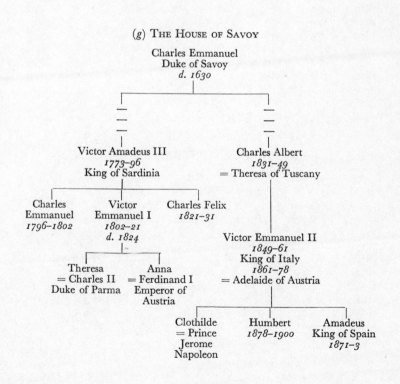

Charles Emmanuel
Duke of Savoy
d. 1630

Victor Amadeus III	Charles Albert
1773–96	*1831–49*
King of Sardinia	= Theresa of Tuscany

Charles	Victor	Charles Felix
Emmanuel	Emmanuel I	*1821–31*
1796–1802	*1802–21*	
	d. 1824	

Victor Emmanuel II
1849–61
King of Italy
1861–78
= Adelaide of Austria

Theresa	Anna
= Charles II	= Ferdinand I
Duke of Parma	Emperor of
	Austria

Clothilde	Humbert	Amadeus
= Prince	*1878–1900*	King of Spain
Jerome		*1871–3*
Napoleon		

2. POPES

Elected	Title	Family Name
1775	Pius VI	Braschi
1800	Pius VII	Chiaramonti
1823	Leo XII	della Genga
1829	Pius VIII	Castiglioni
1831	Gregory XVI	Cappellari
1846	Pius IX	Mastai-Ferretti
1878	Leo XIII	Pecci

3. POPULATIONS

(in millions)

	Great Britain	France	Italy	Habsburg Empire	Germany	Prussia	Russia
(1789)	14·3	26·3				5·7	
1800	15·8	27·3	16·9		22·5	8·8	31·0
1815	19·1	29·0	18·0		26·0	7·9	45·0
1830	24·0	32·5	21·0		30·0		50·0
1840	26·5	34·0	22·4		31·0	15·0	55·0
1850	27·7	35·8	24·3	30·7	36·0	16·0	57·0
1860	29·0	36·7	25·0	31·7	38·0	18·5	63·0
1870	31·0	38·0	26·0	35·8	41·0		77·0

4. COAL, IRON AND STEEL PRODUCTION

COAL
(in millions of metric tons)

	Great Britain	France	Belgium	Habsburg Empire	Prussia	Russia
(1789)		0·25				
1815		0·85				
1830		1·8			1·7	
1840	31·0	3·0	3·9	0·4	3·0	
1850	57·0	4·4	6·0	1·2	5·7	0·04
1860	80·0	8·3	9·6	2·3	12·3	0·15
1865	98·2	11·6	11·8		20·6	
1870	110·4	13·1	13·6	8·6	29·4	0·75

PIG IRON
(in millions of metric tons)

	Great Britain	France	Germany (Prussia)	Russia
1820	0·45	0·22	0·03	
1830	0·67	0·26	0·04	0·2
1840	1·4	0·35	0·18	0·2
1850	2·3	0·5	0·2	0·25
1860	3·8	0·96	0·5	0·35
1865	4·8	1·2	0·99	
1870	6·0	1·4	1·5	0·4

STEEL
(in millions of metric tons)

	Great Britain	France	Germany (Prussia)
1860		0·03	0·09
1865	0·22	0·04	0·15
1870	0·3	0·1	0·3

5. RAILWAY CONSTRUCTION

(in millions of kilometres: 1 kilometre = 0·62 miles)

	Great Britain	France	Germany	Habsburg Empire	Italy	Belgium	Spain	Russia
1840	1·3	0·4	0·4	0·4		0·3		
1850	10·5	2·9	6·0	2·2	0·3	0·9	0·02	0·5
1860	16·7	9·4	11·0	5·1	1·8	1·6	1·6	1·5
1865	21·3	13·5	13·8	6·3	3·9	2·2	4·7	3·9
1870	24·5	17·5	19·5		6·0	3·0	5·5	4·0

BIBLIOGRAPHY

GENERAL HISTORIES AND REFERENCE WORKS

A Select List of Books on European History, 1815–1914, edited by Alan Bullock and
  A. J. P. Taylor, Oxford (2nd edn., 1957)

Modern European History, 1789–1945, A Select Bibliography, compiled by W. N.
  Medlicott, (Hist. Assoc., 1960)

The Cambridge Modern History: Vol. VIII, *The French Revolution;* Vol. IX, *Napoleon;*
  Vol. X, *The Restoration*; Vol. XI, *The Growth of Nationalities*

The New Cambridge Modern History: Vol. VIII, *The Revolutions in America and Europe
  1763–1792*; Vol. IX, *The New Regimes and the Industrial Revolution 1793–1830*;
  Vol. X, *The Zenith of European Power 1830–1870*

The Rise of Modern Europe (ed. W. L. Langer): Vol. XI, C. Brinton, *A Decade of
  Revolution*; Vol. XII, G. Bruun, *Europe and the French Imperium*; Vol. XIII,
  F. B. Artz, *Reaction and Revolution 1814–1832*; Vol. XIV, W. L. Langer,
  Liberalism, Nationalism and Socialism 1832–1852; Vol. XV, R. C. Binkley,
  Realism and Nationalism 1852–1871

Peuples et Civilisations (edd. L. Halphen and P. Sagnac): Vol. XIII, G. Lefebvre,
  La Révolution francaise (3rd edn., 1951), trs. *The French Revolution from its
  Origins to 1793* (1962), and *The French Revolution 1793 to 1799* (1964); G.
  Lefebvre, *Napoléon*; F. Ponteil, *L'éveil des nationalités et le mouvement libéral
  1815–1848*; C. H. Pouthas, *Democraties et capitalisme 1848–1860*; H.
  Hauser, *Du libéralisme à l'impérialisme 1860–1878*

The Fontana History of Europe: George Rudé, *Revolutionary Europe 1783–1815*
  (1964)

I. Collins, *The Age of Progress* – a survey of European History between 1789 and
  1870 (1964)

E. J. Hobsbawm, *The Age of Revolution* – Europe from 1789–1848 (1962)

D. Thompson, *Europe since Napoleon* (1957)

F. M. H. Markham, *Napoleon and the Awakening of Europe* (1954)

A. Wood, *Europe 1815–1945* (1964)

J. McManners, *Lectures on European History 1789–1914* (1966)

L. Namier, *Vanished Supremacies* (1958)

A. J. P. Taylor, *From Napoleon to Stalin* (1950)

A. J. P. Taylor, *Rumours of War* (1952)

THE SOCIAL BACKGROUND

A. Goodwin (ed.), *The European Nobility in the Eighteenth Century* (1953)

H. M. M. Acton, *The Bourbons of Naples* (1956)

A. de Tocqueville, *The Old Regime and the French Revolution* (trs. Blackwell, 1956)

W. H. Bruford, *Germany in the Eighteenth Century* (1939)

A. Young, *Travels in France 1787–89* (ed. C. Maxwell, 1950)

J. Blum, *Noble Landowners and Agriculture in Austria 1815–1848* (1948)

J. Blum, *Lord and Peasant in Russia* (1961)

C. Morazé, *La France bourgeoise* (1946)

C. Morazé, *The Triumph of the Middle Classes* (trs. 1966)

A. K. Greenfield, *Economics and Liberalism in the Risorgimento 1814–48* (1934)

G. Rudé, *The Crowd in History, 1730–1848* (1964)

E. J. Hobsbawn, *Primitive Rebels* (1959)

L. Chevalier, *Classes laborieuses et classes dangereuses à Paris dans la première moitié du 19 siècle* (1958)

ECONOMIC DEVELOPMENT

C. M. Cipolla, *The Economic History of World Population* (Pelican, 1962)

W. W. Rostow, *The Stages of Economic Growth* (1960)

S. B. Clough and C. W. Cole, *Economic History of Europe* (1946)

J. H. Clapham, *Economic Development of France and Germany* (1936)

T. S. Ashton, *The Industrial Revolution* (1950)

T. S. Ashton, *An Economic History of England: the 18th Century* (1955)

W. O. Henderson, *The Industrial Revolution on the Continent* – Germany, France and Russia 1800–1914 (1961)

W. O. Henderson, *Britain and Industrial Europe 1750–1870* (1945)

A. L. Dunham, *The Industrial Revolution in France* (1955)

N. J. G. Pounds and W. N. Parker, *Coal and Steel in Western Europe* (1957)

R. M. Hartwell, *The Industrial Revolution in England* (Hist. Assoc., 1965)

GOVERNMENT, DIPLOMACY AND WAR

M. Beloff, *The Age of Absolutism 1660–1815* (1954)

F. Hartung, *Enlightened Despotism* (Hist. Assoc., 1957)

J. M. Wallace-Hadrill and J. McManners (ed.), *France: Government and Society* (1957)

R. W. Seton-Watson, *Britain and Europe 1789–1914* (1937)

L. C. B. Seaman, *From Vienna to Versailles* (1955)

A. Duff Cooper, *Talleyrand* (1958)

C. K. Webster, *The Foreign Policy of Castlereagh* (1925)

H. V. W. Temperley, *The Foreign Policy of Canning* (1925)

H. C. F. Bell, *Lord Palmerston* (1936)

C. K. Webster, *The Congress of Vienna* (1934)

H. Nicholson, *The Congress of Vienna* (1946)

A. J. P. Taylor, *The Struggle for Mastery in Europe 1848–1918* (1954)

W. E. Mosse, *The European Powers and the German Question 1848–71* (1958)

G. Bonin, *Bismark and the Hohenzollern Candidature for the Spanish Throne* (1957)

G. A. Craig, *The Politics of the Prussian Army* (1955)

G. Davies, *Wellington and His Army* (1954)

B. H. Liddell Hart, *The Ghost of Napoleon* (1933)

M. Lewis, *The History of the British Navy* (Penguin, 1957)

C. Lloyd, *Ships and Seamen* (1961)

C. Oman, *Nelson* (4th edn., 1954)

O. Warner, *Trafalgar* (1959)

C. Woodham-Smith, *The Reason Why* (1953)

M. Howard, *The Franco-Prussian War* (1961)

RELIGIOUS AND INTELLECTUAL

The Pelican History of the Church: Vol. IV, G. R. Cragg, *The Church and the Age of Reason – 1648–1789* (1960); Vol. V, A. R. Vidler, *The Church in an Age of Revolution –* 1789 to the Present Day (1961)

K. S. Latourette, *A History of Christianity* (1954)

E. E. Y. Hales, *Revolution and the Papacy – 1796–1846* (1960)

D. G. Charlton, *Secular Religions in France 1815–70* (1963)

K. Martin, *French Liberal Thought in the Eighteenth Century* (1929)

P. Hazard, *European Thought in the 18th Century from Montesquieu to Lessing* (1954)

J. L. Talmon, *Political Messianism. The Romantic Phase* (1960)

H. Kohn, *The Idea of Nationalism* (1944)

I. Collins, *Liberalism in 19th Century Europe* (Hist. Assoc., 1957)

G. D. H. Cole, *History of Socialist Thought* (1953)

F. E. Manuel, *The New World of Saint-Simon* (1956)

J. Hampden Jackson, *Marx, Proudhon and European Socialism* (1958)

I. Berlin, *Karl Marx, his life and environment* (1939)

R. N. Carew Hunt, *The Theory and Practice of Marxism* (1956)

H. Kohn, *The Mind of Modern Russia* (1955)

H. Kohn, *The Mind of Modern Germany* (1961)

E. Roll, *A History of Economic Thought* (3rd edn., 1954)

J. A. Schumpeter, *History of Economic Analysis* (1954)

REVOLUTIONARY STUDIES

G. Rudé, *Interpretations of the French Revolution* (Hist. Assoc., 1961)

G. Lefebvre, *The Coming of the French Revolution* (trs. R. R. Palmer, 1947)

R. R. Palmer, *The Age of the Democratic Revolution – 1760–1800* (1959)

J. Godechot, *France and the Atlantic Revolution of the Eighteenth Century –* 1770–1799 (trs. H. H. Rowen, 1965)

G. Pernoud and S. Flaissier, *The French Revolution* (1959)

N. Hampson, *A Social History of the French Revolution* (1963)

A. Cobban, *The Social Interpretation of the French Revolution* (1964)

G. Rudé, *The Crowd in the French Revolution* (1959)

M. J. Sydenham, *The Girondins* (1961)

J. Robiquet, *Daily Life in the French Revolution* (trs. J. Kirkup, 1964)

A. Soboul, *The Parisian Sans-Culottes and the French Revolution 1793–4* (trs. 1964)

J. Plamenatz, *The Revolutionary Movement in France 1815–1871* (1952)

H. G. Schenk, *The Aftermath of the Napoleonic Wars* (1947)

R. F. Leslie, *Polish Politics and the Revolution of November 1830* (1956)

F. Fejtö (ed.), *The Opening of an Era, 1848; An Historical Symposium* (1948)

P. Robertson, *Revolutions of 1848: A Social History* (1952)

T. S. Hamerow, *Restoration, Revolution, Reaction –* Economics and Politics in Germany 1815–1871 (1958)

F. Ponteil, *1848* (4th edn., 1966)

D. C. McKay, *The National Workshops; a Study in the French Revolution of 1848* (1933)

A. de Tocqueville, *Recollections* (1896)

K. Marx, *Revolution and Counter Revolution or Germany in 1848* (ed. 1952)

K. Marx, *The Class Struggles in France 1848 to 1850* (ed. 1924)

L. B. Namier, *1848: The Revolution of the Intellectuals* (1946)

G. Brunn, *Revolution and Reaction 1848–1852* (Anvil, 1958)
E. H. Carr, *Studies in Revolution* (1952)
J. Joll, *The Anarchists* (1965)

FRANCE

A. Cobban, *A History of Modern France* (2 vols., 1957, 1961)
C. Wright, *France in Modern Times* – 1760 to the present (1962)
J. P. T. Bury, *France 1814–1940* (1949)
P. Campbell, *French Electoral Systems and Elections 1789–1957* (1958)
I. Collins, *The Government and the Newspaper Press in France 1814–1881* (1959)
A. Goodwin, *The French Revolution* (1953)
J. M. Thompson, *The French Revolution* (ed. 1951)
J. M. Thompson, *Leaders of the French Revolution* (1929)
J. M. Thompson, *Robespierre and the French Revolution* (1952)
F. M. H. Markham, *Napoleon* (1963)
J. M. Thompson, *Napoleon Bonaparte* (1953)
G. Lefebvre, *Napoleon* (1953)
P. Geyl, *Napoleon, For and Against* (1949)
H. Butterfield, *Napoleon* (1939)
Letters of Napoleon (ed. J. M. Thompson, 1934)
F. Artz, *France under the Bourbon Restoration* (1931)
T. E. B. Howarth, *Citizen King* (1961)
J. Dautry, *1848 et la IIe Republique* (1957)
J. P. T. Bury, *Napoleon III and the Second Empire* (1964)
J. M. Thompson, *Louis Napoleon and the Second Empire* (1954)
F. A. Simpson, *The Rise of Louis Napoleon* (ed. 1950)
F. A. Simpson, *Louis Napoleon and the Recovery of France* (ed. 1960)
Th. Zeldin, *The Political System of Napoleon III* (1958)
T. A. B. Corley, *Democratic Despot, A Life of Napoleon III* (1961)
D. H. Pinkney, *Napoleon III and the Rebuilding of Paris* (1958)
A. Horne, *The Fall of Paris. The Siege and the Commune 1870–1* (1965)

GERMANY

K. S. Pinson, *Modern Germany: its History and Civilization* (1954)
H. Halborn, *A History of Modern Germany 1648–1840* (1965)
A. J. P. Taylor, *The Course of German History* (1945)
G. P. Gooch, *Studies in German History* (1948)
W. O. Henderson, *The Zollverein* (1939)
W. N. Medlicott, *Bismarck and Modern Germany* (1965)
F. Darmstaedter, *Bismarck and the Creation of the Second Reich* (1948)
E. Eyck, *Bismarck and the German Empire* (1950)
A. J. P. Taylor, *Bismarck: The Man and the Statesman* (1955)
O. Pflanze, *Bismarck and the Development of Germany: the Period of Unification, 1815–71* (1963)
W. Richter, *Bismarck* (trs. 1964)
W. Carr, *Schleswig-Holstein 1815–1848* (1963)

ITALY

A. J. Whyte, *The Evolution of Modern Italy* (1944)
A. J. Whyte, *The Political Life and Letters of Cavour* – 1848–1861 (1930)
G. F. H., and J. B. Berkeley, *Italy in the Making, 1815–1848* (3 vols., 1932–40)
E. E. Y. Hales, *Pio Nono* (1954)
E. E. Y. Hales, *Mazzini and the Secret Societies* (1956)
D. Mack Smith, *Garibaldi* (1957)
D. Mack Smith, *Italy* (1959)
D. Mack Smith, *Cavour and Garibaldi, 1860* (1954)
G. M. Trevelyan, *Garibaldi's Defence of the Roman Republic* (1907)
G. M. Trevelyan, *Garibaldi and the Thousand* (1909)
G. M. Trevelyan, *Garibaldi and the Making of Italy* (1911)
M. Salvadori, *Cavour and the Unification of Italy* (Anvil, 1961)
A. Ramm, *The Risorgimento* (Hist. Assoc., 1962)

RUSSIA

B. Pares, *A History of Russia* (ed. 1953)
L. Kochan, *The Making of Modern Russia* (1962)
R. Charques, *A Short History of Russia* (1956)
B. H. Sumner, *A Survey of Russian History* (1947)
M. Florinsky, *Russia* (1953)
O. Hoetzsch, *The Evolution of Russia* (1966)
G. Scott Thompson, *Catherine the Great and the Expansion of Russia* (1947)
D. M. Lang, *The First Russian Radical*, Alexander Radishchev, 1749–1802 (1959)
M. Raeff, *Michael Speransky: Statesman of Imperial Russia, 1772–1839* (1957)
A. Mazour, *The First Russian Revolution* (1937)
W. E. Mosse, *Alexander II and the Modernising of Russia* (1958)
J. Erickson, *Pan-Slavism* (Hist. Assoc., 1964)

AUSTRIA AND HUNGARY

A. J. P. Taylor, *The Habsburg Monarchy 1809–1918* (1948)
C. A. Macarteney, *Hungary: a short History* (1962)
H. Kohn, *The Habsburg Empire 1804–1918* (Anvil, 1961)
A. Cecil, *Metternich* (1933)
G. de Berthier de Sauvigny, *Metternich and his Times* (trs. 1962)

EASTERN EUROPE

L. S. Stavrianos, *The Balkans since 1453* (1958)
C. A. Macartney and A. W. Palmer, *Independent Eastern Europe* (1962)
E. S. Forster, *A Short History of Modern Greece* (Revised 1958)
C. M. Woodhouse, *The Greek War of Independence* (1952)
R. W. Seton-Watson, *A History of the Roumanians* (1934)
A. J. Toynbee, *A Study of History*, Vol. VIII (1954)
W. F. Reddaway (ed.), *The Cambridge History of Poland 1697–1935* (1941)

THE IBERIAN PENINSULA

W. C. Atkinson, *A History of Spain and Portugal* (1960)
H. V. Livermore, *A History of Portugal* (1947)

H. V. Livermore, *Spain* (1958)
C. A. M. Hennessy, *Modern Spain* (Hist. Assoc., 1965)
R. Carr, *A History of Modern Spain* (1966)

SCANDINAVIA

B. J. Hovde, *The Scandinavian Countries 1720–1865* (2 vols., 1950)
I. Andersson, *A History of Sweden* (1956)
K. Larsen, *A History of Norway* (1948)
J. Danstrup, *A History of Denmark* (1949)
J. Hampden Jackson, *Finland* (1940)

HOLLAND AND BELGIUM

H. Pirenne, *Histoire de Belgique* (1926)
B. H. M. Vlekke, *Evolution of the Dutch Nation* (1951)
P. Geyl, *History of the Low Countries* (1964)

INDEX

14

3165